THE
LATINO
ENCYCLOPEDIA

THE
LATINO
ENCYCLOPEDIA

Volume 4

López, Trinidad "Trini" – Pescado

Editors

RICHARD CHABRÁN AND RAFAEL CHABRÁN

Marshall Cavendish
New York • London • Toronto

Published By
Marshall Cavendish Corporation
99 White Plains Road
Tarrytown, New York 10591-9001
United States of America

∞ The paper in these volumes conforms to the American National Standard for Permanence of Paper for Printed Library Materials, Z39.48-1984.

Library of Congress Cataloging-in-Publication Data

The Latino encyclopedia / editors, Richard Chabrán, and Rafael Chabrán,
    p. cm.
  Includes bibliographical references and index.
  1. Hispanic Americans—Encyclopedias. I. Chabrán, Richard II. Chabrán, Rafael
E184.S75L357 1995
973′ .0468′003—dc20   95-13144
ISBN 0-7614-0125-3 (set).   CIP
ISBN 0-7614-0129-6 (vol. 4).

First Printing

PRINTED IN THE UNITED STATES OF AMERICA

Contents

THE
LATINO
ENCYCLOPEDIA

López, Trinidad "Trini" (b. May 15, 1937, Dallas, Tex.): Singer. López is considered to be one of the pioneers of LATIN ROCK. His parents, Trinidad López and Petra López, immigrated to the United States in 1927. They crossed the Rio Grande as undocumented persons from Mexico, hoping to find a better life in the United States. López was born in the district of Dallas known as "Little Mexico." He exhibited a love for music at an early age. His father bought him a guitar and taught him rudimentary playing skills when López was eleven years old. Eventually, he took guitar lessons.

When López was in high school, he started a band that played TEX-MEX folk rock. After playing in hotels and nightclubs throughout the Southwest, López and the band ventured to Los Angeles. He became a popular attraction as a solo artist at a number of respected entertainment establishments. In 1963, López signed a recording contract with Reprise Records. His first album was a huge success, selling more than a million copies. The single from the album, "If I Had a Hammer," became an international hit. The song became the number one record in twenty-three countries.

López toured Europe in 1963 and the United States in 1964, appearing on a number of television shows. He continued to record albums during the mid-1960's. In 1967, López costarred in the popular film *The Dirty Dozen* and was named Dallas Man of the Year. López became wealthy as a result of investments and earnings from his music. He has contributed to many charitable and educational institutions.

López, Yolanda (b. 1942, San Diego, Calif.): Artist. Many of López's works of art include religious figures, particularly Our Lady of GUADALUPE. López updates the figures to emphasize Chicano culture and identity. In the place of traditional images of Our Lady of Guadalupe, for example, she has substituted an Aztec deity, her mother, herself, and an Indian woman. She uses Our Lady of Guadalupe as a model, transferring her power and virtue to real-life women as a way of questioning stereotypes and traditional role modeling (*see* STEREOTYPES OF LATINAS).

López received inspiration for her work from her grandmother, who told her family tales of migration and of the changes the family underwent in the United States. López invests her works, which include posters, video, and installation art, with social content. She has worked on behalf of farmworkers and toward improving living and working conditions on the U.S.-Mexico border.

López earned a master of fine arts degree from the University of California, San Diego, in 1978. She has taught painting at the California College of Arts and Crafts.

López del Castillo, Gerardo (b. Mexico City): Actor. One of the leading figures of early Hispanic theater in the United States, López del Castillo began acting at the age of fifteen. He was present at the 1849 inauguration of the grand Pabellon Méxicano in Mexico City. In the 1850's, he went to Hermosillo, where he married Amalia Estrella and became the leading actor in and a director for the Compañía de la Familia Estrella. He was the first Mexican actor to take a company on tour outside of Mexico.

The Estrella company moved its base to San Francisco in 1862 but continued to tour widely. López del

Trini Lopez, pictured in 1964. (AP/Wide World Photos)

Castillo became president of the Junta Patriótica Méxicana de San Francisco. A zealous Mexican patriot, he often used performances to raise funds for the Mexican revolutionary forces and several times interrupted his stage career to become a soldier. In the 1870's, he returned to Mexico City to promote the establishment of a national dramatic literature. Although he was known throughout the southwestern United States and Latin America, López del Castillo took many risks on political material late in his career and died tragically poor.

López Tijerina, Reies. *See* **Tijerina, Reies López**

Lorenzana, Apolinaria (1800—1884, Santa Barbara, Calif.): Religious figure. An abandoned baby found in 1800, Lorenzana grew up in California's missions. She assisted Father Antonio Peyri in the daily operations of Mission San Luis Rey between 1821 and 1830. Lorenzana taught the women to sew and cared for the sick. She later acquired two ranches, Jamacho and La Cañada de los Coches. Lorenzana became blind in later life and died in 1884.

Los Angeles, California: Originally named El Pueblo de Nuestra Señora la Reina de Los Angeles de Porciúncula, the city was founded in 1781 by an expedition from Mexico. It had a prominent role in the development of ALTA CALIFORNIA and again became a major Latino center with large waves of Mexican immigration in the twentieth century. In 1990, Los Angeles was the second-largest city in the United States with 3.5 million inhabitants, 40 percent of them Latino.

The original inhabitants of the area 140 miles north of Mexico were Native Americans, particularly members of the Gabrielino tribe, who called the area Yang-na. Mainly farmers and hunters, the Gabrielinos had a flourishing culture in politically autonomous villages. Both the village chief and the shaman played important roles in public life. Indian culture was nearly eliminated in the process of Spanish colonization and Anglo settlement.

The Founding of the Pueblo. The first phase of the modern city of Los Angeles began with Spanish exploration. Father Juan Crespi, a member of an early exploration team in 1769, described the Los Angeles basin as well suited to farming, as well as suitable for establishment of a mission and a large settlement.

Felipe de Neve, the governor of the Californias and a colonel in the Spanish army, proposed the original pueblos that later became San Jose, Santa Barbara, and Los Angeles. He also drew up regulations for these pueblos and subsequent laws for all of California when it became a colony of Spain. The major motivation for colonization was to establish defenses against Russian expansion from Alaska and British interests in the Pacific Northwest.

The first expedition to found the pueblo left Mexico on February 2, 1781, sailed to San Diego, and reached the Los Angeles basin by land in September, 1781. The group consisted of twenty-three adults and twenty-one children, ranging in age from one to sixty-seven years. Mostly from Sonora in northern Mexico, the group was ethnically mixed. Eight of the adults were Native Americans and ten were of African descent. Only one member had been born in Spain, and one was a mestizo (mixed Spanish and Indian blood). Another member, referred to as a chino (literally Chinese), was probably a Filipino. He had been born in Manila, then a Spanish colony. Nineteen of the children were of racially mixed descent, and two were full-blooded Native Americans.

Although the indigenous culture was nearly wiped out in the course of the Spanish invasion and racial brutality, at the same time there was also a gradual mingling of Native American, European, and African people into an ethnically mixed population. Ethnic balance and harmony characterized Los Angeles society until the middle of the nineteenth century, when it became part of the United States.

The Colonial Period. The original pueblo had an area of thirty-six square miles, compared to its present-day sprawl of 464 square miles. It was organized according to Spanish custom, with building lots of fifty-five-foot frontage around a central plaza. Each settler was permitted to cultivate two seven-acre tracts outside the residential district. In addition, settlers had free range for livestock on pueblo lands lying beyond the residential area. Farming was the main occupation.

During the COLONIAL PERIOD (1781 to 1822), the town became solidly established on the basis of its self-supporting agricultural economy. Through periods of good harvest, drought, and floods, the town grew steadily. By 1810, there were 365 people, not including the soldiers in the garrisons. The pueblo's first public school was funded for 1817-1818 and run by a retired soldier, Maximo Pina. It closed after one year for lack of funds.

Contact with the Spanish and other Caucasians was limited, except in the smuggling trade with the United States and Russia. As a result of frequent intermarriage between Native Americans and settlers from Mexico,

A mural commemorating the founding of Los Angeles. (Martin Hutner)

Native American culture had a strong influence on the society. The first mayor of El Pueblo de Los Angeles was José Vanegas, a Native American from Durango.

The Mexican Period. The Mexican War of Independence caused hardship for the residents. After Mexico's victory over Spain in 1821, however, the Los Angeles community recovered rapidly and prospered. There was increasing maritime trade, both legal and illegal, with foreigners. As a result of the secularization of mission lands in 1833, the economy received a major boost. The cattle industry grew rapidly and came to dominate the local economy. In 1834, annual exports included 100,000 hides, along with soap and tallow. This strong economic growth continued into the 1840's. In 1842, a *VAQUERO* named Francisco López discovered gold in Placeritas Canyon, near the San Fernando Valley. There were a brief gold rush and a surge in population.

In 1830, Los Angeles had a Mexican population of 1,180, with 2,479 Native Americans, the latter mostly concentrated at the missions. By 1844, the Mexican population had grown to 1,841, while the Native American population had declined to 1,200. A well-organized political system developed, marked by clashes among individuals and factions. Residents of Los Angeles played an increasingly prominent role in the affairs of Alta California. Los Angeles became a separate administrative district and was declared a *ciudad* (city) by the Mexican government in 1836.

A regional California identity and forms of cultural expression began to develop during this period. Women had the right to separately own and manage their property under California law. A school was finally established in the 1840's.

In February, 1845, the ruling junta of Alta California removed General Manuel Micheltorena as governor and declared Pío Pico, the senior member of the junta, as governor (*see* PICO FAMILY). The Mexican government recognized this change. Pico moved the capital from Monterey to Los Angeles, as the Mexican Congress had ordered in 1836. The northern CALIFORNIOS, however, refused to accept this move and supported an alternate governor. Under a compromise agreement, the governor and the legislature moved south to Los Angeles, but the Custom House and military authority remained in Monterey in the north.

There were increasing military confrontations between the United States and the Mexicans in Alta California. By 1846, there were pitched battles between Angelenos and U.S. soldiers. Even women participated in the defense of the city. Francisca Reyes helped bury a cannon in her yard to prevent it from being seized by the enemy. This cannon, nicknamed *el pedrero de la vieja* (the old woman's gun) was instrumental in defeating Captain Gillespie, Robert Stockton's assistant who had been left in charge of Los Angeles after its conquest by Stockton and his troops. For their open racism and brutality, Gillespie and his troops earned the wrath of the Angelenos. A group of women presented the defeated Gillespie with a parting gift of a basket of peaches rolled in cactus needles. Later, however, additional troops from the United States arrived, and the Angelenos were defeated. The Treaty of Cahuenga in 1847 ended Mexican control of Los Angeles. In the February, 1848, TREATY OF GUADALUPE HIDALGO, Mexico ceded all of Alta California to the United States.

The Early American Period. Despite conquest by the United States, Los Angeles in a sense continued to be a Mexican city until well into the 1860's. In 1850, 75 percent of the city's population was Mexican. Only by 1860 did the Mexicans, then numbering 2,069, constitute less than half of the population. Los Angeles remained a multicultural community, with Spanish as the common local language.

**LATINO POPULATION OF
LOS ANGELES, CALIFORNIA, 1990**

Total number of Latinos = 4,779,118; 33% of population

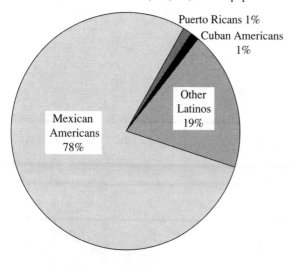

Source: Data are from Marlita A. Reddy, ed., *Statistical Record of Hispanic Americans* (Detroit: Gale Research, 1993), Table 111.

Note: Figures represent the population of the Los Angeles-Anaheim-Riverside, California, Consolidated Metropolitan Statistical Area as delineated by the U.S. Bureau of the Census. Percentages are rounded to the nearest whole number.

A rendering of the city early in its development. (Security Pacific Bank Collection, Los Angeles Public Library)

The GOLD RUSH of 1848 in northern California created a demand for beef. The cattle industry in Los Angeles experienced a boom and, for a short time, the price increased to $1,000 per head of cattle. Throughout the 1850's, a small elite of both Mexican and Anglo ranchers reaped enormous wealth. In 1857, however, beef prices fell sharply, resulting in an economic depression.

Apart from this temporary prosperity, there was a continuous general decline of the economic status of the Mexican population after California became a part of the United States. The Treaty of Guadalupe Hidalgo had recognized the rights of the Mexicans in California, especially property rights. In practice, however, the protection of those rights was only sporadic and tended to favor the economic interests of Anglo settlers.

Meanwhile, with the influx of outlaws, gamblers, and prostitutes, driven out of San Francisco and attracted by the cattle boom of Los Angeles, there was a gradual breakdown of law and order. Violence, specifically targeting Mexicans, increased. Horse stealing, highway robbery, and murder became commonplace.

Changing Residential Patterns. From the 1870's on, the pace of change accelerated. Business interests in Los Angeles, especially city boosters such as the Chamber of Commerce, broadcast the benefits of the climate in Los Angeles and urged people from the eastern part of the United States to emigrate. Thousands of Anglos obliged, helped by the construction of railway lines.

In the late 1880's, an oil boom created new prosperity for some but also led to disruption of the old patterns in the community. Mexicans did not share in the wealth of the city. Increasingly, Mexicans were confined to less skilled jobs, reinforcing overtly racist attitudes of the Anglo population toward Mexicans. The development of industrial areas, the building of the downtown area, and the constructions of roads resulted in several traditional neighborhoods being torn down and in severe dislocation of the Mexican community.

As wealthy residents gradually moved westward to more desirable locations in the city, Mexicans found themselves living in a barrio in the eastern section, increasingly suffering from urban blight. Racist attitudes led to laws excluding Mexicans from several neighborhoods in the city. Even after the laws were repealed, segregation in housing and education continued.

From 1900 to 1910, while the population of Los Angeles tripled from 102,479 to 319,198, the original Mexican barrio near the plaza continued to grow. The Mexican population moved away from the city's central district in a northeasterly direction to settle in new areas that permitted land ownership and a degree of economic stability.

Several newspapers, such as *La Prensa* and *El Heraldo de Mexico*, provided the community with information about the latest developments in Mexico and a forum for discussing issues concerning their life in the United States. *La Prensa*, for example, strongly supported union organizing in order to improve the standard of living of workers and their families at a time of militant opposition from the business community.

New barrios sprang up east of the Los Angeles River. Low-income Mexican families moved to BOYLE HEIGHTS, near Lincoln Park, to Belvedere, and to central Los Angeles. The new lines of the interurban railway system enabled the scattered communities on the east side of the city to become a tightly clustered

This group of Latino youth apparently tried to show willingness to make peace following the zoot-suit riots. (AP/Wide World Photos)

group, an enormous subcultural barrio, by 1930. With a Mexican population of 97,116, Los Angeles surpassed SAN ANTONIO, TEXAS, as the "Mexican capital" of the United States.

Economic and Social Conditions. In the 1930's, Mexican Americans worked primarily in agriculture and in the garment industry. For example, 75 percent of the women working in the city's garment industry were of Mexican descent. On October 12, 1934, with the help of Rose Pesotta, a leading organizer for the INTERNATIONAL LADIES' GARMENT WORKERS' UNION (ILGWU), the Mexican women workers went on strike to compel employers to comply with industry codes as required by law. In November, the employers agreed, and in December the ILGWU became an official union in Los Angeles.

Many Mexican workers had been encouraged to come to the United States in the 1910's and 1920's as a source of cheap labor. During the Depression, how-

ever, they were no longer welcome. The Chamber of Commerce took an active part in the movement to deport those who were not naturalized. By 1935, some 500,000 Mexican workers had been repatriated (*see* DEPORTATIONS, EXPATRIATIONS, AND REPATRIATIONS).

During the 1940's, anti-Latino RACISM again became overt in Los Angeles. Movie theaters were segregated and students in schools were kept from speaking Spanish. Prejudice erupted in the SLEEPY LAGOON CASE and in the 1943 zoot-suit riots, when Anglo servicemen attacked young Latino males.

World War II brought major changes to the entire community. Although Mexican Americans constituted between 5 and 10 percent of the city's population, people with Spanish surnames accounted for nearly 25 percent of the local casualty lists.

Political Developments. After World War II and the Korean War, the CHICANO MOVEMENT, designed to improve the social and political lot of Mexican Americans, gained prominence. The community's dissatisfaction with the War on Poverty, among other social policies, reached a climax in the late 1960's. On college campuses throughout Los Angeles, Chicano students organized groups to discuss common political concerns and work for social reform. In 1967, the Mexican Unity Council was formed and Julian Nava was elected to the Los Angeles school board.

The BLOWOUT of March, 1968, was one of the most significant efforts of the Chicano movement in drawing society's attention to the deplorable conditions in the city's public schools for Mexican American children. Thousands of Chicano students walked out of their classrooms in EAST LOS ANGELES to protest the racist attitudes of many Anglo teachers and the inferior school conditions. On August 29, 1970, the movement organized the NATIONAL CHICANO MORATORIUM ON VIETNAM, a large march and rally to protest U.S. intervention in Vietnam and the high rate of Mexican American war casualties.

The Chicano movement and Mexican American political organizations helped bring more Latino politicians into office. In 1962, Los Angeles city council member Edward Roybal (*see* ROYBAL FAMILY) was elected to the U.S. House of Representatives. Also in 1962, Phillip S. Soto and Manuel Moreno were elected to the California State Assembly. They were first Mexican Americans to be elected to that body since the 1890's. Other prominent Mexican American politicians in Los Angeles in the late twentieth century included city council member Richard ALATORRE and Los Angeles county supervisor Gloria MOLINA. Latino political power in the city has been hampered by the low rate of voter registration and participation, even among those Latinos eligible to vote. Los Angeles was ordered to reconfigure some of its voting districts in the 1980's to ensure better representation for large concentrations of Latino voters.

The 1980's and 1990's. In the 1980's, Los Angeles became popularly known as the "new Ellis Island" for

The city retains early colonial flavor in some of its buildings. (Martin Hutner)

its extraordinary absorption of immigrants from Latin America and Asia since the late 1960's. It was one of the most ethnically diverse cities in the country in 1990, composed of 40 percent Latino, 14 percent African American, 10 percent Asian American, and 0.5 percent American Indian residents. The Latino population was still predominantly Mexican American but became notably more diverse in the 1980's with the influx of large numbers of Central Americans, particularly from El Salvador and Guatemala. South Central Los Angeles, previously a black ghetto, attracted increasing numbers of new Latino immigrants, leading to some interethnic tensions and conflicts over resources. East Los Angeles remained a distinctive Mexican American barrio, but new BARRIOS expanded in the San Fernando and San Gabriel valleys to the north and east of the city. Meanwhile many Latinos were able to leave low-income areas for middle- and upper-middle-class suburbs such as Hacienda Heights.

The strong Latino presence is a major part of the city's character. Spanish is widely spoken, not only in residential barrios but also in the downtown business area, which resembles a Latin American city. The city is home to the prestigious *La Opinion* daily as well as other Spanish-language newspapers and television stations. Spanish-language commercial radio programs have captured the area's largest audiences. Latino cultural centers and organizations abound, as do a wide variety of murals on Chicano and Latino themes. Angelenos can enjoy national and regional foods and music from virtually every Latin American country. The dramatic growth in the number of Latino schoolchildren has changed the face of the city's mammoth school system and forced it to face new challenges. With their participation in the LOS ANGELES RIOTS of 1992, thousands of poor Latinos brought attention to the problems of their community, which tend to be slighted in the mainstream media. Although marginalized and exploited, the Mexican American community in Los Angeles has regained its voice in the late twentieth century and has emerged as an important player in the life of the city.   —*Hari Vishwanadha*

SUGGESTED READINGS: • Hill, Laurance. *La Reina, Los Angeles in Three Centuries.* Los Angeles: Security-First National Bank, 1929. • Nadeau, Remi. *Los Angeles: From Mission to Modern City.* New York: Longmans, Green, 1960. • Rios-Bustamante, Antonio. *Mexican Los Angeles: A Narrative and Pictorial History.* Encino, Calif.: Floricanto Press, 1992. • Rios-Bustamante, Antonio, and Pedro Castillo. *An Illustrated History of Mexican Los Angeles, 1781-1985.*

Los Angeles: University of California, Chicano Studies Research Center Publications, 1986. • Romo, Ricardo. *East Los Angeles: History of a Barrio.* Austin: University of Texas Press, 1983.

Los Angeles riots (Apr. 29-31, 1992): Most destructive riot in American history. On March 3, 1991, Rodney King, a black man, was beaten by four white Los Angeles police officers. The event was videotaped by an observer, and the videotape was seen on nationwide television. On April 29, 1992, an all-white jury in Simi Valley, an almost entirely white community near Los Angeles, found all four officers innocent of using excessive force. Within hours, South Central Los Angeles, a predominantly black, poor area, erupted into rioting. The disturbance quickly spread.

The King verdict was only the immediate cause of the rebellion in Los Angeles. An independent commission appointed by Mayor Tom Bradley shortly after the King beating had concluded that Los Angeles police often used excessive force against members of minority groups. Police Chief Daryl Gates was suspended on April 4, 1992, but this decision was overturned by the city council. At the time of the riots, Gates was still in charge of the police force. Many commentators at the time considered the riots as primarily a rebellion against the police.

Latinos played a large role in the rebellion, even though it was set off by the beating of an African American. Latinos specifically targeted Korean American-owned businesses, as tensions between the two groups had been building for years. More than one-third of the businesses destroyed in the riots were owned by Korean Americans. Many of those were in an area called Koreatown that had a large Latino population.

By the afternoon of April 30, the rioting had spread to the more affluent white suburbs. That day, Gates made a statement that he thought illegal aliens were at the root of the trouble. With this as an excuse, thousands of Latinos were forced to prove their citizenship and about fifteen hundred unregistered Mexicans were deported. At the height of the rioting, it was estimated that 51 percent of arrested persons were Latinos and 36 percent were black.

By the time the violence ended, ten thousand United States Marines had been called in, with one thousand stationed in South Central. Five thousand National Guards had been called in as well. An estimated ten thousand businesses were destroyed, fifty-eight people were killed, and a billion dollars worth of property was destroyed. Other American cities experienced riots set off by the unrest in Los Angeles, but none was as severe.

The most immediate impact of the riots was the passage of Proposition F, an initiative formed by Mayor Bradley's commission to reform the police department. The ballot proposition passed with a 67 percent majority. In broader terms, the Los Angeles riots were seen as a signal that American cities were in trouble. Many Americans saw conditions in the worst parts of big cities for the first time. There were many calls for racial harmony, and huge sums of money were allocated by the federal government to help rebuild Los Angeles. Fears were also fueled, and cries for tougher law enforcement were heard from many sides.

Louisiana: Located in the south-central United States, the state of Louisiana had a population of about 4,220,000 according to the 1990 U.S. Census. About 2.2 percent of the state's residents were Latinos; of those, about one-fourth were of Mexican American heritage.

Louisiana holds a unique place in North American history. Little remains of the original Native American culture, and a series of European, Caribbean, and African cultures have left their mark.

The first Europeans to explore the area arrived in the early sixteenth century. Alonzo ÁLVAREZ DE PINEDA sighted the Mississippi Delta in 1519, and in 1542, Hernando DE SOTO landed in Louisiana. There was no serious attempt at establishing a Spanish settlement until centuries later, after the French appeared.

All lands drained by the Mississippi River were claimed by René-Robert Cavalier, Sieur de La Salle, in the name of France and King Louis XIV in 1682. During most of the next century, when rivals Spain and France controlled most of the Caribbean Sea, the Caribbean islands and Louisiana came into frequent contact. French Creole became the working language of most of the population of what is now southern Louisiana, and Caribbean customs, particularly from Haiti, were taken to Louisiana.

In 1762, the Louisiana Territory was ceded to Spain, which controlled the territory until 1800, when it was ceded back to France, then under the rule of Napoleon Bonaparte. Napoleon held onto the territory only until 1803, when he sold it to the United States to finance intensifying wars in Europe. In 1812, Louisiana became a state.

Despite the facts that Spaniards were the first Europeans in Louisiana and that travel between the state and the Caribbean islands was common for at least a

LATINO POPULATION OF LOUISIANA, 1990

Total number of Latinos = 93,044; 2% of population

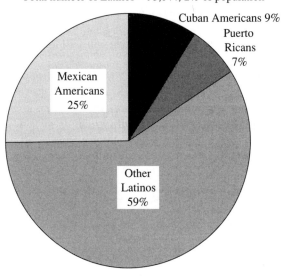

Source: Data are from Marlita A. Reddy, ed., *Statistical Record of Hispanic Americans* (Detroit: Gale Research, 1993), Table 106.

century, the 1990 census showed a Latino population of only 2.2 percent. This figure belies the amount of Spanish influence in architecture, cuisine, and music. Although there has been some immigration from Cuba, much of the Latino culture in the area appeared centuries ago.

Louisiana, in a sense, has two cultures. In the north, the white population is almost entirely Protestant and largely Anglo-Saxon. In southern Louisiana, the Creole culture is very much alive, and French Creole is important as a language. There is a somewhat different French culture as well. The Cajuns are descendants of French exiles who left Nova Scotia (then called Arcadia; "Arcadian" became corrupted over the centuries to "Cajun") when the British won control of that area during the French and Indian War. Although Spanish is rarely heard, Louisiana French contains a large amount of Spanish vocabulary, and the famous Creole cuisine is a mixture of Spanish, French, Native American, and African cooking styles.

Louisiana Purchase (Apr. 30, 1803): Purchase of land from France by the United States. On April 30, 1803, the United States agreed to pay Napoleon Bonaparte, the French dictator, $15,250,000 for 828,000 square miles of land stretching from the Mississippi River to the Rocky Mountains. From 1762 to 1800, the region had belonged to Spain. Napoleon had reacquired it, hoping to send thousands of French colonists into the region to build an empire. While the Spanish had title to the territory, they had granted Americans the right to use the port of New Orleans. In 1802, however, that right was revoked, a move that angered President Thomas Jefferson.

Jefferson offered to buy New Orleans from France for $2 million. Napoleon needed money to finance a recently-renewed war with Great Britain. Instead of one city, however, the French offered all of what was then called Louisiana for about four cents an acre ($15,250,000). The sale angered the Spanish government, as it violated Napoleon's pledge never to sell the territory. The Spanish did not want a long border with the United States, but they were forced to accept the agreement. France transferred control of the land to the United States, nearly doubling that nation's size.

Low riders and low riding: Low riders are both modified cars that ride low to the ground and the subculture of people who drive them, mostly young Chicano men in the Southwest.

Low riding dates back at least to the PACHUCO era of the 1940's. In the postwar period, young Mexican Americans participated in the national automobile craze by rebuilding and stylizing used cars to create a distinctive, clean appearance that became the traditional low rider look. Springs were shortened to lower the car close to the ground, and chrome bumpers and ornaments, extra lights, and skirts were added. Further extras came to include lacquer paint jobs featuring symbols, fancy writing, paintings, and images related to Mexican history and Chicano culture.

Cruising is an important part of low riding. Low riders drive along unofficially designated streets, slowly enough to make eye contact and occasional conversation with others in cars or on the street. The appearance of the "ride" (the car itself), its occupants, and the music coming from the car are all important. Cruising is sometimes compared to the *paseo* in Mexican tradition, in which male and female youth walk around a town plaza exchanging smiles and flirtatious talk.

Low rider cars are traditionally older American models from the 1940's through the 1960's. Although they are still popular and highly sought, such vintage

Cars from the first years of the low rider period remain popular. (Ruben G. Mendoza)

A participant in a "car hopping" contest prepares to raise his car on its hydraulic shocks. (Ruben G. Mendoza)

cars have become prohibitively expensive. Some low riders have opted instead for new, more economical small trucks. They are sometimes equipped with hydraulics such as "dancing beds" that raise, lower, and tilt the trucks' beds.

Although low rider culture is sometimes stereotyped as gang-related, it is actually a tradition that spans several generations and a range of types of people. "Clubbers" are one group of low riders, whose cars are the most highly ornamented. The car club phenomenon dates back to the pachuco era, when community workers established the clubs to guide cruising youths away from gangs. The clubs extend beyond an interest in cars, often participating in community fund-raisers and events. Clubbers compete for trophies and titles at car shows, which are a popular venue for displaying the immaculate shiny engines and velvet upholstery fitted with mini-bars and televisions. Clubbers often cruise together in car caravans, sometimes creating a display of dancing beds moving in unison. Some clubbers have passed on their cars and the low riding tradition to their children.

The *CHOLOS* constitute another large group of low riders. They are economically less well-off, and their cars are usually more conservative models from the 1950's to 1970's. Unlike the clubbers, who prefer contemporary popular music, *cholos* are more likely to listen to tunes from the 1950's and 1960's.

A third and much smaller group of low riders are the "cha chas," who were born in Mexico but reared for the most part in the United States. They drive and customize smaller cars such as Toyotas and Volkswagens.

Low riding has crossed cultural boundaries in the United States as well as overseas. Anglos, Asian Americans, and other groups, as well as youth in Japan, have begun customizing low rider-style cars.

Loyalist: Supporter of the government during the MEXICAN REVOLUTION. A loyalist is anyone who is or remains loyal, particularly to a political cause, party, government, or sovereign. The term was used frequently within Mexican American communities during the Mexican Revolution (1910-1921) to describe an individual's political sympathies. Many Mexicans immigrated to the United States particularly because of their loyalty to one faction or another. In the border towns, particularly El Paso, Texas, many Mexican expatriates helped fund and develop factions that participated in the war. The term "loyalist" frequently referred to those who supported Porfirio Díaz and the government that presided over Mexico prior to the conflict; however, as the conflict wore on and different leaders entered the struggle, the meaning of this term became less certain.

Lozano, Ignacio Eugenio, Sr. (1887, Marín, Nuevo León, Mexico—1953, San Antonio, Tex.): Newspaper editor. For most of the twentieth century, the Lozano family served the Mexican American community by publishing Spanish-language newspapers in the United States. In 1913, Lozano started the newspaper *La Prensa*. A second paper, *La Opinión*, followed in 1926. The papers were influential among Spanish speakers, particularly in California. They took strong positions in favor of workers but always called for calm negotiations rather than violent protests. Compensating for a weakness in the major dailies, *La Opinión* provided the only good coverage of the Latino community for most of its life.

Lozano's son, Ignacio, Jr., began managing *La Opinión* in the 1950's. His son, Jose, served for a time as publisher in the 1980's, and his daughter, Mónica Cecilia, became associate publisher and editor a few years later. *La Opinión* was sold to the *Los Angeles Times* in 1990.

Lucas, María Elena (b. Mar. 22, 1941, Matamoros, Mexico): Labor organizer. A poor Chicana farmworker, Lucas emerged in the late 1970's as a voice for undocumented workers from Central America and Mexico. She began working at the age of five, in the shrimp industry on the Gulf of Mexico. After years of hard work and violence, she came to understand the hardships facing farmworkers as well as the sexism in American society and even within the Latino labor movement. With no knowledge of labor politics or organizations, Lucas joined other farmworkers in Onarga, Illinois, to demand better conditions. Impressed with her work, labor activists introduced her to the ideology and tactics of the UNITED FARM WORKERS. She became an organizer for the Farm Worker Organizing Committee. Mexican folk Catholicism shaped her ideas about women and holiness. She was permanently disabled by exposure to pesticides in 1988 but continued to speak and write on behalf of farmworkers.

Ludlow Massacre (Apr. 20, 1914): During a violent coal strike that lasted almost fifteen months, the Colo-

rado state militia charged and burned a tent colony of strikers, resulting in the deaths of eight strikers, two young mothers, and twelve children. The strike, which claimed sixty-six lives, ended only when President Woodrow Wilson intervened with federal troops.

The Ludlow, Colorado, violence of 1913 and 1914 was a culmination of class conflict and economic grievances that had been building for thirty years in the Trinidad mining district, which was dominated by the Colorado Fuel and Iron Company owned by John D. Rockefeller, Jr. In an earlier strike in 1903 and 1904, the United Mine Workers (UMW) had tried and failed to obtain union recognition and an eight-hour workday. Wages and labor conditions were about average for the time, but the company's policy was one of antiunionism and benevolent paternalism. The company employed miners of different nationalities. Most were recent immigrants from Greece and Southeast Europe, but a considerable number were Mexicans and Mexican Americans.

In early 1913, the UMW returned with an intensive organizational campaign, resulting in widespread support for the goals of the union. After failing to obtain recognition, the UMW on September 23 called for a strike. More than 80 percent of the workers and their families responded with a mass exodus from the company-owned houses to set up several tent colonies, including the one at Ludlow. Tensions grew as the operators sent in several hundred guards and strikebreakers. After eleven deaths, Governor Elias Ammons, who was known to favor management, sent the Colorado National Guard to the area on October 28. This intervention only intensified the enmity and determination of the workers.

On April 20, 1914, bitter fighting broke out at the Ludlow camp, with the militia using machine guns against the strikers. After a zealous lieutenant ordered the troops to charge and to burn down the tents, a group of women and children who sought refuge in a pit perished in the conflagration. That same night, two unarmed union leaders were killed by Guardsmen while in custody.

Following the massacre of April 20, strikers rebelled with unrestrained anger, destroying company property and killing National Guardsmen as well as company employees. Governor Ammons declared that the state was unable to maintain order and called for President Wilson to send in federal troops. After John D. Rockefeller, Jr., refused to agree to federal arbitration, Wilson on April 28 reluctantly ordered the Army to occupy much of southeastern Colorado. Although peace was established by federal troops, Wilson was not able to convince the company to meet with union officials. The UMW admitted defeat and called an end to the strike on December 10, 1914. The company then imposed a settlement that included reforms allowing for representation of workers in a company union.

The Ludlow Massacre and other incidents during the strike led to much adverse publicity about the power of big business and, in the long term, contributed to the belief that workers should have more rights of collective bargaining. The company union that was organized after the strike became a model that enjoyed some popularity until the passage of the Wagner Act of 1935.

Luis, Juan (b. July 10, 1940, Vieques, Puerto Rico): Governor of the Virgin Islands. The family of Juan Luis moved from Puerto Rico to St. Croix, Virgin Islands, when he was two months old. Luis was educated there at the Inter-American University of Puerto Rico.

After serving in the U.S. Army, Luis taught primary school and held administrative positions in various local businesses. His first elected office was that of insular senator, as a candidate of the Independent Citizens Movement in 1972. Luis served as chairman of the legislature's housing and planning committee. He was also vice chairman of the recreational committee and a member of the committees on finance, public safety, health and welfare, and labor and veterans' affairs. In 1974, Luis ran successfully for lieutenant governor. Four years later, he won the seat of governor.

Luján, Gilbert Sánchez (b. 1940, French Camp, Calif.): Artist. Luján, who is known professionally by the name "Magu," spent most of the first few months of his life in a migrant workers' settlement in northern California. His parents, both of whom had Mexican American lineage, relocated to East Los Angeles. Luján spent his elementary and high school years in the suburban towns of La Puente and El Monte, near Los Angeles. His homes were near enough to Los Angeles that he was exposed to the popular culture surrounding the automobile; he became obsessed with customized cars.

After serving four years in the U.S. Air Force, Luján enrolled at East Los Angeles Junior College, where he received his first formal training in art. He transferred

Juan Luis takes the oath of office as governor of the Virgin Islands. (AP/Wide World Photos)

Manuel Luján, Jr., was the first U.S. secretary of the interior to visit the Miccosukee Indian Reservation. (AP/Wide World Photos)

to Long Beach State University, where he earned a B.A. degree, then went on to the University of California, Irvine, where he was awarded a master's degree in fine arts. Luján specialized in ceramic works, later branching into painted wood sculptures and pastel paintings. His work often shows barrio life in Southern California.

Luján had known artist Beto de la Rocha since 1963. The two of them joined Carlos Almaraz and Frank Romero to form an exhibiting group called Los Four. Their first show was in Irvine in 1974. It was expanded for an exhibition at the Los Angeles County Museum of Art.

In 1976, Luján moved to Fresno, California, where he taught ethnic studies and served as chair of La Raza Studies Department at Fresno City College. He became involved in community work with such activities as organizing a health clinic. He returned to Los Angeles in 1981 and began teaching at the Municipal Art Center at Barnsdall Park.

Luján, Manuel, Jr. (b. May 12, 1928, San Ildefonso, N.Mex.): Public official. Luján, a Mexican American, was reared and educated in Santa Fe. He joined the family insurance business after completing his education. He rose to local prominence at a time when Latinos in New Mexico were being urged by Senator Dennis Chávez to play an active role in politics. In 1948, he ran unsuccessfully for governor as a moderate Republican.

Luján won a seat in Congress in 1968, representing the First District of New Mexico. He later served as the ranking Republican member of the House Interior Committee and the Science, Space, and Technology Committee. He served in Congress until President George Bush called upon him to serve as secretary of the interior in 1989. In this cabinet position, Luján advocated policies promoting economic development and environmental protection in tandem. He returned to Santa Fe in 1993.

Luque, Dolf (Adolfo Luque; Aug. 4, 1890, Havana, Cuba—July 3, 1957, Havana, Cuba): Baseball player and coach. Known as "the Pride of Havana," Luque became the first Latin American-born player to appear

Dolf Luque won the final game of the 1933 World Series. (AP/Wide World Photos)

in a World Series game when he pitched five scoreless innings for the Cincinnati Reds in two games of the scandal-marred 1919 World Series against the Chicago White Sox.

Speaking little English and keeping to himself, the diminutive right-hander debuted in the major leagues in 1914 with the Boston Red Sox. After joining the Reds in 1918, Luque spent twelve seasons with the team. He led the National League with 27 wins and a 1.93 earned run average (ERA) in 1923, and he led the league again with a 2.63 ERA in 1925.

Late in his career, Luque became primarily a relief pitcher. As a reliever for the New York Giants, Luque won the final game of the 1933 World Series. He retired after the 1935 season with a career record of 193-179 and a 3.24 ERA. During the late 1930's and early 1940's, he served as a coach for the Giants.

M

McCarran-Walter Act. *See* **Immigration and Nationality Act of 1952**

Machismo: Masculinity. Machismo (literally, "maleness") is a name for characteristics Latino men may exhibit in relationships with their family members and others. Machismo penetrates all social and economic levels of Latino cultures. The term has been popularized in everyday speech by Anglos to mean male chauvinism, but this is not a true definition. Machismo carries both positive and negative aspects. Positive aspects include the importance of family, leadership in the family, loyalty, bravery, and pride in oneself. Negative machismo behavior includes treating women as subordinates, indulgent behavior with the intention of proving one's manhood, and being inflexible. With the growth of feminism, Latinas tended to view machismo as negative.

Machito and His Afro-Cubans: LATIN JAZZ group. Frank Raul Grillo, known as "Machito," was born in Havana, Cuba, on February 16, 1909, and immigrated to the United States in 1937. In 1940, he formed his group, the Afro-Cubans, with trumpeter and arranger Mario Bauza as musical director. Machito was a master of Cuban rhythms, which he combined with jazz to develop the Latin jazz sound. He worked and recorded with Dizzy Gillespie, Charlie Parker, and other jazz giants. He toured throughout the United States and Europe. His sixty albums included two nominated for Grammy Awards. He died in London, England, on April 15, 1984.

McLish, Rachel Livia Elizondo (b. 1958, Harlingen, Tex.): Bodybuilder. Mexican American bodybuilding champion Rachel McLish grew up around dance and fitness. Encouraged by her father, McLish turned her attention to weightlifting when she entered college. After earning a degree in health and physical education, McLish opened the first health club in southern Texas, the Sport Palace, in 1978.

In 1980, McLish took the title at the first U.S. Women's Body Building Championships, and she also won the 1980 Ms. Olympia title. Two years later, she again won Ms. Olympia and added the World Championship to her list of accomplishments. McLish was heralded as both a pioneering female bodybuilder and a positive role model. Early ballet training gave her grace, and she was often called the "feminine bodybuilder." The sport changed, however, by the mid-1980's; bulk replaced tone, and McLish retired.

After leaving competition, McLish became the spokesperson for the Health and Tennis Corporation of America. Advocating drug-free fitness and bodybuilding, she wrote several books on the topic, lent her name to a collection of workout clothing, and acted in the 1992 adventure film *Iron Eagle III.*

Madrugadores, Los: Group of Mexican musicians. Los Madrugadores ("the early risers") were brothers Victor and Jesus Sanchez, Fernando Linares, and radio announcer Pedro J. GONZÁLEZ. In 1929, González started an early-morning radio show and invited the self-taught guitarist/vocalist brothers to play. Later joined by Linares, the group played CANCIONES *mexicanas* and *CORRIDOS*, often by request. In 1931, González began a new morning show and used the name Los Madrugadores to include a range of other musicians who appeared on the show. The name most commonly refers to the original musicians. Los Madrugadores became a household name in the 1930's, attaining great popularity on González's show. The program ended after two years, but the three musicians continued to perform in restaurants and on other radio programs until Jesus Sanchez's untimely death in 1941. The group recorded an estimated two hundred records during the 1930's.

Magazines. *See* **Newspapers and magazines**

Maize: Corn. Maize was domesticated in the Americas and has been important there both as a foodstuff and as a cultural symbol. Maize was domesticated from an unknown wild ancestor sometime before 6000 B.C.E., apparently both in Peru and in Mexico. The earliest forms of corn were tiny, smaller than an adult finger and bearing only a few kernels, but selective breeding gradually produced forms that were larger, more productive, and resistant to climatic challenges. This meant that maize could be grown in various environments, including the cooler sections of North America; it also meant that it was sufficiently productive to become a dietary staple in most parts of the Americas. More than one hundred varieties of corn

Rachel McLish poses in the 1980 Ms. Olympia contest. (AP/Wide World Photos)

are known from pre-Columbian times, and more have been produced by modern agronomists.

Despite its many virtues, corn has three major drawbacks as a staple crop. First, the kernels of many varieties have hard hulls that can cut the gums. To solve this problem, ancient American Indians devised a lye bath to loosen the hulls, producing *nixtamal*, or hominy. Ground, this becomes the MASA used to make Mexican tortillas and other corn preparations. Second, during domestication, the ear of maize became tightly wrapped with a husk and the kernels tightly attached; in short, maize lost its ability to reproduce without human assistance. As long as people continue to plant corn, this is not a real problem. Third, maize is missing essential amino acids, particularly lysine. Fortunately, another American domesticated crop, beans, provides these.

Wherever maize was grown in the Americas, it was revered. The Maya worshipped the corn god, the Aztecs incorporated corn into their depictions of heaven, and the Hopi Indians refer to maize as "Mother Corn." At a festival in honor of the god Huitzilopochtli, Aztecs would produce a giant statue of the god made from ground maize and honey, then parade it around the capital. Priests would break the statue and eat it as the god's blood and bones. Two of the most powerful substances in Navajo curing are maize pollen and ground maize. Maize was at the heart of the economies of most Native American agriculturalists, and they reflected that fact in their ideologies and rituals.

The relatively few places where maize was not grown were ecologically unsuitable for it. Colder areas in North America and in the mountains of Latin America had conditions too extreme for growing maize, and most of these areas had no agriculture whatsoever. In much of the lowland and coastal areas, especially the swampy margins of Central America and northeastern South America, little maize was grown because these environments were better suited to the growing of cassava (yucca) as a staple.

After the European voyages of discovery took maize to the Old World in 1497, it spread rapidly. Italy was growing substantial amounts of maize by 1550, and the rest of Europe was doing so by 1650. India was growing maize as a staple by 1650, parts of Africa by 1700, and parts of China by 1800.

Maldonado-Denis, Manuel (b. 1933, Santurce, Puerto Rico): Educator and historian. Maldonado-Denis' work primarily concerns the history of Puerto Rico and emigration of Puerto Ricans to the U.S. mainland. Several of his books written in Spanish have been translated to English.

Maldonado-Denis holds a bachelor's degree from the University of Puerto Rico. His master's degree and doctorate are from the University of Chicago. He be-

La Malinche translated for Hernán Cortés. (Institute of Texan Cultures)

gan teaching at the University of Puerto Rico in Río Piedras in 1959, eventually earning promotion to the rank of professor. In 1972 and 1973, he worked as professor of Puerto Rican studies at Queens College of the City University of New York.

Malinche, La (also known as Doña Marina and Malitzin; c. 1502, Painalá, México—c. 1528): Translator for Hernán CORTÉS. Baptized as Marina, La Malinche was Cortés' translator and mistress during the Spanish Conquest of Mexico. She was born in central Mexico but had been sold into slavery to the Tabascans of the south and was among the twenty women given to Cortés when he landed in Mexico in 1519. Because she spoke both Nahuatl and Maya, she became Cortés' translator.

La Malinche was by Cortés' side throughout the conquest period. She translated all the conversations between Cortés and Moctezuma and informed Cortés of an ambush at Cholula that would have devastated the Spanish expedition.

In 1524, La Malinche married one of Cortés' soldiers, Juan Jaramillo. She went with Cortés and Jaramillo in an expedition to Honduras and died of an illness around 1528.

La Malinche has become synonymous with treason in Mexico because she betrayed her own race for the Spaniards. Although she was always faithful to Cortés, it is important that she was a female slave in a strong patriarchal society. She was conditioned to serve her master, so it is not surprising that she failed to plot against Cortés. La Malinche is also perceived as the symbolic mother of MESTIZOS, or mixed-race people.

Mambo: An off-beat dance derived from the Cuban RUMBA. Mambo music is in four-four time and carries the accents on the first beat and the second half of the second beat, creating a syncopation accentuated by percussion instruments such as MARACAS, conga drums, and claves. The dance is performed by couples, in embrace or separated, with a hip-rocking motion and with forward and backward steps that begin on the fourth beat. Basically a swinging rumba, the mambo evolved with both Cuban and Mexican musicians. It first appeared in Cuba in the mid-1940's and spread throughout Europe after 1955, later giving birth to the CHA-CHA.

Manifest Destiny: Ideology justifying expansion of the United States into the Southwest and the Pacific Northwest. By the 1840's, many citizens in the United States came to believe that their country's expansion across the North American continent was preordained. John L. O'Sullivan captured this sentiment in 1845 with his coining of the phrase "Manifest Destiny."

U.S. diplomacy promoted expansionism on three grounds. First, God supposedly had blessed the United States, allowing it to grow while punishing Mexico for clinging to Catholicism. Second, as United States pioneers spilled across the Mississippi River, they converted British and Mexican land into free, democratic areas. Finally, the United States was growing so rapidly that the aggressive republic needed more land. The only questions were how far the United States would expand and whether it would use diplomacy or war to do so.

President James Polk strongly favored annexing Texas. He had triumphed in the 1844 presidential election by articulating Manifest Destiny to a boisterous public that boasted of its freedom from European tradition. Polk interpreted his victory as a mandate for expansion. Concerned that the union was shaky, Polk thought that expansionism would unify the republic. As if to underline Polk's views, Congress annexed Texas shortly before Polk's inauguration.

Various groups in the United States supported Manifest Destiny as a means to rationalize agrarian cupidity and increase trade. At a deeper level, it justified racial prejudice and reflected deep insecurity about the future. New England merchants demanded deep-water ports in California as a link to Asian markets and feared that Europeans would seize Western territories first. The South fretted over the possibility of new states becoming free of slavery. The area west of the Mississippi River was full of land speculators, aggressive pioneers, and outright warmongers. A joint Mexican-U.S. claims commission could not satisfy the largely western claimants who demanded payment from the Mexican government for various losses incurred by U.S. citizens.

The forces behind Manifest Destiny finally led to a decisive war with Mexico. John Stockton attempted to provoke war during an 1845 California revolt, during which the Polk Administration instructed various diplomats to obtain California. Polk sent John Slidell, a New Orleans lawyer, to Mexico to obtain agreement on the Rio Grande being the Texas border as well as to purchase New Mexico and California. Tensions increased dramatically when Mexico would not recognize Slidell's credentials. When president Joaquín Herrera appeared ready to receive Slidell, a monarchist group in Mexico overthrew Herrera, making Mariano Paredes the new leader.

Polk then took the initiative. First, he sent general Zachary Taylor to Corpus Christi, Texas, as part of his continued effort to establish the Rio Grande boundary. U.S. warships also dropped anchor off the Mexican coast. Mexico still counted on European support, but Great Britain was about to peacefully settle its dispute with the United States concerning Oregon. At one point, Polk considered sacrificing Oregon if Great Britain could convince Mexico to sell California, but the aggressive president found himself in a position to triumph on both fronts. Finally provoked into fighting, Mexican forces attacked one of Taylor's scouting parties active on the Rio Grande in April, 1846. Polk called for war, claiming that "American blood had been shed on American soil" even though the attack occurred in a disputed area with virtually no U.S. citizens resident. In the ensuing MEXICAN AMERICAN WAR, Mexico lost half of its territory, and the United States gained this land as well as the eighty thousand Mexican Americans living on it. Manifest Destiny was revived later, particularly with regard to U.S. annexation of the Philippines.

Manioc: Central American root. Manioc, also known as manihot, yucca, and cassava, was first eaten about six thousand years ago along the eastern coast of Central America and northeastern South America. The manioc of that time was laden with poisonous oxalic acid, and it was necessary to grate and leach the root before cooking and eating it. During the intervening period, American Indians developed nonpoisonous manioc through selective breeding, and most modern manioc is of this sort.

Manioc resembles potatoes in taste and can be cooked either by boiling or by frying. Manioc processed into a powder and reformed into pellets is tapioca, widely used in puddings and to thicken stews. Manioc juice sold commercially is simmered down with brown sugar and spices to make *cassareep*, a molasses-like condiment used in Caribbean cuisine, particularly for making pepperpot.

Mano: Cylindrical or loaf-shaped stone used to grind corn and other foods. The *mano* and its partner, the *METATE*, have been the most favored grinding implements in folk Mexico and adjacent areas for thousands of years. The *mano* is held in the hands and pushed or pulled over the slablike *metate* to grind anything from dried corn to fresh chiles to spice mixtures. Both *manos* and *metates* are best made of hard volcanic rock, but softer stones sometimes are substituted.

Manuel, Herschel Thurman (Dec. 24, 1887, Freetown, Ind.—Mar. 21, 1976, Austin, Tex.): Educational psychologist. Manuel studied obstacles encountered by Spanish-speaking children in an English-speaking environment and was interested in issues related to BILINGUAL EDUCATION and testing. Along with his work as a teacher, he was president of the National Council on Measurements Used in Education (1954-1955) and director of research for the Texas Committee on Coordination in Education (1935-1938).

Manuel, a Mexican American, was graduated from DePauw University in 1909, then worked as a teacher and administrator in Indiana public schools until 1913. He earned his M.A. at the University of Chicago in 1914 and his Ph.D. at the University of Illinois in 1917. From 1919 to 1925, he taught at Western State College in Colorado. He joined the faculty of the University of Texas at Austin in 1925 and remained at that school until 1976. From 1946 to 1958, he was director of testing and guidance. Among his many publications are *The Education of Mexican and Spanish-Speaking Children in Texas* (1930) and *Spanish-Speaking Children of the Southwest: Their Education and the Public Welfare* (1965), which is considered to be the culmination of his years of research and practice.

Maquiladoras (established in 1965): Twin manufacturing and assembly plants. These Mexican-owned operations have joint-venture contracts with non-Mexican multinational corporations and offer less expensive alternatives for the production of goods for export.

NUMBERS OF *MAQUILADORA* PLANTS AND EMPLOYEES, 1966-1988		
	Number of Plants	*Number of Employees*
1966	12	3,000
1970	120	20,000
1975	454	67,200
1980	620	119,500
1981	605	131,000
1982	585	127,000
1983	600	151,000
1984	672	199,000
1985	760	212,000
1986	890	250,000
1987	1,125	305,000
1988	1,279	329,000

Source: Data are from Leslie Sklair, *Assembling for Development: The Maquila Industry in Mexico and the United States* (Winchester, Mass: Unwin Hyman, 1988), p. 144.

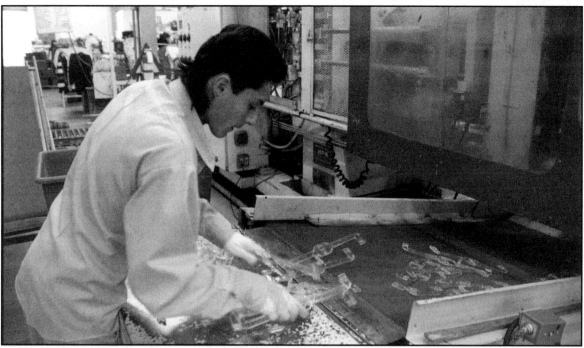

A maquiladora *in Tijuana, Mexico, produces plastic coathangers.* (David Bacon)

History. In 1965, the United States and Mexican governments implemented the BORDER INDUSTRIALIZATION PROGRAM (BIP) for the primary purpose of providing business opportunities along the U.S.-Mexico border. Factories with Mexican majority ownership opened in specified industrial trade zones for the manufacturing and/or assembly of goods for export to the United States. The Mexican government established guidelines for the operation of twin plants, addressing working conditions and environmental concerns. The Mexican government modified the BIP and allowed for corporations not based in the United States to establish *maquiladoras* throughout Mexico.

The BIP required Mexican ownership, but up to 49 percent of foreign investment was allowed. Most *maquiladoras* are clustered around urban areas and have spurred a movement of workers from rural areas. The factories produce a diversified set of goods, most of which are readily available in the United States. *Twin Plant News* reported in 1966 that only twelve *maquiladoras* were in operation along the U.S.-Mexico border. By 1994, each of the thirty-two Mexican states and districts had at least one *maquiladora* industrial park, and more than two thousand twin plants manufactured goods. Products manufactured for export included apparel, appliances, automobiles and parts, electronics, lumber, machinery, petrochemical products, pharmaceuticals, rubber products, resins, and synthetic fibers.

Major exporters for 1993 included Singer (appliances); General Motors, Ford Motor Company, and Chrysler (automobiles and parts); General Electric and International Business Machines (electronics); Dupont (petrochemicals); Kimberly-Clark (lumber); and General Tire (rubber products). *Twin Plant News* reported that in 1993 more than 400,000 Mexican workers were employed in *maquiladora* plants.

Impact on Mexicans. The twin plants vary in size, and employment depends upon the continued existence of product orders. Under BIP guidelines, Mexico is broken into three trade zones that determine the starting salary of workers. The trade zone with the highest pay is mostly along the U.S.-Mexico border and the area around Mexico City. The trade zone with the lowest pay encompasses most of southern Mexico's states and isolated areas of the northern Mexican region. According to *Twin Plant News* the average *maquiladora* direct-labor wage in 1992 was $1.62 per hour. The lowest direct-labor wage rate, $1.26, was in the apparel and textile industry. Workers in the machinery sector were the highest paid at $2.33 per hour.

BIP employer regulations of the early 1990's stipulated a daily minimum starting salary and six paid legal Mexican holidays, with one additional day for the inauguration of a new Mexican president. A common practice among employers was to administer physical exams and educational (dexterity) skill placement tests to potential employees. Potential employees meeting all requirements were given a contract outlining a forty-eight-hour work week with the stipulation that salaries were to be paid in cash. Labor unions were unsuccessful in organizing the work force.

High employee turnover rates are common in the twin plants. An intensive study of *maquiladora* work force conditions by Maria P. Fernandez-Kelly found young single women with an average level of education of seven years to be the most desirable workers. In order to lower training expenses, employers offered incentives to keep employees from leaving, including meals, childcare, health care, and some educational courses.

Impact of NAFTA. The NORTH AMERICAN FREE TRADE AGREEMENT (NAFTA), an agreement among the governments of Mexico, Canada, and the United States to lower barriers to trade, went into effect in 1994. NAFTA provides for import or export of some goods among the three nations without any trade barriers. Mexico planned to establish more *maquiladoras* throughout the nation and to have Mexicans move from rural to urban areas to take advantage of employment opportunities offered by the expected increase in export trade. U.S. Trade Representative Mickey Kantor established NAFTA side agreements in 1993 that ensured workers' rights in all three nations and the protection of environmental conditions within each society. —*Melissa Amado*

SUGGESTED READINGS: • Baerresen, Donald W. *The Border Industrialization Program of Mexico.* Lexington, Mass.: Heath Lexington Books, 1971. • Executive Office of the President. *North American Free Trade Agreement Between the Government of the United States of America, the Government of Canada, and the Government of the United Mexican States.* Washington, D.C.: Government Printing Office, 1993. • Fernandez-Kelly, Maria P. *For We Are Sold, I and My People: Women and Industry in Mexico's Frontier.* Albany: State University of New York Press, 1983. • Kantor, Mickey. "Understanding the NAFTA Side Agreements." *Twin Plant News* 9 (November, 1993): 45. • Seligson, Mitchell, and Edward Williams. *Maquiladoras and Migration: Workers in the Mexico-United States Border Industrialization Program.* Austin: University of Texas Press, 1981. • United States. Congress. House. Committee on Government Operations. *Maquiladora Impact on U.S. Jobs and Trade Competition with Japan: Hearing Before a Subcommittee of the Committee on Government Operations.* 100th Congress, 1st Session, 1987.

At an Aztec cultural workshop, a young girl holds a maraca. (Raymond J. Malace)

Maracas: Pair of oval gourd rattles. Maracas are used by percussion ensembles to provide basic rhythmic accompaniment. Traditional maracas are made from a gourd, including its naturally dried seeds. Imitations can be made of wood, wickerwork, plastic, or metal filled with small beads. Different types of maracas include the *gapachos*, smaller in size, typical of the Andean region; the *clavellinas*, typical of the Llanos region of Colombia; and the Paraguayan *porrongo*, traditionally played exclusively by men. Maracas are generally played in pairs and are held by their handles, one in each hand. They are an essential accompaniment to Latin American music and an integral part of primary school music education.

Maravilla (East Los Angeles, Calif.): Public housing project. Built in the late 1920's, Maravilla was created to relocate low-income residents of the Bunker Hill neighborhood who had been dispossessed as a result of city expansion. Maravilla for years suffered from widespread poverty, gang violence, and squalor. By 1994, the surrounding BARRIO spanned some seventy streets. The area's population in 1990 was more than 90 percent Chicano, with a few African Americans and a few poor whites whose parents and grandparents arrived during the Great Depression.

In the late 1960's, the Maravilla Foundation was established by Esteban Torres (later a U.S. congressman) to help area residents resolve their problems. Through the 1980's and into the 1990's, however, Maravilla's problems continued.

March to Austin (July-September, 1966): Farmworker protest against low wages. On July 4, 1966, several hundred farmworkers began a march of several hundred miles from Rio Grande City, in South Texas, to the state capital of Austin. Led by Eugene Nelson, a disciple of César CHÁVEZ; Father Anthony González, a Catholic priest; and the Reverend James Novaro, a Baptist minister, the marchers pledged nonviolence. Their effort was modeled on the MARCH TO SACRAMENTO earlier that year.

The marchers' goal was to present a petition containing thousands of signatures to Governor John Connally. The petition supported coverage for farm labor-

ers under the Texas minimum wage law, which set a minimum wage of $1.25 per hour but excluded agricultural workers, most of whom earned much less. The marchers reached the capital on Labor Day, but the governor refused to meet with them and made no effort in the legislature in support of the protesters' demands. After a short debate, the Texas Senate rejected inclusion of farm laborers in minimum-wage legislation. The march did help bring the plight of farmworkers to public attention, however, and increased sympathy for their demands.

March to Sacramento (Mar. 17-Apr. 12, 1966): Demonstration in support of grape pickers. On March 17, 1966, sixty grape workers representing the NATIONAL FARM WORKERS ASSOCIATION (NFWA) began a 300-mile, 25-day march from Delano, California, to the state capital to call attention to a boycott against Schenley Industries, a large wine producer. A grape workers' strike had been in progress for several months, and the union hoped that nationwide pressure against the company would help win wage increases for its members.

The number of marchers grew along the way because of the efforts of El TEATRO CAMPESINO (people's theater), which put on skits depicting the plight of

Marchers gather at the capitol in Sacramento. (AP/Wide World Photos)

Juan Mari Brás. (AP/Wide World Photos)

farmworkers in every town the demonstrators visited. By the time the group reached Sacramento on Easter Sunday, more than eight thousand people had joined the march. On the day before the marchers reached their destination, Schenley agreed to recognize the NFWA as sole bargaining agent for field workers and began discussions for a new contract. Despite this victory, Governor Edward "Pat" Brown refused to meet with march leaders, denouncing them as "radicals" and "troublemakers."

Mares, Michael Allen (b. Mar. 11, 1945, Albuquerque, N.Mex): Zoologist. Mares is a zoologist and an expert in the area of mammalian biogeography. The Mexican American scientist received his B.S. from the University of New Mexico in 1968 and his M.S. from Kansas State University and Ph.D. in zoology from the University of Texas in 1973. In 1981, he went to the University of Oklahoma at Norman, where he has served as professor of zoology and director of the Stovall Museum. In addition, he has worked as a research field worker in Argentina and in the southwestern United States. He has held concurrent appointments as adjunct professor of ecology at the Universidad Nacional de Cordoba and the Universidad Nacional de Tucuman. His areas of substantive research are convergent evolution, adaptation and community organization of desert rodents, and the ecology, conservation, evolution, and systematics of South American mammals. Among many awards, he has received a Ford Fellowship to do research at the University of Arizona at Tucson (1980-1981), a Fulbright Residential Fellowship (1974), and a National Chicano Council Fellowship (1978).

Mari Brás, Juan (b. Dec. 2, 1927, Mayagüez, Puerto Rico): Political leader. Mari Brás is a leader of the Puerto Rican Socialist Party. After attending high school in his hometown, Mari Brás attended the University of Puerto Rico, la Universidad Nacional Autónoma de Mexico, Florida Southern College, and Georgetown University. He earned his law degree in 1954.

Mari Brás mastered English and French in addition to his native Spanish. His interests, aside from Puerto Rican politics, are varied and include art, literature, and the theater. He is a member of the Puerto Rican Bar Association and its Constitutional Law Commission.

Mari Brás is also affiliated with the Ateneo Puertorriqueño, the oldest cultural institution in Puerto Rico. The Ateneo has encouraged intellectual and artistic development for more than one hundred years.

Mariachi: The word "mariachi" can refer to a specific type of Mexican musical group or ensemble or to an individual musician in a mariachi group. It can also refer, as an adjective, to a genre or style related to the mariachi, as in mariachi music or mariachi trumpet. Since the 1930's, the mariachi has been widely considered the quintessential Mexican folk-derived musical ensemble and has become an institution symbolic of Mexican music and culture. Mariachi groups are found throughout the Americas and in Europe.

Origins. Professional musicians accompanied Hernán Cortés when he arrived in 1519 in what is now Mexico. Among their instruments were the harp and the vihuela, prototypes of those later used by the mariachi. Natives, who had their own highly developed musical traditions, quickly mastered European musical practices. African music was brought to Mexico during the early colonial period with the importation of slaves. Many regional traditions of mestizo folk music, including that of the mariachi, resulted from the ensuing cultural and musical blending of indigenous and foreign elements.

The mariachi is native to a region of western Mexico that includes what are today the states of Jalisco, Nayarit, Zacatecas, Aguascalientes, Guanajuato, Michoacán, and Colima. The region extends as far north as Sinaloa and Durango and as far south as Guerrero. The exact birthplace of the mariachi is unknown despite frequent attempts to make such an attribution.

Early History. The early development of mestizo folk music in Mexico is largely undocumented, so theories on the early evolution of the mariachi are largely speculative. The earliest known incontrovertible reference to a mariachi appears in a letter written by a priest, Cosme Santa Anna, in 1852. The word can be found earlier as a place name.

Mariachis documented during the second half of the nineteenth century in central western Mexico were commonly associated with the rural fiesta or fandango and with the *tarima*, a wooden platform upon which couples would dance *sones* and *jarabes*, the two most important genres of the early mariachi repertory. Early mariachis wore peasant garb and had little concern for dressing alike. After the Mexican Revolution (1910-1921), however, modest uniforms began to appear. Later, when mariachis could afford to outfit themselves elegantly, they chose the suit of the horseman, or *traje de charro*. The gala version of this suit worn by contemporary mariachis—with its tightly fitting ornamented pants, short jacket, embroidered belt, boots, wide bow tie, and sombrero—was once the attire of the wealthy hacienda owner or the CHARRO.

Etymology. The consensus of modern scholars is that the word "mariachi" is indigenous to Mexico. The now-extinct Coca language of central Jalisco is that most frequently cited as its probable source. Legend erroneously attributes the word to the French intervention of the 1860's, explaining it as a corruption of the French word *mariage* and citing a similarity between "mariachi" (or its archaic variant, "mariache") and the French word for wedding. Historical documents prove that both the word "mariachi" and the ensemble it designates predate the French occupation of Mexico, making the similarity to the French word a phonetic coincidence.

Urbanization. Although its roots are rural, the contemporary mariachi is an urban phenomenon associated with postrevolutionary Mexico City. It was in that city that the urban mariachi was born and where most of its development took place. Vestiges of earlier types of mariachis may still be found in rural Mexico, but the urban mariachi has been the dominant model since the 1930's.

In 1920, Cirilo Marmolejo moved his group from Tecolotlán, Jalisco, to Mexico City. His was the first mariachi group to establish itself permanently in the capital. In 1923, the cantina Salón Tenampa opened on what is now Plaza Garibaldi, where the mariachis of Concho Andrade and Cirilo Marmolejo performed. The Tenampa soon became Mexico City's center of mariachi activity and attracted other groups from rural areas to that plaza.

Although mariachis had performed for official functions under Porfirio Díaz in 1905 and in 1907, it was not until after the Mexican Revolution that the mariachi became widely adopted as a symbol of nationalism. Since Álvaro Obregón's presidential administration (1920-1924), postrevolutionary Mexican leaders have used mariachi music for political events, with Lázaro Cárdenas being the first to officially subsidize it during his term (1934-1940).

The media were crucial to popularization of the mariachi. During the 1930's, radio, cinema, and the phonograph came of age in Mexico, launching what previously had been a rural, regional music to national and international prominence. The principal role of the mariachi in the media became that of accompanying leading vocalists of ranchera music, Mexico's most popular nationalistic musical expression.

Instrumentation. At the beginning of the twentieth century, a typical mariachi consisted of four musicians. Although precise instrumentation could vary with each group, regional tendencies existed. The two most prominent mariachi regions were those of central Jalisco and southern Jalisco. Mariachis of central Jalisco preferred two violins, vihuela (a small, guitarlike instrument with a convex back and five strings), and guitarrón (a large, six-string bass version of the vihuela). Those of southern Jalisco and Michoacán preferred two violins, harp, and guitarra de golpe (the original mariachi guitar).

After the Mexican Revolution, mariachi groups tended to grow in size. Instruments previously associated with specific regional traditions were combined, and existing instruments were doubled. Following a period of experimentation, the instrumentation of the urban mariachi became standardized. The modern classical guitar was adopted, and the vihuela and the guitarrón were retained; the guitarra de golpe and the harp fell into general disuse.

Early in the twentieth century, wind instruments were frequently added to the traditionally all-string ensemble. By the 1920's, mariachis in different parts of Mexico were using the cornet. By the 1930's, however, the trumpet had replaced the cornet and had gained a permanent foothold in the mariachi. It had become a mariachi institution by the 1940's. The two-trumpet combination popularized by Mariachi México de Pepe Villa in the early 1950's is the most recent innovation to take place in the standard mariachi instrumentation.

The standard contemporary instrumentation for a full mariachi is two trumpets, three or more violins, a vihuela, a guitar, and a guitarrón. An additional guitar or trumpet is sometimes added, and the basic ensemble is often reduced for economic reasons. All members may sing.

Mariachi Vargas. The most important group in the history of mariachi music is Mariachi Vargas de Tecalitlán, founded in 1898 by Gaspar Vargas in Tecalitlán, Jalisco. In the 1930's, the group's leadership was taken over by his son, Silvestre Vargas, considered the greatest mariachi organizer and visionary of all time. In 1934, the group moved permanently to Mexico City, where it played a leading role in the evolution of the mariachi. The majority of influential musicians in the genre have passed through its ranks, including arranger Rubén Fuentes and trumpet player Miguel Martínez. Since the 1940's, Mariachi Vargas has been the model ensemble for the urban mariachi tradition, in which its trajectory and influence are without parallel.

Mariachi Music in the United States. Mariachi music has become deeply rooted in the United States, where it has taken on unique characteristics and even influenced its Mexican counterpart. During the late

A mariachi guitarist performs at a Las Posadas festival. (Robert Fried)

1950's and early 1960's, a number of organized mariachi groups immigrated to Los Angeles, an urban area that has in many ways become to the United States what Mexico City is to Mexico as an urban mecca of mariachi music. In 1961, Nati Cano organized MARIACHI LOS CAMPEROS DE NATI CANO, which became the best-known U.S. mariachi and the country's pioneer group in popularizing this music among non-Hispanics. In 1969, the group opened La Fonda restaurant in Los Angeles, the world's first venue designed to showcase a mariachi. Other U.S. groups followed suit, and eventually this concept was adopted in Mexico.

Mariachi Uclatlán, founded in 1961 at the University of California at Los Angeles Institute of Ethnomusicology, pioneered the academic mariachi tradition. Today, educational institutions throughout the Southwest offer classes in mariachi music. Mariachi Cobre, founded in Tucson, Arizona, in 1971, was the first prominent Mexican American mariachi group.

In 1979, a U.S. mariachi movement was born at the First International Mariachi Conference, held in San Antonio, Texas. Since then, mariachi festivals and conferences have proliferated in the United States. Mexico celebrated its first international festival in 1994. Linda RONSTADT's 1988 recording *Canciones de mi padre* heralded the creation of a new audience for mariachi music among non-Hispanics. Ronstadt is a traditionalist. Mariachis such as Sol de México in Los Angeles and Campanas de América in San Antonio seek innovation, combining other musical styles with that of the mariachi.

Conclusion. Mariachi music reached a peak in popularity during the 1950's and 1960's, then increasingly became a nostalgia genre, marginalized by the media that initially catapulted it to fame. With the exception of isolated attempts to infuse new vitality into the tradition from outside sources, relatively little new mariachi music was composed or performed in the late twentieth century. Nevertheless, the mariachi remains in demand for social functions in Mexican and Mexican American communities, where it has become a cultural inheritance. A 1990's revival in the United States has given new life to the mariachi, the appeal of which transcends ethnic groups and national borders.

—*Jonathan Clark*

SUGGESTED READINGS: • Fogelquist, Mark. *Rhythm and Form in the Contemporary Son Jalisciense.* Master's thesis. Los Angeles: University of California, Los Angeles, 1975. • Jáuregui, Jesús. *El mariachi: El símbolo musical de México.* Mexico: Banpaís, 1990.

A mariachi band relaxes before a performance. (Impact Visuals, Slobodan Dimitrov)

• Loza, Steven. *Barrio Rhythm: Mexican American Music in Los Angeles*. Urbana: University of Illinois Press, 1993. • Pearlman, Steven. *Mariachi Music in Los Angeles*. Ph.D. dissertation. Los Angeles: University of California, Los Angeles, 1988. • Rafael, Hermes. *Origen e historia del mariachi*. Mexico: Editorial Katún, 1982. • Saldívar, Gabriel, and Elisa Osorio Bolio. *Historia de la música en México (épocas precortesiana y colonial)*. 1934. Reprint. Mexico: Secretaría de Educación Pública, Publicaciones del Departamento de Bellas Artes, 1987. • Stevenson, Robert. *Music in Mexico: A Historical Survey*. New York: Thomas Y. Crowell, 1952.

Mariachi Los Camperos de Nati Cano: Los Angeles MARIACHI group. Mexican musician Natividad "Nati" Cano became Los Camperos' director in 1961, when the group was playing backup for acts at Los Angeles' MILLION DOLLAR THEATER. In 1962, Los Camperos created a road show, performing as headliners across the United States. In 1967, Cano opened a Los Angeles restaurant where the group presented a mariachi show with music and dance. The group also toured and produced albums, and it recorded and toured with Linda RONSTADT. Cano won a National Endowment for the Arts National Heritage Award and has recruited some of Mexico's best mariachi musicians to play with the fourteen-member group, which remained active into the 1990's.

Marianismo: Female counterpart to MACHISMO. *Marianismo* is a pattern of behavior and attitudes characteristic of some Latin American women, regardless of social class. As usually applied, it assumes women's spiritual superiority to men. Although it is the counterpart to machismo, a well-known (though sometimes misconceived) concept, *marianismo* is much less known to those outside Latin culture. *Marianismo* derives from the Catholic practice of Marianism, which venerates the VIRGIN MARY. *Marianismo* is a secular derivative of this religious practice in which beliefs are centered on the idea that women are spiritually and morally superior to men. *Marianismo* is sometimes seen as oppressive to women's societal roles, although women as well as men contribute to the perpetuation of the beliefs that sustain *marianismo*.

Marichal, Juan (Juan Antonio Marichal y Sanchez; b. Oct. 20, 1937, Laguna Verde, Dominican Republic): Baseball player. A tall right-handed pitcher noted for his high leg kick and his superb control, Marichal

Juan Marichal. (AP/Wide World Photos)

played for amateur teams in the Dominican Republic before signing with the San Francisco Giants in 1958. After two seasons in the minor leagues, he was called up to the Giants in the middle of the 1960 season and threw a shutout in his first start. The "Dominican Dandy" went on to become one of the pillars of the fine Giants teams of the 1960's, winning more games (191) than any other pitcher during the decade. He led the National League in victories in 1963 and 1968, in winning percentage in 1966, in earned run average in 1969, and in shutouts in 1965 and 1969. A ten-time All-Star, Marichal was the winning pitcher in All-Star Games in 1962 and 1964 and was chosen as the Most Valuable Player of the 1965 game. He retired in 1975 with a career record of 243-142. That year, the Giants retired his number 27 jersey. In 1983, he was inducted into the National Baseball Hall of Fame.

Mariel boat lift (Apr. 21-Sept. 26, 1980): A journey by boat of approximately 125,000 refugees from Mariel Harbor, Cuba, to Key West, Florida. On April 1, 1980, six Cubans in a bus crashed through the gates of the Peruvian embassy in Havana and requested political ASYLUM, expressing their wish to leave Cuba. The Cuban government explained this event by claiming that segments of the populace had been misled by Cuban exiles residing in Florida who had been allowed to visit their homeland and had extolled the economic opportunities of capitalist life in the United States. The Cuban government announced that those who wished to leave Cuba should congregate at the Peruvian embassy, where they would be provided with exit documents. Almost immediately, thousands of people assembled on the embassy grounds. Cuban leader Fidel

CASTRO increased the flood of refugees by releasing some criminals and mental patients.

A group of Cuban exiles who happened to be in Cuba at the time returned to Miami and organized a flotilla of some forty fishing boats and small pleasure craft, which they sent to Cuba. The Cuban government gave permission for the boats to leave the island. U.S. president Jimmy Carter announced that anyone leaving Cuba would be welcomed in the United States, and the U.S. Navy and Coast Guard rendered assistance. The United States quickly faced two problems, however: the overwhelming number of immigrants and the fact that some were criminals and mental patients. On May 14, Carter called for an end to the boat lifts, but the influx of refugees continued. Boat owners risked stiff fines, confiscation of their vessels, and prison sentences to bring refugees to the United States.

The U.S. government received the refugees at federal detention centers consisting of "tent cities" and existing prisons located in Florida, Pennsylvania, Wisconsin, Louisiana, and Georgia. In order to be discharged from one of the crowded camps, a refugee needed an American sponsor. Most of the refugees, sometimes referred to as *marielitos*, did not have families in the United States; unable to arrange for sponsors, many stayed in detention for months without representation or prospect of release. The exodus from Cuba abated in mid-June. Castro officially halted the boat lift on September 26 by closing the Port of Mariel.

The Mariel boat lift was the third most important migration of Cubans to the United States, following the post-Cuban Revolution migration of 1959 and the FREEDOM AIRLIFT of the early 1970's. Controversy surrounded the Mariel boat lift because of the refugees who were from Cuban prisons and mental hospitals.

In 1987, an agreement between the Cuban and the U.S. governments provided for the immigration of twenty thousand Cubans to the United States each year. Cuba agreed to take back some twenty-five hundred Cubans jailed in the United States because of their criminal records. By 1990, 85 percent of the *marielitos* were employed in the United States and paying taxes. Others were in American prisons, hospitals, or other institutions, and about four hundred more had returned to Cuba.

Marimba: Type of xylophone of African origin. The marimba (from the Bantu language prefix *ma* meaning

Florida authorities enlisted the aid of U.S. Marines to manage the flow of refugees during the boat lift. (AP/Wide World Photos)

A street performer plays a marimba. (Claire Rydell)

Cheech Marín starred in the satirical Born in East L.A. (AP/Wide World Photos)

cumulative and the suffix *rimba* meaning single notes) is a resonated instrument capable of reproducing many *rimba* (notes). Its origin is disputed. Some experts place it during pre-Columbian times; others ascribe its introduction in the Americas to African slaves. It is still played in Brazil, Ecuador, Nicaragua, Cuba, and Mexico, where it is known as the *zapotecano*. In Guatemala, it has a second keyboard for chromatic range and is considered to be the national instrument.

Marín, Richard "Cheech" (b. July 13, 1946, Los Angeles, Calif.): Comedian and actor. Marín, who was graduated with a degree in English from California State University at Northridge, began his comedy work in partnership with Tommy Chong. The pair, known as Cheech and Chong, produced a series of popular comedy albums (including *The Wedding Album*, for which they received a Grammy Award) and were featured in a number of television specials. Marín cowrote and performed in a number of Cheech and Chong films, including *Up in Smoke* (1978), *Cheech and Chong's Next Movie* (1980), *Cheech and Chong's Nice Dreams* (1981), *Things Are Tough All Over* (1982), *Still Smokin'* (1983), and *Cheech and Chong's the Corsican Brothers* (1984). He has also performed in the features *It Came from Hollywood* (1982), *Yellowbeard* (1983), *After Hours* (1985), *Echo Park* (1986), *Ghostbusters II* (1989), *Troop Beverly Hills* (1989), *Rude Awakening* (1989), and *The Shrimp on the Barbie* (1990). Marín wrote, directed, and starred in the hit 1987 comedy *Born in East L.A.* That film, like many of the Cheech and Chong films, satirized stereotypes of Mexican Americans.

Marketing and advertising: Marketing to Latinos requires particular skills and knowledge of the diversity of Latino subgroups. Many Latinos prefer to be addressed in Spanish, for example, but others prefer English.

With an estimated annual purchasing power of nearly $200 billion and a population composing about 9 percent of the U.S. total in 1990, Latinos are a growing consumer market. According to the U.S. Bureau of

TOP TEN LATINO MARKETS, 1990

Note: The listing is based on the Latino populations of cities.

Billboards and other advertisements increasingly appear in Spanish. (James Shaffer)

the Census, the Hispanic population increased by more than 53 percent from 1980 to 1990, from 14.6 million to 22.4 million. Growth in the Latino market has provided a catalyst for improved marketing to Latinos. As the number of Latino-owned advertising and public relations agencies has grown, expertise in and sophistication of marketing to Latino markets has increased.

Major corporations that at one time used mainstream marketing unsuccessfully to attract Latino consumers have adopted new tools and techniques, incorporating a clearer understanding of Latino culture, history, and mentality. They have realized that there is no single Latino market but instead several distinct markets and audiences based on customs, income, and language. In addition, many first-generation Latinos do not understand or speak English, but their children may not speak Spanish. Studies have shown that as Latinos become more acculturated to the United States they generally show increased income, education, and buying power.

Some observers have noted that the Latino market is united in some ways, such as language (although split between English and Spanish), culture, and religion, but not in other ways, such as economics and politics. Mexican Americans compose approximately two-thirds of Latino households, forming one large bloc. About 70 percent of Latinos in one survey reported that they speak Spanish regularly at home, meaning that advertising in Spanish has the potential to be very effective. Still, important differences remain that necessitate different approaches to different segments of the Latino market.

Among the characteristics of Latinos most important to advertisers are brand loyalty and devotion to the health and welfare of the family. Latinos purchase brand-name products both because they are perceived to be the best and because purchasers obtain a feeling of assimilation or identification with the mainstream U.S. population.

Among the myths about the Latino market is that it is one mass consumer segment best reached through use of the Spanish language. Many ad agencies have made the crucial mistake of attempting to translate non-Latino campaigns into Spanish. The results often were comical and embarrassing. Direct translations may look good on paper, but the essence or marketing message may end up convoluted. Legendary mistakes include trying to sell the Chevrolet Nova in Mexico; in Spanish, *no va* means "it does not run or operate." An airline ad running in the 1980's proudly announced that its passengers would travel in leather seats, or *en cuero*; in some Latin American countries, however, *en cuero* is slang for "naked." Sometimes, literal or inaccurate translations insult Spanish speakers who are offended that the marketer has little or no grasp of the Spanish language and is neglecting the Latino consumer.

Other problems occur because of ignorance of geography or history. A travel agency ad in Miami once confused the land of the Aztecs and the land of the Incas, incorrectly placing the Aztecs in Peru and the Incas in Mexico, alienating many potential customers. As another example, in Latin America, the term "national" has negative connotations. Many Latin American nations have experienced dictatorial rule, and their citizens interpret the term "national" as "the state" or even "the national police."

The Latino market as a whole represents tremendous opportunities for advertisers. Companies must, however, be aware of the diversity within this huge market and must be aware of the cultural, historical, and language issues involved in marketing to Latinos and to various Latino subgroups.

Marqués, René (Oct. 4, 1919, Arecibo, Puerto Rico—Mar. 22, 1979, San Juan, Puerto Rico): Playwright. Marqués, a member of an agrarian family, was studying agriculture in Puerto Rico when he began his writing career in 1944. In 1948, he received a Rockefeller Foundation Fellowship to study playwriting in New York City at Columbia University and the Erwin Piscator Dramatic Workshop. After returning to Puerto Rico, Marqués started the Teatro Experimental de Ateneo. He is best known for *La carreta* (1953; *The Oxcart*, 1969), a full-length play reflecting the experience of immigrants coming from the highlands of Puerto Rico to San Juan and New York.

Marqués' numerous other plays include *El hombre y sus sueños* (1948), *Palm Sunday* (1949), *Otro día nuestro* (1955), *Juan Boto y la dama del occidente* (1956), *Los soles truncos* (1959), *Un niño azul para esa sombra* (1959), and *La muerte no entrará en palacio* (1959). Known for his appeal to traditional Latino values, Marqués is among the most widely produced and most influential of Hispanic American playwrights.

Marriage. *See* **Life cycle customs**

Martí, José (Jan. 29, 1853, Havana, Cuba—May 19, 1895, Dos Ríos, Cuba): Revolutionary. Martí was born in Havana to peninsular parents. His anti-Spanish statements during the Ten Years' War (1868-1878) led to his arrest and exile to Spain in 1871. Martí arrived in New York, New York, nine years later. His abilities as an orator and writer soon made him a central force among Cuban exiles in the United States.

Martí found Cuban expatriates in New York hostile to his plan to organize a broad-based, democratic, revolutionary party. He did find, however, widespread support among communities of cigar workers in Florida. With their help, he formed the Cuban Revolutionary Party in 1892.

Martí's single goal was the independence of Cuba. In his opinion, this entailed full and complete sovereignty from both Spain and the United States. Martí also regarded independence as a preliminary phase of a larger process. He sought to create a Cuba free from racism and economic debilities. Martí fashioned the idea of Cuban independence into a movement commit-

A bust of José Martí stands outside a park in Miami, Florida, named for the Cuban revolutionary. (Martin Hutner)

ted not only to freeing Cubans from Spanish oppression but also to giving them a new place in society. His beliefs influenced subsequent generations of Cuban writers and statesmen, including Fidel CASTRO.

Martínez, Al (b. July 21, 1929, Oakland, Calif.): Journalist. Martínez, a Mexican American, began his career as a journalist in Richmond, California. At the *Oakland Tribune*, he worked as a military writer, feature writer, and columnist from 1955 to 1971. In 1972, he began his illustrious career at the *Los Angeles Times* as a feature writer-reporter for the Metro section. He was also a columnist for the Valley Edition and the Westside section (1984-1988), and in 1988, he became a columnist for the Metro section.

Martínez has written several books, including *Rising Voices: Profiles of Hispano-American Lives* (1974), *Jigsaw John* (1975), *Ashes in the Rain* (1989), *Dancing Under the Moon* (1992), and *Rising Voices: A New Generation* (1994). Other writing credits include three network television series, films, and scripts for MGM-TV, Lorimar Productions, and Columbia-TV.

Martínez has received numerous awards for his thought-provoking, compassionate columns. Most notably, in 1984 he was awarded the Pulitzer Prize Gold Medal for Meritorious Public Services as cowinner for the "Southern California Latino Community" series. He has also received the National Ernie Pyle Award (1991), National Headliner Award (1987 and 1988), National Society of Newspaper Columnists award (1986), and many local honors. Martínez is an outspoken member of the Latino community, yet his columns leave lasting impressions with all readers.

Martínez, Antonio José (Jan. 7, 1793, Abiquiu, N.Mex.—July 28, 1867, Taos, N.Mex.): Religious figure. Shortly after the death of his wife and daughter in 1818, Martínez went to Durango, Mexico, to study for the Catholic priesthood. He took charge of a parish in Taos, New Mexico, in 1824, and two years later established a seminary there.

Martínez served in the state legislature between 1830 and 1836. During this time, he also published a newspaper and wrote books and pamphlets. Martínez held strong views in opposition to the United States. He opposed the land grants given to Americans during the early 1840's and conspired with other influential New Mexicans to drive the Americans from the state after its occupation in 1846. Some historians believe that Martínez instigated the TAOS REBELLION (1847) that the Pueblo Indians spearheaded against the Americans.

Following the American takeover of New Mexico, Martínez became active in territorial politics in an effort to obtain political and educational benefits for native-born New Mexicans. He also resisted the efforts of his new bishop, Jean Baptiste Lamy, to reintroduce tithing, which he saw as harmful to the economic well-being of his parishioners. Martínez's resolve led to his excommunication, but he continued to preside over his church until his death.

Martínez, César (b. 1944, Laredo, Tex.): Artist. Martínez's parents both came to Texas from northern Mexico as children. Martínez's father died when Martínez was less than one year old. After that, he and his mother lived in Laredo with his grandmother and two aunts.

Martínez spent two years at Laredo Junior College, enrolled in a business program because he believed a career in business would be more secure than one in art. He had always enjoyed drawing and painting, and he found that he was uninterested in business courses. He entered Texas Arts and Industries University in Kingsville in 1964 and earned a B.A. in art education in 1968.

After being drafted in 1969, Martínez eventually was posted with a medical battalion in Korea. Equipment for photography was inexpensive there, and he pursued that medium. Following his discharge, he continued to express himself through photography.

Martínez returned to Texas and became involved with the Texas Institute for Educational Development, a Chicano activist organization. He was one of the founders of the periodical *Caracol* and served as photographer, designer, and occasional columnist. He also joined Con Safos, a Chicano visual arts group.

Wanting to concentrate more on his work and less on activism, Martínez left Con Safos in the mid-1970's. He also returned to painting, using his camera primarily for everyday work including taking photographs for real estate listings. Some of his paintings from the late 1970's are populated by the pachucos he saw as a child.

Martinez, Dennis (Jose Dennis Martinez y Emilia; b. May 14, 1955, Granada, Nicaragua): Baseball player. Martinez, the first Nicaraguan to play major league baseball, began his professional career in the Baltimore Orioles' minor league organization in 1974. After being named the International League Pitcher of the Year in 1976, he was called up to the majors. He became a fixture in Baltimore's starting rotation, win-

Dennis Martinez's career improved after he joined the Montreal Expos. (AP/Wide World Photos)

ning fifteen games and leading the American League in innings pitched for the Orioles' 1979 league champions. In 1981, he led the league with fourteen wins.

A drinking problem took its toll on Martinez's performance, however, and he was traded to the Montreal Expos in 1986 after a series of poor seasons. With the Expos, Martinez overcame his alcoholism, leading the National League with a .733 winning percentage (11-4) in 1987. In 1990, 1991, and 1992, he was named to the National League All-Star Team. On July 28, 1991, he became only the fifteenth pitcher in major league history to throw a perfect game, in a 2-0 win against the Los Angeles Dodgers. That year, he also led the league with a 2.39 earned run average and five shutouts. After

posting a 15-9 record for the Expos in 1993, he signed as a free agent with the Cleveland Indians.

Martínez, Elizabeth (b. Apr. 14, 1943, Pomona, Calif.): Librarian. Martínez began her library service in 1966, as a children's librarian for the Los Angeles County Public Library. She worked for the Los Angeles County Library in various positions, including that of regional administrative librarian and chief of public services, from 1972 to 1979. During that time, she helped establish the Chicano Resource Center in East Los Angeles and the Asian Pacific Cultural Center in Montebello. From 1974 to 1976, she taught at California State University, Fullerton, where she helped the school obtain a federal grant for the Institute for Mexican American Librarians.

Martínez became the county librarian for the Orange County public library system in April, 1979. That position originally entailed oversight of twenty-four community and three regional libraries; during her tenure, eight more community libraries were constructed. She left that position in June, 1990, to become city librarian for Los Angeles. As the administrative head of the Los Angeles Public Library, she supervised sixty-three branches in addition to the central library. In August, 1994, she became the executive director of the American Library Association.

Martínez saw the city librarian job as a chance to work in an ethnically diverse community. As a child, she saw books as expanding her world beyond her community in Pomona, which was mostly Hispanic, but she noted that Mexican Americans rarely inhabited the books she read. As a librarian, she saw her job as involving management as well as dispensing information. She earned her B.A. in Latin American studies from the University of California, Los Angeles (1965) and M.A. in library and information science from the University of Southern California (1966). She later earned a certificate in management from the University of Southern California and a certificate in executive management from the University of California, Riverside.

Martínez, Robert "Bob" (b. Dec. 25, 1934, Tampa, Fla.): Public official. Martínez completed his undergraduate studies at the University of Tampa in 1957.

Bob Martínez declares victory in the 1986 Florida gubernatorial election. (AP/Wide World Photos)

He attended the University of Illinois and completed a master's program in labor and industrial relations in 1964. He taught in the Hillsborough County public schools from 1957 to 1962 and again from 1964 to 1966.

Martínez owned and operated the Cafe Sevilla Restaurant from 1975 to 1983. He became involved in local politics and was elected mayor of Tampa as a Republican in 1979. Martínez served in that office until 1987, when he became governor of Florida. While in office, Martínez was named to the White House Conference on a Drug-Free America by President Ronald Reagan. In 1991, he was appointed as director of the Office of National Drug Control Policy by President George Bush.

Martínez, Vilma Socorro (b. Oct. 17, 1943, San Antonio, Tex.): Civil rights leader and lawyer. Martínez was graduated from Jefferson High School in 1961 and, despite counseling that discouraged her from pursuing academic studies, she received a scholarship at the University of Texas at Austin and was graduated in fewer than three years as a political science major.

In an effort to escape the multiple discrimination she experienced in Texas as a woman and a Mexican American, Martínez went to Columbia University's Law School on a scholarship, receiving her degree in 1967. She then joined the Legal Defense Fund of the National Association for the Advancement of Colored People as staff attorney and subsequently worked for a major Wall Street law firm.

Martínez worked with the MEXICAN AMERICAN LEGAL DEFENSE AND EDUCATION FUND (MALDEF), a leading civil rights organization, from its inception in 1968. In 1972, she moved to California and assumed leadership of the organization. In an effort to increase its self-sufficiency and effectiveness, Martínez focused on broadening its funding base and its educational, employment, and political activities. In 1974, she won a pivotal case guaranteeing non-English-speaking children's rights to BILINGUAL EDUCATION in public schools. Martínez stepped down as president of MALDEF in 1981.

Martínez was active on numerous commissions, committees, boards, and panels crucial to Hispanics. She was appointed a member of the University of California Board of Regents in 1976, and in 1984 she became the board's chair.

Martínez-Cañas, María (b. May 19, 1960, Havana, Cuba): Photographer. Martínez-Cañas is known for her photographic collages that combine disparate elements and force the viewer to reexamine images. She has experimented with various processes and materials including amberlith, which blocks light. She has used amberlith, which she cut, to create images resembling an oscilloscope screen. Her more traditional photographs reflect folktales, the culture of Cuba, and Spanish history, often questioning Eurocentric values.

When she was three months old, Martínez-Cañas moved with her family to Puerto Rico, where she spent most of her life through adolescence. Her work sometimes reflects a longing for Cuba. She received an undergraduate degree in photography from the Philadelphia College of Art (1982) and an M.F.A. from the School of Art Institute in Chicago, Illinois (1984). She has received fellowships from the National Endowment for the Arts and the Cintas Foundation, among other awards.

Under a 1985 Fulbright-Hays Fellowship, Martínez-Cañas traveled to Spain to work with maps sketched by Christopher Columbus. She used those maps as a way of getting in touch with her roots, focusing on maps of Cuba. She later settled in Miami, Florida.

Martínez Ybor, Vicente (Sept. 17, 1818, Valencia, Spain—Dec. 14, 1896, Tampa, Fla.): Businessman. Born to wealthy parents, Martínez Ybor immigrated to Cuba as a young man to avoid compulsory military service in the Spanish army. He directed the rise and modernization of the tobacco industry, climbing from apprentice clerk to manufacturer. He created new markets and expanded operations to meet world demand for hand-rolled Havana cigars.

Economic motives as well as empathy for Cubans led Martínez Ybor to support Cuba's independence movement in the late 1860's. Alerted that Spanish authorities had issued an order for his arrest, Martínez Ybor fled to Key West, Florida, in 1869.

By 1885, however, Key West proved inadequate for Martínez Ybor's business. As a result, he relocated his operations to an area east of Tampa that came to be known as YBOR CITY. Soon other cigar factories and many Spaniards, Cubans, and other Spanish-speaking people moved to the new complex. By 1890, Ybor City had become a flourishing Latino colony and the center of CIGAR MANUFACTURING in Florida.

Martínez Ybor remained active inspecting tobacco plantations and supervising his various business interests until the year of his death. He became ill from an infected liver in March, 1896, and died on December 14 of that year.

Martorell, Antonio (b. 1939, Santurce, Puerto Rico): Artist. Martorell is known for his satirical works created for popular audiences, for example, artworks based on playing cards that he created after the 1968 elections in Puerto Rico. He produced large-scale playing cards at his workshop, the Taller Alacrán (scorpion workshop), which he operated with the goal of producing graphic art at affordable prices.

Martorell founded the Taller Alacrán in 1968. It was one of many similar workshops established during the late 1960's, when political agitation and movements for independence gained strength in Puerto Rico. The Taller Alacrán was one of the earliest workshops to concentrate on political art. It provided training for graphic artists and led to the establishment of similar workshops.

Even before establishing his workshop, Martorell was a popular artist. He had several solo and group exhibitions in the early 1960's. His work has been acquired by major collections in Puerto Rico and in the United States, including those of El Museo del Barrio, the Metropolitan Museum of Art, and the American Institute of Graphic Arts in New York, New York; the Library of Congress in Washington, D.C.; and the Art Institute of Chicago.

Mas Canosa, Jorge L. (b. Sept. 21, 1939, Santiago, Oriente, Cuba): Community leader. Mas Canosa attended the University of the Oriente, Santiago de Cuba; the Presbyterian College; and the Instituto Santiago de Cuba. He developed into an advocate of democracy and the free market system as well as an avowed enemy of Cuban president Fidel CASTRO.

During his business career, Mas Canosa has served as president of Church and Tower of Florida, chief operating officer of Neff Machinery, and president of the Mas Group. He has successfully tapped into the passions and emotions of the Cuban exile community to the degree that he is recognized as the unofficial spokesperson for that group in the United States.

In 1993, Mas Canosa joined forces with Congressman Robert Torricelli of New Jersey to pass the Cuban Democracy Act, aimed at further isolating the Castro government. Critics of the legislation complained that the bill would cut off medical supplies and food for the impoverished people of Cuba.

Masa: Fresh corn dough used to make tortillas, tamales, and other dishes. When corn is boiled with lime, it loses its tough hulls and becomes *POSOLE*; when *posole* is ground, it becomes *masa*. Coarse *masa* is used to make tamales, and finer *masa* is used to make tortillas. *Masa harina* is a flour made from *masa* by drying and crushing and has the advantage of keeping well without refrigeration, although its flavor is generally less desirable than that of fresh *masa*. *Masa* literally means "dough," and outside Mexico it refers to any dough.

Mata, Eduardo (b. Sept. 5, 1942, Mexico City, Mexico): Orchestra conductor and composer. Mata studied composition with Rodolfo Halffter at the National Conservatory in Mexico City from 1954 to 1960. He also took composition and conducting lessons with eminent Mexican composer-conductor Carlos Chavez from 1960 to 1965. In 1964, he was awarded the Koussevitzky Fellowship, which resulted in further conduct-

Eduardo Mata. (AP/Wide World Photos)

ing studies with Gunther Schuller and Eric Leinsdorf at the Berkshire Music Center in Tanglewood, Massachusetts.

Mata has had a successful conducting career, working with the Mexico Ballet Company (1963-1964), the Guadalajara Symphony Orchestra (1964-1966), and the Philharmonic Orchestra of the National University of Mexico (1966-1976). In 1970, he began his American conducting career with the Phoenix Symphony Orchestra. He followed with the Dallas Symphony Orchestra from 1977 to 1993. In 1990, he became principal guest conductor of the Pittsburgh Symphony Orchestra.

Mata is also a composer with an impressive list of works, including Symphony No. 1 "Classical" (1962), Symphony No. 2 "Romantic" (1963), Symphony No. 3 (1966/1967), ballet music including "Débora" (1963) and "Los huesos secos" (1967), and several chamber works. His music has been published by Peer-Southern and Ediciones Mexicanas de Música. His recording of the symphonic works of Carlos Chavez was highly praised by critics.

Matachines: Dancers associated with religious ceremonies. *Matachines* perform the *matachin*, a dance of ancient origins introduced by Spaniards to the Americas in the eighteenth century. It is an all-male battle mime with two opposing lines of dancers performing swordplay and intricate formations. A *monarca* calls the changes in figures in falsetto, to an accompaniment of guitar and rattles. In Mexico, the *matachin* is con-

Matachin dancers perform at a festival in San Antonio, Texas. (Institute of Texan Cultures)

nected to Catholic rituals glorifying the Virgin and enacting the evolution of Christianity, while in New Mexico *matachines* pantomime bullfighting and the triumph of good over evil. The *matachin* is performed at fiestas, at funerals, and at churches on Sundays.

Matos Paoli, Francisco (b. Mar. 9, 1915, Lares, Puerto Rico): Poet and political activist. Matos Paoli may have inherited his poetic tendencies from his father, who wrote poetry to ease the pain of adversity. From his mother, he received a religious sense of life and an affinity for mysticism. Matos completed his high school work in Lares, Puerto Rico, before entering the University of Puerto Rico in 1936. Later, he taught at the university, but much of his time was consumed by his poetry writing and his involvement in the Puerto Rican Nationalist Party, for which he served as secretary. As a result of his political activism, he was imprisoned for five years. His *Canto a Puerto Rico* (1952, canto to Puerto Rico) and *Habitante del eco, 1937-41* (inhabitant of the echo) won literary prizes. *Canto a la locura* (1962; canto to madness) has been called his "richest book."

Matthews v. Díaz (426 U.S. 67, 1976): Legal case. A sixty-five-year-old resident alien of the United States named Díaz brought suit to challenge the constitutionality of a provision of the Social Security Act. The provision required that before they became eligible for Medicare, resident aliens must have resided in the United States for at least five years.

The U.S. district court in Florida ruled that this requirement was unconstitutional. The U.S. Supreme Court reversed that decision, stating that Congress could make aliens' eligibility for Medicare or any federal program conditional on citizenship or continuous residence in the United States. Congress only had to show a rational basis for such conditions.

Mauricio Gaston Institute for Latino Community Development and Public Policy (founded in 1971): Research institute. The Gaston Institute was founded as the Survey Research Program. It operates as an integral part of the University of Massachusetts, Boston campus, and is funded in totality by the Commonwealth of Massachusetts.

The institute's primary objective is to analyze public policies affecting Latinos in the Commonwealth of Puerto Rico. The ways in which the institute fulfills its objectives include analyzing research produced by other agencies (such as the Bureau of the Census) and

producing original research. Its research is disseminated through periodic publications as well as target reports commissioned by specific agencies or governmental bodies.

The institute holds periodic conferences, seminars, and discussion groups. The institute's main publication venues are periodic working papers and professional articles in journals. The institute uses the same facilities as the Center for Survey Research, another social research center that is also an integral part of the University of Massachusetts.

Mayan civilization: In recent years, the study of ancient Mayan civilization has been transformed through revolutionary advances in the interpretation and translation of the Maya glyph (writing) system. Both archaeology and epigraphy, or glyph interpretation, have added to the understanding of ancient Maya social, cultural, political, and economic history.

Maya Cultural History. The Maya were indigenous inhabitants of eastern and southern Mesoamerica, the region encompassing the areas of the present-day states of Chiapas and Tabasco in Mexico, Mexico's Yucatán Peninsula, and the countries of Belize, Guatemala, Honduras, and El Salvador. Although the Maya are best known for the ancient monuments and glyphic writings of the Classic era of 300 to 900 C.E., they settled the Maya heartland as early as ten to twelve thousand years ago.

The gradual transition from early hunting and gathering practices to early village lifestyles was facilitated by the advent of agriculture, based on MAIZE or corn cultivation. By 3500 B.C.E., early village farming communities had formed. Over the course of the next three millennia, the Maya coalesced into one of Mesoamerica's premier civilizations.

The Mayan diet, often characterized as the "Mesoamerican triumvirate" or "triad," was one centered on the cultivation and consumption of corn, BEANS, and SQUASH. It has been maintained intact for more than five thousand years. The lack of domesticable animals or other beasts of burden led to a reliance on this agricultural triad. To this diet were added such New World plants as the CHILI, TOMATO, and AVOCADO; cacao; and a host of root crops.

The dense jungles and rain forest areas of the Mayan region necessitated a strategy based on swidden or "slash-and-burn" agriculture. This agricultural approach entailed an initial clearing of forest vegetation, followed shortly thereafter by the setting of fires to burn away the felled vegetation. A farmer could then

AREA OF MAYAN CIVILIZATION

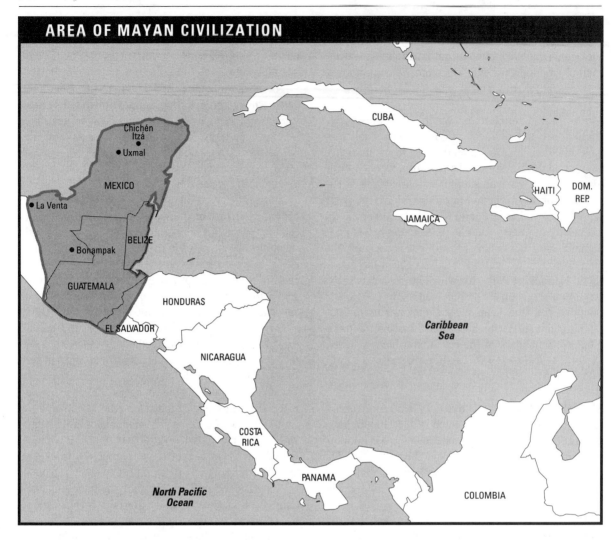

plant crops within the cleared area. The charred vegetation served to enrich the otherwise sterile soils of the jungle floor.

Over time, the Maya devised many sophisticated methods for farming the jungles of the lowlands. Such methods included the reclamation of swamplands through the construction of massive "ridged field" systems, wherein soil was dredged from the bottoms of swamps and used to construct agricultural islands, mounded banks of soil upon which crops could be grown. Use of sophisticated agricultural techniques permitted massive populations to be supported throughout the Peten Maya lowlands and Yucatán Peninsula.

At such sites as El Mirador, Guatemala, the early Maya initiated the construction of massive monuments and temples dedicated to ancient deities such as Kinich Ahau, the ancient Mayan "Sun Lord," and Itzamna, the "Lord of Scribes." Many towering pyramidal plat-

forms have been identified in El Mirador, dating to as early as the fourth century B.C.E.

Influences derived from the OLMEC civilization of the Mexican Gulf Coast provided impetus to the growth of a pan-Mesoamerican religious and mercantile system that became the foundation of all civilizational developments to follow. Much of this broader tradition encompassed the calendrical and glyphic writing traditions generally credited to the Maya. The Maya can be credited with elaborating and reformulating these indigenous Olmec traditions.

The Classic Period. The period of development in the Mayan region identified as Preclassic began around 2000 B.C.E. and ended around 300 C.E., when Mayan civilization flowered into a full-blown regional tradition. The cultural chronology of Mesoamerica is based on the chronology of the Mayan Classic period, extending from 300 to 900 C.E.

Ruins in Palenque, Mexico, date from about 600 C.E. (Claire Rydell)

During the Classic era, the culturally significant Peten lowland tradition first formally used glyphic texts to record dynastic genealogies. This tradition persisted through to the collapse of the Classic tradition. It was during the Classic era that the most spectacular developments associated with Classic arts, architecture, astronomy, writing, and mathematics developed into full-blown Mayan traditions. Such ancient sites as Tikal, Uaxactun, Dos Pilas, Piedras Negras, Yaxchilan, Bonampak, and Palenque characterize Classic developments.

At the culmination of more than fifteen hundred years of continuous development in the arts and sciences, Mayan civilization underwent a dramatic and volatile period of transformation. After 550, Maya lowland civilization in the Peten (which up to that time was centered on ancient Tikal, Guatemala) bore the brunt of a major war between the kingdoms of Caracol, Belize, and Tikal, Guatemala. In the aftermath of conquest, Caracol prevailed.

Tikal underwent a dark age of subordination under the ruling house of Caracol in the years between 550 and 700. Tikal overcame this period of disruption and subordination through a series of shrewd political alliances that culminated in the toppling of the Caracol confederation in the late seventh century. Thus liberated, Tikal embarked on an aggressive campaign to rebuild its city and return legitimacy to its royal house. This process resulted in the erection of some of the most spectacular funerary monuments—"sacred mountains" or pyramidal platforms—ever built in the Peten lowlands of Guatemala.

By the advent of the ninth century, the kingdom of Tikal, once the possessor of more than 450,000 subjects, underwent a precipitous population decline. Deforestation and intensified agriculture led to the collapse of the ecology of the Mayan lowlands and set off a chain reaction echoed through the social and political fabric of the Maya.

From the seventh through the tenth centuries, city after ancient city fell prey to the exploits of interlopers and foreigners seeking new lands and kingdoms to conquer. This process was sped along its course by the collapse of the Peten Maya heartland. By the year 900, the dynastic tradition, large-scale public works projects, hieroglyphic histories and related texts, and the erection of dated stela or commemorative markers had ceased to exist as cultural hallmarks of the Maya.

The Postclassic Era. After 900, Mayan civilization was transformed radically. The period from 900 to 1521 has come to be regarded as the Postclassic era of warlords and Mexicanized cults centered on human sacrifice. The Yucatecan site of Chichén Itzá has come to epitomize the art and culture of this era in the northern Maya lowlands.

Chichén, located at the heart of the ancient salt trade of the northern Mayan lowlands, shows evidence of its long-ranging maritime contacts in its artistic traditions and monumental constructions. Chichén flourished from 700 through 1250 and represents the last bastion of Classic Mayan lowland civilization. Monumental temples and palaces were composed from carefully sculpted limestone masonry blocks. The architectural style of Chichén is eclectic, reflecting the influences of the Puuc, Chenes, and other Mayan regional and pan-Mesoamerican traditions in art and architecture. The presence of images of Chac (the rain deity) and Itzamna within the baroque façades of many of Chichén's monuments is a hallmark of the international style of the northern Mayan lowland Postclassic tradition.

By the mid-thirteenth century, ancient Chichén and the Toltec capital of Tula, located in Mexico's central highlands, had succumbed to conquest. The final centuries of pre-Columbian civilization in the Mayan heartland were dominated by a multitude of multiethnic or Mexicanized Mayan regional kingdoms sharing in a pan-Mesoamerican style dominated by images of death, sacrifice, and the supernatural. Ancient Mayan seaports characterize the commercial and internationalized style of this highly militarized era. The massive walled administrative and ceremonial precinct of Tulum was occupied at the time of the first Spanish forays along the coast in the early sixteenth century.

Pre-Columbian civilization had ended in many areas of Mesoamerica by the mid-sixteenth century as a consequence of military conquest, missionary activity, and the spread of European diseases to which the native populations had no immunity. The Maya continued to resist Spanish, and later Mexican, domination well into the nineteenth century. One of the last major attempts on the part of the Maya to throw off domination of the region by outsiders took the form of the great Caste War of the 1840's, in which the Maya went into rebellion against their Mexican overlords.

Contributions Beyond Technology. The traditions of the Maya related to literacy are the most relevant to New World civilizational development. These include contributions and innovations in the arts and sciences that center on epigraphy and historical texts and on calendrics, including mathematics and astronomy.

The most dramatic and revolutionary recent discoveries concerning the Mayan world have been in the area of epigraphy. Epigraphy, the study of writing systems, has resulted in the deciphering of many early Mayan scripts. Russian epigrapher Yuri Knorosov is credited with breaking the Mayan code through his realization that Mayan glyphic texts were both pictographic and phonetic in character. In other words, one could "read" a Mayan symbol, sign, or image element (e.g., the picture of a jaguar) or rely on the attendant combination of phonetic signs or sound elements to articulate the word corresponding to the picture element.

Scholars have been able to interpret more than 90 percent of the written scripts of the Mayan region. These scripts are recorded on sculpted tablets known as stela, lintels (both of stone and of wood), fresco murals, screenfold deerhide or bark paper books known as codices, tomb paintings, inscribed or painted ceramic vessels, and inscribed or painted jade, bone, stone, and wooden ornaments and related artifacts. Mayan glyphic texts are available for the study of virtu-

ally every type of Mayan artifact ever conceived. Such a ubiquity of social, cultural, religious, political, and economic contexts has opened a tremendous resource for the cultural interpretation of all that was once the Mayan world.

The epigraphy of the Maya provides direct access to a vast body of information on the dynastic history and genealogy of the great royal houses of the Classic Mayan heartland. These ancient texts serve to document the rituals, battles, games, coronations, sacrifices, deaths, and royal marriages of the lords and ladies of such ancient cities as Yaxchilan, Tikal, Bonampak, Palenque, and literally hundreds of other towns and cities of the Classic Maya world.

Calendrics. The Mayan glyphic system reveals a complex calendrical, mathematical, and astronomical system known to scholars as the Maya Long Count. The Long Count is known as such because of its reliance on an initial origins date of August 11, 3114 B.C.E. The Maya counted time from this date in *kin* periods or

The Temple of Warriors, dating from about 1000 C.E., was in Chichén Itzá. (Claire Rydell)

solar days. Time was partitioned into units based on a vigesimal notational system, or one that counts by twenties. Time was reckoned in divisions of one day (*kin*), twenty days (*uinal*), 360 days (*tun*, or a period constituting 18 months or *uinals*), and 7,200 days (*katun*). Numerical symbols included the half-shell representing the "zero" concept (the earliest practical use of the null set or zero concept anywhere in the world), a "dot" to designate the number one, and a "bar" to signify the number five. This system was in turn meshed with a solar calendar of 365 days (rendered by the Maya to 365.2420 astronomical days; the Gregorian calendar computes at 365.2425 days; in actuality, the modern astronomical year is 365.2422 days).

The solar year was known to the ancient Maya as the *haab*. A secondary ritual calendar, based on the agricultural cycle, encompassed a period of 260 days. This latter calendar was known to the ancient Maya as the *tzolkin*. The meshing of the solar and ritual years in turn constituted a cycle of fifty-two vague years.

The Maya calendar was the most accurate astronomical calendar formulated and formally utilized by any ancient society. The coordination of calendrical, mathematical, and astronomical concepts facilitated elaboration of a complex almanac of astrological phenomena, intended for divination, dynastic reckoning, and agricultural planning. The Maya used both calendrical and astronomical information in the fixing of sacred events, the dedication of temples, the launching of wars of conquest, and the coronation of kings.

The Maya employed calendrical, astronomical, and astrological events to define the sanctity of the throne, through the tracing of genealogical and dynastic linkages pertaining to the royal house of the prevailing king or queen. Much of the information translated from Mayan glyphics taken from public contexts centers on the legitimation of kingship and dynastic succession in royal houses torn by problems of succession, war, or problematic royal marriages.

The end of the dynastic tradition of reckoning the exploits of individual kings and their kingdoms coincides with the collapse of the Classic Mayan lowland tradition. A host of modern epigraphers, iconographers, and archaeologists are resurrecting historical accounts and dynastic traditions that were nearly lost to the ravages of time, hoards of looters and plunderers, and the incessant encroachment of jungle vegetation. —*Ruben G. Mendoza*

SUGGESTED READINGS:
• Hunter, C. Bruce. *A Guide to Ancient Maya Ruins.* 2d ed. Norman: University of Oklahoma Press, 1986. A guide to major archaeological zones of the Mayan region of Mesoamerica, with an introduction to the culture, chronology, and religion of the ancient Maya.
• Marcus, Joyce. *Mesoamerican Writing Systems: Propaganda, Myth, and History in Four Ancient Civilizations.* Princeton, N.J.: Princeton University Press, 1992. Provides an anthropological and evolutionary overview of the ancient Mesoamerican writing systems of the Aztec, Mixtec, Zapotec, and Maya.
• Miller, Mary Ellen. *The Art of Mesoamerica: From Olmec to Aztec.* London: Thames and Hudson, 1986. An art history review of the major artistic and cultural traditions of ancient Mesoamerica.
• Miller, Mary, and Karl Taube. *The Gods and Symbols of Ancient Mexico and the Maya.* New York: Thames and Hudson, 1993. An illustrated dictionary of Mesoamerican religion that provides a chronological and cultural outline of Mesoamerican civilization along with definitions and discussion pertaining to the major deities of the region.
• Muser, Curt, comp. *Facts and Artifacts of Ancient Middle America.* New York: E. P. Dutton, 1978. A glossary of technical terms employed in the study of the archaeology and art history of Mesoamerica.
• *Popol Vuh: The Sacred Book of the Ancient Quiche Maya.* Translated by Delia Goetz and Sylvanus G. Morley, from the translation of Adrian Recinos. Norman: University of Oklahoma Press, 1975. A English translation of the Sacred Book of Council and Quichean origins of the Quichean Maya of highland Guatemala.
• Sabloff, Jeremy A. *The New Archaeology and the Ancient Maya.* New York: Scientific American Library, 1990. Examines the revolutionary changes, born of recent advances in the art and science of archaeology, that have affected the course of Maya studies.
• Schele, Linda, and David Freidel. *A Forest of Kings: The Untold Story of the Ancient Maya.* New York: William Morrow, 1990. Reconstructs through epigraphic research the life histories of the kings and kingdoms of the Classic Mayan lowlands.

MECHA. *See* **Movimiento Estudiantil Chicano de Aztlán**

Medicine, pre-Columbian: Medicine, medical theory, and therapeutics as practiced in the New World before the coming of the Spanish. Pre-Columbian medicine includes the contributions of the Aztecs, Maya, and Incas as well as the developments of all Native American groups, especially in herbal medi-

The maguey or agave plant has been used to make medicine and other products since pre-Columbian times. (Ruben G. Mendoza)

cine. The Aztecs made some of the most advanced contributions.

Health practices were highly developed among the Aztecs (*see* AZTEC CIVILIZATION). The Aztecs saw important connections between their religion, worldview, magic, and medicine. Among these is the connection between the macrocosm (Aztec universe) and microcosm (the human body). As in European astrological medicine, there was a reciprocal correspondence and influence between humans and the cosmos.

In turn, Aztec theories of physiology and etiology (the origins of disease) connected with religion and worldview. These theories were important for understanding illnesses and their cures, causes, and prevention. The Aztecs believed that the human body contained multiple souls or animistic forces (spirits), each of which implied specific characteristics for the human body, such as growth, development, and physiology. The most important of these spiritual forces were *teyolia* (located in the heart), *tonalli* (in the head), and *ihiyotl* (associated with the liver). According to the Aztecs, the health of an individual depended on the relative amounts of each of the animistic forces at a given time as well as on the balance of these forces.

Three distinct categories for the origins of diseases were diagnosed by Aztec health practitioners and shamans: supernatural, magical, and natural. Their view of medicine was holistic, and their etiology posited a continuum between the natural and the supernatural. They believed that one's susceptibility to certain illnesses and how one was cured depended upon when one was born and one's relationship to the universe, somewhat like European astrological medicine. Magic, sorcery, and witchcraft also played important roles in the treatment of illnesses.

Aztec cures either could be of a religious nature, including religious rituals, offerings, confession ("talking cure"), expiation, and prayers; or could involve magical and symbolic healing, such as the use of stones and gems for sympathetic magical cures. A significant portion of Aztec medicine involved the empirical treatment of diseases. The Aztecs possessed significant empirical knowledge with respect to medicinal plants and herbs, which they used in their treatment of illnesses (*see* HERBAL MEDICINE). They also had a highly developed medico-botanical taxonomy as well as a sophisticated system of anatomical nomenclature. They were proficient in the treatment of wounds and used medicinal plants for women's health care. It has been argued that much of modern Mexican and Mexican American FOLK MEDICINE developed as a consequence of a blending of Spanish humoral medicine (based on the body containing various "humors") and Aztec medical beliefs.

Mediero: Sharecropper. In New Mexico, particularly during the Spanish and Mexican eras, *mediero* referred to a poor Nuevo Mexicano who worked on a farm and was paid with a share of the crop. Sharecropping was a common feature of Nuevo Mexico. It forced many poor, landless peasants into a condition of debt peonage. *Genizaros* (detribalized Indians, or freed slaves) often fell into this position, but debt peonage also afflicted Spaniards and mixed-bloods. Pueblo Indians were forced to plant and harvest on the large haciendas, preventing them from working their fields for their own subsistence. Once off their pueblos and in a wage relationship, they soon became so indebted that they could never gain their freedom. As for the poor Spaniards and mixed-bloods, frequently these families purchased items from merchants with future crops or

leased land from wealthy landlords, contracting to keep a small share of the profits gained from the crop. Any failure of a crop could place the *mediero* in a state of permanent indebtedness to the landowner.

Medrano v. Allee: Labor litigation. Following a strike by farmworkers in the Rio Grande Valley in 1966 and 1967, workers led by Francisco Medrano filed a class action suit against the TEXAS RANGERS and its Captain A. Y. Allee. The suit charged that the Texas Rangers had interfered with the workers' rights to organize and strike, in violation of the First and FOURTEENTH AMENDMENTS.

A federal district court ruled in 1972 in favor of the workers and prohibited the Texas Rangers from interfering with peaceful organizing and from arresting people without probable cause. Two years later, the U.S. Supreme Court upheld the district court's ruling on appeal. The Court agreed with the district court that the Texas Rangers, in their efforts to intimidate strikers, had used Texas statutes that violated the Constitution and had unconstitutionally used valid laws.

Meléndez, Edwin (b. Aug. 28, 1951, San Juan, Puerto Rico): Scholar. Meléndez immigrated to the United States from Puerto Rico in 1978 after earning a bachelor's degree from the University of Puerto Rico. He holds a master's degree from the University of California, Santa Barbara, and a Ph.D. from the University of Massachusetts at Amherst, both in economics. He began his teaching career in 1984, teaching economics and Puerto Rican studies at Fordham University. Meléndez taught in the department of urban studies and planning at the Massachusetts Institute of Technology from 1986 to 1992 and later directed the MAURICIO GASTON INSTITUTE FOR LATINO COMMUNITY DEVELOPMENT AND PUBLIC POLICY at the University of Massachusetts at Boston.

Meléndez's work focuses on economic development, the labor force, and poverty, along with issues regarding migration from Puerto Rico to the U.S. mainland and back. He is the coeditor of *Hispanics in the Labor Force: Issues and Policies* (1993) and *Colonial Dilemma: Critical Perspectives on Contemporary Puerto Rico* (1993), among other books. Meléndez has served as a consultant to the INSTITUTE FOR PUERTO RICAN POLICY and the Hispanic Office of Planning and Evaluation, among other organizations, and has been associated with several academic journals as either a reviewer or member of the editorial board.

Meléndez, Rosalinda: Actress. Meléndez starred with the Compañía de Revistas y Variedades el Niño Fidencio in the 1940's in Los Angeles and on local tour. El Fidencio was a folk healer from Mexico who was later discredited as a buffoon. Meléndez's son was actor William Lanceford.

Melting pot theory: The melting pot theory proposed that Old World cultures brought to the United States by immigrants would merge to produce a unique American culture. The term "melting pot" was coined by Israel Zangwill, who published a play by the same name in 1909.

A school of melting pot theorists soon developed, based at the University of Chicago and led by Robert Park. Park and his followers began their research in the 1910's, when more than a million immigrants were entering the United States each year, primarily

Bringing together people from different cultures can allow intermixing of and learning about traditions and customs. (James Shaffer)

from Southern and Eastern Europe. Chicago sociologists turned to the question of what happens when people of divergent cultures come into contact and possible conflict.

In his book *Race and Culture* (1950), Park proposed a "race relation cycle" with three stages of contact, accommodation, and assimilation. By assimilation, Park meant something less than an obliteration of ethnic difference. The term referred to superficial uniformity that could conceal differences in opinions and beliefs.

Park also believed that assimilation would lead to a final stage, amalgamation, that would occur through INTERMARRIAGE. Contrary to the claims of his modern critics, he did not predict an abrupt and complete "melting" of ethnic groups. He was careful to point out that the processes of ACCULTURATION and assimilation occur in different ways and at different rates depending on numerous factors.

Ethnic specialists have expressed a shift in opinion on the issue of the desirability of ethnic and cultural assimilation. An earlier generation of sociologists emphasized the tendency among immigrant minorities to assimilate. A more recent group of writers insists that ethnicity is a powerful and enduring factor in American life.

By the last decades of the twentieth century, sociologists had largely abandoned the melting pot theory in favor of CULTURAL PLURALISM or MULTICULTURALISM. It was evident that as members of various cultures lived side by side, some degree of acculturation and assimilation would occur. Diverse ethnic and cultural groups, however, often persisted in maintaining their cultural identity while contributing cultural features to the society at large. This has been the case for Latinos, who have tended to maintain use of the Spanish language and other cultural traits. The CHICANO MOVEMENT of the 1960's emphasized recognition of a unique Chicano culture and stressed the importance of pride in cultural heritage.

Melville, Margarita Bradford (b. Aug. 19, 1929, Irapuato, Guanajuato, Mexico): Scholar and activist. Melville took her vows as a Maryknoll sister in 1949, becoming a Catholic nun. She left the convent to attend Rogers College in Ossining, New York. She received a bachelor of education degree in 1954 and was sent to Guatemala to teach. She also established health and literary programs to empower the peasant population. Although her programs and similar ones were grounded in religious teachings, she and others, including a bishop, left the country in 1967 at the request of the United States embassy and the Guatemalan government.

Back in the United States, she was married to Thomas Melville, a former priest who had also worked in Guatemala. The couple strove to increase American awareness of the presence of U.S. troops in Guatemala and were arrested for burning Selective Service records in Catonsville, Maryland. While she served a federal prison sentence that was reduced to nine months, she and her husband completed a joint master's thesis in Latin American studies at the American University in Washington, D.C. It was published in book form as *Guatemala: The Politics of Land Ownership* in 1971. Their joint autobiography, stressing activism for social justice, was published as *Whose Heaven, Whose Earth?* in 1970.

The Melvilles traveled to Chile in 1973 for work on their doctorate degrees. They both were asked to teach at the Catholic University in Temuco after the coup that overthrew Salvador Allende. After receiving her doctorate in 1976, Melville accepted a position as assistant professor of anthropology at the University of Houston. She continued her outside activities, promoting legal services for immigrants through the Centro para Immigrantes. In 1986, Melville became an associate professor of the University of California, Berkeley. She served as coordinator for Chicano studies and in 1988 was named as associate dean in the graduate division. She continued to speak for the rights of Guatemalans and was also involved in the Chicano-Latino Policy Project at the university.

Mendes, Sergio (b. Feb. 11, 1941, Niteroi, Brazil): Jazz pianist and composer. Mendes began playing the piano as a child and entered the Niteroi Conservatory at the age of nine. By the time he was a teenager, he was already known in Brazil as a leading jazz musician. Before he was twenty, he joined the circle of musicians who created the BOSSA NOVA.

In 1962, Mendes appeared in Carnegie Hall with well-known jazz artists Antonio Carlos JOBIM, João Gilberto, Charlie Byrd, Stan Getz, and Dizzy Gillespie. By 1964, he had toured France, Italy, Japan, and the United States. In 1968, he played with the National Symphony in Washington, D.C., and in 1970 he performed at the White House. In the mid-1960's, he toured extensively with the group Brazil '66 and recorded for the A&M label. The group was enormously successful and is known for "Mas que Nada," among other hits.

Sergio Mendes accepts the 1993 Grammy Award for the best world music album, Brasileiro. (AP/Wide World Photos)

Mendes' unique musical arrangements, blending Brazilian percussion instruments with the female voice, brought him wide success in popular music. The hit songs "So Many Stars" and "Song of No Regrets" show his talents as both composer and arranger.

Mendez, José (Mar. 19, 1888, Cardena, Cuba—Oct. 31, 1928, Havana, Cuba): Baseball player and manager. A right-handed pitcher, Mendez is considered one of the best Cuban players who never played in the major leagues. In his first professional season in 1908, Mendez compiled a 15-6 record in the Cuban winter league. Lured to the U.S. Cuban Stars, he posted a 44-2 record in 1909 on the strength of a blazing fastball and a good curveball. Mendez then returned to his native Cuba for the 1910 and 1911 seasons.

Despite arm trouble, Mendez went back to the United States in 1912 and began playing for the multiracial All-Nations of Kansas City. He then moved to shortstop and also played in the outfield with the Chicago American Giants and Detroit Stars.

Mendez found his greatest success as a player-manager for the Kansas City Monarchs from 1920 to 1926, leading his team to three straight Negro National League pennants from 1923 to 1925 and compiling a 20-4 pitching record. During the 1924 Negro League World Series, he had a 2-0 record with a 1.42 earned run average in four games, including one shutout. Kept out of the major leagues by his color, Mendez nevertheless outpitched such stars as Christy Mathewson and Eddie Plank in exhibition games.

Méndez, Miguel Morales (b. June 15, 1930, Bisbee, Ariz.): Writer. The son of a farmer and miner, Méndez attended schools in El Claro, Sonora, Mexico, for six years. Méndez worked for a time in a Mexican government farming community and, at the age of fifteen, entered the United States as a migrant farmworker.

Later, he became a bricklayer and construction worker in Tuscon, Arizona. In 1970, Méndez became an instructor at the Pima Community College in Tuscon; he has also worked as an instructor at the University of Arizona. His first novel, *Peregrinos de Aztlán*, was published in 1974. He was awarded an honorary doctor of humanities degree by the University of Arizona in 1984.

Méndez has gained critical attention for his poetic depictions of poor members of an uprooted society at odds with the Anglo-American culture that threatens their heritage. He is especially concerned with preserving the oral tradition.

Méndez, Rafael (Mar. 6, 1906, Jiquilpán, Michoacán, Mexico—Sept. 15, 1981, Encino, Calif.): Composer and trumpeter. By the age of ten, Méndez was playing the trumpet for revolutionary Pancho VILLA, who took the Méndez family with him for several months to provide entertainment. Méndez studied composition at the Mexico City Conservatory. His musical gift as a trumpet virtuoso established him as a regular soloist with local orchestras.

Méndez played in numerous bands, including a circus band and, from 1927-1932, a pit band at the Fox Theater in Detroit, Michigan. In 1934, he was featured with the Chicago Symphony at the Chicago World's Fair. He also appeared as guest artist with the Los Angeles Symphony.

Between 1940 and 1950, Méndez was a studio musician in Hollywood and appeared in the films *Holiday in Mexico* (1946), *Fiesta* (1947), and *Luxury Liner* (1948). As a recording artist, he performed such classics as "Carnival in Venice" and "The Flight of the Bumble Bee." With the Rafael Méndez Orchestra, he recorded the ever-popular "La Bamba," "Tea for Two," "El Rancho Grande," and many more songs. Méndez has also written numerous instrumental compositions, including "The Elf Trumpeter" and "Valse Suriano." In 1964, he became the first trumpet player to give a solo performance at Carnegie Hall. F. E. Olds & Son named one of its trumpet models for him.

Méndez v. Westminster School District (Feb. 18, 1946, and Apr. 14, 1947): Education lawsuit. In *Méndez v. Westminster School District*, Mexican American parents in Southern California challenged the SEGREGATION of children of Mexican descent. In 1946, Federal Judge Paul McCormick ruled that this segregation was unconstitutional, and the following year, the Ninth Circuit Court in San Francisco upheld the lower court.

During World War II, Mexican Americans increasingly felt a sense of ethnic pride combined with a resentment of unequal treatment. Organizations such as the LEAGUE OF UNITED LATIN AMERICAN CITIZENS (LULAC) and concerned parents began to voice strong opposition to the segregation of public schools. After Gonzalo Méndez, a prosperous farmer, and other parents in four districts of Orange County, California, failed to convince local school boards to allow their children to attend integrated schools, they decided to take legal action. With the support of LULAC, the parents argued that segregation was contrary to the due-process clause and the equal-protection clause of the FOURTEENTH AMENDMENT. Lawyers for the districts answered that the matter was governed by state law and that the Supreme Court had endorsed the principle of "separate but equal" in *Plessy v. Ferguson* (1896).

Judge McCormick announced his decision on February 18, 1946, ruling in favor of LULAC and the parents. Without directly confronting the *Plessy* precedent, McCormick emphasized that the California law of 1935 mentioned only the segregation of Indians and Asians. Because state law did not refer to separate schools for Latino children, the school boards were taking arbitrary action that deprived citizens of liberty and property without due process of law.

Using the assimilationist ideas of the 1940's, McCormick stated that Spanish speakers might be segregated in the earliest years because of difficulties with the English language but that separate classes were justified only for a limited period of time. Segregation without a compelling reason, moreover, was contrary to the American doctrine of "social equality" because it "fosters antagonisms in the children and suggests inferiority among them where none exists."

The Orange County school boards appealed to the Ninth Circuit Court. By this time the case had attracted national attention, and the plaintiffs were joined by the National Association for the Advancement of Colored People (NAACP) and other liberal organizations. On April 14, 1947, the seven justices of the Ninth Circuit Court unanimously upheld the judgment of the district court. Writing for the majority, Justice Albert Stevens ruled only on the narrow issue that California law did not provide for the segregation of Latino children, and he refused to consider whether de jure segregation was constitutional. In a concurring opinion, however, Judge William Denham took the broader view that segregation created "inequality on its face." Officials of Orange County decided that further appeal was pointless, and integrated schools opened in the four districts with little trouble in September, 1947.

The *Méndez* victory was a landmark in the quest to obtain equal rights for Latinos. The decision did not integrate many schools because it did not address the issue of de facto segregation, but it was an early assault on the idea of state-supported segregation. The controversy did stimulate the legislature to repeal the 1935 law that had allowed segregation of Asian and Indian children, a change signed by Governor Earl Warren. The judicial opinions of *Méndez* did not directly attack the constitutionality of "separate but equal," although Judges McCormick and Denham anticipated many ideas enunciated in BROWN V. BOARD OF EDUCATION (1954).

Mendieta, Ana (d. 1985): Artist. Mendieta spent her childhood in Cuba and immigrated to the United States in the early 1960's, when she was thirteen years old. She received her training in art at the Center for the New Performing Arts at the University of Iowa.

Mendieta developed methods of using her own body, including performances, to create artworks. Much of her early work dealt with blood, and some involved allusions to rituals of the SANTERÍA religion. She returned to Cuba in 1979 and in 1981. Mendieta received significant recognition for her work during her lifetime, including grants from the National Endowment for the Arts and a Guggenheim Fellowship. She was also honored with a posthumous exhibit of her work at the New Museum of Contemporary Art in New York, New York.

Mendoza, Hope (b. 1921, Miami, Ariz.): Labor leader. Before her marriage in 1955 to Harvey Schechter, Mendoza was an industrial worker and union organizer. She later shifted her focus to Democratic Party politics. As a young woman, she left school to work first in the garment industry and then in a defense plant. After World War II, she became an organizer for the INTERNATIONAL LADIES' GARMENT WORKERS' UNION and the Central Labor Council. In 1948, she helped found the COMMUNITY SERVICE ORGANIZATION, later serving on the executive board for seven years. After marrying, she finished her high school education and started her own deposition business. She joined the Mexican American Youth Opportunities Foundation and the Council of Mexican American Affairs, and she was appointed by President Lyndon Johnson to the National Advisory Council for the Peace Corps. Into the 1990's, she continued to serve the Los Angeles Mexican American community and the Democratic Party.

Mendoza, Lydia (b. May 13, 1916, Houston, Tex.): Singer and composer. Mendoza learned to sing and play the guitar with her mother and grandmother. By the age of twelve, she had also learned to play the violin and mandolin.

Mendoza began her career in 1920 with her family group, El Cuarteto Carta Blanca. In the early 1930's, her migrant worker family moved to the Detroit, Michigan, area. They found a receptive audience of Mexican Americans who enjoyed her songs. Later, in San Antonio, Texas, Mendoza sang in Market Square. In 1934, she had her first hit, "Mal Hombre," accompanying herself on her twelve-string guitar. Her tempestuous voice expressed the joy and sorrows of her fellow countrymen and earned her the title of "La Cancionera de los Pobres."

In her sixty-year career, Mendoza recorded more than fifty albums of polkas, RANCHERA MUSIC, *CUMBIAS*, and BOLEROS, including her hit singles "Mal Hombre" and "Mujer Paseada." Mendoza's honors include performances for the president of Mexico in 1950 and for President Jimmy Carter's inauguration in 1977, as well as induction into the Texas Women Hall of Fame in 1984. *Lydia Mendoza: A Family Autobiography* was published in 1993.

Menéndez de Avilés, Pedro (Feb. 15, 1519, Avilés, Spain—Sept. 17, 1574, Santander, Spain): Explorer and settler. Menéndez came from a noble family of the Asturias region of Spain. At a young age, he became a seaman. At first he worked for others, but eventually he owned his own ship. He became well known for fighting corsairs, receiving two royal commissions for this purpose.

In the mid-sixteenth century, competition from other colonial powers forced King Philip II of Spain to make a special effort to settle FLORIDA. The territory was nominally Spain's, but no serious attempts to colonize it had been undertaken since Hernando DE SOTO's expedition. Menéndez received the capitulation to settle Florida on March 20, 1565.

Menéndez took eleven ships and two thousand men. On August 28, 1565, he reached land. He gave the bay where he landed the name of St. Augustine. This became the first permanent European settlement in the modern territory of the United States. On September 20, Menéndez attacked the French colony of Fort Caroline and killed nearly all of its inhabitants.

As a reward for his success, King Philip II named Menéndez governor of Cuba and captain general of a new royal armada to defend the Spanish Caribbean waters against corsairs. The same year, he was recalled to Spain to organize a new squadron to fight the British.

Mental health: Mental health has been defined as simply as "a lack of mental illness." Mental illness often involves limited capacity for self-discipline and lack of willpower to resist conducting oneself or thinking in ways that are not socially or culturally sanctioned.

Need for Study. A major problem for Latinos has been the limited amount of information available regarding their health status. Until the 1980's and 1990's, Latinos were often omitted from national and state data sources. When Latinos were included in surveys, they were often treated as a homogeneous group; therefore, information about specific Latino groups is not available. Many studies focused exclusively on the Mexican American population, and results from those studies have been generalized to other Latinos. The need for more information became more pressing when it was realized that the Latino population was increasing at a rate five times that of the rest of the United States. By the year 2000, the Latino population was estimated to become the largest ethnic group in the country.

Characteristics. The Hispanic Research Center at Fordham University has reported that Latinos with low socioeconomic status are more vulnerable to mental health problems. There is evidence indicating a relationship between migration and mental illness; the relationship has been observed in first-generation immigrants. Strain components of the migration experience include entering a low socioeconomic status, disturbances in the family life cycle, and problems related to adaptation or acculturation to a new environment. Strain in some cases manifests itself in mental illness. ACCULTURATION and DISCRIMINATION have been found to be major problems for Latino youth and young adults, but there is little information regarding the mental health of Latino children and youth. This lack of information was both surprising and discouraging, given that one-third of the Latinos admitted to psychiatric hospitals, according to a study performed in the early 1990's, were under the age of twenty-five.

Some of the most frequent mental health problems associated with Latinos include anxiety, depression, and low self-esteem. These factors of mental health can lead to other health problems, such as drug abuse and ALCOHOLISM. For example, the U.S. Department of Education has reported that among minority high school seniors, Latinos ranked second in alcohol consumption, following Native Americans. The Department of Health and Human Services has reported that Latinos were 2.7 times more likely to be in treatment for problems related to drug abuse than were whites.

Use of Health Services. Compared to other ethnic groups in the United States, Latinos were less likely to use health services, making use of them only in extreme circumstances. One reason for this situation is that a large segment of the Latino population is neither eligible for government medical programs nor covered by private insurance. In addition, Latinos have the lowest levels of education of any ethnic group in the United States. Lack of formal education is associated with poor consumer knowledge about health resources and medical services. The treatment of illness (including mental illness) for Latinos is influenced to a large extent by socioeconomic factors and cultural beliefs.

Illness, as commonly perceived by Latinos, is the result of psychological status (for example, excessive worry), environmental conditions (for example, POVERTY), or supernatural causes (for example, bad luck or witchcraft). Religion is influential in the response of Latinos to mental illness. The use of prayer as a therapeutic agent in response to symptoms of mental illness is typical. The family is an important support system for those experiencing emotional problems. Thus Latinos find treatment for illness within religion and the family rather than from the traditional Western medical establishment.

Folk practitioners called *curanderos* are a major alternative to established health and mental health services (*see* CURANDERISMO). The *ESPIRITISTA* (spiritualist) is the highest-ranking *curandero*. *Espiritistas* have knowledge about how to treat physical ailments and folk diseases (diseases not recognized by the U.S. medical establishment), but they are also perceived to have power to communicate with spirits. They are the main folk resource for dealing with emotional problems. Their services are relatively inexpensive; on some occasions no charge is levied. The affordability of *curanderos* has been indicated as a strong factor motivating Latinos to seek their services.

The spiritual aspect of Latinos' views of illness suggests that interpretation of psychological factors based on the dominant U.S. cultural framework may lead to diagnostic distortion and bias. For example, Latinos with spiritualist beliefs may be interpreted as psychotics.

Latinos' perceptions of mental health are tied to their overall use and perceptions of the medical care system. (Hazel Hankin)

Experts have suggested health care policies directed specifically toward Latinos (*see* HEALTH CARE POLICY). Some of the policies that could be implemented quickly include locating health and mental health clinics within Latino communities. recruiting bilingual and bicultural professionals and paraprofessionals, encouraging Latino students to enter health professional schools, encouraging administrators of health facilities to examine culturally insensitive policies and procedures and institute action for change, and allocating attention and resources in the areas of prevention of illness and health education for Latinos.

—*Carlos I. Ramos*

SUGGESTED READINGS: • Becerra, Rosina, Marvin Karno, and Javier Escobar. *Mental Health and Hispanic Americans: Clinical Perspectives.* New York: Grune & Stratton, 1982. • Boswell, Thomas, and James Curtis. *The Cuban-American Experience: Culture, Images, and Perspectives.* Totowa, N.J.: Rowman & Allanheld, 1983. • Carrasquillo, Angela. *Hispanic Children and Youth in the United States: A Resource Guide.* New York: Garland, 1991. • Furino, Antonio, and Eric Munoz. "Health Status Among Hispanics: Major Themes and New Priorities." *JAMA: Journal of the American Medical Association* 265 (January 9, 1991): 255-257. • Giachello, Aida. "Hispanics and Health Care." In *Hispanics in the United States*, edited by Pastora San Juan Cafferty and William C. McCready. New Brunswick, N.J.: Transaction Books, 1985. • Kaplan, Mark, and Gary Marks. "Adverse Effects of Acculturation: Psychological Distress Among Mexican American Young Adults." *Social Science and Medicine* 31, no. 12 (1990): 1313-1319. • Moore, Joan, and Harry Pachon. *Hispanics in the United States.* Englewood Cliffs, N.J.: Prentice-Hall, 1985. • Novello, Antonia, Paul Wise, and Dushanka

Kleinman. "Hispanic Health: Time for Data, Time for Action." *JAMA: Journal of the American Medical Association* 265 (January 9, 1991): 253-255. • Rogler, Lloyd, et al. *A Conceptual Framework for Mental Health Research on Hispanic Populations.* Bronx, N.Y.: Hispanic Research Center, Fordham University, 1983.

Menudo: Teen music group from Puerto Rico. Menudo was founded in 1977. A member's participation in the five-boy group ended when he turned sixteen or his voice changed, so the group underwent numerous personnel changes. Menudo gained widespread popularity first in Latin America and later in the United States, selling out concerts at large venues such as New York's Radio City Music Hall. Its pop/soft rock music and clean-cut teen-idol image drew mostly young fans. Menudo toured extensively, filmed commercials and a Saturday morning television show, and recorded albums. In 1984, at the height of their popularity, Menudo members were appointed youth ambassadors for the United Nations Children's Fund (UNICEF).

Menudo: Mexican tripe soup. *Menudo* is eaten all over Mexico, but northern Mexico is most famous for its version. All *menudo* consists of long-cooked tripe and various seasonings, usually chile, garlic, onions, oregano, lime juice, and cumin, thickened and flavored with a calf's foot. In northern Mexico, POSOLE usually is added. *Menudo* is most commonly eaten as breakfast in most of Mexico, perhaps in part because it is reputed to be a hangover remedy. In northern Mexico, *menudo* is eaten for any meal. *Menudo* is so popular in Southern California that it is a cultural symbol of Chicanos, and Texas hosts *menudo* cookoffs. Along Mexico's eastern coast, *menudo* usually is called MONDONGO.

Mercedes: Spanish land grants. *Mercedes* were first granted in 1689 in northern Mexico. The *merced* or *gracia* was a land grant through which the Spanish Crown conceded land to individuals or groups of applicants who fulfilled certain legal obligations. These grants were based on the premise that the Spanish Crown had a legitimate right to own and dispose of lands in the Western Hemisphere.

In the *merced*, the Spanish sovereign retained ultimate title to all land granted. Grantees were given only a right of occupation and use. The land would revert to the Spanish Crown if the grantees did not meet the legal requirements. All ungranted lands were denominated *tierras realengas y baldías* (royal and vacant lands) and were retained by the Crown.

There were several types of land grants. A town proprietary grant would be given to an individual to found one or more towns, and groups of ten or more families desiring to establish an agricultural village would be given a community land grant. Land could also be granted to private owners to establish farms or stock ranches, or for other legal purposes. Depending on local conditions and the Crown's interest in attracting settlers, other requirements might be imposed. Indian PUEBLOS also received titles giving them complete possession of the lands they occupied.

Spanish law required that each settler of a town or rural community be given a house lot and ample land to sustain his family. Additional settlers would receive farmland as available. In the community land grant, land unsuitable for farming as well as all pastures and watering sites became the *ejido*, or common lands of the community. These *ejidos* belonged to the land grant community, not the individual settler on the grant. Thus, all residents of the community, despite their financial resources, had equal rights to graze land and make use of other natural resources. Generally, settlers were required to spend a specified period of time on the grant.

Limited knowledge of the vastness of the New World caused many problems. Although the Crown issued grants with the intent of not infringing on Indian rights or those of other parties, some territorial claims did overlap. When Mexico won independence from Spain in 1821, it adopted the Spanish land tenure system, and subsequent overlapping of existing Spanish grants caused legal problems (*see* LAND TENURE ISSUES).

At the end of the MEXICAN AMERICAN WAR in 1848, through the TREATY OF GUADALUPE HIDALGO, the United States committed itself to protecting the civil and property rights of the population of the annexed territories. When disputes arose concerning unsettled land titles, Congress established a specialized Court of Private Land Claims to adjudicate land grant titles in Arizona, Colorado, and New Mexico. The system was so cumbersome, complicated, and expensive that Spanish Americans had difficulty defending their land rights. In the 1960's, Reies López TIJERINA and the Alianza Federal de Mercedes demanded the return of Spanish and Mexican land grants to Spanish Americans and Mexican Americans.

Merengue: Folk music and dance form of Afro-Cuban influence. The music is in rapid two-four meter, show-

A merengue band. (City Lore, Martha Cooper)

ing *cinquillo* and *tresillo* rhythms and call-and-response singing patterns. It is characterized by alternating between the Spanish *copla* (four-line stanza) and the *estribillo* (refrain). Accompaniment is provided predominantly by the CUATRO (four-string guitar), accordion, *charasca* (metal scraper), and *tamboras* and *bajos* (double- and single-headed drums). The merengue originated in the Dominican Republic, where it devel-

oped into a sophisticated dance form executed in four-four time. The merengue is also found in Venezuela and Haiti.

Merienda: Daytime snack. In Mexico and most of the rest of Latin America, *merienda* is the snack between lunch and supper, a direct outgrowth of Spain's mid-afternoon snack of the same name. Occasionally *me-*

rienda is at mid-morning. Urban, middle-class people, especially women, are most likely to meet for a *merienda*. Refreshments at the *merienda* consist of sweet pastries, usually purchased at a *panadería*, accompanied by tea, coffee, or fruit juices; alcoholic beverages are not part of a *merienda*. In some rural places, especially in South America, *merienda* is a picnic; in parts of Michoacán, it is a bedtime snack.

Mesa-Bains, Amalia (b. 1943): Artist. The artwork created by Mesa-Bains relies heavily on Mexican symbols and religious imagery. She has designed altar installations that honor ancestors as well as Mexican historical figures. In her altar installations, Mesa-Bains uses such traditional and context-laden Mexican symbols as skulls, hearts, and crosses.

Mesa-Bains earned a B.A. in painting (1966) from San Jose State University and an M.A. (1971) from San Francisco State University. At the Wright Institute, she earned a second master's degree in 1980, then a Ph.D. in psychology, with an emphasis on culture and identity. Her studies of culture inform her art, which explores how GENDER ROLES and ethnic identity are created within the Latino community. She focuses on female identity.

Mesa-Bains has taught in various locations around the world and has worked with the United States Information Agency as a consultant and lecturer. She has also served on the board of directors of the Galeria de la Raza in San Francisco, California, and was the commissioner of art for that city.

Mesoamerican native communities: The historical achievements of the Mesoamerican Indian tribes are noted throughout the world. These tribes are remembered particularly for the striking architecture of the ceremonial centers of the MAYAN, OLMEC, and AZTEC civilizations; the achievement of glyphic writing forms; and infamous religious practices that included human sacrifice among both the early Mayan high cultures and the later Aztec military/religious civilization complex. There is a growing literature on the ancient Mesoamerican civilizations, but far less is known about the modern descendants of these once-great human societies that predate Spanish arrival by more than fifteen hundred years.

Classification Systems. Recent studies of Mesoamerican native peoples have divided the various cultural forms into general trait-groups for clarification, but the use of classification systems is controversial. Classification systems always involve generalizations.

It is important to keep in mind that native cultures in the Americas occupy vast territories, and tribal traditions seem to merge at the borders, rather like the blending of the colors in a rainbow. Furthermore, Mesoamerican history has involved a tragic series of cultural and physical crises brought about by European immigrants who often saw native people merely as pagans and potential slaves. It is therefore helpful to remember that classification systems are intended not to blur the uniqueness of groups of people but to facilitate introduction to a vast field. In the Mesoamerican cultural areas, a convenient classification system would include the gathering and hunting tribes of northern Mexico; horticultural tribes of northwestern Mexico; Mesoamerican tribes of southern Mexico, Guatemala, and El Salvador; and the circum-Caribbean and Caribbean island cultures.

Gathering and Hunting Tribes. Hunter/gatherers are typified by the age of their lifestyle. Scholars typically assume that farming cultures developed secondarily, in areas where water is easily found and agricultural work results in stable food supplies. Hunter/gatherers have perfected important means of collecting food, such as leaching out inedible parts of a variety of plants, collecting seeds, and using certain tree products such as acorn seeds.

Typical of the social structure of hunter/gatherers are patrilineal descent, nomadic hunting groups, strong presence of witchcraft and rites of maturity, and peacefulness.

Various hunter/gatherer tribal groups have been referred to by the general term "Chichimec." Specific names for smaller cultural units, from north to south in Baja California, are as follows. In the northwest, the Diegueno occupy northern Baja and some regions of the southwestern United States. Further south are the Akwa'ala (who call themselves the Paipai) and the Kiliwa. The latter are reportedly more successful in preserving their identity in the twentieth century. The Cochimi once lived in the Sonoran desert, but they became extinct.

In the south of Baja California are the Waicuru and Cora, and at the tip of the peninsula are the Pericu. Similar to ancient Baja culture were the Seri, across the bay on the western coast of the Mexican mainland.

Most of the Baja cultures became extinct as a result of Spanish invasion and diseases brought by well-meaning missionaries (*see* EPIDEMICS AND INDIGENOUS POPULATIONS). The Seri culture persists, as do remnants of related North American tribes such as the Chumash and Gabrielino. Modern Seri call themselves the Kongkaak (which, as is typical for self-designations, merely means "the people"). In the twentieth century, the Seri took to fishing, and for a time, a market in shark liver oil provided a reasonable income. In modern Mexico, the Seri persist as a small but self-conscious indigenous people centered mostly in Desemboque and Punta Chueca.

Horticultural Tribes of Northwestern Mexico. From the Pima and Papago of what is now the southwestern United States and northern Mexico, and down the "spine" of western Mexico, a cultural spectrum of horticulturally based native peoples dominated in precontact time. Their geographical area includes the Sierra Madre down to the coastal lowlands, where they came into contact with hunter/gatherer seminomadic tribal groups.

The most important agricultural staples were MAIZE, BEANS, and SQUASH. These were supplemented by nuts and fruits. The tribes wove cotton and traded clothing items, along with copper rattles, parrot feathers, shells, and stones. Unlike the "higher cultures" of the lower Mesoamerican tribes, the horticultural tribes had no marketplaces or massive ceremonial architecture. Farming was considerably less intensive.

Northwestern tribal groups lived in neighborhoods and traced descent through both male and female lines. The village neighborhoods practiced a loose form of governance presided over by elders. Clearly differentiated tribal groups were identified by Jesuit missionaries as early as the seventeenth century. Political oppression by Spanish colonists (especially through a program of land grants known as the ENCOMIENDA SYSTEM that allowed grantees to treat resident Indians as virtual slaves) and the resulting cultural influences of nationalism resulted in the loss of precontact cultures and languages.

Surviving tribes have taken on a Hispanicized MESTIZO culture combining remnants of precontact practice with peasant precapitalist lifestyles of modern northern Mexico. Some tribal groups have managed to maintain a clearly recognizable identity, often by combining the remnants of closely related precontact tribal groups, such as the Opata-Edeve-Jova group, which numbered some four thousand in 1960.

Another example of modern survivals from this general culture grouping is the Yaqui. The Yaqui have maintained a clear presence in Mexico (near Seri country on the western coast) and in significant communities around Tucson, Arizona. Related to the Yaqui are the Mayo, who are more deeply impacted by Catholicism.

The Tarahumara persist in the southwestern part of Chihuahua. In the 1970's, their population was estimated to be between forty thousand and fifty thousand. Many maintain indigenous forms of religious belief. In a similar area are remnants of the Tepehuan. The Huichol culture interests some advocates of new age religions who are intrigued with the use of PEYOTE. The highly developed art of the Huichol has been the subject of numerous museum exhibits.

Mesoamerican Tribes of Southern Mexico, Guatemala, and El Salvador. Many scholars define the northern "border" of the high cultures in the Mesoamerican cultural area by the Tarascan, Otomi, Nahua, and Huastec Mayan tribal group boundaries, and the southern border as El Salvador and Honduras. There is a tremendous variety of tribal groupings in this territory, as well as a significant variety of environmental areas, including mountain ranges (the southern Sierra Madre Occidental, and then the Sierra Madre Oriental ranges, which continue into Guatemala) and tropical plains such as the Yucatán Peninsula.

The Spanish found most of the people living in the mountains, the mountain lowlands, and the Yucatán Peninsula, in population centers ranging from small peasant villages to large cities. The urban development of the great Mesoamerican civilizations set this part of Mesoamerican culture apart from the more northern tribal groupings. Urban development is attributed in part to the success of agricultural produce, again mainly corn, beans, and squash, which allowed for a surplus that initiated small business and the growth of a differentiated society around market exchange systems. A series of Mesoamerican civilizations created massive architectural ceremonial centers that stand as witness to the greatness of precontact civilizations that engaged in public sport, elaborate religious rituals, market exchange, astronomical speculation, and written communication.

Archaeologists continue to debate the date of the arrival of the Mesoamerican peoples in this part of the world. Artifacts providing a date of 24,000-20,000 B.C.E. (before the common era, now replacing B.C.) have been found. Most common is to date the people's arrival at 12,000 to 10,000 B.C.E., because that date matches evidence found in North America, assuming (as do the majority of scholars) that Native Americans originated in Asia and crossed the Bering Strait.

In southern Mexico, evidence suggests that the domestication of plants began between 5,000 and 3,000 B.C.E. By the time pottery makes its appearance, scholars no longer refer to the Paleo-Indian or the later

The ruins of the Mayan Temple of the Foliated Cross, in Palenque, Mexico, date from about 600 C.E. (Claire Rydell)

Archaic period, instead referring to the Preclassic period (2,000 B.C.E. to 200 C.E.). At this time, platforms began to be built in larger urban areas. In later eras of the Preclassic period, the city of TEOTIHUACÁN, thirty miles northeast of modern Mexico City, dominated the entire area, with an urban population of 125,000 to 200,000.

Scholars refer to the Classic period as 200-250 to 900 C.E. At this time, the Mesoamerican civilizations reached a zenith of development, with massive ceremonial centers featuring monumental architectural achievements. A widely differentiated religious and civil administration presided over an impressive level of economic exchange and planned agricultural produce. Although the prevailing form of dwelling was the village, urban centers held more than 200,000 people, sometimes living in impressive ADOBE dwellings with more than one story. At the center of each city was the ceremonial plaza, with the palace, pyramids, and ball courts.

The majority of people were still agriculturally based peasants, living in villages surrounding the great civil centers but related to them in their religious and civil lives. Classic period civilizations also developed in southern Guatemala, among the Maya, at this same time. In the last centuries of the Classic period, however, these early civilizations went into decline.

The Postclassic Period. From about 900 C.E., the beginning of the Postclassic period, the TOLTEC people dominated from north of Teotihuacán. Among the people who took advantage of the general decline were a northern mercenary people known as the Mexica, who arrived around 1300 C.E. and used their growing military advantages to found what came to be known as the AZTEC CIVILIZATION. Their capital, TENOCHTITLÁN, stood where Mexico City is now.

At this time, MAYAN CIVILIZATION continued further south. Many scholars dispute the standard divisions of Preclassic, Classic, and Postclassic, which suggest that the Aztec civilization was in some sense a decline from the previous greatness of the classic civilizations.

Mesoamerican agricultural produce included potatoes, peppers, vanilla, cacao, manioc, mesquite, avocados, tomatoes, and papaya. Tortillas, a major part of the Mesoamerican diet, were made from corn. Farming methods went from the standard slash-and-burn method of clearing land and planting it until the soil was depleted (and then moving on), to use of irrigation systems and raised gardens known as *chinampas*. Hunting also provided some food. The Mesoamerican tribes ate a variety of animals, including some reptiles. They kept various forms of poultry, including geese, quail, turkeys, and ducks, but they did not have the larger farm animals more typical of the Old World.

Agricultural needs gave rise to a complex set of gods and rituals. Part of the ritual life of the great Mesoamerican civilizations was advanced artistry, including impressive stone carvings that have survived to the present and a variety of household decorations. Part of their artistic achievement was the making of jewelry and other items from silver, gold, copper, and alloys.

Mesoamerican civilizations are also noteworthy for their level of governance. Aztec and Mayan civilizations had governments consisting of a council of elders from sections of the city. In Tenochtitlán, the Aztec capital, this council elected three main officers: one for economic affairs, one for military/police affairs, and a speaker who served as head of the entire council. Most civilizations had class systems consisting of an aristocracy-priesthood on one side and the peasant majority on the other.

Other Mesoamerican civilizations did not have such a system. The Tarascans, for example, were essentially a dictatorship and ruled over a larger territory. As Aztec rituals demanded more and more prisoners of war as sacrificial victims, Tarascan protection was welcomed. Mayan civilization was broken up into a variety of small city-states.

The Mayan high cultures were significantly different from either the later Aztec or the more southern Andean civilizations of the Inca, in that they were settled in widespread areas and their ceremonial centers were not large centers of population. They were much more susceptible to military conquest because these centers did not serve as "fortresses."

The Circum-Caribbean Tribes. Although largely decimated by the arrival of European settlers, the circum-Caribbean/Central American/West Indian tribes represent an important cultural grouping that scholars recognize because of coastal traditions that persist to the present, such as among the mixed Mosquito Indians of Nicaragua and among some of the southeastern American tribal groups such as the Natchez and Chickasaw. The circum-Caribbean tribes are known largely through historical records maintained by missionaries. From such records, it is clear that there are a number of traits common to the circum-Caribbean cultures that were further developed in the Mayan and Aztec "high cultures." Some scholars suggest that the circum-Caribbean tribes were a source for some of the more important cultural traits that then spread throughout the continent. A second source of migration to the

A model of the Mexican Gulf site of El Tajín, Mexico, shows ballcourts and multitiered platform mounds. (Ruben G. Mendoza)

New World may well have been through the Caribbean region, supplementing that of Asiatic peoples migrating across the Bering Strait.

The high cultures of the Andes such as the Inca can not have developed much later than the more northern Mesoamerican Mayan and later Aztec cultures because the potato, so central to these civilizations, was originally a South American plant. The Andean high cultures shared with the circum-Caribbean cultures certain important traits such as intensive farming, large population centers, and stable settlements. There also developed strong class differentiation and governmental structures, as opposed to rule by family elders. There were religious buildings apart from the well-developed local architecture. Many artistic skills were shared by the high cultures and the circum-Caribbean cultures, such as the use of pottery, feathers, and cotton garments.

The circum-Caribbean societies were coastal peoples practiced in the use of seafaring boats and intensive fishing. Societies divided into three levels: aristocracy and priesthood, commoners, and prisoners of war who were used as slaves. Elements of these and other circum-Caribbean traits have been noted in southern United States groups such as the Natchez and Chickasaw. Certain religious features are shared among these peoples as well, such as the use of a priestly class, which diffuses into shamanism farther from the coast.

The circum-Caribbean cultural complex was devastated by the arrival of Spanish and European conquerors. Today, only remnants of these cultures survive. The once numerous populations of the Caribbean islands are extinct, replaced by Afro-Caribbean/Spanish cultures in Cuba, Haiti, and Jamaica, and on other Caribbean islands. It is thought that remnants of circum-Caribbean tribes are mixed with the peoples of northern Colombia and tribes such as the Mosquito Indians of Nicaragua.

Influence on European Development. Many Native American contributions remain unheralded because much of what benefited European Americans was taken without the active choice of the native peoples. The most obvious cases are the mineral resources of silver and gold.

American mineral resources, including vast amounts of gold and silver, began to have serious inflationary effects on Spain soon after Spanish discovery of the New World. The influx of large amounts of gold drove prices upward and contributed to the decline of Spain's economic dominance of Europe even as it fueled the zeal of Spanish exploration. By 1600, the supply of precious metals had increased nearly eightfold, largely as a result of exploitation of Latin lands, and had inflationary effects as far away as the Ottoman Empire. European financial and industrial development began to surpass that of the Near Eastern societies only with the assistance of New World resources and opportunities for new production. Mesoamerican contributions extend far more widely, however, than simply the exploitation of resources and land previously controlled by the indigenous populations.

Native Agriculture. The introduction of the potato had a major effect on European society, particularly those parts of Northern Europe where grain agriculture was highly susceptible to weather conditions, making famine frequent and devastating. The durable potato produced more nutrition with less labor. The potato could be prepared easily and stored for long periods of time. The impact of potato farming in Poland, Russia (with its cold climate), and Ireland (with a damp climate that makes storage of other foods difficult) is difficult to overestimate. It is difficult to imagine national cuisines of these countries without POTATOES.

American peppers similarly affected the spiced curries of the Indian/South Asian subcontinent and the famous Szechwan spices of South China. Native Americans also contributed TOMATOES, PEANUTS, pecans, strawberries, maple syrup, AVOCADOS, wild rice, sweet potatoes, cranberries, blueberries, chocolate, and vanilla.

Further basic, yet clearly critical, contributions of this nature include sisal (for making rope), and rubber. South American tribes developed the technology for producing rubber-coated clothing, such as jackets and footwear, before the arrival of the resourceful and inventive Europeans. It was not until Charles Goodyear duplicated the native refining process in 1839 that Western society developed a massive industry for rubberized products.

Post-Conquest Mesoamerican Indians. Oliver La-Farge suggested a sequence of postcontact eras that has been accepted by many scholars. They are Conquest (1524-1600), Colonial Indian (1600-1720), First Transition (1720-1800), Recent Indian (1800-1880), and Recent Indian II (1880 to the present).

During the era of Conquest, the impact on much of Mesoamerican Indian civilization was devastating, although some distant groups remained relatively untouched. The center of activity was the Aztec capital. Many Indians were enslaved in the ENCOMIENDA SYSTEM. Others were forced into public works projects to help establish the colonial state system. The CATHOLIC CHURCH was often the source of severe persecution used to destroy pagan religious practices. One of the most interesting aspects of the SPANISH CONQUEST that differentiated it dramatically from enslavement of Africans in North America was the fact that the Spanish began to intermarry with the upper classes of the Indian population, laying the groundwork for the emergence of the unique MESTIZO culture predominant in modern Mexico.

During the First Transition, Spain ended some of the more violent practices directed against the Indian population, and new forms of relations with the Indian peoples emerged. Many Indian groups openly practiced forms of their previous religious life, often mixing it in creative ways with the Catholic Christianity brought by missionaries.

By 1880, the Industrial Revolution brought new conflicts between the industrial nations' need for raw materials and the vast pool of cheap Indian labor. Once again, European civilization entered into a destructive relationship with the native peoples. This was the era of coffee plantations and agricultural exploitation, with massive forced labor campaigns for Indians on commercial farmlands.

Some researchers have estimated that more than nine million people still spoke native Mesoamerican languages as late as 1980. These are identified as belonging to three general linguistic families: the Mayan family of languages known as Macromayan, the Oto-Manguean (the largest complex of modern native Mesoamerican languages), and the Uto-Aztecan, related to many modern North American language groups.

Mesoamerican Religion and Life. The most imposing feature of Mesoamerican religion is the pyramids. On top of these great structures, some of which were more than one hundred feet high, temples were erected, dedicated to some of the more important gods. For example, in TENOCHTITLÁN, the two temples on top of the largest pyramid were dedicated to the war god and the god of rain.

Human sacrifice was an element of Mesoamerican religion. In Mesoamerican belief, however, the dead continued to "live," and there was a belief in ghosts that could return to the present world. Spirits were an essential part of Mesoamerican cosmology.

To generalize about Mesoamerican personality types is risky; nevertheless, scholars have noticed a certain common complex of ideas. Foremost among them is fatalism, accompanied by the belief that the universe is populated by hostile spirits and powers. This results in a pessimistic outlook on life and mistrust of other people. There is correspondingly an extensive ritual of etiquette, for example, in greeting others. The use of intermediaries when arranging marriages or business matters is extensive. Aggression that is suppressed may be expressed through witchcraft, malevolent gossip, or occasional outbursts of violence. Some anthropologists object to this portrayal, citing the fact that Mesoamericans seem able to enjoy life and live at peace a majority of the time.

Contemporary Mesoamerican life is centered on stages in life, beginning with the importance of baptism and continuing with rites often associated with pre-Conquest traditions. Marriage is an important occasion in the life of modern Mesoamericans. Many marriages are arranged by the parents.

In Mayan culture, a variety of men's societies have both political and religious functions, such as presiding over the observances associated with particular saints. Through their responsibilities in these various societies and in other social and civil obligations, young persons rise in the level of responsibility in the wider society of the local villages.

Religious observances of Mesoamericans are highly syncretistic, drawing in diverse elements. Divergence from mainstream Catholicism was viewed with open suspicion by the hierarchy, but it has come into reconsideration in the light of LIBERATION THEOLOGY and its emphasis on making Christian religion an authentic expression of the life of the poor. In this view, syncretism is part of the creative process of expressing a Christian faith that is authentic to the Mesoamerican peoples. St. Peter may take on the functions of the rain god, for example, and other saints may occupy the roles of pre-Conquest gods or spirits. Each community also has its patron saints who are honored regularly by festivals.

In addition to orthodox Christian observances of saints and their roles as intermediaries of the spirit, there are also a variety of beliefs in spirits in control of the forces of nature in many Mesoamerican communities. Gods or spirits are associated with war, rain, crops, wind, storms, and other phenomena. A unique belief of Mesoamerican (and now more widely Mexican) culture is the "Day of the Dead (DÍA DE LOS MUERTOS)," when the spirits of the dead are invited back to the family ALTARS. Finally, magic and witchcraft (*see* WITCHES AND WITCHCRAFT) remain widely used traditions in Mesoamerican culture.

—*Daniel Smith-Christopher*

SUGGESTED READINGS:

• Browman, David, ed. *Cultural Continuity in Mesoamerica.* The Hague: Mouton, 1978. A good collection of technical articles.

• Lyon, Patricia J., ed. *Native South Americans: Ethnology of the Least Known Continent.* Boston: Little, Brown, 1974. Included are Julian Steward's "American Culture History in the Light of South America," George Peter Murdock's "South American Culture Areas," John Howland Rowe's "Linguistic Classification Problems in South America," and the classic essay by Robert Carneiro, "Slash-and-Burn Cultivation Among the Kuikuru and Its Implications for Cultural Development in the Amazon Basin."

• Skar, Harald O., and Frank Salomon, eds. *Natives and Neighbors in South America: Anthropological Essays.* Göteborg, Sweden: Göteborgs Etnografiska Museum, 1987. An important survey of contemporary issues that discusses modern liberation/political movements among natives of Central and South America.

• Steward, Julian. *Handbook of South American Indians.* 7 vols. Washington, D.C.: Government Printing Office, 1946-1959. Remains the standard reference for South American Indians.

• Taylor, Robert. *Indians of Middle America: An Introduction to the Ethnology of Mexico, Central America, and the Caribbean.* Manhattan, Kans.: Lifeway Books, 1989. An excellent source for this topic.

• Weatherford, Jack. *Indian Givers: How the Indians of the Americas Transformed the World.* New York: Crown, 1988. Discusses how Indian cultures have affected the rest of the world.

Mester, Jorge (b. Apr. 10, 1935, Mexico City, Mexico): Orchestra conductor. Mester studied music and conducting at the Juilliard School in New York, New York, where years later he presented the American premieres of many works by contemporary composers, such as Paul Hindemith's "Long Christmas Dinner." Mester also studied with the famous conductor Leonard Bernstein.

Mester made his debut as a conductor in 1955 with the Orquesta Sinfónica Nacional de México. He has conducted many orchestras in the United States and Europe, such as the British Broadcasting Corporation Symphony Orchestra and the Royal Philharmonic Orchestra in London, as well as several opera companies. In 1968, he won the Naumburg Award for conducting.

Mester has served as music director of the Aspen Musical Festival and the Festival Casals de Puerto Rico, chairman of conducting studies at the Juilliard School of Music, conductor of the Kansas City Philharmonic Orchestra (1971-1974), and conductor of the Pasadena Symphony Orchestra beginning in 1984. Mester's long association with the Louisville Orchestra, from 1967 to 1979, produced a distinguished catalog of some two hundred premiere recordings of works by twentieth century composers.

Mestizaje: Mixing of Spanish, indigenous, and African blood. *Mestizaje* (literally, "miscegenation") refers to the racial mixing of Indian, Spanish, and African blood among people in Latin America. *Mestizaje* in Latin America dates to the beginning of the sixteenth century, when Hernán CORTÉS and fellow Spaniards invaded Mexico and used indigenous people to conquer the territory. The conquistadores interbred with native people, and a new race was created that would eventually comprise the majority of the culture. African slaves were imported into some Latin American countries. Slaves and their descendants had children with native persons, creating another type of racial intermixing. The culture created by *mestizaje* was a new one in which some indigenous and African elements were retained while others were lost.

Mestizo: Person of mixed Spanish, Indian, and/or African blood. "Mestizo" refers to a person who is of

A mestiza as depicted by Jose Cisneros. (Institute of Texan Cultures)

mixed Spanish and Indian blood, in some cases with African heritage as well. Mestizos constitute most of the worldwide Latin American population. In the first years following the invasion of Spaniards in the Americas, mestizos were considered neither Spaniards nor Indians. Their culture gradually became less similar to that of their indigenous ancestors and more Hispanicized.

Metate: Slab-shaped stone used to grind corn and other foods. With its partner, the *mano* or handstone, the *metate* is the most common folk implement for grinding foods, especially in Mexico, the American Southwest, and parts of Central America. Modern *metates*, usually made of hard volcanic rock, are usually simple slabs with three or four legs. *Metates* came into use about 7000 B.C.E. Some are ornate, carved with jaguars, parrots, and other motifs.

Mexican-American Anti-Defamation Committee: Antidiscrimination organization. This committee fights DISCRIMINATION through the media and legal means. It was created in the late 1960's to aid the Chicano community in defending its civil and cultural rights. In 1969, it sued the Frito Lay Company. Mexican American leaders had complained about the racist portrayal of a Mexican in a cartoon character Frito Lay called the "Frito Bandito." Frito Lay made a statement promising to replace the advertising but continued to show the commercials for nearly a year, leading to the lawsuit. The organization later changed its name to the Institute for the Study of Hispanic-American Life and History, concerning itself with civil rights and the study of Latino life in the United States.

Mexican American Bar Association: Professional association. This group was established in 1960 with twelve members. In the 1970's and 1980's, its membership swelled as the number of Mexican American attorneys increased. The association's goals are to protect the legal rights of Latinos, increase the welfare of Latino communities, and serve as a support system for Latino lawyers. The organization has committees focusing on immigration and the media, along with various others, and a Spanish-speaking attorney referral service. Members speak in schools to encourage students to consider becoming lawyers. The association has lobbied for Latinos to be appointed as judges.

Mexican American Cultural Center: Center for pastoral education. Established in 1972 by the PADRES

Asociados Para Derechos, Religiosos, Educativos, y Sociales (PADRES), the center is a nondenominational institute promoting the Mexican cultural heritage and the Spanish language. It is a national center for pastoral education and language studies directed at the Hispanic ministry, particularly among Mexican Americans.

The organization responds primarily to the need to prepare future bilingual and bicultural ministers within the Catholic church in the United States. Its classes and programs are conducted in both English and Spanish. The center also administers an institute that provides the necessary communication tools for ministering among Hispanics.

Mexican American Legal Defense and Education Fund

(MALDEF): Founded in 1968 as a nonprofit public interest organization. MALDEF was established through the efforts of Pete Tijerina, a lawyer from the League of United Latin American Citizens (LULAC); Gregory Luna, a Texas lawyer and politician; and Mario Obledo, with funds from the Ford Foundation. Its founding purpose was to continue the work of the NAACP Legal Defense Fund (LDF) and the Southwest Council of La Raza (SWCLR). Important leadership positions have been held by Vilma Martínez and Antonia Hernández.

MALDEF is a public interest group that monitors issues important to the Mexican American and general Latino communities, including immigration, employment, education, housing, voter registration and elections, public funding, and discrimination. It has played a prominent role in civil rights cases, class action litigation, community education, and leadership training since the early 1970's. Its principal objective is to protect and promote civil rights related to employment, education, immigration, political access, and language. It does so through litigation, advocacy, education outreach, and scholarships.

Among MALDEF's major achievements has been the reduction of barriers to political participation. It has offered assistance to non-English-speaking voters by working toward the extension of the Voting Rights Act of 1965 and the application of the Equal Educational Opportunity Act of 1974. Through its development of political redistricting plans that give Latinos a stronger voice in government, MALDEF has also attacked gerrymandering of voting districts that gives unfair advantage to English-speaking residents. For example, *Garza v. County of Los Angeles, California Board of Supervisors* (1991) ruled against the Board of Supervisors' redistricting plan and provided a new plan that established a new L.A. Board of Supervisors district seat.

MALDEF has worked to enhance educational opportunities for the Latino community through cases such as *Serna v. Portales* (New Mexico, 1974), which established the constitutionality of bilingual education, and *Plyler v. Doe* (1982), which determined that undocumented immigrants could not be denied access to free public school education. In addition, MALDEF administers a Law School Scholarship Program to enable promising Latino students to enter the legal profession. It maintains a law library of more than two thousand volumes at its Los Angeles office.

The undercount of Latinos in the U.S. census of 1970 prompted MALDEF to conduct the national 1990 Census Awareness Program, with the slogan *Hágase contar* ("Make yourself be counted"). Members of MALDEF conducted a public relations campaign to inform the Latino community about the importance of participating in the U.S. Census so that there would be an accurate count of Latinos in the United States. (*See* census, treatment and counting of Latinos in the.)

MALDEF maintains a national office in Los Angeles and regional offices in Sacramento, San Francisco, Fresno, and Santa Ana, California; El Paso and San Antonio, Texas; Chicago, Illinois; Detroit, Michigan; and Washington, D.C. In addition to its advocacy and educational programs, it publishes an annual report and two tri-annual newsletters: *Newsletter* and *Leadership Program Newsletter*.

Mexican American Movement:

Youth organization. The Mexican American Movement grew out of Mexican Youth Conferences sponsored by the Young Men's Christian Association in Southern California. Most attendees were college students whose parents had emigrated from Mexico. The organization evolved from a boys' club into a professional organization dedicated to helping youth and creating a new middle-class leadership of professionals in the Mexican American community. It emphasized pride in being Mexican and saw education as the main tool for progress, seeing lack of education as Mexican Americans' primary stumbling block to advancement. This position was criticized by some as overly optimistic.

In 1939-1940, the movement expanded its work to include a women's branch, a teachers' association, and a network with Mexican American leaders. In the late 1940's, membership declined. Many members had graduated from college and left the group. In 1950, organization president Paul Coronel could no longer fund the group, and it dissolved. The Mexican American Movement had a long-lasting effect on the community, however, as the first organization of Mexican American students to face the problems of their community. In addition, many former members went on to participate in other organizations.

Mexican American Political Association (MAPA): Founded in 1959. MAPA is devoted to securing equality for Latinos as well as advocating greater participation of Mexican Americans in the political process, as both voters and candidates.

MAPA was founded in April of 1959 by Bert Corona and Eduardo Quevedo in Fresno, California. The group at first had about 150 volunteer delegates. In succeeding years, Francisca Flores, Grace Davis Montanez, Julia Luna Mont, Ramona Morin, and Dolores Sanchez all played important roles in the growth and development of the organization.

MAPA sought to meet the need for distinctly Mexican electoral organizations by stressing ethnic identity, direct electoral politics, and electoral independence. Upon its formation, MAPA announced that its basic aspiration was to become the political voice in California for the Mexican American community. MAPA has consistently worked toward election of Mexican Americans, regardless of party, though it more consistently supported Democrats.

The peak years of MAPA were between 1960 and 1965. During this time, MAPA contributed to the election of two members of the state assembly, one member of Congress, and six judges in the state of California by endorsing their candidacy. MAPA also worked tirelessly in defense of the Mexican American community in specific situations regarding police brutality, discrimination, immigration, and education. Although endorsement of candidates and advocacy of appointments remained its central concern, MAPA also aided the Hispanic community through its charitable efforts. The association has a history of supporting the organization of Chicano workers into unions and of fighting employer violations of contracts signed with unions. In this regard, MAPA has had its largest effects in central California with the United Farm Workers of America and in fighting for the political rights of undocumented workers.

In 1960, MAPA played a large role in the VIVA KENNEDY movement in support of the election of John F. Kennedy to the presidency of the United States. Although Kennedy lost California in the election, he received 85 percent of the Mexican American vote nationally, largely as a result of the grassroots organization of MAPA and the activism of Edward Roybal (*see* ROYBAL FAMILY). Kennedy was immensely popular among Mexicans Americans, who believed that the Irish Catholic politician would identify with their causes.

Probably the most significant setback to MAPA was the failure of the campaign to incorporate EAST LOS ANGELES in 1961. The association sought incorporation to grant municipal status to a major urban concentration of Mexican Americans.

MAPA remained active in California, securing civil rights and electoral power for Latinos, intervening in civil rights issues, and working to combat negative stereotypes of the Chicano community. As of the early 1990's, MAPA had chapters in eight California regions and more than ten thousand members.

Mexican American Unity Council: Community assistance organization. The council, founded in 1967, is committed to developing the human and economic potential of Hispanics. It focuses on encouraging pride in the Hispanic culture at large and the Mexican American culture in particular. It also encourages participation in the economic mainstream and leveraging public and private resources.

The council seeks to achieve community development by creating jobs through joint ventures among established businesses and by establishing role models through assistance to Hispanic entrepreneurs. It works to expand human resource potential through mental health support services in local communities. The council is committed to achieving economic self-sufficiency for all Hispanic communities by using its financial, political, and social resources toward economic development and by creating employment to give Hispanics the opportunity to experience productive lives.

Mexican American War (May 13, 1846—Feb. 2, 1848): Dispute concerning national boundaries and reparations for seized property. Two years of war resulted in the United States acquiring territory that became all or parts of seven states.

Prelude to War. In a perverse way, the nineteenth century war between Mexico and the United States resembled the Vietnam War some 120 years later. It was characterized by an American administration, headed by President James Polk, that severely under-

General Zachary Taylor's forces won the Battle of Resaca de la Palma. (Institute of Texan Cultures)

estimated the intentions of the Mexican government, and by a sense of nationalism. As in Vietnam, much of the war with Mexico was fought in guerrilla fashion, and disenchantment with the war was expressed by large numbers of American people. Ultimately, the United States had to invade Mexico and occupy the capital to force an armistice.

Roots of the war began with the declaration of independence of Texas from Mexico in 1836 and its establishment as an independent republic. The combination of large numbers of settlers in the Republic of Texas from the United States and the American idea of MANIFEST DESTINY resulted in the annexation of Texas as the twenty-eighth U.S. state on December 29, 1845. Mexico, which had never recognized Texas' independence, broke diplomatic relations with the United States.

Disputes between the two countries revolved around two major issues. Good faith negotiations on these issues might have avoided the war. One area of contention was the precise boundary between Texas and Mexico. Mexico recognized the Nueces River as the boundary, but the American government wished to use the Rio Grande, farther west. The other area of

dispute, one more important in the eyes of many Americans, was the question of Mexican reparations to American citizens for frequent confiscations by the Mexican government. An international tribunal had awarded approximately $2 million from Mexico to American citizens in 1842, but the Mexican government was bankrupt and defaulted on the award. The American government wanted to obtain land owned by Mexico in place of the money. These issues were coupled with the intransigence of Mexican leaders who were unwilling to lose territory they could not afford to maintain and who were more interested in power and wealth for their own sake.

When, in the fall of 1845, the Mexican government refused to see John Slidell, the negotiator sent from Washington, President Polk ordered General Zachary Taylor to move with four thousand troops to the Rio Grande. Taylor established his army at Fort Texas (near Brownsville), refusing a Mexican order to withdraw. In early May, 1846, he was attacked by a Mexican contingent under General Mariano Arista. The Mexicans were driven off in what history calls the Battle of Palo Alto, at which several American soldiers were killed. Taylor followed up this action with a more decisive victory at Resaca de la Palma a day later. On May 13, President Polk requested that Congress pass a declaration of war, which it did.

American Campaigns. American strategy centered on the escalation of military pressure on the Mexican government. The ultimate goals were a settlement of the boundary dispute, with the Rio Grande established as a border, and the American annexation of California and New Mexico territories.

Conquest of California came first. In June, 1846, Captain John Charles Frémont and local rebels called the Bear Flaggers (named for the bear on their flag) opened a revolt in central California against the Mexican authorities (*see* BEAR FLAG REVOLT). Frémont's California Battalion, allied with a naval force under Commodore John Sloat, captured central California in their revolt.

President Polk also authorized a force quartered at Fort Leavenworth, Kansas, under Colonel Stephen Kearny to seize New Mexico and ultimately proceed to California. Kearny, promoted to brigadier general on the trek, and his Army of the West traveled more than eight hundred miles through desert, reaching Sante Fe in August, 1846. Kearny announced the annexation of the territory to the United States, treating the local population with tact and respect, and proceeded to California. In December, 1846, the army under Kearny defeated Mexican forces in heavy fighting in Southern California, effectively completing the conquest.

Meanwhile, in northeastern Mexico, General Taylor continued the occupation of additional territory, aiming for an armistice on American terms. Mexico refused to comply. With an army tired from campaigning in the heat since May, Taylor reached the outskirts of

General Winfield Scott occupied Mexico City on September 14, 1847. (Library of Congress)

Monterey in mid-September. Taylor concluded a controversial armistice with his Mexican counterpart, General Pedro de Ampudia. American forces occupied the town but allowed much of the Mexican army to withdraw.

It became clear that only occupation of the capital, Mexico City, would cause a Mexican surrender. Polk ordered an American force of ten thousand soldiers under General Winfield Scott to land at Veracruz and proceed to Mexico City. Troops were transferred from Taylor's command to supplement those of Scott. Opposing them was the Mexican army, commanded by General (and President) Antonio López de Santa Anna. Santa Anna attacked Taylor's forces near Buena Vista in February, 1847. Outnumbered nearly four to one, Taylor's men held off and defeated the Mexicans.

In March, 1847, Scott occupied Veracruz. Following heavy fighting at Cerro Gordo and Churubusco, he reached the outskirts of Mexico City. On September 12, the Americans captured the fortress of Chapultepec outside the city; they occupied the capital on September 14. Fearing further loss of territory, the Mexican government agreed to an armistice. The TREATY OF GUADALUPE HIDALGO was signed on February 2, 1848.

Aftermath. The United States was satisfied with acquiring the territory requested prior to the war. Some 525,000 square miles, including the future states of California, Nevada, Utah, and Arizona, and parts of New Mexico, Colorado, and Wyoming, were contained in the Mexican Cession. In return, the United States paid Mexico $15 million. Zachary Taylor, considered a hero after the fighting at Buena Vista, was elected U.S. president. The war provided experience to officers who would later lead armies in the U.S. Civil War. The added territories exacerbated the debate concerning slavery, the issue that led to that war.

—*Richard Adler*

SUGGESTED READINGS: • Bauer, K. Jack. *The Mexican War*. New York: Macmillan, 1974. • Bauer, K. Jack. *Zachary Taylor*. Baton Rouge: Louisiana State University Press, 1985. • Brooks, Nathan. *A Complete History of the Mexican War, Its Causes, Conduct, and Consequences*. Chicago: Rio Grande Press, 1965. • McDonald, Archie, ed. *The Mexican War: Crisis for American Democracy*. Lexington, Mass.: Heath, 1969. • Singletary, Otis. *The Mexican War*. Chicago: University of Chicago Press, 1960.

Mexican American Women's National Association: Women's group. The association promotes leadership as well as economic and educational development for Mexican American and other Hispanic women. Areas of concern include pay equity, adolescent PREGNANCY, and children in POVERTY. The group fulfills its objectives by educating Hispanic women through leadership courses at the national and local levels.

The Hermanitas Project provides another avenue for achievement of organizational objectives. This is an annual conference on self-esteem and career counseling that seeks to build Hispanic women's self-image and provide practical advice to the Hispanic high school girls who participate. Each year, the group provides scholarships to promising Hispanic females.

The organization was founded in 1974. By the early 1990's, it had grown to a membership of more than two thousand in a dozen local groups. It is affiliated with the LEAGUE OF UNITED LATIN AMERICAN CITIZENS.

Mexican American Youth Organization (MAYO): Chicano student organization. MAYO was established in 1966-1967 at St. Mary's College in San Antonio, Texas, by José Ángel GUTIÉRREZ and others. Organizers preached a radical rhetoric, unlike that of traditional and established Latino organizations such as the LEAGUE OF UNITED LATIN AMERICAN CITIZENS. They used militant methods such as verbally attacking the white establishment in order to incite Chicanos to action and to draw attention to the plight of Chicanos in Texas. MAYO's actions were pragmatic, however, and leaders worked on numerous social and antipoverty issues. In late 1969, MAYO, which by then consisted of chapters throughout Texas, decided to focus efforts on Winter Garden, Texas, a predominantly Mexican American area where it hoped to create a model Chicano community, with full participation of Chicanos in city government. Gutiérrez was elected to lead this effort, which soon resulted in his starting LA RAZA UNIDA PARTY. MAYO served to support the establishment of party chapters in Texas, and the party eventually replaced MAYO.

Mexican Americans: Mexican Americans were among the first pioneers to venture into the Southwest, in the late sixteenth century, and have constituted a large proportion of late twentieth century immigration into the United States. They were instrumental in the founding of several southwestern cities and helped to develop ranching and mining industries.

According to census data, in 1990 there were 21.9 million Hispanics in the United States, representing about 9 percent of the national population. Of the His-

STATISTICAL PROFILE OF MEXICAN AMERICANS, 1990

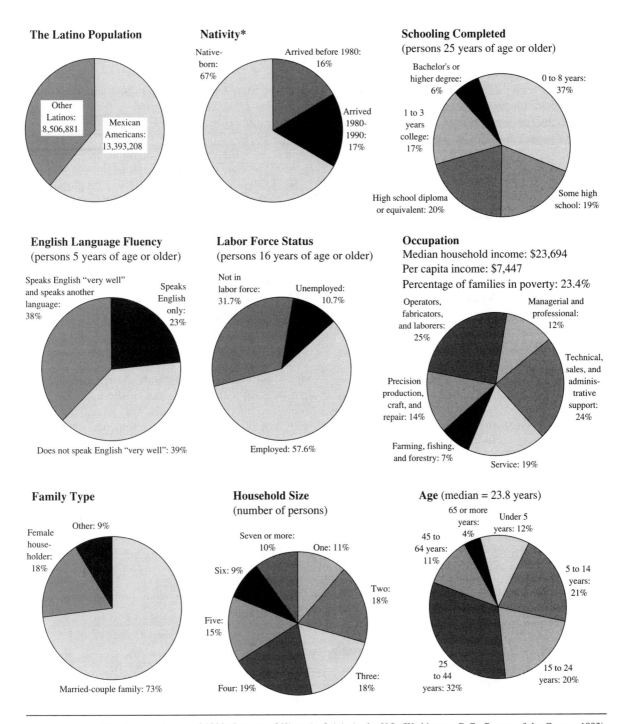

The Latino Population

Other Latinos: 8,506,881

Mexican Americans: 13,393,208

Nativity*

Native-born: 67%

Arrived before 1980: 16%

Arrived 1980-1990: 17%

Schooling Completed
(persons 25 years of age or older)

Bachelor's or higher degree: 6%

0 to 8 years: 37%

1 to 3 years college: 17%

Some high school: 19%

High school diploma or equivalent: 20%

English Language Fluency
(persons 5 years of age or older)

Speaks English "very well" and speaks another language: 38%

Speaks English only: 23%

Does not speak English "very well": 39%

Labor Force Status
(persons 16 years of age or older)

Not in labor force: 31.7%

Unemployed: 10.7%

Employed: 57.6%

Occupation

Median household income: $23,694

Per capita income: $7,447

Percentage of families in poverty: 23.4%

Operators, fabricators, and laborers: 25%

Managerial and professional: 12%

Technical, sales, and administrative support: 24%

Precision production, craft, and repair: 14%

Farming, fishing, and forestry: 7%

Service: 19%

Family Type

Other: 9%

Female householder: 18%

Married-couple family: 73%

Household Size
(number of persons)

Seven or more: 10%

One: 11%

Six: 9%

Two: 18%

Five: 15%

Four: 19%

Three: 18%

Age (median = 23.8 years)

65 or more years: 4%

Under 5 years: 12%

45 to 64 years: 11%

5 to 14 years: 21%

25 to 44 years: 32%

15 to 24 years: 20%

Source: Bureau of the Census, *Census of 1990: Persons of Hispanic Origin in the U.S.* (Washington, D.C.: Bureau of the Census, 1993), Tables 1-5.

Note: All figures and percentages are based on a sample, rather than 100 percent, of the Latino population, as done in reports from the Bureau of the Census.

*Of all "foreign-born" Mexican Americans, 22 percent were naturalized.

panic population, 13.4 million people were Mexican Americans.

New Spain. Mexican pioneers helped to found the first Spanish settlements in what later became the southwestern United States. In 1609, when Santa Fe, New Mexico, was founded, Mexico was called NEW SPAIN. Its northern frontier territories were called *Provincias Internas* (internal provinces). For a time, the seat of government for the provinces was in Arizpe, Sonora, Mexico. The geographic territory of the internal provinces became part or all of the states of Arizona, California, Colorado, New Mexico, Utah, Nevada, and Texas as a result of the TREATY OF GUADALUPE HIDALGO (1848) and the GADSDEN PURCHASE (1854).

Within this northern frontier, Spain built a string of presidios (forts), founded a series of missions, and began numerous RANCHOS that later became PUEBLOS (towns). From 1541 through 1821, when Mexico gained its independence from Spain, explorers from New Spain settled and developed the northern frontier. Both Spain and later Mexico awarded land grants to settlers, many of whom migrated north and introduced new types of crops, cattle, sheep, and horses to the area. Mexican settlers engaged in farming, ranching, MINING, trade, and other endeavors. (*See* AGRICULTURE, LATINO CONTRIBUTIONS TO.)

Cession to the United States. After a prolonged war of independence (1810-1821), the colony of New Spain gained its independence from Spain and became known as Mexico. The name Mexico was ancient, having been derived from "Mechica," the name of one of hundreds of native indigenous tribes that had lived near the ancient Aztec capital TENOCHTITLÁN, which later became Mexico City. Thus, the people of New Spain and its northern frontier, who formerly had cast themselves into distinct racial and social classes, became Mexican. Distinctions and disputes continued, however, among the *peninsulares* (Spaniards), CRIOLLOS (white people born in the colonies), Indians, and MESTIZOS (persons born of unions between whites and Indians). The mestizos continued to grow in number and in time came to dominate Mexico's institutions and its social, economic, and cultural life. As people from many parts of the world settled in Mexico, a new kind of mestizo developed, blending nationalities such as Chinese, German, Irish, and Arabian into the mix. This *MESTIZAJE*, or racial mixing, spread throughout Mexico into Mexico's northern frontier.

Mexico's northern frontier became part of the United States in pieces, through war and by purchase. In 1836, Texas won its independence from Mexico through war. Some Mexicans in Texas at the time revolted against Mexico. After the war, when "Tejas" became a free republic, they became Tejanos. Texas was admitted into the United States in 1845.

Shortly after the MEXICAN AMERICAN WAR (1846-1848), the United States acquired the rest of Mexico's northern frontier. The Treaty of Guadalupe Hidalgo provided that Mexico surrender about half of its territory to the United States. The treaty, signed on February 2, 1848, ended the war and guaranteed the Mexican people living in the newly acquired territory both American citizenship and the right to retain their own lands. Through the Gadsden Purchase (1854), the United States acquired additional Mexican territory.

From 1848 to 1910, the Mexican people who had become American citizens were involved in strife, suffering, and struggle with the non-Hispanic whites from other parts of the United States who sought to gain title to the land grants and properties held by Mexican Americans. As English-speaking populations gained political and economic control and dominated the social and political life of the new territories, Mexican Americans were forced to change their language and culture. As their proportion in the area's population decreased, Mexican Americans continued to lose economic, political, and cultural dominance to the new settlers. The promises of citizenship were misleading: At best, Mexican Americans in the area were second-class citizens, and at worst, they suffered from racial and ethnic discrimination and had their lands taken from them.

Numerous Mexican land grants were lost in New Mexico, California, and Texas. Some of the former owners and ranch hands were displaced and began to wander through the agricultural areas, laboring in the fields as migrant workers. Others went to work in the newly developed copper mines or for the railroad companies, laying and maintaining hundreds of miles of track. As new industries developed, Mexican Americans supplied needed workers.

During these times, Mexican Americans recorded their experiences in songs called *CORRIDOS*, acted out their stories in historical dramas, and recorded their daily life in Spanish-language newspapers. All these methods of recording history had roots in Mexican culture. Mexican Americans organized numerous political groups to protect their rights, social clubs to celebrate their culture, and community organizations to strengthen their economy and citizenship.

Revolution and War. In the early twentieth century, several wars affected the life and future of Mexican Americans. The MEXICAN REVOLUTION (1910-1921)

The Mexican Revolution altered the structure of the Mexican government and encouraged immigration to the United States. (Security Pacific Bank Collection, Los Angeles Public Library)

encouraged thousands of Mexicans to emigrate across the border into the United States. The United States' entry into World War I, coupled with continued rapid industrial and agricultural expansion, created a welcoming climate for immigrants from Mexico, who were willing and ready to work.

World War II, which involved the United States after 1941, changed the lives of Mexican Americans even more. Thousands of men were drafted into the armed forces. When these servicemen returned to their hometowns, they continued to struggle with problems of segregated schools, lack of housing, employment DISCRIMINATION, and many others. On the other hand, thousands used the G.I. Bill of Rights to purchase a home, learn a trade, start a business, or attend college.

Mexican American *mestizaje* continued to evolve, both through unions between Mexican Americans and non-Hispanic Americans and through marriages between servicemen and women from other countries. The new MESTIZO was part of what was called the *raza cosmica,* or cosmic race, by Mexican philosopher José VASCONCELOS.

Two other wars had a large influence on Mexican Americans: the Korean War and the Vietnam War. The latter led to greater political activism among Mexican Americans, as they considered two facts. First, Mexican Americans composed less than 5 percent of the total American population at that time, but their proportional representation in the armed forces was larger. Second, many non-Hispanic Americans refused to serve in Vietnam. Mexican Americans fought bravely and honorably in both wars. The Civil Rights movement and the CHICANO MOVEMENT prompted reflection on injustices at home. Many believed that their patriotism would be rewarded with greater political, social, and cultural equity.

The Chicano Movement. From the Mexican American *mestizaje* emerged a movement that emphasized the worth and dignity of indigenous peoples. Mexican Americans who adopted this point of view began to call themselves CHICANOS. They researched their heritage from the Mexican AZTEC and MAYAN CIVILIZATIONS forward, finding that Mexican cultural contributions rivaled those of Europe in some ways and surpassed them in others.

Several organizations emerged seeking to achieve justice for Chicanos as a minority in American society. These included the CRUSADE FOR JUSTICE, led by

Rodolfo "Corky" GONZÁLES; the NATIONAL FARM WORKERS ASSOCIATION (later the United Farm Workers), led by César CHÁVEZ; and the Alianza Federal de Mercedes, which sought justice in land-grant issues in northern New Mexico and was led by Reies López TIJERINA. Among the many changes sought by political and community organizations were making public schools relevant to Chicanos, with inclusion of CHICANO STUDIES; increasing educational attainment of Mexican Americans; decreasing the high numbers of Mexican Americans in prison; achieving safe working conditions; and obtaining equitable treatment as American citizens in employment, housing, and the criminal justice system.

Demographic Characteristics. In 1980 and 1990, the U.S. Bureau of the Census used the term "Hispanic" to include Mexican Americans. According to a 1994 report by the bureau, 60 percent of the HISPANIC people in the United States were Mexican Americans. The overall Hispanic population in the United States grew by 42 percent between 1980 and 1990, making up 9 percent of the nation's total population by the latter year, an increase from 7 percent in 1980.

The UNEMPLOYMENT rate for Hispanics was 11.9 percent in 1990, much less than the 16.5 percent in 1980 but still higher than the overall national 7.1 percent rate. Jobs that required HIGHER EDUCATION and trained skills often eluded Hispanics. According to census reports, only 50 percent of Hispanics more than twenty-five years of age had high school diplomas, compared to 82 percent of non-Hispanics of the same age.

Lack of education and lower rates of employment translated into less income per family. The median income for Hispanic families increased 11.4 percent from 1982 to 1989, from $23,800 to $26,632, whereas non-Hispanics' family incomes rose by 13.5 percent, from $35,000 to $39,725, during the same period. Like many other Hispanics, Mexican Americans continued to be clustered in blue-collar jobs, many of which were temporary, lacked health insurance and other benefits, and paid the lowest wages. (*See* INCOME AND WAGE LEVELS; OCCUPATIONS AND OCCUPATIONAL TRENDS.)

Mexican Americans were geographically concentrated in 1990, according to census data. Although

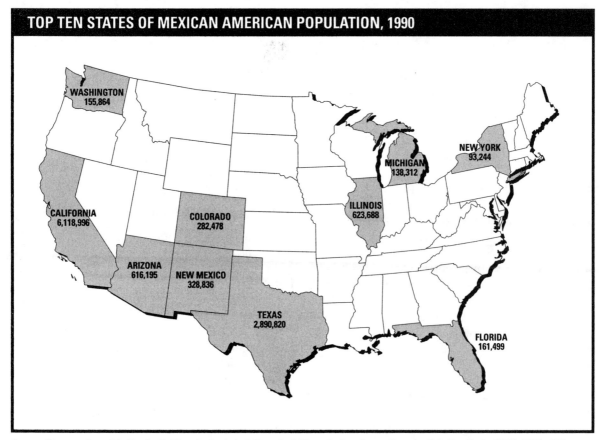

TOP TEN STATES OF MEXICAN AMERICAN POPULATION, 1990

WASHINGTON 155,864

NEW YORK 93,244

MICHIGAN 138,312

ILLINOIS 623,688

CALIFORNIA 6,118,996

COLORADO 282,478

ARIZONA 616,195

NEW MEXICO 328,836

TEXAS 2,890,820

FLORIDA 161,499

Source: Data are from Marlita A. Reddy, ed., *Statistical Record of Hispanic Americans* (Detroit: Gale Research, 1993), Table 107.

MEXICAN IMMIGRATION TO THE UNITED STATES, 1901-1990

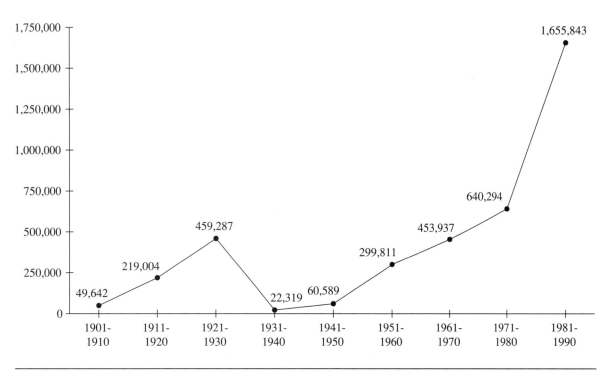

Source: Data are from Marlita A. Reddy, ed., *Statistical Record of Hispanic Americans* (Detroit: Gale Research, 1993), Tables 25 and 26.

some Mexican Americans lived in each state, Arizona, California, Colorado, Illinois, New Mexico, and Texas were home to the vast majority. There were more people of Mexican descent in Los Angeles, California, than in any other city in the world except Mexico City, Mexico.

Education. According to 1990 census data, the median age of Mexican Americans was 23.8, one of the lowest figures of any ethnic group in the country. Mexican Americans thus constituted a disproportionately large share of students in elementary and secondary grades. A study by the NATIONAL COUNCIL OF LA RAZA reported that about one in ten U.S. eighth graders was Hispanic, with 61.8 percent of them considering themselves to be Mexican Americans. In 1988, 90.5 percent of Mexican American students attended public schools, according to a survey conducted by the National Center for Educational Statistics.

Educational attainment for Mexican Americans generally was lower than for the overall U.S. population. Among Mexican Americans twenty-five years of age or older, 6 percent had obtained a bachelor's or more advanced degree. An additional 17 percent had attended college but not received bachelors' degrees. A

high school diploma or equivalent was the highest achievement for another 20 percent; 19 percent had some high school experience, and the remaining 37 percent had not progressed to high school. (*See* EDUCATION AND ACADEMIC ACHIEVEMENT.)

Employment and Income. More than two-thirds of all Mexican Americans aged sixteen and older were in the labor force in 1990. About one-fourth of those employed had jobs in the technical, sales, and administrative support category; another fourth worked as operators, fabricators, and laborers.

A Census Bureau report for March, 1991, indicated that 78 percent of Hispanic men participated in the labor force, compared to 74 percent of all men. The rate for Mexican Americans, 80 percent, exceeded those for Puerto Ricans (66 percent) and Cuban Americans (73 percent) but fell short of that for Central and South Americans (84 percent). Female labor force participation rates were lower for Hispanics than for non-Hispanics, at 51 and 57 percent, respectively. The Mexican American rate was 51 percent, exceeding the 42 percent of Puerto Rican women in the labor force but falling short of the 55 percent of Cuban American women and the 58 percent of Central and

South American women. (*See* LABOR FORCE, LATINAS IN THE; LABOR FORCE, LATINOS IN THE.)

The median family income for Mexican American families in 1990, according to census data, was $23,694. The mean was higher, at $29,151, reflecting a few extremely high incomes. Per capita income was $7,447. Almost 19 percent of families had incomes below $10,000, and 23.4 percent of Mexican American families were below the poverty level. This was the highest poverty rate for any Latino subgroup except Puerto Ricans. At the opposite end of the income scale, more than 4 percent of Mexican American families had incomes of $75,000 or more. Fewer Mexican American families than families of other Hispanic subgroups were in the highest income categories.

Households. Married-couple families, with or without children, constituted 73 percent of Mexican American families. Families headed by women constituted another 18 percent, and families headed by men were another 7 percent. Mexican American families tended to be large, with 10 percent of those families containing seven or more people and only 29 percent having two or fewer (married couples without children and single people with one child or no children).

Mexican American households were slightly more likely than other Hispanic households to own their homes rather than renting. About 44 percent owned their homes, compared to the 39 percent figure for all Hispanic households.

Life Experiences. Mexican Americans have influenced American life in various ways. Mexican Americans contributed to shaping early ranches and mines, working as laborers and introducing new techniques. The Mexican *VAQUERO* and *CHARRO* (cowhand) techniques and dress formed the basis for the American cowboy and Western culture. This ranch culture incorporated horses, saddles, working boots, use of the rope or lariat as a work tool, use of the horse halter, leather

A variety of jobs lured Mexicans north to work in the United States. (Museum of New Mexico, Ella Wormser)

chaps, and the RODEO. The English language incorporated many Spanish words such as mesa, bronco, and corral.

Mexicans were encouraged to migrate by opportunities in ranching, AGRICULTURE, and MINING. They found jobs on the railroads; in mines; in packing plants, steel mills, and factories; in construction; and in service work in urban areas. During the Great Depression, when the need for laborers decreased, immigration was discouraged and many Mexicans and Mexican Americans were repatriated to Mexico (*see* DEPORTATIONS, EXPATRIATIONS, AND REPATRIATIONS).

When the United States entered World War II, Mexican laborers again were encouraged to migrate north and help in the war effort by working in the fields and mines. The United States and Mexico agreed to a temporary contract for laborers in the BRACERO PROGRAM, under Public Law 45 and PUBLIC LAW 78. The program, which lasted until the mid-1960's, allowed Mexican workers to enter the United States temporarily. These braceros worked for lower wages than American workers, forcing wages down. Low pay and often brutal working conditions led to the formation of the NATIONAL FARM WORKERS ASSOCIATION. César CHÁVEZ led organizing and strike efforts among Mexican American farmworkers.

Mexican Americans began migrating from rural areas to cities. By 1960, 80 percent lived in urban areas. The employment markets there demanded higher levels of education and technological skill. Mexican Americans faced the urban ordeals of achieving upward mobility, finding adequate housing, attaining professional skills, and fighting discrimination. The barrio life of POVERTY, low-paying jobs, and family dissolution contributed to problems of dropping out of school, gang membership, drug abuse, and crime (*see* BARRIOS AND BARRIO LIFE; DROPOUTS AND DROPOUT RATES; GANGS AND GANG ACTIVITY). There were also successes. Mexican Americans in increasing numbers were graduated from high school and college. This EDUCATION afforded entrance into professional and business fields, and many Mexican Americans became entrepreneurs.

Mexican Americans also became integrated into the U.S. religious community. The majority of Mexican Americans belong to the CATHOLIC CHURCH. Through the *CURSILLO* MOVEMENT, which stressed short courses in Christianity for conversion and social action, and other Hispanic ministry action, Mexican Americans were encouraged to increase their involvement with the Catholic church. Some Mexican American bishops were appointed in dioceses of the Southwest. Mexican Americans also increased their participation in and gained new positions of leadership in other religious congregations.

International Cooperation. The border between the United States and Mexico is approximately two thousand miles long. The BORDER REGION, which stretches for several hundred miles to the north and south of the border, has been misunderstood by both the nations that govern it. The area, which had been given to subsistence ranching and farming, changed dramatically during the 1960's.

The governments of the United States and Mexico agreed in the 1960's to establishment of factories called *MAQUILADORAS* in Mexico. U.S. companies could ship components of products duty-free into Mexico for assembly into finished products. These products could be shipped back to the United States and not be subject to the usual duties.

The *maquiladora* system adversely affected Mexican Americans in several ways. Mexicans moving to the border areas searching for work found low wages and not enough jobs in the border factories. These conditions encouraged workers to cross into the United States for jobs. This migration increased competition for employment and depressed wages. The flow of thousands of people into border cities stressed the cities' capacity to provide services, causing health and environmental problems. On both sides of the border, people faced such problems as unpaved streets, inadequate sewage facilities, and poorly constructed housing.

The *maquiladora* program and the NORTH AMERICAN FREE TRADE AGREEMENT (NAFTA), which became effective in 1994, did create opportunities for Mexican and Mexican American entrepreneurs. NAFTA promised to open the borders of Mexico, the United States, and Canada to increased trade among the three countries. Marketing and advertising in Spanish radio, television, video, and written materials blossomed. Companies owned by Mexican Americans were in a unique position to take advantage of the provisions of the agreement, as they had connections in Mexico. During the early 1990's, businesses owned by Latinos increased in number and gross receipts.

Social and Political Participation. Established Mexican American organizations such as the LEAGUE OF UNITED LATIN AMERICAN CITIZENS (LULAC, founded in 1929 in Corpus Christi, Texas), the AMERICAN G.I. FORUM, and the NATIONAL COUNCIL OF LA RAZA, along with numerous newer groups, assisted

The Catholic church in the United States, along with other churches, has welcomed Mexican Americans. (James Shaffer)

Mexican Americans and other Latinos. They provided programs to improve social and economic status; eliminate inequities in such areas as education, POLITICAL REPRESENTATION, and CRIMINAL JUSTICE; and increase awareness of the cultural contributions of Latinos. Such organizations helped establish a foundation for recuperation of a lost heritage and for promoting a new future for Mexican Americans. *—Santos C. Vega*

SUGGESTED READINGS:

• Elizondo, Virgilio. *Galilean Journey: The Mexican-American Promise*. Maryknoll, N.Y.: Orbis Books, 1983. Provides interesting conceptions of *mestizaje* and the relationship of the Mexican American people to Christianity.

• Galarza, Ernesto, Herman Gallegos, and Julian Samora. *Mexican-Americans in the Southwest*. Santa Barbara, Calif.: McNally & Loftin, 1969. Based on numerous interviews and observations of Mexican Americans in regard to their life and experience. Discusses various issues including population distribution and employment.

• Gann, L. H., and Peter J. Duignan. *The Hispanics in the United States: A History*. Boulder, Colo.: Westview Press, 1986. The result of a large-scale survey about Hispanics, including Mexican Americans, from different perspectives including history, politics, and culture. Examines the effects of these factors on demographic composition.

• Moore, Joan W., with Alfredo Cuéllar. *Mexican Americans*. Englewood Cliffs, N.J.: Prentice Hall, 1970. Presents the Mexican American people from different aspects including history, immigration, employment, education, family, politics, income and poverty, and involvement in the Great Depression.

- Samora, Julian, ed. *La Raza: Forgotten Americans.* Notre Dame, Ind.: University of Notre Dame Press, 1966. Gives a historical perspective on Mexican Americans in the Southwest. Covers demographic characteristics, history, culture, and education.
- Servin, Manuel P. *An Awakened Minority: The Mexican-Americans.* 2d ed. Beverly Hills, Calif.: Glencoe Press, 1974. A comprehensive book that traces and interprets the varied life history and experiences of Mexican Americans as a minority group in the United States.
- Weber, David J., ed. *Foreigners in Their Native Land: Historical Roots of the Mexican Americans.* Albuquerque: University of New Mexico Press, 1973. An anthology of writings based on personal testimonials by persons who lived the history of the Southwest. The first dates from 1595.

Mexican Museum (San Francisco, Calif.): Inaugurated on November 20, 1975. The Mexican Museum collects, preserves, and exhibits works of art that express the great contributions of artists of Mexican ancestral heritage.

In 1954, artist Peter RODRÍGUEZ made his first trip to Mexico. It occurred to him that a museum in the United States dedicated to the art and artists of Mexican heritage would be an important addition to the artistic community. On November 20, 1975, the Mexican Museum opened. Rodríguez's holdings of art from colonial Mexico, pre-Columbian objects, and FOLK ART pieces formed the museum's first collection.

The Mexican Museum divides its collections into five sections: pre-Hispanic art, colonial art, Mexican fine arts, Mexican American fine arts, and folk arts. Pre-Hispanic art is the art of the ancient cultures of Mexico, such as the Aztec and the Maya. Colonial art is work produced after the conquest of Mexico by Spain. Mexican fine arts are works such as paintings, drawings, and sculptures produced by artists in Mexico. Mexican American fine arts are works produced by artists of Mexican descent working in the United States. Folk art is works of art that employ traditional techniques and are made by unschooled artisans, particularly carved and brightly painted wood figures.

In 1985, the Mexican Museum was the recipient of a portion of the Nelson A. Rockefeller Collection of Mexican Folk Art. The addition of these items was a boost to this young institution, promoting its existence as both an exhibition space and as a center of learning.

The need for a Mexican museum was made clear when Rodríguez noted the lack of art work of Mexican and Mexican American artists in many of the mainstream art museums and galleries. The few works owned by such museums were exhibited infrequently. The founding of the Mexican Museum ensured the Mexican artistic community of a place in which to exhibit works and to educate others by increasing awareness of their artistic contributions. The establishment of this organization gave a sense of identity and vitality to the community it serves.

Mexican artists speak with a specific language of images. These images have their roots in a rich cultural heritage. The Mexican Museum makes it possible to communicate that cultural heritage to those who are outside that experience. Its goal is to inspire and educate by sharing the Mexican heritage and its unique cultural values.

The Mexican Museum has a library that is available for research. The museum publishes a quarterly newsletter as well as catalogs of its collections and exhibitions. The museum shop sells books, folk art pieces, and other museum-related items.

Mexican Revolution (1910-1921): The political disorder, social upheaval, population movements, and United States military interventions associated with the Mexican Revolution altered that nation's history and increased Mexico's influence on the United States.

The Mexican Revolution was one of the twentieth century's major social upheavals. Its civil strife, economic disruptions, and mass migrations had effects in the United States as well as in Mexico. In this time of disorder, the boundary that separated the two countries proved to be porous. Revolutionaries, soldiers, arms, and ammunition crossed and recrossed the border, and many Mexicans sought refuge from the tumult by migrating to the United States. Both the revolutionary struggles and the mass migrations formed broad patterns that linked the histories of the two countries.

The Revolutionaries. Two of the revolutionary instigators, Ricardo FLORES MAGÓN and Francisco Madero, used bases in the United States to launch their movements. A native of the Mexican state of Oaxaca, Flores Magón was an important figure in the early phases of the revolution. Moving first to Texas, then to Missouri and California, he propounded his anarchist ideology in verbal assaults against the dictatorship of Porfirio Díaz. Madero, however, emerged as the central figure because of his role in the overthrow of Díaz in 1911.

Francisco Madero served as Mexico's president. (Library of Congress)

Madero, the son of a wealthy landowner from Coahuila, used San Antonio, Texas, as the center of his revolutionary activities in the crucial months before the collapse of Díaz's government. Madero became Mexico's first revolutionary president (1911-1913) as a champion of democratic idealism, but his political career was cut short by assassination. Flores Magón also met a tragic fate. Incarcerated by United States officials largely because of his anarchist ideology, he died in the penitentiary at Leavenworth in 1922 after a series of debilitating illnesses.

Francisco "Pancho" VILLA was probably the most widely known revolutionary in the United States. A daring horseman and popular figure from the border state of Chihuahua, Villa created a panic in the southwestern United States with his audacious and bloody raid on the small town of Columbus, New Mexico, in March of 1916. The United States mobilized approximately 100,000 soldiers along the border and sent General John Pershing into the rugged terrain of northern Mexico in search of Villa (*see* PERSHING EXPEDITION). Pershing's intervention force of ten thousand troops soon discovered that Villa's knowledge of the mountains and deserts of his home territory made him an elusive opponent. In March of 1917, after a year of frustration, Pershing's forces completed their withdrawal from Mexico. Villa had escaped their grasp.

Changes in Mexican Government. Disorder and violence tended to overshadow efforts to bring fundamental institutional changes to Mexico. Article 27 of the

Armed revolutionaries spread violence across Mexico. (Security Pacific Bank Collection, Los Angeles Public Library)

Constitution of 1917, for example, contained provisions for the national government to take control of private property in order to answer peasant demands for land reform. Article 27 also established the basis for government control of key mineral resources such as petroleum. The revolutionary governments were unable to enforce the provisions of the new constitution immediately because of civil strife and political disagreements, but succeeding administrations used these laws in their dealings with American and other foreign corporations.

Migration to the United States. The disruptions of the revolution imposed hardships on the Mexican people, motivating many of them to leave their villages and farms to seek refuge in the United States. Destroyed harvests, inflated food prices, the threat of starvation, and widespread violence made life difficult throughout the nation. The southwestern United States had much to offer the Mexican immigrant, not only in security from the rampages of combat but also in terms of job opportunities in the expanding agricultural and mining operations. Modern irrigation opened formerly dry lands, from California to Texas, to cotton cultivation. Sugar beet production expanded along fertile river valleys in Colorado. Copper mining flourished in Arizona.

Increased demand for fiber, food, and minerals during World War I added more stimulus to an economy that absorbed the newly arrived workers. Under these conditions, many Mexicans remained in the United States and eventually became U.S. citizens. More than 200,000 Mexicans formally immigrated to the United States between 1910 and 1920. Others, particularly single men, moved to the United States to work for several months and then returned to their homes with much of their earnings saved. The number of these temporary migrants is difficult to determine, but responsible estimates reach nearly one million for the decade after 1910.

Although these immigrants spread throughout the Southwest, approximately 70 percent settled in Texas, with the city of San Antonio serving as a center for the refugees from the revolution. Mexicans encountered both hospitality and hostility in Texas, as in other states. Farms and businesses welcomed them as a plentiful and inexpensive source of labor, but many civic and cultural leaders criticized their illiteracy, their poverty, and the burden that they placed on public services. Undaunted by this ambivalent reception, immigrants crossed the Rio Grande in a steady stream.

Impact. The legacy of the Mexican Revolution reaches beyond death and destruction to include substantial social and economic changes that altered Mexican society. The idealism and radical ideas of the revolution, along with the migration of hundreds of thousands of Mexicans, also had effects in the United States. The revolution caused closer ties to be developed between the two countries, as a result of shared (although at times divisive) historical experiences and through the ever-increasing movement of people and commerce across the border. —*John A. Britton*

SUGGESTED READINGS: • Cardoso, Lawrence. *Mexican Emigration to the United States, 1897-1931.* Tucson: University of Arizona Press, 1980. • Eisenhower, John. *Intervention!: The United States and the Mexican Revolution, 1913-1917.* New York: W. W. Norton, 1993. • Hall, Linda, and Don Coerver. *Revolution on the Border.* Albuquerque: University of New Mexico Press, 1988. • Harris, Charles, and Louis Sadler. *The Border and the Revolution.* Las Cruces: New Mexico State University Press, 1988. • Knight, Alan. *The Mexican Revolution.* 2 vols. Lincoln: University of Nebraska Press, 1990. • MacLachlan, Colin. *Anarchism and the Mexican Revolution.* Berkeley: University of California Press, 1991. • Raat, W. Dirk. *Los Revoltosos: Mexico's Rebels in the United States, 1903-1923.* College Station: Texas A&M Press, 1981.

Mexican schools: Much of Mexico's educational history has been closely tied to the CATHOLIC CHURCH. Before Spain officially recognized Mexico's independence in 1821, many of Mexico's schools were developed by the Jesuit order and were heavily involved with classical studies, theatrical representations, philosophy, literature, and public arts. The Jesuits also brought students into contact with European ideas.

At the time of Mexico's independence, the Lancastrian system of schooling was in use. It tended to rely on large classes and student tutors. During the presidency of Benito Juárez, in 1856, the federal government took over many church possessions, including the schools. From that time onward, education was a function of the state.

The Juárez Administration attempted to increase the number of free primary schools. Free and compulsory education was provided under his leadership, but municipalities, the state, and various religious bodies were allowed to administer it. Thus, the Catholic church once again became a leader in the nation's various educational pursuits.

Even though enrollment doubled between 1874 and 1907 in the country's public and private elementary schools, the expansion of school facilities barely kept pace with population growth. By the turn of the century, only about 25 percent of the country's elementary-age children were enrolled in school. In 1917, Mexico's constitution stated that it was the duty of every Mexican to attend school until the age of fifteen. The Mexican states subsequently enacted their own school laws in keeping with this constitutional provision, but considerable divergence existed from state to state.

Secondary schools in Mexico historically have consisted of a five-year program, divided into two segments. The first two years are normally under the control of the Ministry of Education, but the last three years often come under the control of the universities because this segment has tended to focus on college preparatory work.

Making education available to the masses became a major goal in the second half of the twentieth century. There has been a trend toward helping students become independent lifelong learners. As a result of nationwide economic problems and problems associated with Mexico's rural population, the delivery of education to all Mexican students has proved to be difficult. One promising development for the future was the signing of the North American Free Trade Agreement with the United States and Canada. This agreement was expected to encourage vocational education and a higher level of funding for Mexican schools.

Mexican War for Independence (1810-1821): Mexico's struggle, characterized by civil war, repression, and compromise between Mexico's upper classes and the Spanish government, to gain independence from Spain.

The Hidalgo Revolt. On September 16, 1810, Father Miguel HIDALGO Y COSTILLA summoned his flock to the village church of Dolores, in the intendancy of Guanajuato. Issuing a call that would later be known as El GRITO DE DOLORES, Mexico's cry for independence, Father Hidalgo urged his impoverished Indian and mestizo followers to rise against their Spanish masters.

Hidalgo's proclamation was not truly a call for independence. Hidalgo swore loyalty to the king of Spain but attacked the exploitative Spaniards who ruled Mexico in the king's name. The Indians and mestizo peasants of central Mexico hungered for land and an adequate standard of living. Three hundred years of Spanish rule was the cause of their poverty. By declaring war against the Spanish rulers, Hidalgo triggered the long struggle for national liberation.

Rallied behind the banner of the Virgin of GUADALUPE, Mexico's patron saint and the symbol of Mexican identity, Hidalgo's army marched on the city of Guanajuato. Along the way, it raided the haciendas of rich Spaniards and *CRIOLLOS* (Mexican-born Spaniards), acquiring badly needed provisions and firearms. The ranks of the rebel army grew as peons from pillaged haciendas joined the cause. Within days, the rebels had taken Guanajuato and other towns of the Bajío region, Mexico's rich agricultural and mining heartland.

Hidalgo's army moved toward Mexico City, but obstacles stood in the way. The rebels lacked discipline. They often broke ranks and descended on defenseless villages and farms in search of food and valuables. As the rebels approached Mexico City, they encountered little support for their cause, even among peasant communities. Hidalgo managed to hold his army together and engage Spanish forces in an important battle on the outskirts of Mexico City. Hidalgo's army suffered staggering losses but repelled the enemy. Although Hidalgo could have controlled Mexico City, he inexplicably withdrew his troops and moved north, away from the capital.

Hidalgo's decision to spare Mexico City remains one of the great mysteries in Mexican history. The move marked the beginning of his demise. He soon lost control of his army. With its supplies exhausted and under harassment from regrouped Spanish forces, Hidalgo's army began to melt into the countryside. Although many soldiers fought on with Hidalgo, many abandoned the cause and scrambled home in panic. On January 17, 1811, Spanish forces destroyed the rest of Hidalgo's army outside Guadalajara. The rebel priest was captured in March and executed four months later. Spanish authorities displayed his head in the plaza of Guanajuato as a warning to other would-be rebels.

José María Morelos. Leadership of the rebel cause passed to José María Morelos, a mestizo priest and close friend of Hidalgo. Morelos proved to be an excellent military leader. From his hideouts in the mountains of Guerrero and Oaxaca, Morelos waged a successful guerrilla war against Spanish authorities. His forces harassed viceregal garrisons, seized important towns, and interrupted supply lines between Mexico City and Acapulco. At one point, Morelos' forces surrounded the capital.

While his army fought, Morelos and other leaders discussed the political future of Mexico. Together they proclaimed Mexican independence at Chilpancingo in 1813. They also wrote what was to be Mexico's first national constitution. The Constitution of Chilpancingo

Mexican insurgent soldiers. (Institute of Texan Cultures)

guaranteed the equality of all Mexicans before the law and banned the Spanish Inquisition, slavery, and other oppressive colonial institutions. Despite their unity on these matters, Morelos and his compatriots failed to agree on land reform. Most leaders believed that it was too radical an idea. Morelos withdrew his plea for land reform to maintain unity among the rebel leaders.

The constitutional debate distracted Morelos from the war, and his forces began to lose battles. He fell prisoner to Spanish forces late in 1815 and later joined Hidalgo as a martyr of Mexican independence. With Morelos and Hidalgo gone, social justice for Mexico's peasant masses would be delayed indefinitely, but the rebellions indelibly etched in the Mexican mind the desire for liberty and self-determination.

The Conservative Reaction. The Hidalgo and Morelos insurrections resulted in a backlash that slowed the course of independence. Alarmed by the specter of continued war and economic devastation, most upper- and middle-class Mexicans refused to support the rebellion, thereby depriving the movement of valuable resources and leadership.

The rebellions also provoked repression in the countryside. Between 1813 and 1817, Spanish forces pursued and destroyed the remnants of rebellion in the Bajío and in the south. Thousands of executions took place. Many rebels went into hiding. With the exception of a few pockets of resistance in the south, Mexico was pacified by 1818.

The Plan de Iguala. By 1821, political events in Spain and the independence wars in other parts of the Spanish Empire had undermined Spanish authority in Mexico. The CRIOLLOS realized that they could take power without bloodshed and without making concessions to the Indian and mestizo masses who had devastated the countryside. Under the skillful diplomacy of Augustín Iturbide, a *criollo* from Michoacán, conservatives and remaining rebel leaders joined forces under the Plan de Iguala in February, 1821.

Representing yet another declaration of independence, the Plan de Iguala was a conservative compromise. The plan retained monarchy as a system of government, with King Ferdinand VII of Spain or another European prince on the Mexican throne. The plan also ensured the dominance of the Catholic church in Mexico's cultural and spiritual life. The plan did little to change Mexican society. Once independence was achieved, white-skinned *criollos* would govern the "politically irresponsible" dark-skinned masses. United and secure, the *criollos* demanded self-rule from the Spanish king.

Seeing the futility of reimposing Spanish authority, the last viceroy, Juan O'Donojú, recognized Mexico's independence by signing the Treaty of Córdoba late in 1821. King Ferdinand reluctantly accepted the treaty but refused to accept the Mexican throne. On May 12, 1822, the newly installed Mexican congress crowned Iturbide as Agustín I, Emperor of Mexico. Iturbide's rule lasted only until 1823 but severed forever Mexico's political ties with Spain.　　—*Pablo R. Arreola*

SUGGESTED READINGS: • Hamill, Hugh M., Jr. *The Hidalgo Revolt: Prelude to Mexican Independence.* Gainesville: University of Florida Press, 1966. • Meyer, Michael C., and William Sherman. *The Course of Mexican History.* 4th ed. New York: Oxford University Press, 1991. • Robertson, William S. *Rise of the Spanish American Republics, As Told in the Lives of Their Liberators.* New York: Free Press, 1965. • Ruíz, Ramón Eduardo. *Triumphs and Tragedy: A History of the Mexican People.* New York: W. W. Norton, 1992. • Timmons, Wilbert H. *Morelos: Priest, Soldier, Statesman of Mexico.* El Paso: Texas Western College Press, 1963.

Mexicano: Ethnic identification. Originally, Mexicanos were Nahuatl-speaking people indigenous to Mexico's Valle de Mexica. In common usage, however, the term refers to natives of Mexico who live in the United States or persons of Mexican descent who were born in the United States but identify with Mexico. Both common meanings imply strong linguistic and cultural bonds with Mexico. The word "Chicano," according to some sources, has its origin in the word "Mexicano."

Mexico: With a population of eighty-one million (1990 census) and an area of 756,198 square miles, Mexico is the colossus of Middle America. Politically, the country is subdivided into thirty-one states and the Federal District. Mexico City, the nation's capital, is one of the largest cities in the world.

History. Present-day Mexico holds the reminders of major Native American civilizations that developed in the central and southern portions of the country. Ceremonial centers such as TEOTIHUACÁN, Cholula, and Monte Albán are magnificent displays of their accomplishments in art and architecture.

Between A.D. 250 and 900, the Mayan culture flourished in the tropical rain forests of what are now the state of Tabasco and the neighboring country of Guatemala. From its heart in the tropical lowlands, the MAYAN CIVILIZATION diffused northward into the drier

Yucatán Peninsula, where the ceremonial centers of Uxmal and Chichén Itzá are located. The Maya excelled in mathematics and astronomy. At the time of the Spanish Conquest, most ceremonial centers had been abandoned, but Mayan agriculture and trade were still thriving.

By 1500, the Aztec state dominated the highlands of central Mexico (*see* AZTEC CIVILIZATION). The Nahuatl-speaking Aztecs built their capital, TENOCHTITLÁN, on an island near the shore of Lake Texcoco. From there, they spread southward and eastward into the tropical lowlands, conquering on their way other Indian groups from whom they collected tribute in the form of grain, cacao, cotton, and gold. The Aztec state came to an end in 1521 when Spanish conquerors destroyed Tenochtitlán and built Mexico City upon its ruins.

The pre-Columbian population of Mexico had a well-developed agriculture. They domesticated a large number of plants. The most important food crops were MAIZE, BEANS, and SQUASH. They practiced irrigation in areas with long dry seasons and built terraces on hill slopes. In addition, Indians in central Mexico developed a system of land reclamation known as the *chinampa*, by which marshy areas and shallow lakes were converted into productive agricultural fields.

The Spanish Period. Spaniards began to explore the coast of Mexico in 1517. Francisco Fernández de Córdoba, Juan de Grijalva, and Hernán CORTÉS were among the first explorers. In 1519, Cortés founded the port of Veracruz, the first Spanish settlement in Mexico. Later that year, a group of Spaniards under the leadership of Cortés arrived at Tenochtitlán, where they captured the Aztec emperor MOCTEZUMA II. After a military defeat in 1520, the Spaniards attacked and destroyed Tenochtitlán in 1521 and went on to conquer the entire Aztec Empire.

The conquerors rewarded themselves with huge amounts of land and large ENCOMIENDAS (entrustments) of Indians to work for them. Gold and silver were mined. *Obrajes*, or sweatshops, were established to manufacture cloth. Between 1519 and 1650, brutal working conditions and European diseases reduced by

Hernán Cortés led the attack against the Aztec Empire. (Institute of Texan Cultures)

MEXICO

UNITED STATES

1b

2

3

6

7

1a

Pacific
Ocean

4

5

Gulf of Mexico

8

10

11

12

9

29

14

15

16

30

13

17

18

19 31

21

23

28

20 22

27

24

25

26

1a Baja California Sur
1b Baja California Norte
2 Sonora
3 Chihuahua
4 Sinaloa
5 Duranog
6 Coahuila
7 Nuevo León
8 Zacatecas
9 San Luis Potosi
10 Tamaulipas
11 Nayarit
12 Aguascalientes
13 Jalisco
14 Guanajuato
15 Querétaro

16 Hidalgo
17 Colima
18 Michoacán
19 México
20 Morelos
21 Tlaxcala
22 Puebla
23 Veracruz
24 Guerrero
25 Oaxaca
26 Chiapas
27 Tabasco
28 Campeche
29 Yucatán
30 Quintana Roo
31 Distrito Federal (Federal District)

two-thirds the Indian population of the valley of Mexico. *Peninsulares* (those born in Spain) held the most important positions in government and in the church; creoles or CRIOLLOS (persons of Spanish ancestry born in the New World) began to resent this arrangement.

The fight for Mexico's independence started with an event known as El GRITO DE DOLORES. On the eve of September 16, 1810, in the town of Dolores, Miguel HIDALGO Y COSTILLA, a creole priest, gathered his parishioners and issued a call for independence. Hidalgo was defeated and killed by government forces. The struggle for independence continued under the leadership of José María Morelos y Pavón. Mexico became independent in 1821, and Agustín de Iturbide was declared emperor in 1822. He was driven from power in 1823.

The Mexican Republic. In 1824, Mexico adopted a constitution that established a federal republic with a three-branch national government (executive, legisla-

tive, and judicial) and a bicameral Congress. Guadalupe Victoria, a former follower of Hidalgo, became Mexico's first president.

In 1833, Antonio López de Santa Anna was elected president of Mexico. Texas was then Mexican territory. Many people from the United States settled in Texas, and eventually they outnumbered the Mexican population. Americans in Texas rebelled against the government of Santa Anna and, in 1836, established the Republic of Texas. Santa Anna and the Mexican army defeated the Texans in the battle of the ALAMO at San Antonio on March 6, 1836, but on April 21 of the same year, Santa Anna was defeated at San Jacinto and taken prisoner. In exchange for his freedom, Santa Anna recognized the independence of Texas; the Mexican government found this agreement unacceptable and removed Santa Anna from office.

The United States annexed Texas in 1845. A dispute arose over the area between the Nueces River and the

Rio Grande. In April, 1846, the United States sent troops into the disputed area. These troops were attacked by Mexican forces, and the United States declared war on Mexico. In September, 1847, U.S. forces marched into Mexico City. Mexico was defeated on September 13 in the battle of Chapultepec, and on February 2, 1848, the TREATY OF GUADALUPE HIDALGO was signed. Mexico surrendered an enormous territory, including California, most of New Mexico and Arizona, and parts of Colorado, Nevada, and Utah, for a payment of $15 million.

The Reform. In 1857, a new constitution incorporated important reforms promulgated by Mexico's liberals. Benito Juárez, a lawyer of Zapotec Indian origin, played a leading role in the formulation of laws that broke up the large estates of the church and the communal landholdings of Indian villages. Conservatives and liberals were divided over these laws, and the War of the Reform broke out in 1858. Juárez fled to Veracruz, and the conservatives took control of the government in Mexico City. The liberals were able to take over Mexico City in 1861, and Juárez was elected president.

The French Invasion. Mexico was unable to pay debts to France, Spain, and Great Britain. In 1862, forces of the three countries occupied Veracruz. The Spaniards and the British soon withdrew, but the French marched toward Mexico City. Mexican forces defeated the French near Puebla on the fifth of May (celebrated as the holiday of CINCO DE MAYO), but the French were able to reach Mexico City in 1863. Juárez fled to El Paso del Norte (later Ciudad Juárez), and Napoleon III of France named Maximilian, an Austrian archduke, emperor of Mexico. Under pressure from the United States, the French left Mexico in 1867. Maximilian was shot, and Juárez returned to Mexico City.

The Porfiriato. In 1876, General Porfirio Díaz took over the government by force. He did not seek re-election in 1880, following his own No Re-election slogan. Díaz became president again in 1884, and he remained in office until 1911, when he was forced out. The theme of the Porfiriato, as the Díaz period of government is known, was "peace, order, and progress." Railroads were built, mining and industrialization expanded, exports increased, and Mexico's population doubled. Despite this development, the great majority of Mexicans remained in extreme poverty. Many agricultural laborers and miners were paid not with cash but with scrip (a certificate or note) that could be exchanged for merchandise only at the company store (*tienda de raya*). Peasants were usually in debt. Agriculture emphasized export crops and cattle, and Mexico became a large importer of food. Economic gains from exports benefited primarily the rich and foreign investors.

The Revolution. Opposition to Díaz grew. In November, 1910, Francisco Madero, son of a Coahuila landowner, encouraged Mexicans to rebel against Díaz. Uprisings occurred in different parts of the country. In May, 1911, Díaz resigned and left Mexico for Europe. Madero became president, but his term was short. In 1913, General Victoriano Huerta took over the government, and Madero was murdered. Huerta was opposed by revolutionaries such as Emiliano ZAPATA, Francisco "Pancho" VILLA (born Doroteo Arango), and Venustiano Carranza. Huerta resigned in 1914, after U.S. forces occupied Veracruz, and Carranza assumed control of the Mexican government.

In 1917, during the Carranza regime, Mexico adopted a new constitution. This document limited the president to one four-year term, removed control over primary education from the church, gave the state the right to expropriate and redistribute land, and introduced extensive labor reforms. Beginning in 1922, much expropriated land was given to peasant agrarian communities known as *ejidos*.

Mexico After the Revolution. In 1920, General Alvaro Obregón rebelled against Carranza and became president of Mexico. During Obregón's term, the economy grew. Mexico became a leading petroleum producer. Obregón allowed modest land and labor reforms. Further land reform was encouraged by Plutarco Elías Calles, who became president in 1924. Calles also expanded education, extended the presidential term from four to six years, and formed the National Revolutionary Party.

Lázaro Cárdenas was president from 1934 to 1940. During his term, the agrarian system based on large estates (haciendas) was broken. Cárdenas distributed more land among peasants than all previous presidents combined. He strengthened the national labor union and raised the minimum wage. The National Revolutionary Party was reorganized as the Mexican Revolutionary Party (renamed PARTIDO REVOLUCIONARIO INSTITUCIONAL, or Institutional Revolutionary Party, in 1946). Cárdenas also nationalized Mexico's petroleum industry.

The Mexican economy continued to grow during the 1940's, 1950's, and 1960's. Industrialization and urbanization expanded, and agricultural exports increased. Despite this progress, many Mexicans re-

Porfirio Díaz ruled Mexico for more than twenty-five years but was forced out of office by revolutionaries. (Institute of Texan Cultures)

mained poor. During the 1970's, new petroleum deposits were discovered, but the demand for petroleum decreased during the 1980's. The government borrowed heavily to support industrialization and faced an economic crisis when oil revenues declined. President Miguel de la Madrid Hurtado (1982-1988) introduced an austerity program, but unemployment and poverty rose. To stimulate the economy, President Carlos Salinas de Gortari (1988-1994) encouraged foreign investment, privatized national firms, and advocated Mexico's signing of the NORTH AMERICAN FREE TRADE AGREEMENT (NAFTA).

Geography. Mexico has six main physiographic regions: the Mexican Plateau, the Pacific Northwest, the Gulf Coastal Plain, the Southern Highlands, the Chiapas Highlands, and the Yucatán Peninsula. The Mexican Plateau, the largest and most populous of Mexico's physiographic regions, is bounded on the west by the Sierra Madre Occidental, on the east by the Sierra Madre Oriental, and on the south by a row of volcanoes, the Sierra Volcánica Transversal. The surface of the plateau is a series of low mountains separated by basins. The southern portion, known as Mesa Central, contains the basins of Mexico, Toluca, Puebla, Guadalajara, and the Bajío of Guanajuato. These basins have long been important areas of settlement and still produce much of Mexico's food. Rainfall is generally sufficient for wheat cultivation; in some basins, maize predominates. Irrigated areas produce a variety of fresh vegetables.

North of the Bajío, the elevation of the plateau decreases from about eight thousand feet to less than four thousand feet. The climate in the northern portion of the plateau, Mesa del Norte, is dry. Cattle ranching occupies large areas; better-irrigated lands produce wheat and alfalfa. The Mexican Plateau is rich in sil-

Guanajuato developed during the nineteenth century as a result of silver mining in the area. (Ruben G. Mendoza)

ver, lead, and zinc. Coal is found in the Sabinas Basin, and high-grade iron ore in the states of Chihuahua, Coahuila, and Durango. The city of Monterrey, located in the foothills of the Sierra Madre Oriental, is an important steel center.

The Pacific Northwest. This is a dry region that includes the peninsula of Baja California and the coast along the Gulf of California and along the Pacific Ocean southward to about Banderas Bay. Because of the dry climate of Baja California, its vegetation is primarily desert scrub. In the north, the Colorado River has built a fertile alluvial plain. The area on the mainland west of the Sierra Madre Occidental is composed of a series of terraces dissected by streams along with a generally narrow coastal lowland. Precipitation and the length of the growing season increase along the southern part of the coast. Agriculture flourishes in the Colorado River delta plain and along the valleys of rivers that descend from the Sierra Madre Occidental.

The Gulf Coastal Plain. This lowland extends from the Rio Grande to the Yucatán Peninsula. Its width varies from about one hundred miles in the state of Tamaulipas to approximately ten miles north of Veracruz. Swamps, barrier beaches, and lagoons are common along this coast. The climate is dry in the northern portion, but south of Tampico the coastal lowland is tropical in climate and vegetation. Several rivers cross the Coastal Plain, including the Rio Grande, which serves as a boundary with the United States; the Rio Tamesí, near Tampico; the Coatzacoalcos, in southern Veracruz; and the Grijalva, in Tabasco. Tropical agriculture thrives in this area, which produces sugarcane, coffee, rice, bananas, tobacco, cacao, and vanilla. The vast petroleum resources of the Gulf Coast are of extreme importance to Mexico's economy. The gulf ports of Coatzacoalcos and Ciudad del Carmen ship most of Mexico's petroleum products. Also important are the ports of Tampico, farther north, and Veracruz, which remains Mexico's major port of entry.

The Southern Highlands. Separated from the Mexican Plateau by the hot and dry Balsas Depression, the Southern Highlands of Mexico include the Sierra Madre del Sur, a mountain range bordering the Pacific Ocean, and, to the east, the Oaxaca Plateau, or Mesa del Sur. The terrain is extremely rugged: Only 20 percent of the area is level. The mountain ranges rise to an average elevation of more than seven thousand feet, with some peaks exceeding ten thousand feet. Streams have carved deep valleys with steep slopes. The Sierra Madre del Sur descends abruptly almost to the ocean; thus, there is only a narrow coastal lowland from Cabo Corrientes to the Isthmus of Tehuantepec. On the Pacific Coast, Acapulco, a leading colonial port, has become a popular resort. The rural population of the Southern Highlands is composed mostly of Indians who cultivate subsistence crops.

The Chiapas Highlands. East of the Isthmus of Tehuantepec, the Highlands of Chiapas comprise a series of surface features that run roughly parallel to the Pacific Coast. Within twenty miles of the coast, the mountain range known as the Sierra Madre de Chiapas rises to elevations of more than nine thousand feet. Behind this range, the valley of Chiapas stands at fifteen hundred to three thousand feet above sea level. Northeast of this depression, there are high-altitude tablelands that have been deeply dissected by streams. Most of the population lives in the valley of Chiapas. The high tablelands are inhabited mostly by Maya-speaking Indians. Agricultural products include cotton, bananas, cacao, and sugarcane from the Pacific coastal plain, along with coffee from the steep slopes of the Sierra. Pastures of the Chiapas Valley have been increasingly turned to crop cultivation.

The Yucatán Peninsula. This is a limestone lowland with no surface streams in its northern half. Rainwater sinks through the porous limestone that dissolves easily in water, producing underground channels and caverns. Where the roofs of these caverns have collapsed, steep-walled sinkholes, or cenotes, make underground water available at the surface. The soil is generally shallow and not very fertile. Northern Yucatán is dry and is covered by scrub forest. Rainfall increases toward the south and east, where the vegetation is tropical rain forest. Yucatán has a large population of Maya-speaking Indians, most of whom are subsistence farmers. Important economic activities include the cultivation and processing of the henequen plant (a source of industrial fiber) and tourism.

The People. Mexico's 1990 census reported a national population of eighty-one million. An outstanding characteristic of Mexico's population has been its rapid rate of growth. In 1940, Mexico's population had not yet reached twenty million. After World War II, falling mortality and high fertility produced a high rate of population growth. During the 1970's, Mexico's population growth rate approached 3.5 percent per year. In 1973, the government announced its desire to stabilize the growth of the population, and family planning programs were introduced. After the 1970's, rates of population growth began to decline, reaching 2.3 percent per year by 1994. At this rate, Mexico's population would double in less than thirty years.

As in pre-Columbian times, Mexico's population is concentrated in the central and southern portions of the plateau, the Mesa Central. The Southern Highlands and Chiapas are only moderately populated. Historically, the dry northern portion of the Mexican Plateau has been sparsely populated, but expansion of irrigated agriculture into this region and industrialization in cities along the United States border have attracted a large number of migrants from other parts of the country. Some coastal regions also have experienced rapid growth.

Indian Populations. The overwhelming majority of Mexicans are MESTIZOS, persons of mixed Indian and European ancestry. In Mexico, mestizos are defined in cultural as well as in racial terms. Thus, persons who are racially Indian may be considered mestizos if they speak Spanish and have abandoned the traditional Indian way of life.

Mexico's traditional Indians remain concentrated in four areas of the country: the eastern Mesa Central, the Southern Highlands, the Chiapas Highlands, and Yucatán. Indian languages still in use include Nahuatl, the language of the Aztecs, spoken by about 1.5 million persons in the east-central part of the Mexican Plateau; Maya, spoken by seven hundred thousand persons in Yucatán; Zapotec and Mixtec, used by the Indians of Oaxaca; Otomí, spoken in the eastern section of the Mesa Central; and Tarascan, spoken in Michoacán. Mexico's Indians are generally poor and have low social status. By contrast, Mexico's whites, who constitute 5 to 10 percent of the population, tend to be in the upper classes. The white population is concentrated in Mexico City and other urban areas.

Urbanization. Mexico is becoming an increasingly urban nation. By the 1990's, 70 percent of the population lived in urban places. Rapid population growth and cityward migration underlay the urbanization process. As rural populations grew and agricultural land became more scarce, large numbers of rural persons migrated to the cities. Most of the urban growth has occurred in and around the Mexico City area; from there, urban sprawl extends along an east-west axis from Puebla to Guadalajara.

Mexico City, with a population of more than 15 million (1990 census), is by far Mexico's largest city as well as the country's political, economic, and cultural core. Other large cities include Guadalajara (3 million), Monterrey (2.5 million), and Ciudad Juárez (2 million). Rapid urban growth has also occurred along the Mexico-U.S. border. TIJUANA, Ciudad Juárez, and Mexicali are among the fastest-growing cities in the country. This growth is mainly the result of enhanced employment opportunities in assembly plants, or MAQUILADORAS, that corporations have established in those locations. Rapid urbanization has also taken place along the southern Gulf Coast. Petroleum-related development brought unprecedented growth to the port of Coatzacoalcos, neighboring Minatitlán, and Villahermosa.

Mexican cities generally have been unable to absorb their rapidly growing populations. Problems related to housing, employment, provision of services, and pollution have become severe. Squatter settlements without paved streets and lacking urban services such as running water, electricity, and sewage have mushroomed around every major city. One of these settlements is Netzahualcoyotl, located east of Mexico City. Its population of about two million is usually included with that of the Mexico City urban agglomeration; if counted separately, Netzahualcoyotl would be one of Mexico's largest cities.

Immigration to the United States. Mexican immigration to the United States increased steadily beginning in the 1940's. From 1942 to 1964, a U.S.-Mexico agreement known as the BRACERO PROGRAM allowed a large number of Mexican temporary workers to enter the United States. Legal, permanent immigration to the United States continued after the program was terminated, despite passage of the IMMIGRATION AND NATIONALITY ACT OF 1965, which limited to 120,000 the annual number of immigrants from the Western Hemisphere as a whole. The number of legal Mexican immigrants was further reduced by the 1976 amendment to the 1965 act. This amendment set an annual quota of twenty thousand immigrants per country, excluding immediate relatives of U.S. citizens. It is estimated that during the 1980's an annual average of sixty-seven thousand Mexican immigrants was admitted into the United States.

Undocumented Migration. High rates of population growth and limited employment opportunities in Mexico accelerated the movement of people to the United States during the 1970's and 1980's. Of particular interest is the increase in undocumented (illegal) migration. Reliable data on the number of undocumented immigrants are not available. Estimates suggest that as of 1990 between 3.5 and 6 million UNDOCUMENTED PEOPLE, most of them Mexicans, resided in the United States. Some sources indicate that during the 1970's, an annual average of 110,000 undocumented Mexican immigrants settled in the United States; for 1980-1986, that figure increased to 135,000. In 1986, the Congress

U.S. Border Patrol agents attempt to prevent people without proper authorization from crossing the Mexico-U.S. border. (Impact Visuals, David Maung)

of the United States passed the IMMIGRATION REFORM AND CONTROL ACT (IRCA). This law provided amnesty and legal status for migrants who entered the country before January 1, 1982. It also sanctioned U.S. employers who knowingly hired undocumented persons. The impact of IRCA on Mexican immigration to the United States remains unclear.

The majority of Mexican emigrants of the 1980's and early 1990's were male, young, unskilled, and poorly educated. The emigration of these persons relieved somewhat the population pressure and associated socioeconomic problems at their places of origin. Furthermore, cash remittances sent home alleviated the economic problems of the migrants' families, often bringing significant revenue to entire villages. A small minority of migrants consists of highly skilled technicians and educated professionals. Their emigration causes a "brain drain" to the nation, a loss of individuals who could contribute substantially to the socioeconomic development of their country.

In the United States, Mexican immigrants tend to concentrate in specific locations. The majority of the Mexican population in the United States resides in the western states, primarily California. The state of TEXAS is the second largest area of concentration. Selected midwestern cities such as CHICAGO, ILLINOIS, and DETROIT, MICHIGAN, also have significant Mexican communities. Moreover, migrants from the same origins in Mexico tend to have the same areas of destination. Emigrants from Jalisco and Michoacán are concentrated in California, but those from central Mexico, particularly San Luis Potosí and Guanajuato, have settled overwhelmingly in Texas.

Relations with the United States. During the nineteenth and early twentieth centuries, events such as the proclamation of the Republic of Texas (1836), the annexation of Texas (1845), the defeat of Mexico by American troops in Mexico City (1847), and the American occupation of the port of Veracruz (1914) marred the relations between Mexico and the United States. Mexico-United States relations were again strained in 1938 with the nationalization of Mexican petroleum, an action that angered the large oil companies based in the United States and prompted an American boycott of Mexican petroleum. As a result of actions such as these, Mexicans have developed resentment toward the United States and American involvement in Mexican national affairs. At the same time, Mexicans admire the high living standards and political stability of the United States.

Mexico-United States relations since World War II have been described as cordial. Tensions arise, mainly because of the wide economic disparities between the two countries. Relations between Mexico and the United States have often been asymmetrical, with Mexico in a position of dependence vis-à-vis the United States. Two major issues are central to Mexico-United States relations: energy and trade. President José López Portillo (1976-1982) viewed Mexico's massive oil reserves as an opportunity for his country to achieve greater economic independence. In 1982, the Bilateral Energy Consultation Group (BECG) was created as a forum for discussions between American and Mexican energy specialists. The BECG proved to be instrumental in enhancing Mexico's position, allowing negotiation as an equal partner with the United States.

Trade is another key issue between the two countries. As of the early 1990's, the United States was Mexico's largest trading partner, and Mexico ranked third among the United States' trading partners. Moreover, trade between the two nations was increasing, with further increases likely. Policy changes in Mexico made the country more open to international trade. In 1986, Mexico joined the General Agreement on Tariffs and Trade (GATT), an organization that promotes international trade. Mexico's previous refusal to join GATT was the source of some friction with the United States, a strong advocate of the international agreement. Also significant was the endorsement of the NORTH AMERICAN FREE TRADE AGREEMENT (NAFTA) by President Carlos Salinas de Gortari.

—Jorge A. Brea

SUGGESTED READINGS:
• Grayson, George W., ed. *Prospects for Democracy in Mexico.* New Brunswick, N.J.: Transaction Publishers, 1990. A useful collection of papers dealing

---

FACTS AT A GLANCE

Capital: Mexico City

Area: 756,066 square miles

Population (estimated, 1994): 95,939,000

Percentage living in urban areas: 75

Estimated 1991 Gross National Product (GNP): $252.381 billion

Type of government: federal republic

NAFTA drew opposition from American workers whose jobs were threatened by competition from Mexico.
(Impact Visuals, Piet van Lier)

with political, economic, and U.S.-Mexico bilateral issues.

• Harris, Fred R. "Mexico: Historical Foundations." In *Latin America: Its Problems and Its Promise*, edited by Jan Knippers Black. 2d ed. Boulder, Colo.: Westview Press, 1991. An overview of Mexico's history from the Spanish Conquest to the 1980's.

• Needler, Martin C. "Contemporary Mexico." In *Latin America: Its Problems and Its Promise*, edited by Jan Knippers Black. 2d ed. Boulder, Colo.: Westview Press, 1991. A discussion of Mexico's socioeconomic characteristics and political structure.

• Purcell, Susan Kaufman, ed. *Mexico-United States Relations*. New York: The Academy of Political Science, 1981. An interesting collection of articles on a variety of topics including political and social issues, economic interdependence, exploitation of natural resources, and Mexico-United States relations.

• Rees, Peter W. "Mexico and Central America." In *Latin America and the Caribbean: A Systematic and Regional Survey*, edited by Brian W. Blouet and Olwyn M. Blouet. 2d ed. New York: J. Wiley & Sons, 1993. A geographic discussion of Mexico's and Central America's physical environment and cultural landscape.

• Vernez, Georges, and David Ronfeldt. "The Current Situation in Mexican Immigration." *Science* 251 (March 8, 1991): 1189-1193. Analysis of Mexican immigration into the United States and its causes. The author discusses socioeconomic characteristics, sociocultural integration, and impact on the American labor force of Mexican immigrants.

• West, Robert C., and John P. Augelli. *Middle America: Its Lands and Peoples*. 3d ed. Englewood Cliffs, N.J.: Prentice Hall, 1989. Major geographic work on all countries of Middle America.

Mexico Lindo: Nationalist movement. The mentality of "beautiful Mexico" prevalent among *Mexicanos de afuera* (Mexicans living in the United States) manifests itself in the many parades and fiestas held by Mexican American communities in celebration of Mexican holidays. The Mexico Lindo movement began around the 1920's. This strong identification with the country of origin has been interpreted by historians in two significant ways. Chicano historian F. Arturo Rosales argues that the movement began as a Mexican American grassroots response to the adverse conditions experienced by many Mexicanos in the United States. Historian George Sánchez has challenged this interpretation by suggesting that the Mexican consulate has been the moving force behind these celebrations, in an effort to continue patriotic sentiments among *Mexicanos de afuera*.

Miami, Florida: "Latin America's newest capital city" and "the Cuban capital in exile" are nicknames that have been applied to this semitropical southern resort city and international trade center. The city itself had a 1990 population of 358,548 according to the U.S. Census. The Miami-Fort Lauderdale area had a population of almost 3.2 million, of whom about one-third were Latinos. Cuban Americans constituted more than half of the Latino population of the area.

History. Developers and promoters gave Miami's architectural features and street names a Spanish-Moorish flavor to reflect Miami's mild Mediterranean climate and attract tourists. The city's most prominent minorities, however, were African Americans and Jewish retirees from northern cities who concentrated in Miami Beach. The "Hispanicization" of this city on Biscayne Bay began with the arrival of Cuban exiles in the 1960's and continued with the appearance of other Latin American immigrants.

The Cuban Influence. The short distance between the Caribbean island nation of Cuba and the Florida peninsula, along with nearly identical climates of the two regions, attracted Cuban political refugees, revolutionary conspirators, and resort-bound vacationers as early as the nineteenth century. Prior to the 1960's, several thousand Cubans lived in Miami, primarily individuals who migrated during the repressive dictatorships of Gerardo Machado y Morales and Fulgencio Batista y Zaldívar in the early 1930's and the 1950's.

Dramatic growth of Miami's Cuban community began in January, 1959. About three thousand supporters of deposed dictator Fulgencio Batista boarded airplanes to Miami, fleeing Fidel CASTRO's triumphant revolution. Castro's eventual decision to transform Cuba into a Communist state and society set off an enormous exodus into the United States via Florida.

The exodus occurred in three major waves and transformed Miami into the world's second-largest Cuban city. Hundreds of thousands of people left Cuba between 1959 and 1962 and between 1965 and 1973. An additional 125,000 traveled to southern Florida during the MARIEL BOAT LIFT of March-October, 1980. During interim periods and after 1980, when emigration was banned or tightly restricted, Cubans continued to arrive in smaller numbers via illegal flights and hazardous boat trips across the narrow Florida Straits. The educated upper and middle classes were the most conspicuous among the earliest refugees. They were

The Mariel boat lift added to Miami's Latino population. (AP/Wide World Photos)

followed by refugees more representative of the general Cuban population. The *marielito* group, those arriving during the Mariel boat lift, contained a larger proportion of the young and poor, as well as of Afro-Cubans fleeing economic hardship.

Beginning in the early 1960's, the U.S. government attempted to relieve pressure on southern Florida and the Miami metropolitan area by resettling Cuban refugees throughout other areas of the country. The attractions of Miami's congenial and familiar climate, in addition to its established enclave of Cuban-Spanish culture, lured many back to the Miami metropolitan area, thus reinforcing its Cuban character. In the early 1990's, more than half of all Cuban Americans lived in southern Florida.

The early contingents of post-1959 émigrés concentrated in a central district of the city that became known as "LITTLE HAVANA." In this community of Cuban businesses and residences, it became possible to live almost completely immersed in a Spanish-speaking world and traditional Cuban environment. All routine business could be conducted and daily personal needs met through use of the Spanish language and Cuban-owned enterprises.

In 1973, DADE COUNTY, which comprises the integrated governmental unit of Greater Miami, became officially bilingual in recognition of its huge Spanish-speaking population. Legal documents, street signs, election ballots, and instruction in public schools were to be presented in both Spanish and English. Spanish-language newspapers, radio stations, periodicals, and film theaters abounded.

Unquestionably, Cubans have become the dominant political, economic, and cultural force in Miami. Cuban influence and power was evidenced by the election of Cuban-born Xavier L. SUÁREZ as mayor of Miami in 1985. Cuban Americans have held county commission and municipal council seats, the mayoralties of several Dade County suburbs, and seats in the U.S. Congress.

Miami's Other Latinos. Beginning in the 1980's, Miami's Latino character and location attracted other Latino subgroups, particularly from Central and South America. Notable among these newcomers were Nicaraguans.

The growth and development of Miami's Nicaraguan community have followed a pattern similar to that of the Cuban American community. Nicaraguan immigrants to the United States left their country in response to the establishment of a left-wing revolutionary regime in 1979. Successive separate waves of Nicaraguan refugees and their changing social composition mirrored the Cuban experience, with the wealthy and privileged arriving first, followed by members of the working class. Because of their similar political experience and ideological orientation, the Nicaraguan refugees received strong support from the established Cuban American community.

Other Latin American arrivals in the 1980's and 1990's included Colombians, Venezuelans, Dominicans, and Brazilians. National origins statistics from the 1990 U.S. Census for Dade County listed "Other Hispanics" (other than of Cuban, Puerto Rican, or Mexican descent) as constituting almost one-third of the population of the Miami-Fort Lauderdale area.

Ethnic Neighborhoods. By the 1990's, Cuban Americans had spread out from their original residential zones and were found in every Dade County census unit, but several heavy ethnic concentrations remained. The most famous of these was "Little Havana," also nicknamed "La Saguesera," a Cuban slang term referring to its location southwest of the downtown area. LITTLE HAVANA is a four-square-mile sector whose main artery is S.W. Eighth Street, better known by its Spanish name of CALLE OCHO. Little Havana was a neighborhood in decay during the 1950's, before Cuban immigrants refurbished and revitalized it into a lively, colorful, and economically active sector of the city.

Another area of Latino concentration was Hialeah, a suburban community to the northwest of the city near the international airport. Westward migration out of Little Havana also resulted in large Cuban populations in Greater Miami communities such as West Miami, Westchester, and Sweetwater, which is close to the edge of the Everglades. Other Latinos gravitated to many of these same areas for cultural and linguistic reasons. Working-class Nicaraguans generally moved into the poorer sections of Little Havana, while their more affluent countrymen clustered alongside Cuban Americans in middle-class suburbs such as Sweetwater. The western and southern edges of Dade County also attracted new arrivals.

The Cultural Scene. Little Havana in the early 1990's offered an exotic Latino environment. Business signs were in Spanish. Maps of Cuba and portraits of Cuban national hero José MARTÍ adorned the walls of Cuban bookstores. Cuban food products were sold at vending stands and street markets. Cuban cafés, *bodegas* (small grocery stores), and other small street shops proliferated.

In parks and outdoor cafés, Cuban Americans could be seen playing dominoes or cards. Young men, in colorful GUAYABERA-type shirts, and young women con-

Miami's streets and shops show evidence of the city's diverse Latino influences. (Martin Hutner)

versed on street corners. In Cuban nightclubs and piano bars, couples indulged their fondness for dancing.
Numerous BOTÁNICAS stocked items used by followers
of SANTERÍA, an Afro-Cuban religion. Cuban neighborhoods in the Miami area could be recognized by
wrought-iron grillwork and Spanish tiles decorating
homes and buildings, as well as by yard shrines honoring various Catholic patron saints.

Cuban American contributions to the arts were also
evident in Miami. Artists and painters exhibited their
works, and theater and dance companies staged original plays and musical productions in Spanish. Entertainers and musical groups, such as the popular MIAMI
SOUND MACHINE with Gloria ESTEFAN, performed
music with a Latin flavor.

The Economic Enclave. Beginning in 1959, wealthy
Cuban exiles joined a small, established Miami community of earlier Cuban immigrants in the district now
called Little Havana. These new arrivals founded new
businesses there, buying up vacated buildings. The

following years witnessed the establishment of a Cuban economic enclave. Its growth was sustained by new waves of exiles who became managers, owners, and laborers.

This enclave, where business was transacted in Spanish and according to Cuban business customs, was oriented largely toward Cuban American and other Latino markets. By the early 1990's, there were approximately twenty thousand businesses owned by Cuban Americans in the Miami metropolitan area. Many of these businesses focused on traditional Cuban industries of manufacturing cigars, garments, textiles, leather products, and furniture. Most were small firms with ten or fewer employees. Cuban Americans also had a significant presence in wholesaling, retailing, construction, finance, car dealerships, and the professions.

The Cuban American economic enclave helped to stimulate the overall growth of Miami's economy. The economic activities and strong presence of Cuban Americans and other Latinos opened new economic opportunities for the Miami area as a link to Latin America. A large percentage of U.S. trade with Latin America occurred through Miami by the early 1990's. Branch firms, investors, and traders from other regions of the globe, as well as from Latin America, gravitated to the city. As a result, about one-fourth of Miami's economy was tied to international trade and tourism.

Political and Social Issues. For more than a decade following arrival in Miami of the first large wave of refugees from Castro's Cuba, these immigrants enjoyed a positive image because of their reputation as being responsible, hard workers.

Eventually Miami experienced some of the racial, ethnic, and cultural tensions that often result after a large influx of newcomers enter an area. The once-dominant non-Hispanic white population became a minority. Local African Americans faced economic competition in sectors of the job market they had once dominated. Some people resented the success of the recent arrivals and noted their favored treatment by the U.S. government. BILINGUALISM and the advancement of Latino culture provoked some nativist reactions. The fact that fluency in Spanish became essential for many jobs in the metropolitan area upset many non-Hispanics. Furthermore, a tide of Hispanic and Haitian refugees placed financial strains on Florida's ability to absorb them.

As anti-Communist refugees, Cubans brought with them an extreme dislike of left-wing politics. Their adherence to conservative Republican politics marked a change in Miami's traditional liberal Democratic orientation. Liberal Miamians were disturbed by the right-wing political extremism, fanaticism, and intolerance of some Cubans. In July, 1990, Miami's Cuban mayor caused a furor among black residents when he refused to welcome South African leader Nelson Mandela because of the latter's friendship with Fidel Castro.

A rising crime rate and illicit trafficking in drugs (*see* DRUG TRADE) also drew comment and prompted concern. Anti-Cuban and anti-immigrant sentiment grew after the 1980 MARIEL BOAT LIFT. The Cuban government deliberately sent a small number of habitual criminals with the *marielitos*. Despite these problems, Miami's Latino community has enriched the metropolis and contributed to its economic progress.

—*David A. Crain*

SUGGESTED READINGS:

• Boswell, Thomas, and James R. Curtis. *The Cuban-American Experience: Culture, Images, and Perspectives.* Totowa, N.J.: Rowman & Allanheld, 1984. Contains a useful chapter titled "Miami: Cuban Capital of America." Illustrations, bibliography, charts, maps, and index.

LATINO POPULATION OF MIAMI, FLORIDA, 1990

Total number of Latinos = 1,061,846; 33% of population

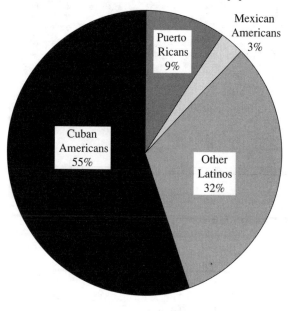

Cuban Americans 55%

Puerto Ricans 9%

Mexican Americans 3%

Other Latinos 32%

Source: Data are from Marlita A. Reddy, ed., *Statistical Record of Hispanic Americans* (Detroit: Gale Research, 1993), Table 111.

Note: Figures represent the population of the Miami-Fort Lauderdale, Florida, Consolidated Metropolitan Statistical Area as delineated by the U.S. Bureau of the Census. Percentages are rounded to the nearest whole number.

• Cosford, B. "Heat of the Moment." *Rolling Stone* 598 (February 21, 1991): 33-36. A short but interesting article on the Latino cultural milieu of the city. Good photographs.

• Didion, Joan. *Miami*. New York: Simon & Schuster, 1987. A prominent feminist author discusses political intrigue and activities of right-wing Cubans in Miami.

Galanoplos, Ruth. "Miami's Little Havana." *Travel* 144 (November, 1975): 46-51. Dated in regard to population figures and statistics, but offers a good discussion of the ethnic color, cultural flavor, and environment of Cuban Miami in the 1970's.

• Linehan, Edward. "Cuba's Exiles Bring New Life to Miami." *National Geographic* 144 (July, 1973): 68-93. A positive look at the city's Cuban American community, stressing its work ethic and economic success. Many color photos.

• Llanes, José. *Cuban Americans: Masters of Survival*. Cambridge, Mass.: Abt Books, 1982. Based largely on interviews with immigrants. Contains some interesting descriptions of Cuban Miami, its inhabitants, the environment, and the distinctive culture that developed there.

• Portes, Alejandro, and Alex Stepick. *City on the Edge: The Transformation of Miami*. Berkeley: University of California Press, 1993. The primary focus is on race relations in the city. Contains chapters on both the Cuban and Nicaraguan communities. Illustrations, charts, maps, bibliography, and index.

• Rieff, David. "The Second Havana." *The New Yorker* 63 (May 18, 1987): 65-83. A good overview of Miami's Cuban community. Also discusses other ethnic groups, race relations, politics, and the city's economic prospects.

Miami Sound Machine: Cuban American music group from Miami. Miami Sound Machine began as the Miami Latin Boys in the mid-1970's. Original members were Cuban Americans Emilio Estefan, Jr., Enrique Garcia, and Juan Marcos Avila. After singer Gloria ESTEFAN joined, the group changed its name, also adding percussion and horn sections. It originally played Spanish-language pop music and became famous in Latin America. Popularity in the United States emerged later, in 1986, with the release of the group's first English-language album, *Primitive Love*. That album sold more than one million copies. Lead singer Gloria Estefan gained popularity as a soloist, and the group has produced gold albums. Recordings of the late 1980's and early 1990's included an album of traditional Cuban music as well as Spanish-language versions of the group's hits.

Michelena, Beatriz (b. San Francisco, Calif.—d. Spain): Actress and singer. The daughter (perhaps through adoption) of a Spanish-born father who sang with the San Francisco Tivoli Opera Company, Michelena began singing and performing at an early age. By the early 1910's, she was a fixture on San Francisco's musical comedy stages. In 1914, she made her screen debut in *Salomy Jane*, a feature produced by the California Motion Picture Corporation. She soon became the company's leading lady, appearing in eleven of its feature films before its bankruptcy in 1920. During the 1920's, she returned to the stage, touring with her own musical comedy group throughout the United States, Latin America, and Spain.

Midniters, Thee: Chicano rock group. Thee Midniters formed in EAST LOS ANGELES in 1964 and included among its eight members lead singer Willie Garcia, trombonist Romeo Prado, saxophonist Larry Rendon, and bassist Jimmy Espinoza. The group played covers and originals of rock songs and ballads. The band's musical talent was said to be on a par with top popular groups. Thee Midniters recorded several albums, and singles such as "Whittier Boulevard" made the *Billboard* chart and became local anthems in Los Angeles. The group is best known not for record sales, however, but for its highly polished and choreographed live performances. The group disbanded in 1970.

Midwest: The Midwest is a vast region in the central United States that includes Ohio, Michigan, Indiana, Illinois, Wisconsin, Iowa, Minnesota, Missouri, Kansas, Nebraska, and North and South Dakota. For 1990, the U.S. Bureau of the Census counted 59,669,000 Midwesterners, of whom approximately 1,727,000 (2.9 percent) indicated that they were Hispanic.

History of Latinos in the Midwest. Latinos have played a major but often unheralded role in the development of the Midwest. Along the SANTA FE TRAIL, which originated in western Missouri, Mexicans usually drove and cared for the animals in wagon trains and pack trains. That they almost always remained anonymous in the annals of Midwestern life written before the 1950's reflected the widespread assumption that Latinos, no matter how long they had lived in the United States, were somehow not real Americans. One exception is Miguel Antonio Otero, Sr. Born in Valencia, Mexico, in 1829, this lawyer, merchant, banker,

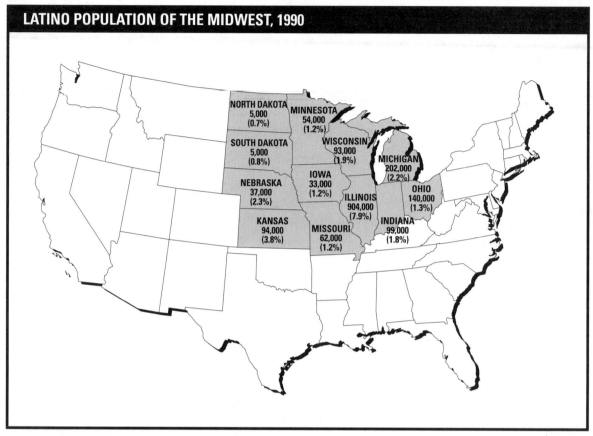

LATINO POPULATION OF THE MIDWEST, 1990

NORTH DAKOTA
5,000
(0.7%)

MINNESOTA
54,000
(1.2%)

SOUTH DAKOTA
5,000
(0.8%)

WISCONSIN
93,000
(1.9%)

MICHIGAN
202,000
(2.2%)

NEBRASKA
37,000
(2.3%)

IOWA
33,000
(1.2%)

ILLINOIS
904,000
(7.9%)

OHIO
140,000
(1.3%)

KANSAS
94,000
(3.8%)

MISSOURI
62,000
(1.2%)

INDIANA
99,000
(1.8%)

Source: Data are from Marlita A. Reddy, ed., *Statistical Record of Hispanic Americans* (Detroit: Gale Research, 1993), Table 92.
Note: Population figures are rounded to the nearest thousand. The total 1990 Latino population of the Midwest was 1,727,000, 2.9% of the total population of the area.

U.S. congressman, and acting governor of New Mexico began a mercantile business in Westport (now in Kansas City, Missouri) in 1861. His firm, Otero, Seller & Company, became one of the largest wholesale merchandising and overland freighting companies in America. Until its demise in 1877, this company brought supplies to travelers on the Santa Fe Trail, Kansas towns, military posts, and workers laying railways over the Midwestern prairie.

By 1900, changing circumstances in Mexico and the Midwest set the stage for greater Mexican immigration. The opening of northern Mexico to railroads and industrialization drew many Mexican workers to cities and towns near the U.S.-Mexico border. The high-handedness of the Porfirio Díaz regime (1877-1880, 1884-1911) caused widespread unrest that culminated in the MEXICAN REVOLUTION and civil war. During this time, the Midwest prospered because of a recently completed transcontinental railway system, the introduction of large-scale irrigation, and the westward expansion of many industries.

By crossing the border, Mexican laborers could double or triple their wages. The U.S. government encouraged Mexican workers to immigrate up until 1924. Although immigration was more difficult after that date, the BRACERO PROGRAM (1942-1964) permitted about five million seasonal farm laborers and railroaders to work temporarily in the United States. Many braceros came to the Midwest; from 1942 to 1945, more than fifteen thousand Mexican railroad workers were brought to Chicago alone.

Until the mid-1950's, it was common for people of Mexican origin to suffer from institutionalized DISCRIMINATION in the Midwest. They were denied access to many businesses, most public schools, and public facilities such as town swimming pools. The invisibility of Latinos encouraged Euro-Americans to treat them even more unjustly during periods of sharp downturn in the U.S. economy. In the 1930's and again during OPERATION WETBACK in 1954, millions of people of Mexican origin, including many U.S. citizens by right of birth, were forcibly repatriated to

Mexico (*see* DEPORTATIONS, EXPATRIATIONS, AND RE-PATRIATIONS).

Although people of Mexican origin are the largest Latino group in the Midwest, many Puerto Ricans, Cuban Americans, Dominican Americans, Central Americans, and South Americans also live in the region. Many of these individuals are in management and professional positions. Some moved to the Midwest from other parts of the United States, particularly California, in search of a more tranquil lifestyle.

Distribution of Latinos in the Midwest. According to U.S. Census Bureau figures, the total number of Midwestern Hispanics in 1990 was 1,727,000, of whom 1,153,000 (67 percent) were of Mexican origin, 258,000 (15 percent) were Puerto Rican, 37,000 (2 percent) were Cuban, and 279,000 (16 percent) were other Hispanics. In all the Midwestern states except Ohio, people of Mexican origin outnumbered all other Hispanics in 1990. Ohio differed in having the highest proportion of Hispanics that were Puerto Rican, 33 percent.

In 1990, slightly more than half (898,000) of all Midwestern Hispanics resided in the consolidated metropolitan statistical area containing CHICAGO, ILLINOIS; Gary, Indiana; and Kenosha, Wisconsin. The seven other largest metropolitan statistical areas and consolidated metropolitan statistical areas in the Midwest had much smaller Hispanic communities, ranging from 105,000 in the DETROIT area to 9,000 in the Cincinnati area.

Midwestern Hispanic communities can also be found in smaller towns with railroad yards or with meatpacking, sugar-beet processing, or other labor-intensive industries. For example, Chicanos and Mexican immigrants have relocated in Garden City, a county seat in western KANSAS, since the early 1900's, first to work on the Santa Fe Railroad and in sugar-beet production and later to labor in beef-packing plants and a farm-machinery factory. In 1990, about one-fourth of the town's population of 24,097 was Hispanic.

The longstanding Midwestern Hispanic communities are enjoying growing political and economic power. The 1987 economic census counted 21,875 Hispanic-owned firms in the Midwest. In 1990, every Midwestern state except the Dakotas had Hispanic local or state officials. Much of this progress can be attributed to the numerous Hispanic organizations in the Midwest. Sometimes these organizations are chapters or regional offices of nationwide groups such as the LEAGUE OF UNITED LATIN AMERICAN CITIZENS. Usually, however, they are grassroots organizations emphasizing self-help, the welfare of local Hispanics, or the local preservation of Latin American cultures.

—*Steven L. Driever*

SUGGESTED READINGS: • Año Nuevo Kerr, Louise. "Mexican Chicago: Chicano Assimilation Aborted, 1939-1954." In *Ethnic Chicago*, edited by Melvin G. Holli and Peter d'A. Jones. Rev. ed. Grand Rapids, Mich.: William B. Eerdmans, 1984. • Hope, Holly. *Garden City: Dreams in a Kansas Town*. Norman: University of Oklahoma Press, 1988. • Padilla, Felix M. *Latino Ethnic Consciousness*. Notre Dame, Ind.: University of Notre Dame Press, 1985. • Rhodes, Richard. *The Inland Ground: An Evocation of the American Middle West*. Rev. ed. Lawrence: University Press of Kansas, 1991. • Shortridge, James R. *The Middle West: Its Meaning in American Culture*. Lawrence: University Press of Kansas, 1989.

Midwest Voter Registration Education Project (MVREP): Organization dedicated to registering Latino voters. The MVREP was founded in 1982 and is headquartered in Chicago, Illinois. It organizes voter registration campaigns for eligible Latinos in the Midwest. Prior to elections in the early 1980's, it reported registering about one million Latino voters in the ten states it covered. The MVREP has performed surveys of Midwest Latinos regarding education, voting history, languages spoken, employment, political preferences, and political issues such as immigration and bilingual programs for children. It also has organized and lobbied for the Democratic Party. The MVREP maintains contact with the SOUTHWEST VOTER REGISTRATION EDUCATION PROJECT and Latino leaders around the nation.

Migra: Slang term for IMMIGRATION AND NATURALIZATION SERVICE (INS) officials and Border Patrol agents. *La migra* often invokes fear and anxiety among Spanish-speaking immigrants because of the INS's aggressive policies of pursuing and deporting people who did not enter the United States through legal means. Immigrants often use the word as an alarm or signal to others that the INS is present. Short for the Spanish word *inmigración*, *migra* has become an accepted part of the Spanish-speaking American lexicon and frequently appears in Spanish- and English-language newspapers throughout the United States.

Migrant education: "Migrant education" refers to educational programs designed to meet the needs of migrant families, who move often as they follow the

EDUCATION LEVELS OF MIGRANT WORKERS, 1985

(workers 25 years of age or older)

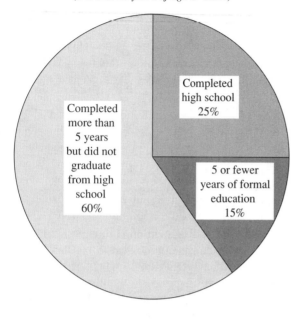

Completed high school
25%

Completed more than 5 years but did not graduate from high school
60%

5 or fewer years of formal education
15%

Source: Data are from Carol Foster et al., eds., *Education Reflecting Our Society?* (Wylie, Tex.: Information Plus, 1992), p. 30. Percentages are approximations.

growing seasons in order to harvest crops. Federal funding has been designated specifically for the purpose of helping to educate children of these families. As a result of their families' constant mobility, migrant children are often two or more grade levels below their age peers. They are less likely to persist in school after the eighth grade and have only a slim chance of being graduated from high school. Since 1965, federal funds have been available to provide compensatory education for migrant children. Every state except Hawaii has a program for migrant education using these federal funds (often augmented by state funds). In many states, a large percentage of migrant workers and their families are of Mexican, Puerto Rican, or other Latino heritage.

To obtain federal eligibility as a "migrant child," a child must generally have moved from one school district to another during the past six years to enable a parent or guardian to seek or acquire temporary or seasonal employment in agriculture, fishing, or related activities. Regulations that govern migrant education are discussed in chapter 1 of the Education and Consolidation Act.

Approaches. The above-mentioned funding is used by various states in different ways. Some of the approaches used in migrant education include the following: tracking for funding purposes on a nationwide database, tutorial programs to augment public-school education, Migrant Head Start (family-centered programs for preschool children), and Secondary Credit Exchange (a program to assist high-school children of migrant families in earning high-school diplomas).

Given the transitory nature of migrant children, a nationwide database, the Migrant Student Record Transfer System, has been established to keep academic and health information on migrant students. Census operators visit migrant locations and enter qualified students into the database. From that point, as long as the student remains part of a family doing qualified MIGRANT LABOR, he or she is qualified for compensatory help. Often this help is in the form of tutorial work, which supplements whatever education the child receives in public school.

Tutorial programs often offer intensive one-on-one instruction in reading, writing, mathematics, and bilingual education. The keys to these programs' success are a cadre of tutors who can meet migrant children and a set of resources (books, magazines, and manipulables) upon which these tutors can draw. Parent education and parental involvement are other components of workable migrant education programs.

Migrant Head Start provides comprehensive services to migrant parents of preschool children, focusing on education, health, nutrition, social services, and parent education. The purpose of the program is to assist preschool children of migrant families so that they will be able to compete successfully with their peers when they enter school.

The Secondary Credit Exchange, like the Migrant Student Record Transfer System, is a part of the migrant education program. In this project, students can continue to pursue secondary credits in a home base while residing in another state. Such students follow the same schedule of classes and course of study that are followed in their home state. Credits are then transferred back to the home-base school on an official school transcript. Another variation of this program, the Portable Assisted Study Sequence (PASS), allows correspondence study.

Contrasts with Traditional Education. Traditional education is based on the premise that students stay in the same school district at least for the school year. Progression from grade to grade and the scope and sequence of the curriculum all tend to be based on the assumption that students are fairly stable. In migrant education, students may stay in one location only for the length of a specific picking season. In addition, financial pressures often dictate that migrant children also work in the fields, necessitating shorter school days or time lost from school. Migrant education programs must be flexible, recognize the family structures and issues present in migrant families, and attempt to advance students' knowledge in the short time the students are in one place.

Controversies. One area of controversy involves the issue of "compensatory education" (adding funds and programs to deal with specific areas of need). Migrant education is one form of "compensatory education"

Almost all the 1994-1995 students at César E. Chávez School in Parlier, California, were children of migrant farmworkers. (Impact Visuals, Thor Swift)

that attempts to funnel categorical aid to areas historically "in need." Some critics advocate other approaches, such as complete system overhaul, instead of compensatory programs. Movements such as the effective schools movement oppose compensatory education and categorical aid.

Another area of controversy is funding itself. Federal funding is extremely political and tenuous. Migrants are historically politically weak, dispersed, and subject to emotional and physical exhaustion. Given these facts, they must find strong advocates to plead their case when federal funds threaten to dry up. In 1986, for example, migrant education was recommended for a 15.9 percent decrease in funding when all other education funding was decreased only 3.7 percent.

Impact. Migrant education programs have the promise of a positive impact on Latinos. A large proportion of migrant workers are Latino, and their children suffer from the interruption of school as a result of frequent moving; the disfranchisement of parents from the public schools; the inability of parents to obtain influential positions (such as school-board membership) as a result of their transience; and, often, language bias. If migrant education programs are sensitive to the needs of Latinos, if they involve parents in planning for the education of their children, and if they stress bilingual/bicultural programming, they may help the educational situation of the Latino.

—*M. C. Ware*

SUGGESTED READINGS: • Atkin, S. Beth, ed. *Voices from the Fields: Children of Migrant Farmworkers Tell Their Stories.* Boston: Little, Brown, 1993. • Diaz, Joseph O., Robert Trotter Prewitt, and Vidal A. Rivera. *The Effects of Migration on Children: An Ethnographic Study.* State College, Pa.: Centro de Estudios Sobre la Migracion, 1989. • King-Stoops, Joyce. *Migrant Education: Teaching the Wandering Ones.* Bloomington, Ind.: Phi Delta Kappa Educational Foundation, 1980. • National Commission on Migrant Education. *Invisible Children: A Portrait of Migrant Education in the United States.* Washington, D.C.: National Commission on Migrant Education, 1992. • Valencia, Richard R., ed. *Chicano School Failure and Success: Research and Policy Agendas for the 1990's.* New York: Falmer Press, 1991.

Migrant Health Act (1962): Law establishing funding for health services. This federal law, signed by President John F. Kennedy in September of 1962, set aside funds to be used as grants to provide health services to migratory farmworkers in the United States. Because of the migratory nature of their work and the lack of permanent county residence in many cases, these workers often did not get health care of the same quality provided to others. The bill benefited the large population of Mexican and Mexican American farm laborers working in the United States, resulting in a dramatic improvement of their quality of life. Because employment of these workers involved matters of interstate commerce, federal action was required for changes to be made.

Migrant labor: Migrant agricultural workers provide seasonal labor necessary for the production of fruits and vegetables and are among the poorest and most disadvantaged workers in the United States. Since the early twentieth century, many Mexican Americans and Mexican immigrants have worked as farmworkers. In 1990, approximately 71 percent of the total farm labor work force was Latino.

Virtually all the produce eaten by Americans was picked by hand by a migrant farmworker. In this way, the work of migrant laborers is directly connected to the life of nearly every American consumer. Despite the central role that migrant workers play in agricultural production, farm work is one of the least desirable jobs in the United States.

Working Conditions. According to the National Agricultural Workers Survey (NAWS), in 1992, the average income of the nation's one million migrant farm laborers was approximately $6,500 per year, with some categories of workers earning as little as $3,500 per year. Although most farmworker families included multiple wage earners, half of all agricultural laborers lived below the poverty line.

The U.S. Department of Labor has ranked farm work as the second most dangerous job in the nation, and farmworkers are specifically excluded from many basic state and federal labor protections. In addition, farmworkers are commonly threatened, cheated out of their wages, and provided with unsafe housing. In the most extreme cases, agricultural employers have been convicted of enslaving their workers.

Historically, the migratory patterns of farmworkers have been understood as involving three "migrant streams," corresponding to the western, central, and eastern regions of the United States. Each of these streams is defined by a "base state"—California, Texas, or Florida—where migrants spend the winter, and a number of "stream states" to which farmworkers travel, following the harvest of a variety of fruits and vegetables. Although studies conducted during the

Migrant worker housing can be as rudimentary as a roof supported by beams. (Impact Visuals, Kathleen Foster)

1980's suggest that the perspective of three migrant streams may no longer be accurate, farmworkers continue to travel extraordinary distances each harvest season. The ten states with the most migrant farmworkers in 1990 were California, Texas, Florida, Washington, Oregon, Michigan, Idaho, North Carolina, Georgia, and Arizona.

The Structure of U.S. Farm Labor. The need for migrant farmworkers arises from large-scale agricultural production. Although modern farms are highly mechanized, certain tasks, particularly harvesting fresh fruits and vegetables, cannot be accomplished efficiently with machines. American agriculture is therefore dependent on large numbers of laborers who work on a variety of farms for relatively short periods of time.

The seasonal nature of farm labor makes it a profoundly unstable job and requires workers to travel hundreds or thousands of miles each year to piece together enough seasonal jobs to earn a living. The extreme POVERTY of farmworkers is not simply the result of low agricultural wages but is also the product of chronic underemployment: Workers spend a significant amount of time either between jobs or waiting for a job to provide full-time employment.

Because growers need large numbers of workers for relatively short periods of time, they often hire middlemen, known as crew leaders or farm labor contractors, who provide farms with crews of migrant laborers. Farm labor contractors generally supervise their crews and arrange a series of different jobs throughout the year, in an effort to provide full-time employment. Many of the worst abuses experienced by migrant laborers are associated with the crew leader system.

To a large degree, the exploitation of farmworkers is a function of migrant laborers' profound dependence on their employers. Migrants commonly live in employer-provided housing known as labor camps and rely on growers or crew leaders for food, transportation, and even communication with the outside world. Farmworkers' lives are so profoundly determined by their employment that the normal distinctions between work and personal life are commonly blurred.

Because migrant farmworkers travel from place to place and generally have little direct contact with local residents, many Americans have no idea that farmworkers live and work in their communities. In addition, many migrants are recent immigrants who cannot speak English, do not vote, and are unfamiliar with U.S. culture. The farmworker community can be understood as socially invisible and politically powerless.

Early History of Migrant Labor. Although the history of migrant agricultural labor in the United States varies from region to region, farmworkers consistently have been recruited from the most vulnerable members of the labor force, in particular, recent immigrants, minorities, and the dispossessed.

The nation's first migrant crews worked in California's large grain farms in the mid-1800's. Many early farmworkers were Chinese immigrants originally brought to the United States to build railroads and work in mines. As these workers began to dominate the agricultural work force in the late nineteenth century, the protests of native-born workers and small farmers led to passage of the Chinese Exclusion Act (1882), which ended the immigration of Chinese workers. In the late nineteenth and early twentieth centuries, recent immigrants from Japan were recruited to labor in California, and European immigrants were encouraged to work on grain farms in the Midwest and truck farms in the East. Gradually, Japanese workers moved out of agriculture and were replaced in the West by Mexican and Filipino workers. In the South, farmworkers were generally African Americans and poor whites, many of whom labored as tenant farmers or sharecroppers.

Since the early twentieth century, Mexican immigrant workers have provided the majority of labor for farms in the southwestern United States. During World War I, a special temporary worker program was enacted that enabled almost seventy-seven thousand Mexican workers to travel to the United States to work in agriculture. Similarly, Mexican workers seeking temporary admission to the United States were exempted from the immigration quotas established by the IMMIGRATION ACT OF 1917.

In the 1930's, as a result of technical advances in agriculture, tenancy and sharecropping systems collapsed, giving rise to the need for migrant farmworkers throughout the rural South. At the same time, the mass migration of Dust Bowl refugees to California displaced many Mexican farmworkers. During the Depression decade of the 1930's, more Mexicans left the United States than entered. This resulted in large part from a massive DEPORTATION program under which even some legal residents were transported across the Mexican border.

Wartime and Postwar Developments. With the start of World War II, western farmers feared a labor shortage. In 1942, the U.S. government responded to these concerns by instituting the BRACERO PROGRAM. It was the largest contract worker program in U.S. history, lasting from 1942 to 1964 and admitting a total of between four and five million Mexicans to the United States to work in agriculture. At its peak in 1956, the program admitted 445,000 workers, and one-third of all farmworkers in California were braceros. The program established close migratory ties between many Mexican and U.S. communities, and it enabled a large number of Mexican citizens to establish permanent U.S. residency. The program was suspended in 1964 after vigorous opposition from organized labor.

Over the years, the U.S. government established a number of smaller contract worker programs, including the British West Indies Program (1943-1953), which brought Jamaican and other West Indian workers to the United States, and the H-2 PROVISION (instituted in 1952), which allowed Caribbean and Mexican workers to work for particular employers who claimed they could not find adequate sources of domestic labor. In addition, after World War II, Puerto Rican workers were extensively recruited as farm laborers. Between 1948 and 1990, more than 427,000 Puerto Ricans were contracted as farmworkers. This program peaked in 1968, when almost 23,000 workers were brought to the mainland. By 1990, the number of Puerto Rican contract workers had dropped to slightly more than 2,000.

Until the late 1950's, Puerto Rican workers made up the vast majority of Latino farmworkers in the East and Midwest. Beginning in the early 1960's, however, Mexican immigrant workers began to displace African Americans and other farm laborers in virtually every part of the country. From the 1970's through the

1990's, foreign-born Latino workers became an increasingly large percentage of the U.S. farm labor work force. According to the NAWS, by 1992 60 percent of farmworkers were foreign born, 55 percent of all agricultural workers were born in Mexico, and only 3 percent of migrant workers were non-Latinos born in the United States. During the 1980's, several new ethnic groups entered the farm labor work force, particularly Haitian immigrants who worked in the East, Central American refugees, and growing numbers of indigenous Mixtecs and Zapotecs from rural Mexico.

Because farm employment is temporary and often informal, it provides particularly appropriate employment for undocumented immigrants, who commonly take the least desirable agricultural jobs. Many undocumented farmworkers gained legal residency status following passage of the IMMIGRATION REFORM AND CONTROL ACT OF 1986 and the Special Agricultural Worker (SAW) program, through which more than one million farmworkers gained work permits and legal residency. These immigration laws were designed to decrease the influx of undocumented workers, but they did not succeed. One reason is that once migrant workers gained legal residency status, they left the farm labor force for more desirable jobs, opening agricultural jobs to a new batch of UNAUTHORIZED WORKERS.

Migrants' Legal Rights. Historically, farmworkers have been denied many of the basic labor protections afforded virtually all other U.S. workers. It is striking how farmworkers were deliberately excluded from almost all the major New Deal labor legislation, including minimum wage laws, child labor protections, and the right to collective bargaining. Most legal protections for farmworkers in the 1990's were the product of social reform policies of the 1960's and subsequent legislation that had only begun to redress the legal inequities facing farmworkers.

It was not until 1966, almost thirty years after Congress passed the original FAIR LABOR STANDARDS ACT, that some farmworkers were provided with minimum

The Bracero Program ended in 1964, on the day this photo was taken in California. (AP/Wide World Photos)

wage protections. Although additional amendments in 1974 and 1978 extended minimum wage coverage to the majority of farmworkers, as of 1994, federal law still denied farmworkers the right to overtime wages and allowed children as young as twelve years of age to labor in the fields.

Although most U.S. workers were covered by Social Security protections beginning in 1935, farmworkers did not receive these benefits until 1950, and it was not until 1976 that they were eligible for unemployment insurance. In addition, farmworkers remain excluded from protection under the NATIONAL LABOR RELATIONS ACT (1935, also known as the Wagner Act), which established the legislative framework for organizing unions and engaging in strikes and collective bargaining. Although farm work is an extremely dangerous profession, as of 1992, farmworkers were provided with only limited workers' compensation coverage in twenty-five states and lacked mandatory coverage in fourteen states.

In 1963, Congress passed the Farm Labor Contractor Registration Act (FLCRA) in response to numerous reports of deplorable living and working conditions of migrant farmworkers. This act required all farm labor contractors to register with the federal government, keep wage records, and provide accurate information to their workers regarding the employment promised. The FLCRA focused enforcement attention on crew leaders because it was believed that they were particularly responsible for abuses. When the FLCRA failed to improve the conditions of migrant workers, Congress passed the Migrant and Seasonal Agricultural Worker Protection Act (MSAWPA) in 1983. This act expanded some of the protections afforded to migrant workers and adopted the "joint employer" doctrine, which defined both the grower and the crew leader as responsible for protecting migrant workers' rights.

Over the years, the U.S. government has set up a number of programs to provide migrant workers with services to address the many social problems resulting

A 1988 United Farm Workers gathering in San Francisco, California, protested what it claimed was dangerous use of pesticides on table grapes. (AP/Wide World Photos)

from a life of constant movement. These include special programs to provide workers and their families with appropriate health care, legal services, and education.

The Future. Increased illegal migration of workers from Mexico to the United States in the late twentieth century created a large surplus of farm laborers, many of whom were desperate enough to accept low wages, job instability, and relatively dangerous living and working conditions. The extraordinary influx of Latino migrants beginning in the 1960's created a paradoxical situation in which even as farmworkers are granted increased legislative protection, the overall wages and living conditions of migrant farmworkers failed to improve. Unless there is a significant shift in the structure of farm labor, the American agricultural industry could expect to continue to depend on a large group of exceptionally poor workers in order to provide consumers with fresh fruits and vegetables.

—Daniel Rothenberg

SUGGESTED READINGS:

• Coles, Robert. *Migrants, Sharecroppers, Mountaineers.* Boston: Little, Brown, 1967. A well-written, moving account of African American migrants working in the rural South during the 1960's.

• Conover, Ted. *Coyotes: A Journey Through the Secret World of America's Illegal Aliens.* New York: Vintage Books, 1987. A personal story of a young American journalist who crosses the U.S.-Mexico border with a group of undocumented immigrants and then works with them in the fields.

• Goldfarb, Ronald. *Migrant Farm Workers: A Caste of Despair.* Ames: Iowa State University Press, 1981. A detailed description of the ways in which farmworkers have been exempted from fundamental legal protections.

• Griffith, David, Ed Kissam, et al. *Working Poor: Farmworkers in the United States.* Philadelphia: Temple University Press, 1994. Documents recent changes in the farm labor force. Includes a number of case studies of particular farmworker communities throughout the United States.

• McWilliams, Carey. *Factories in the Field.* Boston: Little, Brown, 1939. A classic journalistic exposé of the abuse of farm laborers through modern agricultural production.

Mijares, Jose Maria (b. 1921, Havana, Cuba): Artist. Mijares has recalled not being encouraged to be an artist because there were so many sacrifices involved in art as an occupation. He attended the Academia de Bellas Artes de San Alejandro in Cuba in 1945 on a scholarship. He learned to restore photographs from Fidelio Ponce, earning some money at that occupation to supplement his scholarship.

Cuban culture gained prestige in the 1940's, when Mijares was learning to be an artist. At the time, good paintings could be bought relatively cheaply because only the members of the professional and upper middle classes acquired paintings. Mijares traveled to New York, New York, in 1950 after winning the First National Prize in Painting and Sculpture. He returned to Cuba and did not leave again until 1968, making the decision to leave because of the lack of freedom in the country. He settled in Miami, Florida, and won Cintas Foundation fellowships in 1970 and 1971.

Military participation: Latinos began participating as soldiers in the armed forces of the United States in the nineteenth century. Every conflict from the Civil War to the Vietnam War involved Latino soldiers; in some conflicts, entire military units were composed of Latino soldiers. Latinos shared the mixed feelings about war held by the rest of the population, and Latinos were among the many protesters against the Vietnam War.

Latinos as Soldiers. During the U.S. Civil War (1861-1865), Mexicans living in the United States fought for the Union as well as for the Confederacy. Some Confederate units, including Company C of the famous Third Texas Cavalry, were composed entirely of Mexicans. Colonel Santos BENAVIDES commanded one all-Mexican regiment against Union forces.

The Union government also enlisted Mexicans to serve in its armies. In New Mexico, Colonel Miguel Pino led a Mexican American regiment in an unsuccessful bid to stop the flow of arms across the Mexico-Texas border. The Union's Mexican irregular militia elements, led by Gaspar Ortiz y Alrid, José Ignacio Martinez, and Néstor Gonzalez, harassed the enemy with guerrilla tactics. Antonio Vigil led a band of cavalry that terrorized the Confederate forces in the Southwest. Private Orlando Carerra received the first CONGRESSIONAL MEDAL OF HONOR awarded to a Mexican American.

The World Wars. Although no Latinos received the Medal of Honor for service during World War I, the United States armed forces honored many Latino soldiers with the Distinguished Service Cross. Private Marcelino Serna received that honor even though he was a Mexican citizen; he enlisted in the U.S. Army in the town of Asiendo Robinso in the state of Chihuahua, Mexico.

During World War II, the U.S. armed forces opened recruiting offices in Mexico on a larger scale. One

Mexican recruit earned the Congressional Medal of Honor.

Latinos on both sides of the Rio Grande enlisted in the U.S. military to fight the Axis Powers. Of the 250,000 Mexicans who enlisted during World War II, 14,000 saw combat and 1,000 received the Purple Heart. The Mexican Twentieth Fighter Squadron battled the Japanese air force in the South Pacific from the Allied base in Luzon, Philippines. The Brazilian Expeditionary Force, nicknamed the Smoking Serpents, fought alongside the U.S. Army in Italy during the invasion of Southern Europe. Military forces from Latin American countries fought alongside those of the United States, creating a hemispheric defense system that lasted for decades.

Hundreds of thousands of Latinos from within the United States also served during World War II. Ten Mexican Americans earned the Congressional Medal of Honor for service in that war. Service was not always equitably recognized, however, and following the war Mexican Americans who had fought in the war, along with others, began demanding civil rights. This battle for rights, waged primarily in the Southwest, occurred at about the same time that African Americans fought for their own rights, primarily in the South.

SERVICE IN THE MILITARY BY NATIVE-BORN LATINOS, 1989-1990

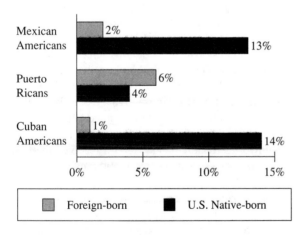

Source: Data are from the Latino National Political Survey, which polled a representative sample of 1,546 Mexican Americans, 589 Puerto Ricans, and 682 Cuban Americans in forty metropolitan areas in 1989-1990. See Rodolfo O. de la Garza et al., *Latino Voices: Mexican, Puerto Rican, and Cuban Perspectives on American Politics* (Boulder, Colo.: Westview Press, 1992), Table 2.22.

The Korean War. Puerto Rico provided the U.S. Army with a combat regiment during the Korean War. Soldiers of the Fighting Sixty-fifth United States Infantry received 125 Silver Star awards and four Distinguished Service Crosses fighting for the high ground of Chorwan.

Segregated units no longer existed, and Latinos served in units from all the services of the U.S. armed forces. Of the 131 recipients of the Congressional Medal of Honor from the Korean War, nine were Latinos. The United States Marines, perhaps the most prestigious branch of the U.S. armed forces, had an increasing percentage of Latino members.

The Vietnam War. Many Mexican Americans and Puerto Ricans willingly served during the Vietnam War, and many died in combat. Some Latino organizations demonstrated against involvement in Southeast Asia and against the foreign policy of the United States. During the mid-1960's, Mexican Americans in Los Angeles, California, created the BROWN BERETS. Mexican Americans demonstrated against the war during the Chicano Moratorium in 1967 and the NATIONAL CHICANO MORATORIUM ON VIETNAM in 1970, and they battled police in another demonstration at Obregon Park on December 20, 1969. The Puerto Rican Student Union demonstrated against the conflict on December 22, 1972. Its members peacefully handed out antiwar flyers in New York City's Herald Square. The Vietnam War split the Latino community in the same way it split the United States citizenry as a whole.

The Gulf War and Beyond. The war in the Persian Gulf saw participation of Latinos in all capacities, from front line activity to service and supply functions. Latinos served in peacekeeping forces in Somalia with the United States Army and Marines. Following the advent of the all-volunteer military, service became a way of life for many Latinos.

According to a 1992 congressional report on minorities in the United States armed forces, Latinos made up 11 percent of all U.S. military personnel. That proportion can be compared with the approximately 9 percent Latino population of the country. Like most enlistees, many Latinos joined the military as a means of moving up the social and economic ladder. The offer of steady employment, educational benefits, and retirement pay made the armed forces a promising career choice. Latinos tended to use the educational benefits offered by the military to a greater extent than did any other identified minority group.

—*Michael A. Warren*

Guy Gabaldon (seated) captured two thousand Japanese soldiers as a U.S. Marine serving in World War II. Here he advises actors in the 1960 film Hell to Eternity, *which tells of his heroics.* (AP/Wide World Photos)

SUGGESTED READINGS: • Editors of Boston Publishing Company. *Above and Beyond: A History of the Medal of Honor from the Civil War to Vietnam*. Boston: Boston Publishing, 1985. • Harris, W. W. *Puerto Rico's Fighting Sixty-fifth U.S. Infantry: From San Juan to Chorwan*. San Rafael, Calif.: Presidio Press, 1980. • Lonn, Ella. *Foreigners in the Confederacy*. Chapel Hill: University of North Carolina Press, 1940. • Lonn, Ella. *Foreigners in the Union Army and Navy*. Baton Rouge: Louisiana State University Press, 1951. • MacLachlan, Colin M., and William H. Beezley. *El Gran Pueblo: A History of Greater Mexico*. Englewood Cliffs, N.J.: Prentice Hall, 1994. • Servin, Manuel P., comp. *An Awakened Minority: The Mexican-Americans*. 2d ed. Beverly Hills, Calif.: Glencoe Press, 1974. • Thompson, Jerry D. *Mexican Texans in the Union Army*. El Paso: Texas Western Press, 1986. • U.S. Congress. House. Committee of Veterans' Affairs. Subcommittee on Education, Training, and Employment. *The Effect of the Military on Minorities and Low-Income Individuals*. 102d Congress. Washington, D.C.: Government Printing Office. • Wynn, Dennis J. *The San Patricio Soldiers: Mexico's Foreign Legion*. El Paso: Texas Western Press, 1984. • Zaroulis, N. L., and Gerald Sullivan. *Who Spoke Up? American Protest Against the War in Vietnam*. New York: Doubleday, 1984.

Millan, Felix (Felix Bernardo Millan y Martinez; b. Aug. 21, 1943, Yabucoa, Puerto Rico): Baseball player. Nicknamed "The Cat" for his defensive reflexes, Felix Millan was a dependable second baseman

Second baseman Felix Millan makes the first out of a double play. (AP/Wide World Photos)

Workers carry bags of silver from a Mexican mine. (Library of Congress)

for the Atlanta Braves and the New York Mets. Recruited by the Kansas City Athletics and drafted by the Braves, Millan made his major league debut in 1966. A three-time All-Star, Millan won Gold Glove Awards for defensive excellence in 1969 and 1972. He was a regular on the Braves' 1969 National League Western Division championship team and on the Mets team that won the 1973 National League pennant. A career .279 hitter, he had his best year with the bat in 1970, when he hit .310 and scored 100 runs. He retired in 1977.

Million Dollar Theater (Los Angeles, Calif.): Theater popularized as a showcase for Mexican acts. The Million Dollar Theater was established in 1918 by Sid Grauman. It is a large and ornate building, with winding staircases and elaborate inside detail. In the 1950's it began featuring Latino acts and became associated with Mexican culture. The Million Dollar Theater featured live acts and films, hosting some of the top names in Mexican and Chicano music. During the 1950's, shows included famous performers such as Agustin Lara and Pedro Infante. The building later was converted from theater to church use.

Mining: Mining was a major industry in the Southwest beginning in the mid-nineteenth century and continuing into the twentieth century. Latinos, particularly Mexicans, made important contributions to this industry, both in mining techniques and as laborers.

The discovery of gold in California in 1848 began the mining boom in the Southwest (*see* GOLD RUSH, CALIFORNIA). Among the many groups of prospectors rushing to the mines were Latinos, including South Americans, CALIFORNIOS (Californians of Mexican descent), and Mexicans, primarily from the region of Sonora. These Latinos contributed their knowledge of mining techniques, acquired through centuries of mining in their own countries, to the California gold mines. These techniques included the use of a *batea* or gold pan for river mining, crushing gold-bearing quartz with an *arrastra*, and the patio process for gold recovery.

In spite of their contributions, Latinos were discriminated against in the California mines. Many non-Latinos felt threatened by the Latinos' mining experience and resented what they perceived to be foreigners' extraction of the United States' resources. As a result, discriminatory policies and laws were adopted against

Latinos and other foreigners. Mining camp codes enforced by vigilance groups excluded foreigners from many diggings. In 1850, the California legislature enacted the FOREIGN MINERS' TAX LAW, which required all non-U.S. citizens to pay a fee of twenty dollars per month for mining privileges. The hardship of this tax forced many to leave the mines.

As mining activity extended from California to other Southwestern states in the second half of the nineteenth century, Latino participation in mining grew more significant. Important gold, silver, and copper discoveries made in Arizona, Nevada, and Colorado from 1850 to 1870 encouraged large influxes of Latino, especially Mexican, laborers to the mines. By 1870, an estimated thirty-seven hundred Mexican immigrants had settled in the Arizona mining region south of the Gila River.

During the late nineteenth and early twentieth centuries, technological advances in the mining industry brought even greater numbers of Mexicans to Southwestern mines. The development of mechanized deep-shaft mining during the 1870's, for example, was a major impetus for the quick growth of the Mexican immigrant population in Arizona, which increased from approximately four thousand in 1870 to more than nine thousand in 1880. The development of open-pit copper mines in Arizona near the beginning of the twentieth century created an even larger demand for Mexican miners. This demand was reflected by the fact that an estimated 60,000 to 100,000 Mexican immigrants entered Arizona in 1901.

Latinos provided an abundant labor source for the Southwestern mining industry but faced challenges as a result of their minority status. As was the case in the first California mines, ethnic prejudices were rampant in most Southwestern mines during the nineteenth and twentieth centuries. Because of these prejudices, the Latinos' role in the mining industry seldom progressed beyond that of low-wage laborer.

Minority group status of Latinos: Following enactment of civil rights legislation during the 1950's and 1960's, Latinos were gradually included with African Americans and other minority groups as a population requiring protection from societal discrimination. Although the majority of the Latino leadership supports this protected status, some voices within and outside the Latino community believe that Latinos have been hindered by it rather than having benefited from it.

History of Discrimination Against Latinos. Since the MEXICAN AMERICAN WAR of 1846-1848, Latinos

in the United States, particularly Mexican Americans, have experienced DISCRIMINATION in education, housing, political access, and employment. Despite the TREATY OF GUADALUPE HIDALGO in 1848, which attempted to protect their political, economic, and cultural rights, discrimination has excluded them from full participation in the nation's public, social, and economic life.

After the Mexican American War, Mexican Americans became a subordinate people within what was formerly their homeland. Mexico ceded about half of its territory through the Treaty of Guadalupe Hidalgo. Landowners were guaranteed rights, but those rights often were not honored and Mexicans had a difficult time defending titles. The change in political boundaries thus served indirectly to transform Mexican Americans from landowners to farm and factory workers. These social and economic processes of exploitation were coupled with measures of social control that included violence and the legal system. Institutions such as the TEXAS RANGERS, political machines, and even the Ku Klux Klan served to render the Mexican American population subordinated and powerless.

Other Latino groups, as they later became a part of U.S. society, also experienced discrimination at different levels. Discrimination against social groups in the United States, specifically racial and ethnic groups, has varied according to a number of factors including mode of incorporation into American social life and racial background.

Both Mexican Americans and Puerto Ricans became part of American society as a result of the political and geographic expansion of the United States. The United States' conquest of Mexico incorporated the Mexican populations of the areas that are now California, Texas, Arizona, Colorado, and New Mexico into the United States. The defeat of Spain during the SPANISH-AMERICAN WAR of 1898 led to Puerto Rico becoming an unincorporated territory of the United States. For both Puerto Ricans and Mexicans, these changes meant being placed in a subordinated social status within American society.

Mexicans have continued to migrate to the United States. Many of these new immigrants also fell into the subordinated status that the early inhabitants of northern Mexico experienced when they became part of the expanding nation. Despite legal and social advances made during the Civil Rights movement during the 1950's and 1960's, racial prejudice and discrimination against non-Europeans persisted in American culture. The racially mixed background (*MESTIZAJE*) of a significant number of Mexican Americans served as a focus for their social treatment as a nonwhite racial group.

Puerto Ricans. The Puerto Rican experience as a minority group includes two dimensions: membership in a national group and membership in a minority group on the United States mainland. Although Puerto Ricans on the island are United States citizens, they do not vote for the president of the United States, nor do they enjoy representation by a voting member of Congress. On the mainland of the United States, Puerto Ricans experience high levels of discrimination in housing and jobs, accounting in part for the high levels

SOCIOECONOMIC CHARACTERISTICS OF LATINOS, AFRICAN AMERICANS, AND ASIAN AMERICANS, 1991

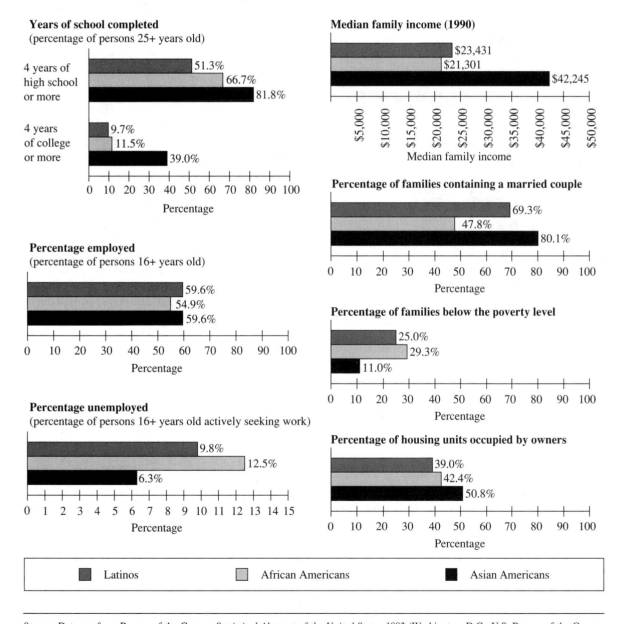

Source: Data are from Bureau of the Census, *Statistical Abstract of the United States 1992* (Washington, D.C.: U.S. Bureau of the Census, 1992), Tables 41, 42, and 44.

STATES IN WHICH LATINOS WERE THE LARGEST MINORITY GROUP, 1990

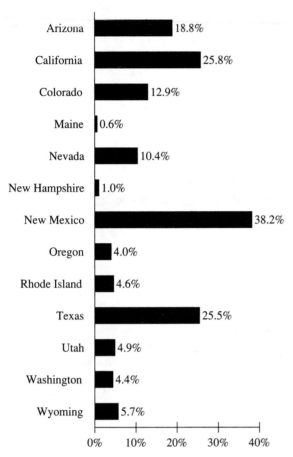

Arizona 18.8%
California 25.8%
Colorado 12.9%
Maine 0.6%
Nevada 10.4%
New Hampshire 1.0%
New Mexico 38.2%
Oregon 4.0%
Rhode Island 4.6%
Texas 25.5%
Utah 4.9%
Washington 4.4%
Wyoming 5.7%

0% 10% 20% 30% 40%

Percentage of the State's Population That Is Latino

Source: Data are from Marlita A. Reddy, ed., *Statistical Record of Hispanic Americans* (Detroit: Gale Research, 1993), Table 92. That table was constructed with data from the 1990 U.S. Census.

of POVERTY experienced by this community. Puerto Ricans, like Mexican Americans, often have a mixed racial background that leads to them being treated as nonwhite. Many Puerto Ricans have black SKIN COLOR, and some have even chosen to identify themselves as black rather than as Puerto Rican.

Cuban Americans. Small communities of Cubans resided in the United States prior to the CUBAN REVOLUTION of 1959. That event began a massive emigration of Cubans fleeing from the regime of Fidel CASTRO. Although Cuban Americans have been only the third-largest Latino subgroup in the United States, they

have enjoyed the highest social and economic status of all Latino subgroups. Despite this status, they also have experienced significant levels of discrimination, particularly in southern Florida, where the bulk of the Cuban community is established.

Challenges to Latino Minority Group Status. Whether Latinos as a group should be accorded protected status as a minority group is debated by some individuals within and outside the community. Some writers, such as Linda CHÁVEZ in her *Out of the Barrio: Toward a New Politics of Hispanic Assimilation* (1991) and Peter Skerry in his *Mexican Americans: The Ambivalent Minority* (1993), argue that Mexican Americans in particular should not be considered similar to other minority groups such as African Americans. In fact, they argue, a protected status impedes their smooth assimilation into the mainstream. This contention does not have the support of a majority of students of race and ethnicity.

One result of Latinos being identified as a minority group is lack of recognition of the diversity of experiences that exists within the Latino community. Historically, the experiences of some Latino subgroups are more similar to the experiences of European immigrant groups than they are to the experiences of other Latino subgroups. Central Americans, for example, in the 1980's and 1990's fled from their countries to escape political persecution, much as Cubans fled their homeland in the 1960's. Mexican Americans, in contrast, have a history of conquest and absorption into U.S. society. In some senses, then, Latinos cannot be viewed as a single minority group, but as subgroups viewed and acting alone, they do not carry the political clout to obtain legislation protecting their rights.

—*Victor M. Rodriguez*

SUGGESTED READINGS: • Acuña, Rodolfo. *Occupied America: A History of Chicanos.* 3d ed. New York: Harper & Row, 1988. • Chávez, Linda. *Out of the Barrio: Toward a New Politics of Hispanic Assimilation.* New York: Basic Books, 1991. • Moore, Joan, and Harry Pachon. *Hispanics in the United States.* Englewood Cliffs, N.J.: Prentice Hall, 1985. • Rodriguez, Clara. *Puerto Ricans: Born in the U.S.A.* Boston: Unwin/Hyman, 1989. • Skerry, Peter. *Mexican Americans: The Ambivalent Minority.* New York: Free Press, 1993.

Minoso, Minnie (b. Nov. 29, 1922, Havana, Cuba): Baseball player. Minoso, a speedy right-handed outfielder, played professionally in his native Cuba and earned the attention of major league scouts with his

Minnie Minoso in a 1955 practice session. (AP/Wide World Photos)

Carmen Miranda with her famous headdress. (AP/Wide World Photos)

play for the New York Cubans in the Negro Leagues in 1946 and 1947. Signed by the Cleveland Indians just as Jackie Robinson was breaking the major league color line, Minoso spent two seasons in the minor leagues before making his major league debut with Cleveland in 1949. Traded to the Chicago White Sox at the beginning of the 1951 season, Minoso, who was still considered a rookie, hit .326 and led the American League in triples and stolen bases. A hustling, aggressive baserunner and line-drive hitter, he also led the American League in steals in 1952 and 1953, in triples in 1954 and 1956, in doubles in 1957, and in hits in 1960. He was named to six All-Star teams, and in 1957 he won a Gold Glove Award for defensive excellence.

Minoso was traded between Chicago and Cleveland three times in the 1950's, and he also played briefly for the St. Louis Cardinals and Washington Senators before retiring in 1964. A popular player, Minoso remained in the White Sox organization as a coach. In 1976 and 1980, he was brought out of retirement by the White Sox for a handful of hitting appearances, making him only the second major leaguer to play in five different decades.

Miranda, Carmen (Feb. 9, 1909, Marco de Canaveses, Portugal—Aug. 5, 1955, Beverly Hills, Calif.): Singer and actress. Miranda grew up in Rio de Janeiro, Brazil, where she later became a nightclub entertainer with her own band and radio show. By 1938, she had made four films and was considered a star not only in her own country but throughout South America. In 1939, she appeared in the Broadway musical *The Streets of Paris*, singing "The South American Way" wearing six-inch heels and a fruited headdress that were to become her trademarks. This performance launched her Hollywood career. She became known as "The Brazilian Bombshell" and made nineteen American films, appearing in secondary roles with such legends as Betty Grable, Groucho Marx, Don Ameche, and Alice Faye.

The height of Miranda's popularity in the 1940's coincided with the American craze for Latin music. Miranda captivated American audiences with her Brazilian songs and dances, performed in a unique style. There was always a sense of self-parody in her performances. Miranda made about 150 recordings and sang regularly with Xavier CUGAT and Desi ARNAZ. Among her most popular songs were "I Yi Yi Yi Yi," "Chica Chica Boom Chic," "Boa Noite," and "Cuando Te Gusta."

Miruelo, Diego: Explorer. Miruelo was a Spanish explorer who sailed from Cuba to Florida in 1516, three years after Juan PONCE DE LEÓN made the first trip to the Florida coast. Miruelo went on a single vessel and reached the coast, where he traded some Spanish toys to the natives for their gold. When he returned to Cuba, he embellished his accounts of the coast, generating interest in the area.

A man named Diego Miruelo was a pilot in Pánfilo de NARVÁEZ's ill-fated expedition to the Florida coast in 1528. All but four members of that expedition perished. It is not clear whether this is the same Diego Miruelo.

Mission architecture: Mission architecture refers to the architecture of the mission churches and related structures established by the Spanish friars, primarily Franciscans and Jesuits, in the area of Spanish colonization. This area included the Southwest from California to Texas, the Gulf Coast, and coastal areas from Georgia to Florida.

Architectural Style. Spanish architecture brought to the Americas had been influenced by the Greeks, Phoenicians, Romans, and Moors. A cosmopolitan architectural style of Spain affected the styles of the missions.

Some factors determining the architecture of missions were availability of construction materials, the expertise of the workers, and environmental conditions. New Mexico, for example, had limited resources and was isolated from colonial metropolitan centers. The materials of choice were locally available ADOBE and rough-hewn wood, and the buildings reflect an adaptation of the already established Indian construction. The buildings are nonintrusive and seem to follow the contours and colors of the landscape. In desert Arizona, the architecture of the missions was influenced by that of desert northern Africa. The buildings feature lavish ornamentation and are covered in white stucco or plaster. In Texas, stone, adobe, and burned brick were used in mission construction. In California, the structures were simple and free flowing, utilizing adobe, burned brick, and terra-cotta tiles.

Each mission was actually a complex of buildings, most commonly including the church, quarters for the clergy, a convent, a school, workrooms, storerooms, stables, and other buildings. Generally, the buildings were laid out around a patio or courtyard that contained a fountain or well. Large gates provided access to the courtyard. The layout of the complex allowed efficient use of and access to all buildings. At the same

The Espada Mission in San Antonio, Texas, illustrates the use of stone in construction. (Institute of Texan Cultures)

time, the fortress-like arrangement of the buildings and gates made the mission a safe haven for the population it served in the event of an attack.

The friars were on their own in the construction of the missions. They had neither professional advice nor training as architects. They relied on their experience in building churches in Mexico. The buildings in the Southwest, however, were simpler and smaller than the monumental churches in Mexico.

History of the Missions. The construction of missions in the United States began in New Mexico, shortly after the Spaniards first colonized the area in 1598. The last missions were built in the 1840's, shortly before the United States took over the Southwest.

The first missions were constructed in New Mexico in the early 1600's. POPÉ'S REVOLT, an Indian uprising in 1680, forced the Spanish colonists to retreat to El Paso. They returned to New Mexico in 1693. In the interim, many of the structures were destroyed, but five adobe missions predating the Indian uprising remain intact.

The form and style of these churches is similar to that of later construction. The Spaniards preferred a cruciform layout, as used in Spain and Mexico, but without the vaults and domed crossings. Those features were beyond the technical capabilities of the builders. Sometimes the buildings were in the form of a rectangle, with one aisle. The materials used were adobe and stone laid in mortar. The roofs were flat, with wooden beams, and were covered with turf. On the façade, the churches had single or twin towers, with a low projecting vestibule, or with a balcony between the heavy end buttresses. The walls usually were undecorated. The mission could have *portales* (covered walks). The church interiors were plain except for the sanctuary, which had an altar. Behind the altar were niches with carved SANTOS or *RETABLOS* showing various religious images.

The missions in California were founded between 1769 (San Diego) and 1823 (San Francisco). They were constructed of stone, burned brick, ADOBE, wooden beams, and terra-cotta. The walls, which were solid and massive, were covered inside and out with white plaster or stucco and were supported with piers and buttresses. The roofs had shallow slopes and were covered in red terra-cotta tile. They featured wide projecting eaves and curved pedimented gables. The buildings had terraced bell towers with a dome-crowned lantern or pierced wall belfries. Arcaded cloisters surrounded the patio or covered the front of the mission.

SAN XAVIER DEL BAC MISSION in Arizona was founded in 1700. In the Arizona missions, the walls, roofs, and domes were built mainly of adobe and burned brick. The churches were of basilica or cruci-

The San Xavier del Bac mission. (Justine Hill)

The Alamo was the first mission in the San Antonio area. (Library of Congress)

form style, with double terraced towers at the front or a single tower on one side. The massive walls were plastered or stuccoed white, with no adornments except for intricate plaster scrollwork crowning the walls and towers. The interiors of the churches have elegant carved *retablos* and gilded altars.

The mission of San Antonio de Valero (the Alamo), founded in 1718, was the first mission in the San Antonio area. The principal materials used in the construction of the Texas missions were adobe, burned brick, and stone laid in lime and sand mortar. The church plan was either a simple basilica or cruciform layout with single or double towers or pierced wall belfries. The roofs had masonry domes or tunnel vaults. Walls were plain, built of heavy masonry, and had no adornment except on the beautifully articulated and decorative façades and around the larger openings, where the stone or brick was lavishly carved.

The Post-Independence Period. After the War of Independence and the establishment of the Mexican Republic (1821), the missions that had been maintained by the Spanish friars were secularized. In California, the result was that the church lands were sold and the buildings fell into disrepair. Beginning in the

1850's, the buildings began to be returned to the church. In the early 1900's, interest in the missions and appreciation for the heritage that the MISSION SYSTEM represented led to a start on their restoration. Today, most of the mission churches in California serve the people in the manner for which they were established and allow visitors to see them as living monuments to the multicultural heritage of California.

The distance and isolation of New Mexico from the colonial and Mexican centers of power resulted in its mission churches generally being maintained, to a great extent, by the laity, who had prolonged periods of time with minimal or no service from the clergy. A long tradition of piety and personal association with the churches permitted the preservation of indigenous santo and *retablo* production as well as independent customs as practiced by the PENITENTES. The mission churches in New Mexico suffered the indignity of being modernized with the addition of foreign decorative elements. Beginning in the 1950's, however, efforts were made to restore them to their simple and rustic original state.

Influence on American Architecture. After the Southwest became a part of the United States as a result of the Mexican American War and the GADSDEN PURCHASE, the Americans who settled in the area tried to import and establish the structures and architecture they remembered from their previous homes. They found it difficult to understand, much less appreciate, the culture and styles of the descendants of the original Spanish settlers and the Mexicans who had moved into the area. Nevertheless, there began a slow development of an appreciation for the charm of the local architecture, leading to an eventual marriage of local and imported forms. In California, the blend of mission and New England architecture led to the rise of the Monterey style. In New Mexico, a recognition of the simplicity of the mission and its adobe construction led to the development first of the "territorial architecture" used extensively during the period when New Mexico was a territory, and subsequently the "Santa Fe" style. The latter was an adaptation of architecture and home furnishings.

NOTABLE MISSIONS

New Mexico

San Agustín	Isleta
San Francisco de Asís	Ranchos de Taos
San José	Laguna Pueblo
San Miguel	Santa Fe
Santa Cruz	Santa Cruz
Santuario de Chimayó	Chimayó

California

San Carlos	Carmel
San Diego de Alcalá	San Diego
San Juan Bautista	San Juan Bautista
San Juan Capistrano	San Juan Capistrano
San Luis Rey	San Clemente
San Luis Rey de Francia	Oceanside
Santa Barbara	Santa Barbara

Texas

San Antonio de Valero (the Alamo)	San Antonio
San Francisco de la Espada	San Antonio
San José y San Miguel de Aguayo	San Antonio

Arizona

San Xavier del Bac	San Xavier Indian Reservation

The missions served as inspiration and patterns for a number of variations of architectural styles, including Spanish Pueblo, Spanish colonial, Mediterranean, California, and Southwestern. These styles represent efforts to adapt to the special needs of the environment of mountains, deserts, and the sun-drenched lands of the Southwest. Examples of this modern architecture can be seen on the campus of the University of New Mexico in Albuquerque, which has a series of buildings showing many variations of the adaptation of the Spanish Pueblo style to serve a number of purposes. The University of New Mexico has been using this beautiful style since 1908. Other examples include the New Mexico State Capitol Building, the Christo Rey Church, and the International Folk Art Museum in Santa Fe; the Missouri-Kansas-Texas Railway Station in San Antonio, Texas; the Beverly Hills Hotel in California; and the National Center for Atmospheric Research in Boulder, Colorado. —*Francisco A. Apodaca*

SUGGESTED READINGS:

• *The California Missions: A Pictorial History*. Edited by the editorial staff of Sunset Books. Menlo Park, Calif.: Lane, 1964. Describes events and people relating to the building and use of each mission. Very readable.

• Campa, Arthur L. *Hispanic Culture in the Southwest*. Norman: University of Oklahoma Press, 1979. A cultural history of the Hispanic Southwest.

• Espinosa, José E. *Saints in the Valleys: Christian Sacred Images in the History, Life, and Folk Art of Spanish New Mexico*. Rev. ed. Albuquerque: University of New Mexico Press, 1967. The premier analysis of Hispanic religious art, by a scholar who lives and feels the meaning of the art.

• Grizzard, Mary. *Spanish Colonial Art and Architecture of Mexico and the U.S. Southwest*. Lanham, Md.: University Press of America, 1986. Reviews and summarizes research on Spanish colonial art.

• Hall, Douglas Kent. *Frontier Spirit: Early Churches of the Southwest*. New York: Abbeville Press, 1990. Contains photographs and descriptions of early churches as they appeared in the 1980's.

• Jackson, Helen Hunt. *Father Junipero and His Work*. El Cajon, Calif.: Frontier, 1966. The story of the man who established the California missions.

• Kessell, John L. *The Missions of New Mexico Since 1776*. Albuquerque: University of New Mexico Press, 1980. Contains descriptions and photographs of New Mexico missions.

• Kubler, George. *The Religious Architecture of New Mexico*. 4th ed. Albuquerque: University of New

Mexico Press, 1972. A scholarly study of historic churches in New Mexico, with emphasis on architectural descriptions.

- Prince, L. Bradford. *Spanish Mission Churches of New Mexico.* Glorieta, N.Mex.: Rio Grande Press, 1977. A reprint of one of the first studies (1915) of the New Mexican missions, by a leader of the state at the beginning of the twentieth century.
- Weigle, Marta, et al., eds. *Hispanic Arts and Ethnohistory in the Southwest: New Papers Inspired by the Work of E. Boyd.* Santa Fe, N.Mex.: Ancient City Press, 1983. Contains articles by various scholars on different aspects of historical Hispanic arts and crafts in the Southwest.
- Whiffen, Marcus. *American Architecture Since 1780: Guide to the Styles.* Cambridge, Mass.: MIT Press, 1969. An illustrated survey of architecture in the United States.

Mission District (San Francisco, Calif.): Primarily Latino residential and shopping district. The Mission District was originally inhabited by Costanoan Indians. Its first white settlers were Spaniards who founded the Mission San Francisco de Asis, known today as Mission Dolores. Middle-income professionals built detailed Victorian-style homes in the area in the 1860's. After World War II, nearby freeway construction and the creation of new subdivisions prompted many residents to move to newer neighborhoods, and the district became affordable to lower-income people.

The Mission District has been home to various immigrant groups including Italians and Irish people in the 1940's and 1950's, Mexicans in the 1960's, Central Americans in the late 1970's to mid-1980's, and Chinese and Southeast Asians in the 1980's and 1990's.

La Misión, as the district is called in Spanish, covers an area of about three hundred square blocks, from Fourteenth Street to Thirtieth Street north to south, and from Potrero Avenue to Dolores Street from east to west. Mission Street is the main artery of the mostly residential district. Its old Victorian houses are often split up into apartments, with shops often occupying the bottom flat. Mission Dolores, restored since the gold rush days, is one of the area's many historical landmarks.

The Mission District is a remarkably diverse area with a distinct Latin flavor. More than half of its roughly fifty-eight thousand residents are Latino, and many of them are recent immigrants. Palm-lined Mission Street is a colorful bustle of activity with *ta-querias*, fruit markets, Mexican bakeries, Latin music stores, Spanish-language bookstores, wall murals, and Mexican and Central American restaurants. The area serves as an important cultural and political hub for Latinos in the Bay Area, with the Galeria de la Raza and Mission Cultural Center producing art, music, film, and theater events. Various Latino service agencies and activist groups also operate out of the district. Two yearly street festivals, Carnaval and Festival de las Americas, draw people from the surrounding Bay Area.

Other influences add to the Mission District's cosmopolitan atmosphere. Low rents attract many non-Latino artists, musicians, and political activists as well as theaters, small cafés, and bookstores. The district is home to the city's first distinctly lesbian neighborhood. Remnants of the area's European immigrant past survive in several businesses and restaurants alongside newer Asian fish and produce markets.

The Mission District is not without problems, notably alcoholism, drug dealing and addiction, poverty, unemployment, deteriorating housing, and prostitution. Pockets of the neighborhood have some of the city's highest crime rates. Gang activity increased in the 1980's and early 1990's, a sign to some of the lack of opportunities for youth. Many of the area's young people are immigrants, some from war-torn Latin American nations, and services to them as well as other immigrants are limited. Citizen and business groups have gone to City Hall to demand better services and conditions in their community. With increased GENTRIFICATION, the influx of Asian-owned businesses, and foreign investors buying up inexpensive property, some Mission District residents became concerned in the 1990's about preserving the Latin flavor of the neighborhood.

Mission schools: From the 1560's to the 1820's, more than 150 missions and *asistencias* (minor missions built for Indians) were established in an area covering the present states of Florida, Georgia, Alabama, Texas, New Mexico, Arizona, and California. This activity ended in 1821 with Mexican independence from Spain and the 1834 secularization of the missions.

Through the missions, Spain tried to establish its dominion in the New World against competition from other European nations. In the sixteenth century, Spain claimed most of the Americas. It tried to advance the frontiers of its empire using a three-pronged approach: the missions, PRESIDIOS (military fortress settlements), and PUEBLOS (civilian townlike settlements).

The annual Carnaval festival is a popular Mission District event. (David Bacon)

The purpose of the missions was to convert Indians into good Catholics and loyal Spanish citizens (*see* MISSION SYSTEM). This strategy was designed to meet Spain's need for new colonists, because Spain otherwise lacked the manpower to settle its territories.

Missions were usually under the supervision of two friars and a handful of soldiers. Most missions were not only churches for indoctrination in the Catholic faith but were also industrial schools, agricultural pueblos, and primitive factories. Many missions actually built schools, but all educated the Indians.

Indians were persuaded to live together at the missions and to be taught the Catholic religion, the Spanish language, and the basics of the Spanish way of life. In addition, they were required to work and were taught trades such as blacksmithing, tanning, carpentry, masonry, construction, architecture, leatherwork, tile and brick manufacturing, agriculture, spinning, weaving, mural painting, winemaking, church music, irrigation, management of livestock, and European medicine. Reading and writing were seldom taught, because the missionaries believed that such knowledge might lead the Indians to rebel.

Indians were considered subjects of Spain, with rights to the protection of its monarchy and with souls to save. The plan called for Indians to become Spanish through religion, language, labor, culture, and the gradual mixture of blood; Indians were to be required to work and live in the missions for a period of ten years. In theory, the cattle, land, and crops belonged to the Indians and were to be held in trust by the missionaries. Every mission was temporary; each was to be secularized ten years after its founding. At that point, the mission pueblo was to receive a grant of four square leagues of land (a league equals three miles, more or less), and the fields, town lots, and other property were to be parcelled out among the Indians.

According to the plan, local government was to pass to native officials trained for that purpose. Indians were to be released from mission discipline to take their place as full members of colonial society. Finally, the mission church was to be turned over to parish priests, while the missionaries were to begin work at a new site in a continuous effort of frontier expansion.

Despite the ten-year plan, most missions continued for decades or for more than a century. Although the Laws of the Indies provided that mission Indians should receive real training for self-government, the missionary fathers regarded Indians as little more than children and turned them into dependents. In many cases, missionaries did protect the natives against the worst cruelties of the soldiers, slavers, miners, and merchants. At the time of secularization in 1834, however, the mission community disintegrated, leaving the dependent Indians without protection. In spite of the missionaries' devotion to their apostolic and educational work, they failed to empower and prepare their charges for participation in the larger society.

Many historians believe that the missionaries mistreated the Indians. The missionaries' activities brought destruction of native cultures, ways of life, and religions. Although Spain did not adopt a policy of extermination, the country's activities resulted in a high death toll. Thousands of Indians died from exposure to European and African diseases (smallpox, for example) for which there was no native immunity (*see* EPIDEMICS AND INDIGENOUS POPULATIONS). The imposition of an alien discipline, harsh punishment for violation of mission rules, and exploitation in the work of building the missions also killed many. Strong Indian resistance to Hispanization led to many deadly uprisings. It is estimated, for example, that the coastal native population from San Francisco to San Diego declined from seventy-two thousand to eighteen thousand during the mission period.

The impact of the missions is apparent throughout the modern southern United States. Mission influence lives on in architecture, in agricultural development and water systems, in names of towns and places, and in religious and cultural traditions. The missions' contributions also include the parochial school, an American institution. Perhaps a more enduring legacy is the difficult question of whether, as most missionaries deeply yearned, their work was an agent for good.

Mission system: The Spanish colonization of much of North America was accomplished in part by the enforced Christianization of indigenous populations. Missions played an important role in that religious conversion.

The Strategy of the Crown. The mission system was part of a three-pronged advance by the Spanish. The mission (religion), the PRESIDIO (military), and the PUEBLO (civil authority) were designed to assist one another in the outreach to and education of new Spanish subjects, in order to prepare them for civilization under the Spanish Crown. The friars were to gather Indians living in scattered communities into villages, baptize them, and eventually catechize them. The neophytes would be taught agricultural techniques and crafts, such as blacksmithing and sewing; learn to read and write; and develop an understanding of Spanish

Castillo de San Marcos, St. Augustine, Florida. (St. Augustine and St. Johns Chamber of Commerce)

law and government. The presidio was to protect neophyte communities from attack by hostile tribes and foreign enemies. Eventually, the missions were to be reduced to the role of parish churches, and the villages would become pueblos with a secular government.

La Florida. Pedro MENÉNDEZ DE AVILÉS, a Jesuit, founded the settlement of St. Augustine in 1565, but missionary efforts in the region were impaired by unfriendly relations between the Spanish and the Native Americans. The killing of several Jesuits by Indians resulted in the Jesuits' withdrawal in 1572. The Franciscans, however, filled the gap the next year.

Missions were founded in 1587 among the Guale and Timucua tribes. The Franciscans advanced westward and, by 1633, their presence was established throughout what is now the northern portion of Florida and the southern edges of Georgia and South Carolina. The ease with which the missionaries moved through the region was a result of the apparently genuine interest of a number of important chiefs in the religion of the Franciscans.

The mission system soon included missions at Santa Catalina de Guale, Santa Catalina de Amelia, and St. Augustine along the Atlantic coast; Santa Fe, Fig Springs, and Baptizing Springs among the Timucua tribe; and San Luis and Patale in Apalachee Province (what is now the northwest corner of Florida and the eastern edge of Alabama). Important mission villages, or *doctrinas*, were under the jurisdiction of a resident friar, who might also control neighboring minor villages. The provincial outposts provided labor (chiefs were responsible for sending an annual allotment of laborers) and supplies that could pass with relative safety along the mission route. In this way, the Spanish colonial effort in La Florida thrived until 1702.

Spanish interaction with the Indians appears to have been somewhat less coercive than in some of the contemporaneous settlements in the Southwest. Indian chiefs, or CACIQUES, were treated as heads of state, and rights to land, including hunting and gathering grounds, were for the most part recognized by the Spanish. The archaeological record suggests an unusual degree of assimilation on the part of the Spanish; for example, two hundred years of interracial marriage and concubinage, as well as servitude, seemed not to have Europeanized the region's cooking methods or implements, even in Spanish or mixed-blood households.

The effects of introduced disease and enforced agriculture, however, were as devastating as in other areas of European settlement. Cattle ranching, encouraged by the friars to provide income for missions, resulted in the displacement of villages and the concentration of Indian populations that were vulnerable to viruses to which they had no immunity. As areas were depeopled, the empty or nearly empty land was opened for Spanish settlement. The Florida Panhandle was awarded to influential Spaniards as land grants beginning in the 1640's.

British forces and their Indian allies drove the Spanish from the region in a series of raids between 1702 and 1704. The missions were deserted or destroyed, and the Spanish missionary presence, except in the immediate vicinity of St. Augustine, vanished.

Nothing but scarce archaeological traces remains of the Franciscans' missions in the Gulf states. Even the locations of a number of the mission sites are a matter of speculation. Excavations begun in the 1980's had, by the mid-1990's, only started to bring to light much that was lost to the historical record for two hundred years.

The Southwest. The first foray of Catholic Spain into what later would be New Mexico was made in 1540. Fray Juan de PADILLA accompanied the young Captain Francisco Vázquez de CORONADO, seeking the lost Seven Cities of Antillia—a utopian mission, though hardly a Christian one. Instead, the expedition discovered a thriving and strategically located (and defended) center of trade called Cicuye or Pekush, later called Pecos.

Initial attempts to convert the Pueblo tribe living there did not appear promising. As a trading center, the city had already been informed of Spanish accomplishments elsewhere. Not until the Juan de OÑATE expedition in 1598 was a Spanish presence established in the region. Spanish persistence eventually resulted in the founding of missions as far as Hopiland. The well-organized and distant Hopi resisted conversion, offering shelter to fleeing Pueblos and driving away the determined Franciscans.

The Spanish presence in the Southwest was strong by the late seventeenth century. The land was poor in agricultural or mineral wealth, but the padres saw the region's rewards in terms of souls. Ninety pueblos yielded sixty thousand converts, and twenty-five missions were founded as far away as SANTA FE, NEW MEXICO, and SAN ANTONIO, TEXAS. Civil government

officials, however, quarreled openly and sometimes violently with the ecclesiastics, each denouncing the other to the Spanish Crown. Although armed and powerful, the Spanish were also divided. They were not prepared when the Pueblo, led by a shaman named Popé from San Juan, revolted. POPÉ'S REVOLT (1680) was the largest and most effective such rebellion, and it ended the missionary endeavor in the region for twelve years.

Eusebio Francisco KINO, a Jesuit, was relatively successful in his ministry along what was known as the "Rim of Christendom." A gentle and reasonable man, he toured the perimeter of the Spanish frontier (in what is now Arizona) introducing cattle and new crops to the natives, gaining the trust and affection of converts and nonconverts alike, and enlisting the aid of the Pimas in repelling Apache attacks. Through his efforts Christianity had come to the San Pedro and Santa Cruz valleys by 1692, and in 1700, a mission was established at Papago Village of Bac, where SAN XAVIER DEL BAC MISSION was finally erected one hundred years later. San Xavier, called the "Dove of the Desert," is widely considered the most beautiful of all the remaining and reconstructed missions in North America.

After the expulsion of the Jesuits from New Spain in 1767, Francisco Tomás GARCÉS, a Franciscan priest, began his mission by living among the Indians. He was respectful of the indigenous lifestyles and even learned to speak Pima. Garcés traveled far, establishing missions among the Yuma, including an important site at the crossing of the Gila and Colorado rivers, though he was no more successful with the Hopi than his predecessors had been. He accompanied Juan Bautista de ANZA on his expedition across the desert, successfully establishing a route to San Diego, where Junípero SERRA had already founded the first California mission. Although Garcés was widely loved and respected, he was not spared in the 1781 Yuma rebellion. Before his death, he had written of the mission effort, "We have failed. It is not because we haven't tried. It is because we have not understood."

California. The Jesuits were the first Christian missionaries to work among the Indians of CALIFORNIA. After their expulsion, missionary efforts were carried on by the Franciscans. Interest in settling California became intense at this time, and by 1769 Serra had founded the first California mission in San Diego. Twenty-one missions were eventually opened along the CAMINO REAL.

The mission system in California was essential in the settling of the territory by non-Indians. Until well

San Xavier del Bac mission. (Library of Congress)

The mission at San Juan Capistrano, California, prior to an 1812 earthquake that destroyed the tower. (Security Pacific Bank Collection, Los Angeles Public Library)

into the nineteenth century, however, the missions effectively precluded widespread settling by Spanish farmers and ranchers. The twenty-one missions lay in a line, the land claims of one adjacent to the next, preventing residence or even lengthy visits by non-Indians other than the padres assigned to the missions. Although the Franciscans owned no land themselves, they monopolized most of the arable acreage in California.

Neophytes were expected to work for the missions, and although the seven-hour workday was not particularly arduous, it was compulsory. The Indians were forced to forfeit a free and relatively leisurely lifestyle for field work, the monetary benefits of which did not return to them. Their free time was largely consumed by religious observation, and the practice of indigenous religions was strictly forbidden.

By 1834, when secularization was well under way, the estimated assets of the California missions included 424,000 horned cattle, 100,000 slaughtered cattle, 70,000 bushels of wheat, 30,000 bushels of other grains, and movable stock valued at $3 million. This did not include buildings, vineyards, or orchards. The growing wealth of the Franciscans had not gone unnoticed by civil authorities, who pressed continuously for secularization of the missions. The padres had become so entrenched, however, that when the first decree was issued in 1813, ordering the transfer of missions more than ten years old to the control of bishops and the reassigning of missionaries to new fields, it had no effect.

Secularization was finally accomplished between 1833 and 1836. Many neophytes fled the missions, seeking out tribal members who had eluded the missionaries' grasp, regrouping, and recovering to some extent old tribal ways. Others remained, attempting to claim the land guaranteed them by the official decree. Many of the mission buildings were abandoned, with the properties auctioned by the new government in California. Buyers were scarce, however, and the once-rich missions fell into neglect and eventual ruin.

The Legacy of the Mission System. The establishment of missions frequently resulted in the depopulation of vast areas that were then available for

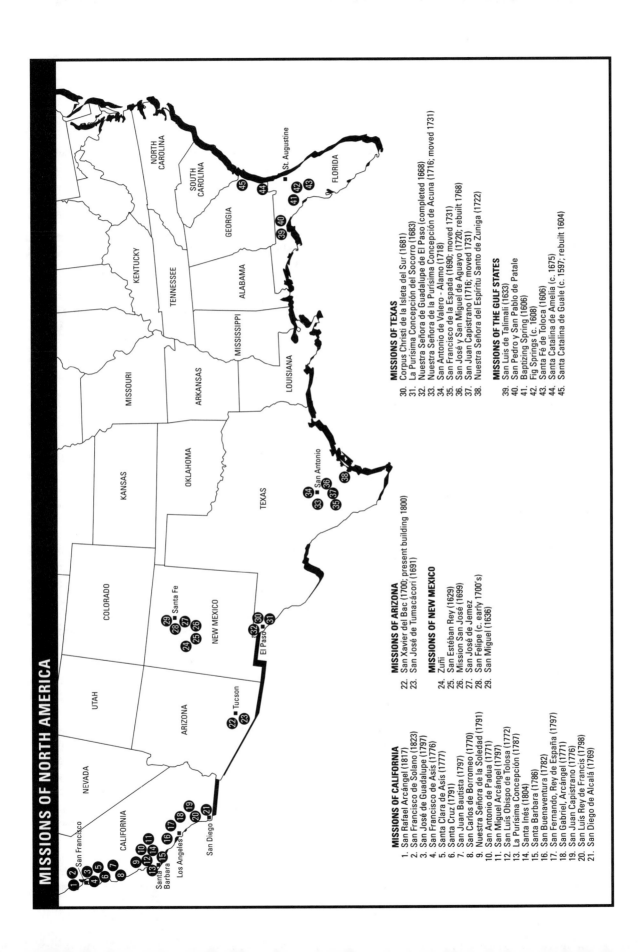

MISSIONS OF NORTH AMERICA

MISSIONS OF CALIFORNIA
1. San Rafael Arcángel (1817)
2. San Francisco de Solano (1823)
3. San José de Guadalupe (1797)
4. San Francisco de Asís (1776)
5. Santa Clara de Asís (1777)
6. Santa Cruz (1791)
7. San Juan Bautista (1797)
8. San Carlos de Borromeo (1770)
9. Nuestra Señora de la Soledad (1791)
10. San Antonio de Padua (1771)
11. San Miguel Arcángel (1797)
12. San Luis Obispo de Tolosa (1772)
13. La Purísima Concepción (1787)
14. Santa Inés (1804)
15. Santa Barbara (1786)
16. San Buenaventura (1782)
17. San Fernando, Rey de España (1797)
18. San Gabriel, Arcángel (1771)
19. San Juan Capistrano (1776)
20. San Luis Rey de Francis (1798)
21. San Diego de Alcalá (1769)

MISSIONS OF ARIZONA
22. San Xavier del Bac (1700; present building 1800)
23. San José de Tumacácori (1691)

MISSIONS OF NEW MEXICO
24. Zuñi
25. San Estéban Rey (1629)
26. Mission San José (1699)
27. San José de Jemez
28. San Felipe (c. early 1700's)
29. San Miguel (1636)

MISSIONS OF TEXAS
30. Corpus Christi de la Isleta del Sur (1681)
31. La Purísima Concepción del Socorro (1683)
32. Nuestra Señora de Guadalupe de El Paso (completed 1668)
33. Nuestra Señora de la Purísima Concepción de Acuna (1716; moved 1731)
34. San Antonio de Valero - Alamo (1718)
35. San Francisco de la Espada (1690; moved 1731)
36. San José y San Miguel de Aguayo (1720; rebuilt 1768)
37. San Juan Capistrano (1716; moved 1731)
38. Nuestra Señora del Espíritu Santo de Zuniga (1722)

MISSIONS OF THE GULF STATES
39. San Luis de Talimali (1633)
40. San Pedro y San Pablo de Patale
41. Baptizing Spring (1606)
42. Fig Springs (c. 1608)
43. Santa Fé de Toloca (1606)
44. Santa Catalina de Amelia (c. 1675)
45. Santa Catalina de Guale (c. 1597; rebuilt 1604)

Spanish settlement in the form of land grants. As the missions were secularized, more land became available, and the PUEBLOS where important missions had been active grew with new Spanish and mixed-blood settlers. Even at the close of the twentieth century, Spanish was still the primary language in some communities of former New Spain.

The mission buildings themselves had tremendous influence on regional architecture, contributing to the development of the Mission, Monterey, and Santa Fe styles (*see* MISSION ARCHITECTURE). In addition to being treasured historical landmarks, some missions still served active congregations throughout the twentieth century.

The cattle introduced by Father Kino have been blamed for much of the ecological degradation of Arizona. Agricultural developments, as with everything the padres brought with them, altered forever the landscapes of the regions they served. —*Janet Alice Long*

SUGGESTED READINGS:

• Fergusson, Erna. *New Mexico: A Pageant of Three Peoples*. Albuquerque: University of New Mexico Press, 1973. A compact history of New Mexico, with a good overview of the role of the padres in development of the state. Bibliography and index.

• Kessell, John L. *Kiva, Cross, and Crown: The Pecos Indians and New Mexico 1540-1840*. Washington, D.C.: National Park Service, U.S. Department of the Interior, 1979. A thorough history of the Pecos, with much information about the relations among the padres, the governor, the military, and the Indians. Notes, bibliography, and index.

• McEwan, Bonnie G., ed. *The Spanish Missions of La Florida*. Gainesville: University Press of Florida, 1993. An excellent compilation of current archaeological findings, written by archaeologists working at mission sites in the Gulf states. Many maps and tables, notes, bibliography, and index.

• Nava, Julian, and Bob Barger. *California: Five Centuries of Cultural Contrasts*. Beverly Hills, Calif.: Glencoe Press, 1976. An illustrated history of California with a concise section on the California missions. Index.

• Webb, Edith Buckland. *Indian Life at the Old Missions*. Lincoln: University of Nebraska Press, 1983. A thorough study of the lives of Indians residing at the California missions. Bibliography and index.

Missionary impulse: Conversion of the Amerindians to Christianity was a major stimulus to, and the chief rationalization for, the Spaniards' exploration and sub-jugation of the Americas. Christopher Columbus' voyage in 1492 opened to the Spanish another world, filled with strange plants and animals and alien peoples. From the outset, Spaniards planned to evangelize the Amerindians. Supported by theologians and the monarchy in Spain, friars and priests embarked upon a missionary campaign that Christianized most Amerindians in Spanish America to some degree.

Much of the indigenous population of the Caribbean died from abuse and disease before the Spaniards organized an effective missionary effort there. Prior to 1520, however, clerics led the Spanish Crown to adopt policies that provided the rationale for evangelization on the mainland. They decided, for example, that Amerindians were humans and possessed souls, and thus were suited to become Catholics. In justifying conquest, they rationalized that God allowed Spaniards to occupy Indian lands and profit from them because Spain accepted the burden of carrying Christianity to the Amerindians. The Caribbean also produced Bartolomé DE LAS CASAS, the most tenacious advocate of indigenous rights and a leading theoretician of the missionary crusade.

The most dramatic missionary effort unfolded in Mexico. "The Conqueror" himself, Hernán CORTÉS, had destroyed Aztec idols and temples. In May, 1524, twelve Franciscans arrived and were soon joined by Dominicans and Augustinians. With the Franciscans in the lead, these religious orders carried out the "spiritual conquest" of Mexico. In part because of the civil turmoil that enveloped Peru after its conquest, conversion proceeded less rapidly and with less fervor there than in Mexico. During the seventeenth century, the Jesuits carried out the evangelization of the Guaraní in Paraguay, where they established their own theocratic kingdom.

Many motives lay behind such evangelization. In their crusade to drive the Moors out of Spain, Spanish Catholics had become religious militants. They were no more willing to tolerate religious diversity in their American possessions than in Spain. Furthermore, missionaries found the Indians alien and their religions troubling. It was easier to remake the Indians in a Spanish and Catholic mold than to accept their differences, even if coercion was required to do so. The friars believed in a world of opposites: good and evil, divine and demoniac. Unable to question the goodness and divinity of their own culture and theology, they necessarily assumed that indigenous religions were evil and must be eradicated. Religion tinged virtually all aspects of Indian life, and to achieve their ends the missionaries destroyed much of the intellectual and artistic heritage of indigenous cultures in the name of Christian exclusivity. The Franciscans in Mexico anticipated Christ's imminent return and hoped the Indians' conversion would complete preparation for it. On the frontier, missionaries served a political purpose. Their missions, usually founded along with military garrisons (presidios) helped pacify and protect such regions (*see* MISSION SYSTEM; PRESIDIO SYSTEM).

Most Indians in Spanish America became at least nominally Christian, and many were devoted to their new religion. Some continued to practice their old rites surreptitiously or assimilated them into a Christian guise. The result was a mestizo Christianity that was neither fully Spanish nor Indian.

Mistral, Gabriela (Lucila Godoy Alcayaga; Apr. 7, 1889, Vicuña, Chile—Jan. 10, 1957, Hempstead, N.Y.): Poet. Petronila Alcayaga Rojas, Lucila's mother, made a living as a seamstress. Lucila idolized her father, Jerónimo Godoy Villanueva, a teacher who eventually abandoned his family.

When she was eleven years old, Lucila entered the Escuela Superior de Niñas de Vicuña. She wrote her first poems while attending that school. Beginning in 1904, her poems appeared under various pseudonyms

Gabriela Mistral lectures on Argentine poet Alfonsina Storni. (AP/Wide World Photos)

Moctezuma receives Hernán Cortés. (Library of Congress)

in *La voz de elqui*, a Vicuña periodical, and in *El Coquimbo*. In 1905, she decided to devote herself to teaching and got an assignment in the school in Campañía Baja, where she moved with her mother. She wrote daily and occasionally published in local papers. She later obtained positions in several other schools and lived and worked in several Latin American countries, Europe, and the United States.

Mistral's major books of poetry include *Desolación* (1922), *Ternura* (1924), and her long narrative poem *Poema de Chile* (1967). She was awarded the Nobel Prize in Literature in 1945. Mistral considered herself to be the direct voice of the poets of her race and the indirect one of the noble Spanish and Portuguese tongues.

Moctezuma II (c. 1480, Tenochtitlán, Mexico—1520, Tenochtitlán, Mexico): Aztec emperor. The Aztec nobility elected Moctezuma (also known as Montezuma) to become emperor in 1503, when he was about twenty-three years old. Moctezuma's strengths for the position lay in his religious knowledge. He had also demonstrated military abilities when he suppressed a rebellion in Oaxaca.

Moctezuma knew that newcomers had arrived when Hernán Cortés reached the Mexican coast in 1519. He was aware of the power of the Spanish because of previous encounters between Spaniards and Indians. Moctezuma tried to convince Cortés to leave; when his efforts failed, Moctezuma decided to welcome Cortés in order to keep the peace. He said that Cortés' arrival matched religious prophecies of the coming of Quetzalcóatl, an Aztec god of creation. Moctezuma signed a vassalage treaty with Cortés, but some of his advisers disagreed with him and attacked the Spaniards. Moctezuma died in one of the following battles.

Moctezuma has been criticized for his inaction and inability to confront Cortés. It is important to note he was in the middle of a complex political situation, trying to maintain a tenuous alliance among three states. He knew that outside forces could destroy the balance of power and wreak havoc on the Aztec empire.

Mofonguitos: Small balls of fried plantains and pork cracklings. *Mofongo* has African roots, and its name is derived from an African word. *Mofongo* is made by frying plantain slices into *TOSTONES*, separately sautéing cubes of salt port ("cracklings"), and crushing the two ingredients together with garlic. The crushed mass is formed into balls and served alone or with a sauce. Cuban *mofongo* is made into a single large ball from which portions are taken, while Puerto Rican *mofongo* is made into smaller balls, usually about two inches in diameter. *Mofonguito* refers to *mofongo* of the Puerto Rican size or smaller.

Mohr, Nicholasa (b. Nov. 1, 1935, New York, N.Y.): Artist and writer. Like many Puerto Rican migrants, Mohr and her family settled in El Barrio, New York's Spanish Harlem. Between 1953 and 1969, Mohr studied at the Art Students League, the Brooklyn Museum of Art School, and the Pratt Center for Contemporary Printmaking. She was married to a clinical child psychologist, Irwin Mohr, who died in 1957; they had two sons. During the 1970's, she was an art instructor in New Jersey and New Hampshire and was later writer-in-residence and artist-in-residence in New York City public schools. She also lectured in creative writing in Illinois, Wisconsin, and Connecticut and produced videos on the cultural heritage of Caribbean Hispanic Americans. Her books, including *Nilda* (1973), *El Bronx Remembered* (1975), and *Going Home* (1986), focus on the plight of Puerto Ricans who came to the United States only to find life an unending struggle for survival. Her books have received numerous awards.

Mojado: Literally, "wet one." The term refers to an illegal immigrant from Mexico. *Mojado* is the Spanish equivalent of the pejorative term "WETBACK," applied to Mexican immigrants who enter the United States illegally. Mexican Americans used the label extensively after World War II for *recién llegados* (recent arrivals) arriving predominantly from Mexico. During "OPERATION WETBACK," a program of the Immigration and Naturalization Service begun in 1954, many second- and third-generation Chicanos used the derogatory term to distinguish themselves from the undocumented.

Mojica, José (Sept. 14, 1895, Jalisco, Mexico—Sept. 20, 1974, Lima, Peru): Singer. Mojica took voice lessons with José Pierson and made his opera debut in the tenor role of *The Barber of Seville* in 1916. He moved to New York, New York, but had to work in menial jobs while performing secondary roles in an opera company.

The famous Enrico Caruso heard him sing and recommended him to the Chicago Lyric Opera. He later sang at the Metropolitan Opera House with opera stars Amelita Galli-Curci and Lily Pons.

The Edison recording company hired Mojica as an exclusive artist, and he recorded thousands of operatic and popular Mexican songs. In 1928, he made his first Hollywood movie, *El precio de un beso*, followed later by *El rey de los gitanos* (1932), *La cruz y la espada* (1937), and *El capitán aventurero* (1938).

In 1940, he decided to become a priest and retired to a Peruvian convent. He was ordained seven years later. Commissioned by his superiors, Mojica started to sing in 1949 to help establish a convent in Arequipa, Peru. To help raise funds to reconstruct the college, he wrote an autobiography, *Yo pecador*, which sold more than one million copies in Spanish and was translated into the English *I, a Sinner* (1963).

Molcajete: Mortar used with a pestle to grind spices and other foodstuffs. Used for thousands of years throughout most of Latin America and part of North America, the *molcajete* is a small bowl, usually with three legs, in which chiles, nuts, herbs, and other foods are ground with a cylindrical pestle. *Molcajetes* most commonly are made of black volcanic rock, and fine-grained rock is the best. In parts of Mexico, particularly along the coast, ceramic *molcajetes* are made. Their interior bottoms are roughened with cross-hatching incised in the clay before firing. This ceramic form appeared first in the ancient city of TEOTIHUA-CÁN, around 100 C.E.

Mole: Class of thick, dark Mexican sauces and the dishes made with them. *Moles* were made by the Aztecs, and a variety of *moles* exist in modern Mexico. All feature thick, cooked chile sauces, made of puréed vegetables and ground nuts or seeds, served over cooked meat. The most famous of *moles*, *mole poblano*, is a puréed sauce made from chiles, chocolate, tomatoes, almonds, raisins, and garlic, served over baked turkey. Many *moles* once were festive dishes and came into common use.

Molina, Gloria (b. May 13, 1948, Los Angeles, Calif.): Public official. Molina has served in the California State Assembly, on the Los Angeles City Council, and on the Los Angeles County Board of Supervisors. In each case, she was the first Mexican American to be elected to that governing body. Molina learned responsibility at an early age, having to support her family at the age of nineteen. She worked as a legal assistant while completing her college education at California State University.

Molina was active in community-based organizations before becoming an elected official. Prior to her own election, she worked as an administrative assistant to Assemblyman Art TORRES. Molina also worked in the administration of President Jimmy Car-

A molcajete, at left, shown with a mano *and a* metate. (Ruben G. Mendoza)

Congressman Edward R. Roybal congratulates Gloria Molina after administering her oath of office as a member of the Los Angeles County Board of Supervisors. (AP/Wide World Photos)

ter as a deputy for presidential personnel. Her political career began in 1982, with her election to the California State Assembly. Molina developed an aggressive grassroots campaign that has since become her trademark. In 1987, Molina won a seat on the Los Angeles City Council, and four years later she became a county supervisor after being embroiled in a redistricting battle concerned with creating a district likely to elect a Latino supervisor. The redistricting plans ended up in court, with judicial rulings coming in GARZA V. COUNTY OF LOS ANGELES, CALIFORNIA BOARD OF SUPERVISORS.

Mondongo: Caribbean tripe soup with chunks of starchy root vegetables. The word *mondongo* is of African origin and refers to tripe in circum-Caribbean Spanish. The name has been extended to the traditional soup made from tripe. This soup features honeycomb tripe and calf's foot and has chunks of various starchy

roots in it. Versions of this soup are consumed all along the Atlantic coast of Central and South America as far south as Venezuela, but *mondongo* does not penetrate beyond the coast. Both Puerto Rico and the Dominican Republic have versions of *mondongo*, some of which include macaroni. Mexican communities along the Gulf Coast have tripe soups called *mondongo*, but they usually do not have starchy roots added and are more truly versions of Mexican MENUDO.

Monolingualism in Spanish: Only 2.68 percent of the population of the United States is monolingual (speaking only one language) in a language other than English, according to data derived from the 1990 U.S. Census. Question 15c of the census form asked "How well does this person speak English?" Monolinguals were classified as people who answered "not well" or "not at all" to this question. People of Dominican and

Central American background were more likely than members of other Latino groups to not speak English "very well," according to the census report.

Spanish-speaking monolinguals in the United States included 643,457 persons aged five to seventeen, 3,425,937 aged eighteen to sixty-four, and 434,639 aged sixty-five and over. A total of slightly more than 4.5 million people therefore were monolingual in Spanish. Monolingualism is particularly prominent in the Southwest, a region with a large percentage of Latinos in its population.

Relationship to Immigration. A direct correlation can be seen between people who have recently immigrated to the United States and monolingualism in Spanish. California, for example, has experienced heavy recent immigration. In 1990, it had nearly 1.8 million Spanish monolinguals, about 40 percent of the U.S. total.

Many Latino rural migrant workers retain the language, and other cultural characteristics, of their country of origin. Isolation from other communities or a concentration of Spanish-speaking people in certain locations allows Spanish monolingualism to persist.

Except for recent arrivals and residents of isolated rural areas, the majority of the Latinos in the United States speak English as well as Spanish. In urban areas with large concentrations of Spanish-speaking people, however, a significant minority of Latinos are monolingual in Spanish. These areas include New York, New York; Los Angeles, California; and Miami, Florida. A gradual but definite shift from Spanish to English as the dominant language occurs in many Latino

In some U.S. ethnic enclaves, knowledge of English is unnecessary and monolingualism in Spanish is only a minor handicap. (Martin Hutner)

communities. Spanish-speaking immigrants seem to follow the same assimilationist pattern as other language groups in the United States.

Europeans arriving in the nineteenth and early twentieth centuries often settled in rural areas of the United States and were able to maintain their own languages and traditions for a considerable time while experiencing little pressure to learn English. Immigrants who moved to urban areas learned English, as did their children, but settlement in ethnic neighborhoods made retention of their native language easy.

The shift to English is becoming more rapid for several reasons. The first is the greater influence of the mass media. Immigrants are more likely to be exposed to English than they were in the past. Public education is more common than in the past, and students in public schools are systematically taught English so that they can experience the mainstream education. Weaker factors in the increased speed of English language acquisition include increased numbers of mixed ethnic marriages and the establishment of more diverse neighborhoods. Most immigrant families now acquire English as a primary or at least secondary language by the second generation.

English-Only Movements. It is ironic that even as the United States is promoting proficiency in foreign languages as a way of becoming more competitive in the international market, the high retention of Spanish is viewed by some Americans as threatening. Official policy emphasizes a global economy and political cooperation through such documents as the NORTH AMERICAN FREE TRADE AGREEMENT, yet unofficial policy seems to discourage the use of Spanish.

Throughout the United States, nearly all "English only" movements have targeted Spanish speakers (*see* ENGLISH-ONLY CONTROVERSY). Paradoxically, states with Spanish names and large populations of Spanish speakers—California, Florida, and Colorado—have approved amendments that make English the official language in government documents and institutions. Bilingualism is perceived differently depending on the dominant language of the speaker. BILINGUALISM among Anglos is viewed as enriching, whereas bilingualism among language minorities is often characterized as a handicap, with use of two languages acting as a source of cognitive confusion.

Acquisition of English. Some immigrant groups shift more rapidly than others from their home language to English. The rate of shift is influenced by educational level, social class, and age at immigration of the individual group members, as well as by the

influx of new immigrants from the same language community. Latinos have successfully maintained use of Spanish in the United States, although many also speak English frequently or even primarily.

Retention of Spanish is common. Among the first Mexican Americans were many who did not cross the border; instead, they were enveloped by a new government and language following the territorial expansion of the United States. The same thing happened to Puerto Ricans, whose government and citizenship changed as a result of circumstances beyond the control of individuals. In 1990, about 79 percent of Latinos spoke Spanish at home according to Census Bureau data. Of the 21.9 million people of Hispanic origin in the country, 17.3 million spoke Spanish or Spanish Creole at home. The Spanish language is closely tied to the Latino identity and forms a meaningful part of the lives of Latinos.

—*M. Cecilia Colombi*

SUGGESTED READINGS: • Hakuta, Kenji. *Mirror of Language*. New York: Basic Books, 1986. • Padilla, Amado M., Kathryn J. Lindholm, and Andrew Chen. "The English-Only Movement: Myths, Reality, and Implications for Psychology." *American Psychologist* 46 (February, 1991): 120-130. • U.S. Department of Commerce. Economics and Statistics Administration. *We the American—: Hispanics*. Washington, D.C.: Government Printing Office, 1993. • Veltman, Calvin. *The Future of the Spanish Language in the United States*. New York: Hispanic Policy Development Project, 1988. • Zentella, Ana Celia. "Language Politics in the U.S.A.: The English-Only Movement." In *Literature, Language, and Politics*, edited by Betty Jean Craige. Athens: University of Georgia Press, 1988.

Monroe Doctrine and Roosevelt Corollary: Statements of foreign policy. On December 2, 1823, President James Monroe informed the nations of Europe that the United States would not allow them to establish any new colonies in the Western Hemisphere. Monroe's message came in the aftermath of successful wars for independence conducted by many countries in the Americas. The United States wanted to control trade with the new republics. Monroe feared that the Spanish would try to regain control of the region, and his message was a warning not to make that attempt. The British supported the American view. The policy proved successful, as American and British companies gained control of Latin American markets.

On December 6, 1904, President Theodore Roosevelt expanded the scope of the Monroe Doctrine in his

Ricardo Montalbán. (AP/Wide World Photos)

corollary. After Venezuela and the Dominican Republic got into financial trouble and failed to repay German investors, Germany threatened military action. The Roosevelt Corollary said that the United States would provide financial supervision and a police force, if necessary, to Latin American governments so that they could repay their loans. Europeans would not have to intervene. Between 1904 and 1916, the corollary was invoked in the Dominican Republic, Nicaragua, and Haiti.

Montalbán, Ricardo (b. Nov. 25, 1920, Mexico City, Mexico): Actor. Montalbán made films in Mexico in the early 1940's before moving to the United States. His more than twenty American films include *Fiesta* (1947), *Kissing Bandit* (1948), *On an Island with You* (1948), *Neptune's Daughter* (1949), *Mystery Street* (1950), *Mark of the Renegade* (1951), *Latin Lovers* (1953), *Sombrero* (1953), *Sayonara* (1957), *Private Warrior* (1961), *Love Is a Ball* (1963), *Sweet Charity* (1968), *Star Trek II: The Wrath of Khan* (1982), and *Naked Gun* (1988).

Several of Montalbán's early films explored social problems dealing with Latinos, and he continued to display a deep interest in the rights and welfare of Latinos as his career progressed. In 1969, he founded the group NOSOTROS to work for the furthering of Latino interests. The group developed the Golden Eagle Awards, the presentation of which became a nationally televised event.

Montalbán became a regular on television as the suave star of *Fantasy Island* (1978-1984), for which he won an Emmy Award in 1978. He starred on *Dynasty* from 1986 to 1987 and was also featured in numerous television commercials. In 1988, Montalbán received the Golden Aztec Award from the Mexican-American Foundation.

Montano, Louis R. (b. Jan. 18, 1928, Roswell, N.Mex.): Public official. Montano, a Mexican American, was educated for the priesthood at the Immaculate Heart of Mary Seminary in 1949. He also attended the College of Santa Fe from 1953 to 1957 and completed the Boys Club Training Program at the University of New York in 1957.

Montano served as director of the Santa Fe Boys Club from 1957 to 1984. During that time, he was also elected to public office. From 1974 to 1978, Montano was a city councilman in Santa Fe. He was mayor pro tem from 1978 to 1982 and mayor from 1982 to 1986. Montano then joined the New Mexico Department of

Labor, where he served as director of the Labor and Industrial Division. Montano has also served on state and local commissions on recreation.

Montez, Lola (1819, Limerick, Ireland—Jan. 17, 1861, New York, N.Y.): Entertainer. Montez began her dancing career in Spain. She became famous for taking a series of lovers, the most famous of whom was Ludwig I, King of Bavaria. Political events forced her to flee Europe. She arrived in New York to commence a tour in 1851.

Montez traveled to California two years later. California during the gold rush offered tremendous opportunities to women with musical or theatrical abilities, and Montez captivated her audiences with the Tarantella. This risqué dance portrayed a woman under attack by spiders that climbed everywhere, including into her undergarments. She performed in San Francisco, Sacramento, and Marysville. Montez was married to and divorced from a prominent California attorney. She bought a cottage in Grass Valley, where she entertained frequently and elaborately.

After two years in California, Montez left for Australia in 1855. She could not sustain her initial success and returned to California in July, 1856. By September, however, Montez had announced her retirement from the stage. In November, 1856, she left for New York to begin a career as a lecturer. Montez suffered a stroke in the fall of 1859 and died two years later.

Montez, María (María Africa Antonia Gracia Vidal de Santo Silas; June 6, 1920, Barahona, Dominican Republic—Sept. 7, 1951, Paris, France): Actor. Montez had a brief modeling career in Europe before going to New York to act. She made her motion-picture debut in 1941 in *The Invisible Woman* and quickly established herself as an exotic and provocative screen temptress. She became the star of a series of Universal Technicolor "Easterns," including *Arabian Nights* (1942), *Ali Baba and the Forty Thieves* (1943), *Sudan* (1945), *Tangier* (1946), *Pirates of Monterey* (1947), and *Siren of Atlantis* (1948), in which she costarred with her husband, Jean-Pierre Aumont.

Montez achieved her greatest fame in the title role of *Cobra Woman* in 1944. Although defined by their sensuality, her characters also tended to be strong authority figures. Her other film credits include *That Night in Rio* (1941), *Moonlight in Hawaii* (1941), *South of Tahiti* (1941), *The Mystery of Marie Roget* (1942), *White Savage* (1943), *Gypsy Wildcat* (1944), and *The Exile* (1947).

María Montez (at left) with actor husband Jean Pierre Aumont at a 1948 premiere of Corridor of Mirrors, *starring Edana Romney (right).* (AP/Wide World Photos)

As their Hollywood careers began to wane, Montez and Aumont went to Europe, where they appeared in a number of French, Italian, and German films. In 1951, Montez died suddenly and tragically by drowning in a scalding bath, possibly after suffering a heart attack.

Montoya, José (b. May 28, 1932, near Escoboza, N.Mex.): Artist. Montoya spent his childhood in New Mexico and California. As a result of frequent moves associated with the family's employment as migrant farmworkers, he received sporadic and fragmented education. After completing high school, he joined the U.S. Navy and served in the Korean War.

Following military service, Montoya enrolled at San Diego City College to study art. He was awarded a scholarship in 1959 to the California College of Arts and Crafts in Oakland; he was graduated in 1962 with a bachelor of arts degree.

While working on his master of fine arts degree, Montoya taught art at Wheatland High School in California. In 1971, he began teaching at Sacramento State University in California. Montoya helped develop a program of barrio art in Sacramento. In addition to creating his visual art, Montoya has written poetry that has been published in the journal *El Grito* and in anthologies.

Montoya, Joseph Manuel (Sept. 24, 1915, Peña Blanca, N.Mex.—June 5, 1978, Washington, D.C.): Politician. Montoya traced his descent to eighteenth century Spanish immigrants to New Mexico. He earned a B.A. degree from Regis College in 1934 and a J.D. degree from Georgetown University in 1938.

In 1936, Montoya was elected to the New Mexico House of Representatives, becoming the youngest representative in New Mexico's history. Two years later,

Joseph Montoya interrogates John Dean III during the Watergate hearings in 1973. (AP/Wide World Photos)

he was reelected and named Democratic floor leader. In 1940, he won election to the state senate.

Montoya served four terms as lieutenant governor of New Mexico between 1947 and 1957, when he began the first of four terms in the United States House of Representatives. In 1962, he became a member of the U.S. Senate, filling the seat of Dennis CHÁVEZ, who died in November of that year. Montoya won his own seat in the Senate in 1964.

As a senator, Montoya advocated measures to aid the poor, American Indians, and the elderly. He was also an early opponent of American involvement in Vietnam. His popularity waned in the 1970's, and he was defeated in his 1976 reelection bid. Montoya's health steadily deteriorated from that point on. He underwent surgery for cancer, then died of complications.

Montoya, Juana Alicia. *See* **Alicia, Juana**

Montoya, Malaquías (b. June 21, 1938, Albuquerque, N.Mex.): Artist. Montoya began lecturing and teaching in the early 1960's. He became involved in the Chicano movement while attending the University of California, Berkeley, from which he was graduated in 1970 with a bachelor's degree in art. As a student, he was involved in numerous activist groups and did the cover for *El Plan de Santa Bárbara: A Chicano Plan for Higher Education* (1969).

Throughout the 1970's, Montoya concentrated on posters, working with various activist groups and for activist causes. His work also appeared in numerous individual shows and group exhibitions throughout California. Montoya has taught at the California College of Arts and Crafts in Oakland. He is best known for his silkscreens but has also produced murals, paintings, and drawings.

Montoya, María Teresa: Theater manager. Montoya was manager of the Teatro Princesa in Los Angeles during the early days of Los Angeles theater. In January of 1922, she established her own company, the Gran Compañía María Teresa Montoya, but it met with poor reception and soon went bankrupt. Montoya blamed the company's failure in part on the Americanization of Mexicans in the United States. In 1956, she published her autobiography, *El teatro en mi vida* (the theater in my life).

Mora, Patricia "Pat" (b. Jan. 19, 1942, El Paso, Tex.): Poet and educator. Born to Raul Antonio, an optician, and Estella Delgado Mora, Mora received her educa-

tion at Texas Western University and at the University of Texas at El Paso, where she completed her master's degree in 1967. A longtime teacher, Mora in 1988 became director of the El Paso Independent School District. She held that position for about three years before becoming an English and communications instructor at El Paso Community College. In 1979, she joined the part-time faculty of the University of Texas at El Paso. She has also served as judge for the Texas Institute of Letters and on the literary advisory council for the Texas Commission on the Arts. Her books include *Chants* (1985) and *Borders* (1986).

Moraga, Cherríe (b. Sept. 25, 1952, Whittier, Calif.): Editor and writer. Moraga is the daughter of a Chicana mother, Elvira Moraga, and an Anglo father, Joseph Lawrence. After earning a master's degree from San Francisco State University, in 1981, she became cofounder of the Kitchen Table/Women of Color Press. A Hispanic American arts center in New York City, INTAR, invited her to be playwright-in-residence in 1984. In 1986, Moraga began working as a part-time instructor of writing at the University of California at Berkeley. In 1986, she received the American Book Award from the Before Columbus Foundation for her coeditorship of and contributions to *This Bridge Called My Back: Writings by Radical Women of Color* (1981).

Morales, Alejandro (b. Oct. 14, 1944, Montebello, Calif.): Novelist. Morales, a Mexican American, spent his youth in East Los Angeles, California, and completed his undergraduate study at California State University, Los Angeles. He later earned master's and doctoral degrees in Spanish from Rutgers University.

After completing his formal education, Morales returned to California and advanced through the academic ranks to become a professor in the department of Spanish and Portuguese at the University of California, Irvine. His first novels, *Caras viejas y vino nuevo* (1975; *Old Faces and New Wine*, 1981) and *La verdad sin voz* (1979; *Death of an Anglo*, 1988), were first published in Mexico. These novels explore generational conflicts in a barrio family. His later novels include *Reto en el paraíso* (1982; challenge in paradise), *The Brick People* (1988), and *The Rag Doll Plagues* (1992). They are imaginative works based on historical research.

Morales, Esai (b. Oct. 1, 1962, Brooklyn, N.Y.): Actor. Morales left his family home at the age of fourteen to attend New York City's High School of the Performing Arts. His first major stage appearance was in a 1981 New York Shakespeare Festival production of *The Tempest*. His other stage credits include Miguel PIÑERO's prison play *Short Eyes*, *Tamer of Horses*, and *El Hermano*.

Morales made his film debut in 1983 in *Bad Boys*, playing opposite Sean Penn as Paco Moreno, a prisoner with a personal vendetta. This character set the tone for many of his later film portrayals. He played Ritchie VALENS' envious older brother in the hit film *La Bamba* (1987), and he starred as a Hispanic youth warlord in *The Principal* (1987). Morales' other films include *Rainy Day Friends* (1985), *L.A. Bad* (1985), *Bloodhounds of Broadway* (1989), *Naked Tango* (1990), *A Climate for Killing* (1991), and *Amazon* (1991).

On television, Morales has appeared in the 1986 film *On Wings of Eagles* and in such series as *The Equalizer*, *Miami Vice*, and *Fame*. He has been honored with a Golden Eagle Award from NOSOTROS as most promising actor and with a New York Image Award. Morales has also established his own production company, Richport, named to honor his Puerto Rican heritage.

Morales, Noro (Jan. 4, 1911, San Juan, Puerto Rico—Jan. 4, 1964, San Juan, Puerto Rico): Composer, conductor, and pianist. Morales began his career as the pianist in the Orquesta Hermanos Morales, a well-known Puerto Rican popular band composed of family members and conducted by his father. After his father's death, Morales took over and led the band.

In 1935, Morales and several of his brothers decided to move to New York, New York, then at the peak of the rumba craze. They began a career in the Teatro Hispano at 116th Street, in the area known as El Barrio.

Morales formed his own band in 1939 and performed in nightclubs such as El Morocco and Harlem's popular Stork Club. He soon became one of the major names among Latin musicians. His big band included singers Tito Rodríguez and MACHITO. In 1947, Morales won a *La Prensa* newspaper poll of popularity of various artists.

Morales' unique compositions and recordings for MGM, including "Bim Bam Bum," "Perfume de Amor," "If You Only Knew," "Walter Winchell Rumba," "Oye Negra," and "Rum and Soda," made him a crowd pleaser. Numerous musicians, including Xavier CUGAT and Percy Faith, sought his work.

Morales, Pedro Pablo, Jr. (b. Dec. 5, 1964, Chicago, Ill.): Swimmer. Morales, a Cuban American, was forced to learn to swim by his mother, who had almost

drowned as a youngster. His early instructors had little praise for his swimming abilities, but at the age of ten he became the national champion in the ten-and-under division for the 50-yard butterfly. He would repeat as national champion in the twelve-, fourteen-, and sixteen-year-old divisions.

During his senior year in high school, Morales broke Mark Spitz's sixteen-year-old record in the 100-yard butterfly. Heavily recruited, Morales chose to attend Stanford University. While at Stanford, he

Pablo Morales holds his gold medal for the 100-meter butterfly in the 1992 Olympics. (AP/Wide World Photos)

broke the world record for the 100-meter butterfly. At the 1984 Los Angeles Olympics, Morales won a gold medal in the medley relay and silver medals in the 100-meter butterfly and 200-meter individual medley.

After failing to make the 1988 U.S. Olympic team, Morales turned his attention to law school. He returned to competition for the 1992 Barcelona Olympics, however, and was named the U.S. team captain. At Barcelona, he won his fourth Olympic medal, a gold in the 100-meter butterfly.

Morales, Sylvia: Filmmaker. An acclaimed filmmaker whose work explores contemporary Latino and women's issues, Morales in 1979 directed *Chicanas*, a short documentary focusing on the role of Hispanic women in society. Her 1984 *Los Lobos: And a Time to Dance* was a short public-television special profiling the popular Latino musical group Los Lobos. In the narrative drama *Esperanza*, Morales showed the predicament of a young immigrant girl separated from her mother and left on her own in the United States. Her *SIDA Is AIDS*, a documentary made for public television, was broadcast in both English and Spanish. Her documentary *Values: Sexuality and the Family* examined health issues in the Chicano community. In *Faith Even to the Fire*, she profiled the tenacious faith of three outspoken nuns.

Morbidity and mortality: No single cause of death is prevalent among all Latinos, but three large subpopulations exhibit similar patterns. Young male Latinos have a relatively higher annual rate of mortality per capita than do non-Hispanic whites; middle-aged and elderly Latinos have relatively low mortality rates.

Concept of Death. Latinos, especially those of Mexican origin, celebrate the annual holiday Día de los Muertos, or Day of the Dead. The symbolic beginnings of this holiday are with the Last Supper.

Candy skulls are popular on this day in Mexico, and families often set a place at the table for a deceased family member or friend. The significance of this day and the feeling for death are captured in folk art that often depicts dancing and laughing skeletons. Death itself is not seen as particularly positive or negative but simply as a necessary part of life. The Day of the Dead gives families an opportunity to honor those who have died, thus celebrating their spiritual and tangible contributions to the living. At the same time, the living affirm their own lives and the continued promise that life holds while they also accept and embrace the eventuality of their own deaths.

Mexican people are not necessarily less afraid of death than others but are generally more comfortable with talking and joking about it. Death may be perceived with irony or disdain, but it is viewed directly. Death is a reason for celebration and is an amusement for the mind; it is somewhat less mysterious for Latinos than for Anglos, who are historically not as comfortable with it.

Rates of Mortality. Young male Latinos show a higher rate of death by homicide than do young male non-Hispanic whites. The Latino community shows a rate of homicide comparable to the black community in the United States. Homicide is the only form of death in which Hispanics show a marked disadvantage relative to the total U.S. population. For the three main groups of Latinos in America—people of Mexican, Cuban, and Puerto Rican descent—who make up 80 percent of the Latino population, the adjusted death rates for homicide are about five times as high as those for the total white population.

The highest annual per capita death rates among Latinos are for Cuba-born males between the ages of twenty-five and forty-four. Mexico-born males from the ages of fifteen to twenty-four have the second-highest mortality rate, followed by Puerto Rico-born males aged twenty-five to forty-four. The death rate of young male Latinos is approximately twice the rate of whites of the same age. Latinas do not show similar patterns of homicide, suicide, or accidental death, and there is no consistent cause of death among young Latinas.

Among middle-aged and elderly Latinos, death rates are similar to Asian groups in the United States, who have comparably low mortality rates at all ages. The statistics for cancer and heart and lung diseases at middle and elderly ages are all comparable to mortality and morbidity among the white and black populations of North America. Puerto Rico-born people have a higher mortality rate than do whites up to the age of fifty-five. After that age, death rates of Puerto Rico-born people are generally lower than those for all U.S. whites as a group.

Selective Migration. In all three main Latino subgroups, with the possible exception of Puerto Rico-born males, mortality from all causes is higher in the country of origin than in the United States. This introduces the idea of selective migration: Only the most psychologically and physically healthy people of other countries are likely to move from their country of birth. In fact, people who emigrate from Latin American countries do, on the whole, live longer than the general populations of their countries of origin.

The Day of the Dead is an opportunity to remember and honor deceased relatives and friends. (Diane C. Lyell)

Cuba-born people have the lowest overall annual rates of death per capita in the United States, followed by Mexico-born and Puerto Rico-born people, then native whites and blacks. Mexico shows the most marked difference in life expectancy of the three Latino countries of origin. Life expectancy was considerably lower in Mexico than among people of Mexican origin living in the United States.

The mortality rates for the children of immigrants are roughly the same as those for the general population in the new country. The first generation of U.S.-born Latinos, whose health is not selected by migration, may show a higher rate of accidental, self-inflicted, or violent deaths. This generation is typically less integrated into the traditional family networks of the old country and is also at odds with the traditions and expectations of the new culture and country; thus, levels of suicide are higher in this generation. The children of Latino immigrants also show a higher rate of psychiatric disorders than do their foreign-born parents.

As second- and third-generation Latinos integrate into the cultures and habits of the majority populations of the United States and Canada, they become less tied to their heritage. Simultaneously, they become more homogenous with the trends of morbidity and mortality typical of the host North American countries.

Causes of Death. Heart disease, cancer, and stroke are the three leading causes of death in the United States and Canada. Latino males show a lower mortality rate for these than do their Anglo counterparts. Among the three subgroups, there are distinct variations in cause-specific deaths: Cuba-born people are less likely to die from diseases of the heart or chronic pulmonary disorders, cerebrovascular disease, accidents, or DIABETES; Mexico-born people show comparatively lower mortality as a result of suicide and malignant neoplasms; and Puerto Rico-born individuals rarely die of lung cancer.

Health Risks. The single most obvious cause of morbidity and mortality in North America is cigarette smoking, which accounts for 25 percent of all deaths and is the most readily identifiable reason for the difference in life expectancies of males and females. Men smoke more and women smoke less; thus, women live longer as a group. Smoking patterns between men and women may be converging, however; as the number of male and female smokers equalizes, the life expectancies of men and women are likely to follow suit.

Mexican Americans smoke less than their non-Hispanic counterparts; those who do smoke tend to smoke fewer cigarettes. Puerto Ricans in the United States also tend to smoke less. Among U.S. ethnic Latino subpopulations, Puerto Rico-born people die of lung cancer least often, followed by Mexico-born and Cuba-born Americans.

In the United States, many people die of coronary heart disease. Changes in health behavior, however, have led to declines in heart-disease mortality in the general population. By smoking less, exercising more, and reducing intake of saturated fats, people are extending their life expectancies. Medical improvements and advances are made constantly and add incrementally to the number of years a person can expect to live. As people become more health conscious and better informed about healthy diet and exercise programs, many chronic heart disorders can be delayed or prevented altogether. Among U.S. Latinos, Cuba-born people have the lowest heart-disease mortality rate, followed closely by Mexico-born and Puerto Rico-born people.

The consumption of alcohol is directly correlated to cirrhosis of the liver, homicide, and motor vehicle fatalities. Latinos drink less alcohol than Anglos, but there are proportionately more heavy drinkers among Latinos (*see* ALCOHOLISM). Although Puerto Ricans drink relatively less beer and wine, they have an extremely high per capita intake of hard liquor. Not surprisingly, the Puerto Rican death rate from cirrhosis of the liver almost doubles that of people born in Cuba or Mexico. Puerto Ricans also have a higher rate of homicide deaths.

Latino females drink more wine and liquor than beer, but they drink less frequently and in smaller quantities than Latino men do. Thus, alcohol mortality rates among women are lower. Latino men drink greater quantities of beer, wine, and hard liquor and drink more often than women; they are thus more likely to acquire cirrhosis of the liver in later life or to die a violent death as a young person. Latino females drink alcohol and smoke less as youths and live longer as a result. Women are less likely than men to die of lung cancer or cirrhosis of the liver. They do, however, suffer a comparable number of deaths from obesity, high blood pressure, and diabetes.

Diabetes and High Blood Pressure. Mexican Americans have more cases of DIABETES per capita than do people of the other two major subgroups. Type II diabetes mellitus is two to five times more common among Mexican Americans than among the general population. Latinos show higher rates of obesity and exhibit less inclination to exercise and engage in physical activity than Anglos do. Death from diabetes is highest for people of Mexican or Puerto Rican heritage. African Americans are also more susceptible to diabetes than are members of the other groups. Cuban and non-Hispanic white Americans acquire diabetes half as often as the rest of the population.

High blood pressure is the cause of many deaths in the United States and in Canada. Massive coronary attacks, stroke, and heart paralysis are frequent results of high blood pressure. High blood pressure is caused by a number of factors, including physical or psychological stress, poor diet, lax exercise patterns, and heredity. The rates of high blood pressure are nearly equal among Latinos, but Puerto Ricans have the highest rates, followed by Cuban Americans and Mexican Americans. Anglos and Mexican Americans have about the same rates of high blood pressure, but Mexican American males do not take blood pressure medications as often as Anglos and are therefore less successful in controlling HYPERTENSION.—*Beaird Glover*
SUGGESTED READINGS:

• Kearl, Michael C. *Endings*. New York: Oxford University Press, 1989. Gives historical and modern sociological perspectives on death and dying relative to a wide range of ethnicities.

• Markides, Kyriakos S., and Charles H. Mindel. *Aging and Ethnicity*. Newbury Park, Calif.: Sage Publications, 1987. A gerontological study applying to all ethnic groups in the United States.

• Paz, Octavio. *The Labyrinth of Solitude*. Translated by Lysander Kemp. New York: Grove Press, 1961. Essays concerning national characteristics of Mexico and Mexican culture.

• Rosenwaike, Ira, ed. *Mortality of Hispanic Populations: Mexicans, Puerto Ricans, and Cubans in the United States and in the Home Countries*. New York: Greenwood Press, 1991. Studies in population and urban demography.

Moré, Benny (Bartolomé Maximiliano Moré Gutierrez; Aug. 24, 1919, Cienfuegos, Cuba—Feb. 19, 1963, Havana, Cuba): Singer and bandleader. Moré's musical career began in his native Cuba, where he played the guitar and sang in cafés and bars.

In the early 1940's, he went to Havana and joined the bohemian circle of musicians, also singing with the Cuarteto Cordero and the Sexteto Cauto on local radio station programs. He made his recording debut with the famous group of Miguel Matamoros and also traveled to Mexico, where he met Pérez PRADO, with whom he also toured and recorded.

In 1953, back in Cuba, Moré organized a big jazz band, Banda Gigante, composed of twenty-one musi-

cians with a central rhythmic section. The band became popular throughout the Caribbean and in both South and North America. It gathered, among others, the pianist Peruchín Justiz, trumpeter Alfredo "Chocolate" Armenteros, trombonist Generoso Jiménez, and Moré's brother Delfín.

Moré's numerous recordings of songs, *sones*, BOLEROS, MAMBOS, *GUARACHAS*, and many other musical forms have been issued by various record companies. For example, the seven-volume collection *Benny Moré: Sonero Mayor* contains the best blend in terms of musical forms and Moré's powerful interpretations. *Magia Antillana* and *The Most from Benny Moré* have been reissued on compact disc.

Moreira Guimorva, Airto (b. Aug. 5, 1941, Itaiópolis, Brazil): Jazz percussionist and singer. At a very early age, Moreira learned to sing and play various instruments. He traveled around Brazil collecting hundreds of musical instruments.

Airto Moreira performs at the 1978 Newport Jazz Festival. (AP/Wide World Photos)

In 1968, Moreira became one of the original members of the jazz-rock group Weather Report. The group developed an unconventional style of playing, discarding the traditional jazz role of soloist and accompanist, letting each player take the lead by turn, thus creating continuously changing sound textures.

After moving to New York, Moreira made his first recordings with Miles Davis. He then became first percussionist and drummer for Chick Corea's group Return to Forever.

In the 1970's, Moreira became one of the best-known percussionists in American jazz. He employed a wide range of traditional and self-invented musical devices, including bells, rattles, shakes, and bows, to achieve new musical colors and create unusual rhythmic patterns.

Moreira may be the single most influential of all Brazilian musicians to come to the United States. His album *Identities* is considered by many to be his most adventurous and successful experiment. It is a fusion of rock, Afro-Brazilian, and Amerindian elements. Moreira was married to Brazilian singer Flora PURIM, and they performed together in numerous concerts and on albums.

Moreno: Having a dark complexion. *Moreno*, meaning "brown," is an adjective referring to the color of a person's skin. Latin Americans with dark hair and skin are sometimes referred to as *moreno* by their peers. The term is not derogatory but merely descriptive. *Moreno* and its female counterpart, *morena*, are sometimes used as terms of endearment.

Moreno, Antonio (Antonio Garrido Monteagudo y Moreno; Sept. 26, 1887, Madrid, Spain—1967): Actor. After his father's early death, Moreno moved with his mother to Gibraltar, where he learned to speak English. He was brought to the United States at the age of fourteen by a wealthy American couple for whom he had served as an interpreter in Gibraltar. While attending school, he acted with a traveling stock theater company and developed his performing skills.

Moreno made his motion-picture debut in 1912 in a D. W. Griffith feature. Over the next two decades, he appeared in more than one hundred feature films. His credits include *The House of Discord* (1913), *The Quality of Mercy* (1915), *The Secret of the Hills* (1921), *My American Wife* (1923, opposite Gloria Swanson), *The Exciters* (1923, opposite Bebe Daniels), *One Year to Live* (1925), *Mare Nostrum* (1926), and *Romance of the Rio Grande* (1929).

Moreno was the prototype of the "Latin lover" later personified by Rudolph Valentino. With the advent of talkies in the late 1920's and early 1930's, however, Moreno's career waned, and he was typecast in smaller, stereotypically Latino character roles. Nevertheless, he continued working into the 1950's in such films as *Rose of the Rio Grande* (1938), *Captain from Castile* (1947), and *Creature from the Black Lagoon* (1954).

Moreno, Luisa (1906, Guatemala—c. 1990, Mexico): Labor union organizer. During a thirty-year career as a labor activist, Moreno organized garment workers in New York, cigar workers in Florida, pecan shellers in Texas, and workers of many kinds in California. In 1938, she founded the National Congress of Spanish Speaking People (El Congreso de los Pueblos de Habla Español), one of the first national organizations to fight for civil rights for Latinos. Also active in established union organizations, she rose from editor to the position of international vice president of the UNITED CANNERY, AGRICULTURAL, PACKING AND ALLIED WORKERS OF AMERICA (UCAPAWA). She helped bring important Mexican government figures to Los Angeles to observe the treatment of Mexicans there; this led to strained relationships between the United States and Mexico. She was deported under the McCarran-Walter Immigration Act, which called for the deportation of "radical" foreigners and communist sympathizers. She never returned to the United States.

Moreno, Rita (Rosa Dolores Alverio; b. Dec. 11, 1931, Humacao, Puerto Rico): Actress and dancer. Moreno began performing as a child and soon developed her dancing, singing, and acting skills to professional levels. In 1945, at the age of fourteen, she made her Broadway debut. As a teenager, she also sang in nightclubs and dubbed U.S. films into Spanish for foreign release.

After signing with Metro-Goldwyn-Mayer (MGM), Moreno made her film debut in 1950 in *So Young, So Bad*. Her other early films include *Singin' in the Rain* (1952), *The Fabulous Señorita* (1952), *The Ring* (1952), *Cattle Town* (1952), *Latin Lovers* (1953), and *Jivaro* (1953). She was featured on the cover of *Life* magazine in 1954; two years later, she appeared on Broadway in *The King and I*. Her other Broadway credits include *The Sign in Sidney Brustein's Window* (1964), *Elmer Gantry* (1969), *The Ritz* (1975), and the female version of *The Odd Couple* (1985).

Rita Moreno holds her Oscar for her role in West Side Story. (AP/Wide World Photos)

Moreno is the first performer to have won all four major U.S. entertainment-industry awards: a 1962 Oscar as best supporting actress in *West Side Story*, a 1973 Grammy for best recording for an *Electric Company* sound track, a 1975 Tony for best supporting actress in *The Rink*, and 1977 and 1978 Emmys for appearances on *The Muppet Show* and *The Rockford Files*.

Moreno Reyes, Mario. *See* **Cantinflas**

Morfi, Juan Agustín (c. 1710, Galicia, Spain—Oct. 20, 1783, Mexico): Priest and writer. Morfi traveled to the colony of New Spain in 1752. He taught theology at Santiago de Tlatelolco. Later, he traveled extensively through the colonies of New Spain, New Galicia, and New Vizcaya. In 1777, he went with Teodoro de Croix to territories north of the Rio Grande. His duty was to convert the natives to Christianity. He returned to Mexico and died in 1783.

Morfi's impact came from his writings. During his travels, he made copious notes on the geography and peoples of the regions. His *History of Texas, 1673-1779* (1935, translated by Carlos Eduardo Castañeda) has become a major source for the study of Texas during the colonial period.

Morín, Raul R. (July 26, 1913, Lockhart, Tex.—1967): Author and civic leader. Morín, a Mexican American, received his early education in Texas, including a commercial art education. After service in the Civilian Conservation Corps, Morín settled in Los Angeles in the mid-1930's, enrolling in the Frank Wiggins Trade School and later opening a sign-printing business.

As an infantryman in World War II, Morín was wounded in the Battle of the Bulge. He read extensively and took journalism, among other classes, during his hospital recovery, which lasted nearly two years. After his discharge, he returned to his sign-painting business with a greater awareness of the discrimination Mexican Americans suffered despite their courage and sacrifice during the war.

In a personal effort to improve race relations, Morín finished his work on Hispanic valor and service during the war, *Among the Valiant*. After ten years, it finally was published through the efforts of the AMERICAN G.I. FORUM, the Chicano veterans' organization.

Morín was active in Mexican American Democratic politics, organizations, and veteran and civic groups during the 1950's and 1960's. He was appointed to many commissions and boards, including the Mayor of Los Angeles' Advisory Committee. In 1968, a veteran's memorial in East Los Angeles was dedicated as the Raul R. Morín Memorial Square.

Mormons: Religious denomination. Although Mormons (members of the Church of Latter Day Saints) have traditionally been European American, the church has increasingly reached out to potential Latino converts in the twentieth century.

Initial contact between Spanish-speaking peoples and the Mormons occurred when Mormon pioneers arrived in 1847 in the area that would eventually become Utah. The entire region was still part of the sovereign nation of Mexico, but the MEXICAN AMERICAN WAR (1846-1848), which would transfer the intermountain zone to the United States, was near its end. This change of sovereignty meant that any Hispanic inhabitants of the region who remained behind in U.S. territory faced changes in citizenship and uncertain protection from the government.

Utah and other former Mexican zones with substantial Mormon and Hispanic populations (Nevada and Idaho) did not become states for a number of decades. Very few conversions of Hispanics to Mormonism occurred in this period of time.

By 1900, however, several events changed relations between the two communities. First, a rising (but definitely still minority) population of non-Mormons had established themselves in the intermountain zone to work in the booming mining industry or on the transcontinental railway. As a result of this demographic change, certain religious groups, particularly Roman Catholics, became determined to mark their presence in an area that was predominantly Mormon (*see* CATHOLIC CHURCH AND CATHOLICISM). Because the Hispanic minority in the region was traditionally Catholic, this emphasis on Catholic ecclesiastical presence (Salt Lake City is one of the few intermountain cities to have a cathedral) can be seen as a desire to provide Latinos with the assurance that their religious heritage need not be put to question. Increased Mormon concern for proselytism among Latinos soon followed.

By the 1920's, enough Latinos in Utah had converted to Mormonism to impel them to call for the creation of their own ward, or administrative/religious subcommunity. This specifically Latino ward bore the name Lucero (light). Unlike more typical wards for families living in an immediate neighborhood, the Lucero ward was designed to provide a central gathering place for both worship and community information services for Latino Mormons in and beyond the region.

In later decades, widespread missionary operations by the Latter Day Saints began in many countries of Central and South America. Many young Mormon men and women are called yearly to fulfill missionary obligations in Spanish-speaking countries and increasingly in Latino communities in the United States. For example, in the heavily Latino San Gabriel Valley east of Los Angeles in 1994, one-third of Mormon missionaries were assigned to convert Latinos, and Latinos represented 20 percent of the Mormon membership in the area.

To prepare such missionaries, the church maintains formal training programs in Spanish and Latin American culture. The goal is to gain enough converts to establish wards throughout Latin America and the United States to meet the needs of new Mormon communities.

Moroles, Jesús Bautista (b. Sept. 22, 1950, Corpus Christi, Tex.): Sculptor. As a child, Moroles helped his father, who had emigrated from Mexico, renovate a house for the family in Oak Cliff, Texas. He was trained in construction by an uncle, who helped him obtain construction jobs. As a teenager, Moroles attended Crozier Tech, a vocational school in Dallas, Texas, and focused his coursework on commercial art. He received both his first job offer and a draft notice shortly after graduation.

In 1973, following four years in the Air Force that included service in Thailand, Moroles enrolled in El Centro Junior College in Dallas. After two years of required courses and courses in art, Moroles earned his associate of arts degree. He then enrolled at North Texas State University, where he strengthened skills in drafting, electronics, math, and woodworking that would aid in his later artistic work. He met artist Luis Alfonso JIMÉNEZ, Jr., in 1978, during his final year at North Texas State University, and later apprenticed for a year with Jiménez. Following his apprenticeship, Moroles traveled to Italy for a year to study the stone sculptures there. He returned to Texas and began constructing sculptures of his own that have been featured in numerous individual shows. His sculptures have been displayed at various locations including the Museum of Fine Arts in Santa Fe, New Mexico, and the University of Houston.

Mortality. *See* **Morbidity and mortality**

Morton, Carlos (b. Oct. 15, 1947, Chicago, Ill.): Playwright. The son of Mexican American parents, Morton was graduated from the University of Texas at El Paso in 1975 and received a master's degree in playwriting from the University of California, San Diego, in 1979. In 1987, he received a doctorate from the University of Texas at Austin. He has taught at the University of California, Riverside.

Morton's first important writing was a chapbook of poems, titled *White Heroin Winter*, that he produced in 1971. In 1974, he wrote *El Jardin*, a play that has been produced widely at universities and Hispanic community arts centers and has helped to make him one of the most widely produced Latino playwrights in the United States. His other plays have been published in two collections, *The Many Deaths of Danny Rosales and Other Plays* (1983) and *Johnny Tenorio and Other Plays* (1991).

Morton's *The Many Deaths of Danny Rosales* has been presented at the Los Angeles Bilingual Foundation for the Arts, and *Pancho Diablo* has been staged at the New York Shakespeare Festival. His plays, which reflect the street life of Hispanic American communities, are written in urban dialects that combine English and Spanish.

Mota, Manny (Manuel Rafael Mota y Geronimo; b. Feb. 18, 1939, Santo Domingo, Dominican Republic): Baseball player. Mota, a small right-handed hitter, made his major league debut with the San Francisco Giants in 1962. Traded to the Pittsburgh Pirates the following season, he excelled as a role player and occasional starter, capable of playing the outfield, second base, and third base and once even filling in as a catcher. He also developed the skill for which he would become best known: the ability to come off the bench in the late innings and deliver a key pinch hit.

In 1966, Mota batted .332, and he hit better than .300 in six of the following seven seasons. In 1969, he played briefly with the Montreal Expos before settling in as the Los Angeles Dodgers' pinch-hitting specialist. He hit .600 as a pinch hitter in three National League playoff series; in the third game of the 1977 playoffs, his ninth-inning double led the Dodgers to a come-from-behind win over the Philadelphia Phillies. He remained a remarkably effective pinch hitter past the age when most players have retired, posting averages of .395, .303, .357, and .429 in consecutive seasons after his thirty-ninth birthday. After the 1980 season, he retired to become a full-time

Manny Mota. (AP/Wide World Photos)

coach, but in 1982 the Dodgers activated the forty-four-year-old Mota for a pinch-hitting appearance (he did not get a hit). His total of 150 career pinch hits is a major league record.

Mothers of East L.A. (MELA): Group formed to protect the quality of life in EAST LOS ANGELES. MELA was established in 1986 by five mothers who met to discuss a proposed state prison to be built in East Los Angeles. These women, all long-term residents of the area, went door to door to educate neighborhood residents on the prison issue and used their connections in the community through parish groups, school groups, and neighborhood watch teams to help create a base of support. They eventually filed a lawsuit to make sure the state would abide by constitutional provisions and statutes regarding the project. MELA developed a large membership and grassroots network of activists, including various Catholic clergy and Mexican American government representatives. MELA has organized against other proposed projects in East Los Angeles including a plan to build a toxic waste incinerator.

Mount Pleasant riots (May 5 and 6, 1991): Two days of civil disturbances in the Latino community of Mount Pleasant, an area of WASHINGTON, D.C., focused attention on the social conditions faced by recent Central American immigrants. On May 5, 1991, two Washington police officers arrested two people for disorderly conduct. During the arrest, a third person, Salvadoran Daniel Enrique Gomez, became "disorderly," according to police. One officer fired, wounding Gomez. Police contended that Gomez had pulled a knife and had lunged at one of the officers. Witnesses to the shooting, however, said that Gomez was already handcuffed behind his back when he was shot.

The incident ignited smoldering hostility between Mount Pleasant's established African American and Anglo communities and the area's recent immigrants from Central America, particularly El Salvador. The shooting sparked two nights of riots that resulted in damage to thirty-one businesses and twenty-one city buses. Seventeen fires were set, and 125 immediate arrests were made.

Mount Pleasant is a racially and economically diverse neighborhood in the northwest part of Washington, D.C. At the time of the disturbances, the ethnic breakdown for the area was 35 percent African American, 35 percent Anglo, and 27 percent Latino. Mount Pleasant borders Adams-Morgan, an affluent Washington neighborhood.

The Latino population in Washington increased rapidly in the 1980's, largely as a result of civil war and strife in Central America. The 1990 U.S. Census reported 31,358 Latinos in Washington, more than ten thousand of whom were from El Salvador. The remainder of the Latino population consisted of people of Mexican, Puerto Rican, Cuban, Guatemalan, Honduran, Nicaraguan, and Dominican descent. This diverse population was divided by a host of complexities, including a dissimilarity in dialects, tensions between rural newcomers and urban residents, and differences in ideological beliefs, religious beliefs, and immigration status. The riots were stoked by this uneasy mixture as well as by an enormous population growth in a short span of time in a constricted place.

The first night of the riots was entirely spontaneous, prompted by the unfairness described by witnesses to the Gomez shooting. Anger and racial injustice felt by the Latino community literally and figuratively fueled the fires that night. On the second night, local news organizations began to broadcast from the neighborhood before evening fell, speculating as to when and where rioting would commence. City residents observed that this decision by broadcasters may have played a part in inviting even more destruction of property.

Police figures indicated that of the 230 people charged in connection with the riots and subsequent curfews, 25 percent were Hispanic and 16 percent were juveniles. *The Washington Post* conducted its own survey of 105 of the 193 adults arrested and found that more than half were African American, 38 percent were Hispanic, 8 percent were Anglo, and 1 percent were Asian.

The D.C. Latino Civil Rights Task Force was organized as a result of the riots and their underlying causes. The task force made specific recommendations to improve communications between the city government and the Latino population.

In January, 1993, the U.S. Commission on Civil Rights issued a report that acknowledged, among other factors, that a pattern of miscommunication and mistrust had developed between the Latino residents and the city police department. As a result, the city government pledged to work more closely with the Latino community.

Movimiento Estudiantil Chicano de Aztlán, El (MECHA): Chicano student group. In 1969, at the Conference of Santa Barbara, Chicano college students and faculty decided to unite the various Chicano

MECHA participates in a variety of political causes, often in concert with other groups. (Tony Cuevas)

student groups already in existence under a central umbrella organization with one ideology and common purpose. The result was MECHA, a name that included the new concepts of Chicano and AZTLÁN (the mythical origin of Aztec civilization). MECHA's organizers outlined their goals in *El PLAN DE SANTA BÁRBARA: A CHICANO PLAN FOR HIGHER EDUCATION*.

MECHA galvanized new levels of organized political commitment among Mexican American students. Its demands were radical. Primary among those demands was establishment of CHICANO STUDIES PROGRAMS at four-year colleges. Students fought for more control of educational opportunity programs on campus to increase recruitment of Mexican American students. They also forged links with the Chicano community by creating tutoring and mentoring centers, participating in local politics, and working with other organizations. By constantly challenging existing limits, MECHA succeeded in achieving many of its goals while raising the political consciousness of Mexican Americans.

By the early 1970's, Chicano student activism began to decline, both as part of a larger trend in the CHICANO MOVEMENT and as a result of internal

schisms in MECHA. Some of MECHA's original leaders had graduated, leaving behind a new generation of students. More specialized Chicano student groups emerged that were focused on specific professions or academic fields of interest and were more concerned with individual advancement than with collective political concerns. Some college administrations had also clamped down on MECHA activities.

In 1973, ideological struggles within MECHA came to a head at a planning conference. Some leaders believed that CULTURAL NATIONALISM should provide a framework for the group's ideology, while others believed in Marxist principles. The Marxists walked out of the conference and left MECHA, considerably denting the group's membership and level of activism.

During the 1980's, MECHA membership rose and fell. Many observers saw the group as more social than activist during this period, although political activity varied from chapter to chapter. Internal struggles continued over ideological issues such as membership qualifications and the role of women. New guidelines stressing tolerance were established in California.

In the 1990's, MECHA saw a resurgence in interest and commitment. Among its primary concerns were affirmative action, the high dropout rate of Chicano students, elimination of bilingual programs, discrepancies in funding among school districts, college funding cuts, immigration, and farmworker issues.

Movimiento Pro Independencia (MPI): Political party. The MPI had as its goal independence of Puerto Rico from the United States. Beginning in 1961, the MPI, a radical offshoot of the Popular Independence Party, proclaimed that boycotting the entire electoral process was the best strategy to achieve a free Puerto Rico.

Although not embracing violence, the MPI was not opposed to using violence as a means to achieve its ends. It embraced a Marxist-Leninist ideology popular at the time. The Partido Socialista Puertorriqueño was formed as a result of an MPI assembly held on November 28, 1971. The MPI sought to form an electoral front with the Independence Party; thus, it made the move to convert itself into a political party. The coalition of the MPI and the Independence Party was not accepted, so the Partido Socialista Puertorriqueño did not participate in the 1972 election.

Moya del Pino, José (1891, Cordova, Spain—1969, Ross, Calif.): Artist. Moya del Pino, a muralist, did much of his work in the 1930's under WORKS PROGRESS ADMINISTRATION programs of the federal government. During the 1930's, he painted murals in the Coit Tower in San Francisco, California, as well as in Stockton, Redwood City, and Lancaster, all in California. In 1933, he completed murals incorporating Aztec and Mayan motifs for the Aztec Brewery in San Diego. These murals were saved in the late 1980's when the brewery, which had been out of operation for more than three decades, was scheduled for destruction.

Moya del Pino's murals were painted specifically for their locations, incorporating elements particular to the area. For example, the Redwood City mural depicts the important agricultural activities of the area, and the Lancaster mural shows water pipe being hauled to the area, which is a desert valley. Most of Moya del Pino's murals were done in California.

Mujeres Activas en Letras y Cambio Social: Research and activist group. Founded in 1982, this group seeks to facilitate its members' research and writing on Chicanas and other Latinas. All members are currently employed in higher education and are seeking to fight "race, class, and gender oppression in universities." The group seeks to bridge the gap between intellec-

tual work and active commitment in Hispanic communities.

The group works to develop strategies to promote social change. It also seeks to promote college-level courses on Chicanas and/or Latinas in the United States. It documents, analyzes, and interprets the Chicana experience in the United States and the condition of women in the home and the workplace.

The organizational philosophy is one of social and political justice as promoted by academic and community involvement. The struggle for social and economic justice is an integral part of organizational objectives. The group operates a speakers' bureau and offers placement services as well as maintaining biographical archives. It annually publishes monographical works under the title *Trabajos Monográficos: Studies in Chicana/Latina Research*.

Multicultural education: Educational reform movement. Multicultural education seeks to restructure schools so that students of all races, cultures, and social classes and of both genders will have equal opportunities to learn. In addition, multicultural education attempts to assist students in developing values, attitudes and beliefs, skills, and knowledge that will help them function cross-culturally and appreciate people with cultural backgrounds different from their own.

Approaches. A number of approaches to multicultural education, used alone or in combination, could help to achieve the goals mentioned above. Some approaches are curricular, adding to or changing the content of what is taught. Some emphasize achievement and thus work to increase the academic achievement of students traditionally disadvantaged by the schools, such as those from lower income groups, students of color, women, students with disabilities, and gay and lesbian students. Another approach is intergroup education or prejudice reduction, which seeks to develop positive attitudes in all students toward those different in some ways from themselves.

Curricular approaches can involve such activities as celebrating the holidays, heroes, and heroines of different cultures; workshops for teachers; or use of textbooks with a multicultural focus. Examples of achievement-oriented approaches include attempts to match learning styles with teachers and teaching styles, bilingual and bicultural programs, targeted programs in fields such as science, math, and computer skills for female students (traditionally underrepresented in these areas), and separate schools for certain

A member of a Mayan theater troupe performs for a group of schoolchildren. (Impact Visuals, Tom McKitterick)

groups (for example, male African American students). Intergroup education approaches include prejudice reduction activities such as those of the National Coalition Building Institute and World of Difference, desegregation of schools (with accompanying interventions to prevent "resegregation"), and cooperative learning. (*See* DISCRIMINATION, BIGOTRY, AND PREJUDICE AGAINST LATINOS; SEGREGATION, DESEGREGATION, AND INTEGRATION.)

Curriculum changes are often categorized as "curricular infusion" or "curricular transformation." In curricular infusion, topics and issues from various cultures or perspectives are brought into the existing curriculum in places where they seem appropriate to teachers and curricular experts. In other words, it is an "additive" approach. Often this infusion is well-meaning in theory but tends to continue an Anglo or Western perspective, with information and ideas from other perspectives tacked on as asides.

Curricular transformation, considered more desirable by most multicultural education experts, is somewhat harder to bring about. In curricular transformation, the goal is to understand concepts, events, and people from different cultural, ethnic, and gender-related perspectives and points of view. This requires much of teachers, including a recognition that knowledge is a social construction. Teachers must also find and bring alive resources that will illustrate the voices, thoughts, and feelings of a variety of peoples affected by such things as events in history, scientific discoveries, and even English grammar. Because the training of many teachers has focused on Western culture and thought, this transformation would be difficult to achieve and would require conscious efforts and possibly retraining on the part of teachers.

Contrasts with Traditional Education. Multicultural education differs from what could be labeled the "traditional" education of the United States in that multicultural education recognizes that each person sees the world from a unique perspective and that the "traditional" curriculum has shown the world from a Eurocentric, middle-class perspective. Perhaps unintentionally, traditional curriculum materials often picture the "typical" family as white, with two parents, two children, and perhaps a dog, in a suburban setting. Multicultural texts might, for example, picture persons with different skin hues and names such as García, Runningstone, and Antonici instead of Smith, Jones, and Williams.

Controversies. Efforts to implement multicultural education are controversial. One controversy concerns the concept of assimilation, or the "MELTING POT." One school of thought holds that people of cultures should blend in, with the implicit assumption that the Anglo culture will dominate. The opposing school believes that different cultures and beliefs should coexist and be appreciated by everyone.

Multicultural education, with its tenet of "social construction of knowledge," threatens many people because it raises questions regarding the "canon" and the nature of truth. Teachers often worry, in addition, that adding content to the curriculum will necessitate inadequate, superficial instruction because of the volume of topics requiring some attention. Proponents of multicultural education answer that it can entail a different way of viewing the current curriculum rather than additions to that curriculum.

Impact. Implications for Latinos are many. In the area of curricular transformation, many items of traditional content would undoubtedly be changed if studied from the perspectives of Cuban Americans, Mexican Americans, Puerto Ricans, and other Latino groups. Hiring of more Latino teachers would help to transform the curriculum by providing role models and those who could add the perspective of their history and culture. Textbooks in all fields using illustrations

Language classes can offer introductions to different cultures. (James Shaffer)

of Latinos would stimulate interest in students who currently do not see themselves in the books they read. Bilingual and bicultural programs could improve the academic achievement of Spanish-speaking students (*see* EDUCATION AND ACADEMIC ACHIEVEMENT).

In terms of other programs to improve the academic achievement of Latinos, programs to match teachers with their students' learning styles could help, as could programs to show teachers techniques that would reward rather than punish varied learning styles and cultural differences (*see* TEACHERS AND TEACHING STYLES). Finally, intergroup education programs that help students appreciate, not demean, those who are different hold the promise of helping those of all races and cultures to coexist in schools and communities.

—*M. C. Ware*

SUGGESTED READINGS: • Banks, James A. *An Introduction to Multicultural Education*. Boston: Allyn and Bacon, 1994. • Banks, James A., and Cherry McGee Banks. *Multicultural Education: Issues and Perspectives*. 2d ed. Boston: Allyn and Bacon, 1993. • Banks, James A., C. E. Cortes, G. Gay, R. L. Garcia, and A. Ochoa. *Curriculum Guidelines for Multicultural Education*. Washington, D.C.: National Council for Social Studies, 1992. • Bennett, Christine I. *Comprehensive Multicultural Education: Theory and Practice*. Boston: Allyn and Bacon, 1990. • Sleeter, C. E., and C. A. Grant. *Making Choices for Multicultural Education*. Columbus, Ohio: Merrill, 1988. • Tiedt, Pamela L., and Iris M. Tiedt. *Multicultural Teaching: A Handbook of Activities, Information, and Resources*. 3d ed. Boston: Allyn and Bacon, 1990.

Multiculturalism: Recognition of the concurrent existence of various cultures within the same society. Proponents of conscious multiculturalism try to discourage any one culture within a society from being perceived as dominant, even if some traits of one culture predominate. Having an official language, for example, does not imply having an official culture.

Americans of color, including Latinos and African Americans, began using the term "multiculturalism" in the 1980's to stress the need to include cultural diversity in public life and education. They perceived mul-

Students can gain exposure to different cultures by learning about their classmates. (James Shaffer)

ticulturalism as a way of empowering previously marginalized groups.

Multiculturalism is both a fact of life in American society and an ideology. Diversity in the population, with about one of four Americans in 1990 being people of color, called for attention to cultural differences. Members of culturally different groups have experienced alienation from mainstream society and have called for recognition of the value of their cultures.

The MELTING POT THEORY of assimilation states that as people of different cultures enter a society, their cultural traits will mix, with a common culture emerging (*see* ACCULTURATION VERSUS ASSIMILATION). This theory has been abandoned in large part in the United States as various groups have made increasingly vocal demands that their cultural identities be recognized and celebrated rather than being lost through mixing.

More people are accepting the pluralistic nature of culture in the United States. As an ideal, multiculturalism encourages treating members of a culturally diverse society with dignity, respect, and responsibility. According to proponents of multiculturalism, members of identifiable groups rather than scholars from other backgrounds should be the primary source of information about those groups' situation, condition, and future direction. Multiculturalism recognizes that populations are heterogeneous and that each person is unique; thus, stereotypes should be avoided. Institutions dealing with social and cultural issues, such as schools, should have well-defined policy statements and curricula that reflect recognition of the importance of multiculturalism.

Education is crucial to achieving the ideal of multiculturalism, and much of the debate and activity concerning multiculturalism has taken place in educational settings. Multiculturalism demands that educators be aware of RACISM and alienation as well as the spectrum of diverse heritages within American society. In 1972, the Commission on Multicultural Education of the American Association of Colleges of Teacher Education issued a statement proclaiming that multiculturalism "recognizes cultural diversity as a fact of life in American society, and it affirms that this cultural diversity is a valuable resource that should be preserved and extended."

A multicultural approach to various cultures may consider the many elements that form those cultures. Among these are sociopolitical factors, the culture's history of oppression, the experience of prejudice and racism, poverty within the culture, language and the arts, religious practices, child-rearing practices, family roles and structure, and the degree of opposition to acculturation. A multicultural society encourages the parallel development of different cultures, considers the needs of each, and recognizes the enrichment this diversity brings to the society as a whole.

Anthony Muñoz. (AP/Wide World Photos)

Muñoz, Anthony (Michael Anthony Muñoz; b. Aug. 19, 1958, Ontario, Calif.): Football player. Muñoz, a 6-foot-6-inch, 285-pound offensive lineman, was considered a top professional prospect during his college career at the University of Southern California (USC). Although he suffered a series of knee injuries while at USC, his size and speed convinced the Cincinnati Bengals of the National Football League (NFL) to select Muñoz, a Mexican American, with the third overall pick of the 1980 NFL draft. Muñoz had a tremendous rookie season. Although the Bengals lost the Super Bowl to the San Francisco 49ers, the young player took NFL Lineman of the Year and Cincinnati Bengal Man of the Year honors. He followed his promising start by solidifying his status as one of the league's top linemen, earning ten Pro Bowl nominations in eleven seasons. When he retired after thirteen seasons with the Bengals, he was considered to be a certain future Hall of Fame inductee.

Carlos Muñoz, Jr. (David Bacon)

Muñoz, Carlos, Jr. (b. Aug. 25, 1939, El Paso, Tex.): Educator, writer, and historian. A writer on Chicano protest and politics, Muñoz is the author of *Youth, Identity, Power: The Chicano Movement* (1989). In 1973, he was one of the founders of the National Association for Chicano Studies. Earlier, he co-founded El MOVIMIENTO ESTUDIANTIL CHICANO DE AZTLÁN and La RAZA UNIDA PARTY.

Muñoz attended East Los Angeles College and earned his A.A. at Los Angeles City College in 1964. He holds a B.A. in political science from California State University, Los Angeles (1967) and a Ph.D. in government from Claremont Graduate School (1973). Muñoz worked as an instructor at California State University, Los Angeles, from 1968 to 1969, becoming the founding chair of the first Mexican American Chicano Studies department in the United States in 1968. He joined the faculty of Pitzer College of the Claremont Colleges in 1969. In 1970, he was made an assistant professor at the University of California, Irvine. In 1976, he joined the staff of the University of California, Berkeley, as an associate professor. He was a key adviser during Jesse Jackson's 1988 presidential campaign.

Muñoz Marín, Luis (Feb. 18, 1898, San Juan, Puerto Rico—Apr. 30, 1980, San Juan, Puerto Rico): Politician, journalist, and poet. Muñoz Marín was the son of Amalia Marín and Luis MUÑOZ RIVERA, who served in the cabinet of the autonomist government of Puerto Rico in 1898 and 1899 and was resident commissioner from 1910 to 1916, representing Puerto Rico in the U.S. Congress with the right to speak but no vote. While his father served as resident commissioner in Washington, D.C., Muñoz Marín studied journalism at Georgetown University. He later spent considerable amounts of time in Greenwich Village in New York City, writing and familiarizing himself with U.S. politics.

Muñoz Marín believed in the independence of Puerto Rico and in 1920 joined the Socialist Party in Puerto Rico. In 1924, he left the party and Puerto Rico to return to the mainland, where he wrote for publications such as *The Nation* and *The American Mercury*. In 1931, he returned to Puerto Rico and joined the Liberal Party. He was elected as a senator in 1932 and took over *La Democracia*, which had been his father's newspaper.

Muñoz Marín believed that Puerto Rico's economy had to be strengthened before the country could gain its freedom. He and others, such as Felisa Rincón de Gautier, set out to combat hunger, disease, and poverty by forming the PARTIDO POPULAR DEMOCRÁTICO, or Popular Democratic Party, in 1938. It launched a massive grassroots campaign among the *jíbaros* (farmers) of Puerto Rico's countryside under the slogan "Pan, Tierra, y Libertad" (bread, land, and liberty). Muñoz Marín was elected senator. In 1940, he became president of the Puerto Rican Senate, and by 1944 the PDP had control of the legislature. Under his guidance, Puerto Rico developed a plan to create jobs and build hospitals, schools, roads, housing projects, and power plants, primarily by luring U.S. companies to relocate their factories through tax incentives and cheap labor. This plan, known as Manos a la Obra (OPERATION BOOTSTRAP), helped Puerto Rico to become the Latin American country with the highest per capita income.

The U.S. Congress granted Puerto Rico the right to elect its own governor, and in 1948 Muñoz Marín won that position. Under his leadership, in 1952 Puerto Rico became officially known as the Estado Libre Asociado or ELA (Free Associated State), a self-governing entity with its own constitution, subject to the U.S. Congress. It was the first time that Puerto Rico collectively unfurled its own flag and sang its own national anthem.

Luis Muñoz Marín casts his ballot in the 1948 election for the governorship of Puerto Rico. (AP/Wide World Photos)

In 1963, Muñoz Marín became the first Puerto Rican to receive the Presidential Medal of Freedom, awarded to him by President John F. Kennedy. Muñoz Marín served four consecutive terms; he chose not to run for re-election in 1964.

Muñoz Rivera, Luis (July 17, 1859, Barranquitas, Puerto Rico—Nov. 15, 1916, Santurce, Puerto Rico): Politician. By the late 1890's, Muñoz Rivera was known as the editor of the Ponce newspaper *La Democracia* and as an outspoken critic of Spanish rule. In 1897, he was a member of the autonomist commission that persuaded Spain to grant an autonomist constitution for Puerto Rico.

Muñoz Rivera insisted on retaining home rule after the SPANISH-AMERICAN WAR, but this sentiment clashed with American estimates of Puerto Rican abilities. As a result of the FORAKER ACT of 1900, Puerto Rico had a nonvoting representative in Congress, but that representative had little influence even on matters pertaining to Puerto Rican interests.

Muñoz Rivera did not accept this political humiliation. He served as resident commissioner (representative in Congress) in Washington, D.C., between 1910 and 1916. In that capacity, he battled to obtain home rule for Puerto Rico from a reluctant U.S. Congress. He returned to Puerto Rico in September, 1916, but a ruptured gall bladder caused an infection, and he died two months later. His efforts, however, were not in vain. In 1917, Congress passed the JONES ACT, which granted American citizenship to Puerto Ricans and instituted popularly elected houses of the legislature.

Mural art: The Latino mural movement in North America has roots in the Mexican mural renaissance of the 1920's as well as in the influences of the masters—Diego RIVERA, José Clemente OROZCO, and David Alfaro SIQUEIROS—during their respective sojourns in North America in the 1930's. Like the Mexican mural tradition, the contemporary mural movement is centered on the themes of cultural identity and pride, ethnic heritage, and a social and political consciousness born of an activist agenda.

Historical Antecedents. The Latino-dominated muralist tradition in North America has ancient roots in the Americas. From wall paintings of the early Olmec culture (c. 500 B.C.E.) in Juxtlahuacan, Guerrero, Mexico, to the elaborate frescoed murals of Teotihuacán, Mexico (c. 250-650 C.E.), pre-Columbian artists painted the walls of a multitude of public and private structures.

The seventh and eighth century C.E. battle murals of Cacaxtla, Tlaxcala, Mexico, are among the ancient Mexican murals most recently to have become the focus of art historical inquiry into the Mexican mural tradition. Painted in true fresco technique, with paints applied to wet stucco, these murals provide a vivid and graphic sociopolitical statement of the Epiclassic world order of c. 600 to 900 C.E. Propaganda, power, and identity are the focal points of the Cacaxtla mural message.

A justly famous example of muralism in ancient Mexico is that provided by the ancient Maya center of Bonampak, Chiapas. Three elaborately painted rooms document the exploits of the royal house of Bonampak, particularly the preparations, actions, and aftermath of a war of conquest waged against a neighboring kingdom.

In late AZTEC times (c. fifteenth century C.E.), the message was much the same as that at Cacaxtla and Bonampak. Icons, symbols, signs, and other images were used to communicate the powerful dictates of both supernatural and earthly overlords. The remnant mural panels from the Templo Mayor—the great Aztec temple of TENOCHTITLÁN—and the related works from Tlatelolco provide other public contexts within which muralism was presented in the pre-Columbian world. Themes center on blood sacrifice, the Mexica pantheon of gods and goddesses, and the relation of humans to the cosmic order.

The Colonial Period. During the Colonial period, the pre-Columbian or indigenous mural tradition was fused with the European ecclesiastical art tradition. Early examples of this fusion of indigenous and European ecclesiastical art can be found in the sixteenth century churches of Acolman, Actopan, Cuernavaca, and Puebla, Mexico. Through the course of the Colonial period (1521-1824), the mural tradition was sustained and nurtured in the ecclesiastical art and architecture of much of Spanish colonial America. This larger tradition was recurrently transformed by the infusion of European traditions, including the romanesque, gothic, and renaissance styles in art and architecture. By the seventeenth century, the baroque traditions of Italy had shown tremendous influence on Spanish colonial ecclesiastical art styles in New Spain (Mexico).

At the end of the eighteenth century and at the beginning of the nineteenth, the neoclassic artistic tradition of Europe swept New Spain. The neoclassic style was in large part a reaction to the ultra-religious baroque styles of the earlier Colonial period. The neo-

The murals on the wall of a San Luis, Colorado, art gallery resemble pulqueria *murals.* (James Shaffer)

classical style emphasized a return to romanesque and classical themes, in stark contrast to the ornate religiosity of the sixteenth through eighteenth century ecclesiastical traditions.

By the mid-1800's, *pulquerias*—establishments catering to the consumption of *pulque*, a fermented indigenous beverage produced from the sap of the *maguey* or agave plant—had taken on muralism as a means of promoting the consumption of this ancient beverage. The so-called *pulqueria* murals depicted idyllic scenes from Mexican history, culture, and landscapes. These murals graced the façades of *pulquerias* and were public proclamations of the art, culture, and history of Mexico. *Pulqueria* themes ranged from images of Aztec warriors and maidens to landscapes of the Mexican countryside. Themes from *pulqueria* art were eclectic and individualistic, reflecting the motivations of business owners and the skills of the artists.

The Mexican Mural Movement. By the 1920's, *los tres grandes*, the so-called Big Three—Diego RIVERA, José Clemente OROZCO, and David Alfaro SIQUEIROS—emerged as leaders of the Mexican mural movement. Art historian Jean Charlot has characterized the period from 1920 to 1925, when Rivera, Orozco, and Siqueiros produced some of their earliest public art projects, as the era of the "Mexican mural renaissance." Drawing upon European modernism, particularly cubism, expressionism, and futurism, the Mexican mural masters formulated a new tradition of socially motivated realism. Socially motivated realism in the works of the Big Three deployed revolutionary new compositional styles and formats.

During the 1920's and 1930's, public support for Mexican and Mexican-inspired mural projects in the United States reached a peak. The Mexican masters themselves were recruited by U.S. artistic and cultural

A mural by David Martinez connects Chicano culture to the state of Arizona. (Ruben G. Mendoza)

institutes to exhibit or to create commissioned works. Whereas Rivera's collage-like compositions juxtaposed diverse elements, Orozco integrated distorted forms and exaggerated expressions of light and dark, and Siqueiros altered traditional perspective with extreme foreshortening that made forms appear to come out of the wall. These mural masters and their respective innovations and styles influenced the development of the contemporary mural movement in North America.

Expressions of Social Themes. The WORKS PROGRESS ADMINISTRATION and NEW DEAL murals sponsored by the U.S. federal government in the 1930's promoted the growth of the social realist mural movement. With themes that embraced the plight of the working class, war, poverty, industrialization and alienation, social reform, and progress, more than twenty-five hundred murals of the New Deal era promoted social agendas that by World War II were seen as inspired by socialism or communism.

Because the works of the Big Three embraced the socialist agenda and openly promoted Marxist-Leninist thinking, agrarian reform, revolution, and anti-imperialist themes, it was only a matter of time before these works

were deemed politically incorrect. The U.S. works of Rivera, Orozco, and Siqueiros soon became the targets of anticommunist coalitions intent on eradicating works deemed subversive to American democracy. Murals by the Big Three in Detroit, San Francisco, Los Angeles, and New York were systematically dismantled, whitewashed, defaced, or otherwise hidden from the public eye during World War II and the subsequent anticommunist McCarthy era. These murals and their painters became suspect as a result of their socialist rhetoric and for their monumental political statements espousing the socialist transformation of North American culture and society. Public murals, Orozco's "disinterested form" of art, were thereafter relegated to the marginalized genres of the art world, in large part as a result of the equation of public art with communist agendas and of muralism with the rhetoric of the working class and the plight of the urban poor.

The Contemporary Mural Movement. In the 1960's and 1970's, the contemporary mural movement flowered in tandem with the growth of the social, political, and cultural agendas of the Civil Rights movement. This was a period when the cause of civil rights in the

Latino, Asian, and African American communities was taken to the streets in the form of demonstrations, civil unrest, and revitalization of the social realist mural tradition. Public arts projects and community murals of the 1960's and 1970's, then often the domain of politically active artists working without sponsors, became a new forum for expressing and experiencing social discontent and mediating potential unrest.

The need for such a forum was soon recognized and met through the creation of tens of thousands of murals across North America. Unlike the works of their Mexican counterparts, the works of the artists of the Chicano mural movement in North America were not sponsored by the government but signified a struggle by the people themselves against the status quo. These new murals were located in the barrios and ghettos of the inner cities. They served as an inspiration for struggle, a way of reclaiming a cultural heritage, and a means of developing self-pride.

The murals of this era were first seen as folk art. They were born of the frustrations and challenges of politically active professional and community artists, advocated civil rights themes deemed unpopular in the commercial art world, and generally were located within working-class neighborhoods, urban barrios, and ghettos. They therefore did not fit within the mainstream art tradition.

The intense and radicalized imagery of Latino urban artists has been characterized as largely marginal to the North American art community, despite the emergence of Latino and African American art coalitions and professional guilds. The traditional art community questioned the aesthetics of the muralists. The emergence of the Civil Rights movement, with its emphasis on social protest and challenge, ethnic identity, and cultural diversity, gave a place to this art.

The very thing that brought the contemporary mural movement into existence—its community participa-

A section of The Great Wall of Los Angeles, *a mural painted under the direction of Judy Baca.* (Martin Hutner)

tion and social agenda—is the very dynamic that has served to sustain the muralist tradition in North America. This art form has been redefined by art historians in recent years as a "people's art" for North America. The contemporary mural movement is significant for having spawned two generations of urban artists specialized in the production and perpetuation of these sociopolitical—and thereby, ephemeral—landscapes of the human condition.

Particularly important in this regard is the fact that these works of public art have long targeted racism, discrimination, unfair employment and housing practices, urban violence, drug abuse, imperialism, and war. At the same time, these works are expressions that recurrently serve to revitalize cultural pride and identity, particularly as they call attention to the struggle for civil rights and social equality and demand that the contributions of women and people of color be acknowledged. The growing international reputations of Chicano muralists such as Malaquías Montoya, Judith F. Baca, José Montoya, Ray Patlán, Carlos Almaraz, Alfredo Hernández, Patricia Rodriguez, and various groups of artists are testaments to the aesthetic worth of works deemed inappropriate at one time within the more conservative and largely institutionalized art circles of the United States. These artists and their respective arts organizations—many of whom have produced both community and commercial works—continue to focus on social protest, ethnic and cultural pride, and spiritual and heroic themes arising from within the social and cultural landscapes of the inner city. —*Ruben G. Mendoza*

SUGGESTED READINGS:

• Barnett, Alan W. *Community Murals: The People's Art*. Philadelphia, Pa.: Art Alliance Press, 1984. An art historical overview of the origins, development, styles, and contemporary crisis in the community mural tradition.

• Charlot, Jean. *The Mexican Mural Renaissance: 1920-1925*. New Haven, Conn.: Yale University Press, 1967. Documents in autobiographical format the author's observation of creation of early works of Rivera, Orozco, and Siqueiros.

• Cockcroft, Eva Sperling, and Holly Barnet-Sanchez, eds. *Signs from the Heart: California Chicano Murals*. Venice, Calif.: Social and Public Art Resource Center, 1993. A photographic essay and art historical review of the California Chicano mural movement and its works.

• Cockcroft, Eva, John Weber, and Jim Cockcroft. *Toward a People's Art: The Contemporary Mural Movement*. New York: E. P. Dutton, 1977. A comprehensive overview of the origins, development, and artists of the contemporary mural movement in the United States.

• Fondo Editorial de la Plastica Mexicana. *La Pintura Mural de la Revolución Mexicana*. 2d ed. Mexico: Author, 1967. A comprehensive photographic survey, incorporating a historical overview from pre-Columbian times to the present, of the Mexican mural tradition, especially as this pertains to works documenting the Mexican Revolution.

• González, Alicia M. "Murals: Fine, Popular, or Folk Art?" *Aztlán: International Journal of Chicano Studies Research* 13 (Spring/Fall, 1982): 149-163. A scholarly treatment and assessment of the artistic and social underpinnings of the Chicano mural movement and its works.

• Greenberg, David, Kathryn Smith, and Stuart Teacher. *Big Art: Megamurals and Supergraphics*. Philadelphia, Pa.: Running Press, 1977. A photographic essay of monumental public art and commercial muralism from throughout the United States, Canada, and Mexico.

• Hurlburt, Laurance P. *The Mexican Muralists in the United States*. Albuquerque: University of New Mexico Press, 1989. Documents the early works of the three great Mexican mural masters—Orozco, Rivera, and Siqueiros—whose U.S. commissions caused considerable controversy in the 1930's.

• Marling, Karal Ann. *Wall-to-Wall America: A Cultural History of Post-Office Murals in the Great Depression*. Minneapolis: University of Minnesota Press, 1982. A comprehensive assessment of the post office murals painted throughout the United States during the Depression.

• Smith, Bradley. *Mexico: A History in Art*. New York: Harper & Row, 1968. An art historical overview and cultural chronology of the broad span of Mexico's artistic traditions from pre-Columbian times to the 1960's.

Murieta, Joaquín (also known as Murrieta; c. 1832, Sonora, Mexico—July, 1853, California): Folk hero. According to legend, Murieta migrated from Sonora, Mexico, to the California gold fields when he was eighteen years old. He endured the insults of American miners for one year before embarking on a path of revenge.

In mid-January, 1852, he began a series of robberies. Vigilantes repeatedly gave chase to him and his group of bandits. By March, 1853, the "Joaquín scare," a hysteria of unprecedented proportions, had spread across the state. Consequently, the legislature created a special ranger company for his capture (but without clearly defining his surname). The governor also put up a $1,000 reward on his own authority. As the time limit on the bounty was about to expire, the ranger company returned with a head pickled in a whiskey jar. It was never proved that this was actually the head of Murieta. A grateful legislature nevertheless awarded $5,000 to the captain of the ranger company.

Although the question of Murieta's existence will probably never be settled, his authenticity is of secondary importance. Both CALIFORNIOS and Americans believed in his existence. The former saw in him a means to strike out against American control, and the latter's belief in Murieta illustrates the depth of fear of the bandit activity that intensified in California during the 1850's.

Music and musicians, Caribbean: According to Bartolomé DE LAS CASAS (1474-1566) and other early chroniclers, the aboriginal peoples of Cuba, Puerto Rico, and the Dominican Republic performed AREITOS (dances featuring antiphonal singing). Following the SPANISH CONQUEST, genocide, and exposure to Old World diseases, none of these peoples or their cultures survived except in archaeological remains. Aboriginal contributions to the islands' present musics are minimal. Archaeological evidence indicates that the Cuban Siboneye and Taino Indians used stone and ceramic whistles, conch-shell trumpets, and bird-bone flutes. MARACAS, or gourd rattles, are still used in contemporary Cuban music. The Arawak Indians of Puerto Rico used gourd rattles and the "baston," an ornamented stick struck on the ground.

Colonial Period. The first documented European music in the Spanish West Indies was sacred music

Caribbean musicians perform in the "Musica Tradicional" series in New York City. (Impact Visuals, Hazel Hankin)

performed in cathedrals. In Cuba, Esteban Salas (1725-1803) was the organist at the Cathedral of Santiago and the first significant Cuban composer, writing in a style similar to that of the Italian composer Giovanni Pergolesi. In the Dominican Republic, Cristobal de Llerena (c. 1540-1600) was the first European-trained musician to serve at the Cathedral of La Vega. In Puerto Rico, cathedral records are incomplete regarding specific musicians who served as organists or choirmasters. The records, however, show that from early in the sixteenth century, organists and singers were in the cathedral's employ and provided the island's first formal music instruction.

In Cuba, the earliest documented secular music was performed in the late sixteenth century by musicians in the employ of the Cathedral of Santiago. Micaela and Teodora Gines, black sisters from the Dominican Republic, composed and performed the extant "Son of Ma-Teodora," an Afro-Cuban dance piece, at dances in Santiago. In Puerto Rico before the nineteenth century, secular music often accompanied public celebrations for the accession of Spanish monarchs. Eighteenth and nineteenth century musicians from Spanish military garrisons played for balls and in symphony and opera concerts; many stayed on as performers, instructors, and founders of musical families. In the Dominican Republic, secular music by the seventeenth century included popular dances such as the *zarabanda*, *calenda*, *fandinguete*, and *tumba*.

In Cuba, the CONTRADANZA (derived from English "country dance") arrived with immigrating Haitian planters and their enslaved Africans after the Haitian revolution of the late eighteenth century. It later evolved into the nineteenth century DANZÓN. The *contradanza habanera* became internationally popular during the nineteenth century. In Puerto Rico, military bands introduced the *contradanza*, which later evolved into the Puerto Rican DANZA.

During the nineteenth century, the piano became a popular instrument in the Hispanic Caribbean. Some of the earliest stirrings of Caribbean nationalism may be found in the piano *danzas* and *contradanzas* of Ignacio Cervantes (1847-1905) and Manuel Saumell (1817-1870) of Cuba; in the *danzas* of Juan Morel Campos (1857-1896) and Jose Ignacio Quinton (1881-1925) of Puerto Rico; and in the *danza*-like *dominicanas* of Pablo Claudio (1866-1899) in the Dominican Republic. These works showed European (especially Spanish) influence in their melodies and harmonies but African influence in their syncopation (off-beat accents) and polyrhythms (multiple rhythms). The

contradanza and *danza* were also fashionable in nineteenth century urban ballrooms in the Dominican Republic, along with the MERENGUE, *carabine*, *mangulina*, and *yuca*. Military band concerts also played an important role in Dominican musical and social life.

Nineteenth century composers in Cuba, Puerto Rico, and the Dominican Republic often straddled the areas of classical art music and popular music. For example, Cervantes wrote music for orchestra, chamber groups, and opera in addition to *contradanzas*. The Dominican composer Juan Bautista Alfonseca (1810-1875) composed popular dances as well as two Masses. Quinton in Puerto Rico composed music for the church, theater, and chamber groups as well as the popular *danzas*.

Visiting and resident operatic and ZARZUELA (Spanish operetta) troupes found success in the nineteenth century Hispanic Caribbean. The works of Italian composers enjoyed popularity among Creoles, who also heard operatic arrangements at outdoor band concerts and in piano recitals given in private salons. Visiting virtuoso singers and pianists (especially the Louisiana-born Louis Moreau Gottschalk) enriched the concert life of the islands. A number of native-born singers and instrumentalists achieved international prominence, among them the Puerto Rican tenor Antonio PAOLI (1871-1946) and the Cuban mulatto violinist/composer José White (1836-1918).

Twentieth Century. In the field of art music, nationalist composers dominated the first half of the century. They drew upon a rich legacy of dances and folk songs, although initially within the context of late-nineteenth century Romanticism. In Cuba, the zarzuelas and popular songs of Gonzalo Roig (1890-1970) and Ernesto Lecuona (1895-1963) occasionally incorporated Afro-Cuban folklore and music. The research of Fernando Ortiz (1881-1969) into Afro-Cuban music and ritual helped to inspire a new generation of composers during the 1920's and 1930's. The orchestral works of Alejandro Garcia Caturla (1906-1940) and Amadeo Roldan (1900-1939) received international acclaim for their inclusion of Afro-Cuban genres, rhythms, and percussion instruments within a 1930's avant-garde musical vocabulary.

In Puerto Rico, the change of sovereignty from Spain to the United States in 1898 and a devastating hurricane in 1899 brought a period of economic depression, and traditional sources of musical patronage declined. From 1949 through 1958, however, the island's government sponsored a series of cultural initiatives. Among them was the creation of Free Music

A group of Puerto Rican musicians using traditional instruments. (Hazel Hankin)

Schools to provide preconservatory training in the principal cities, the founding of a new symphony orchestra, the creation of government-owned educational radio and television stations, and the establishment of the Division of Education for the Community, which commissioned film scores from Puerto Rican composers. During the 1940's, Puerto Rican composers adopted a self-consciously nationalist stance, creating music that drew on the island's Taino, Spanish, and African roots. In 1957, Spanish cellist Pablo Casals (1876-1973) founded the annual international music festival that bears his name. As a catalyst to the founding of the conservatory and symphony orchestra, Casals helped to improve the island's performance standards in classical music.

In the Dominican Republic, the oratorios and other sacred music of José de Jesus Ravelo (1876-1952) were pivotal in the transition from Romanticism to nationalism. Esteban Peña Morell (1897-1938) and

Juan Francisco Garcia (1892-1974) were among the first Dominicans to compose nationalist symphonies. Garcia's *Quisqueyana* (1935) used quotations and variations of folk music, especially the Dominican MERENGUE. Enrique de Marchena (b. 1908) is the Dominican composer most familiar abroad. Casal Chapi, a Spanish emigrant, directed the National Symphony from 1941 to 1945 and taught a new, more progressive generation of composers, of which the most outstanding was Manuel Simó (b. 1916).

Since the 1950's, composers in Cuba, Puerto Rico, and the Dominican Republic have embraced an internationalist musical vocabulary—one that includes folklore but also aleatoricism (chance music), serialism (music based on twelve-tone rows), mixed-media, and other later twentieth century idioms. Composers who have followed these trends include José Ardévol (b. 1911), Julian Orbon (1925-1991), Aurélio de la Vega (b. 1925), Harold Gramatges (b. 1918), and Leo

Brouwer (b. 1939) of Cuba; Hector Campos Parsi (b. 1922), Jack Delano (b. 1914), Ernesto Cordero (b. 1946), and Roberto Sierra (b. 1953) of Puerto Rico; and Manuel Simó, Margarita Luna (b. 1921), and Miguel Pichardo-Vicioso (b. 1939) of the Dominican Republic.

Folk and Popular Music. Many dance and song genres of the Hispanic Caribbean contain Spanish and African influences. Numerous genres are related to the Spanish *romance* (narrative song), *villancico* (Christmas carol), CANCIÓN de cuna (lullaby), DÉCIMA (ten-line verse form), and *salve* (hymn). Hispanic influence includes European harmony, melodies in thirds, a tendency toward triple meter and "colonial rhythm" (two- and three-beat measures in simultaneity), and the use of the guitar and its variants. Guitar variants native to the Hispanic Caribbean include the Cuban nine-string *tres* and the Puerto Rican ten-string CUATRO.

The guitar-based *punto*, which exhibits Spanish traits, is found throughout the rural Hispanic Caribbean. In Puerto Rico, the *jíbaros* (country folk) sing and dance the SEIS (related to the *décima*) to the accompaniment of guitars, GÜIRO (scraper), and BONGOS. The Cuban *décima guajira* and the Puerto Rican *seis de controversia* are frequently sung in contests, with improvised lyrics. Other popular Puerto Rican Hispanic genres include the CORRIDO and AGUINALDO, related respectively to the *romance* and *villancico*. The Dominican *merengue cibaeño* (rural folk MERENGUE, also known as *perico ripiao*) is sung to the accompaniment of guitars or accordion, MARIMBA (a xylophone-like instrument, similar to the Cuban *marímbula*, which provides bass), *tambora* (drum), and GUAYO (scraper). During the Rafael Trujillo dictatorship (1930-1961), the *merengue cibaeño* lost some of its traditional function as a vehicle for acerbic social and political commentary.

Many Afro-Caribbean genres reflect African heritage in the use of responsorial form (in which a lead singer alternates with a choral response) and occasional blue notes (pitches derived from a West African scale). In rhythm and timbre, African survivals are especially strong. They include polyrhythms (multiple meters and rhythms), syncopation (weak-beat accents), and use of a variety of percussion instruments including drums, scrapers, gourd rattles, and bells. The African timeline—an unchanging, repetitive pattern, played on bells or kept through hand-claps, which functions as an orienting rhythm for performers—survives in the *clave* rhythms common to Afro-Caribbean (especially Cuban) music. Many Afro-Caribbean dance genres are

also defined partly by their recurring rhythmic formula, or "cell." The least acculturated Afro-Caribbean music is that performed by various cult groups (especially in Cuba and Haiti) preserving West African religious practices syncretized with Catholicism. Cult music includes drumming, invocations of *orishas* (African deities), and ritual trances.

The best-known secular Afro-Caribbean dance genres include the Cuban SON, CONGA, and RUMBA, the Puerto Rican BOMBA and PLENA, and the Dominican *plena*. The African influence of the merengue has been disputed by some Dominican scholars, perhaps as a result of latent nationalism and anti-Haitianism (Haiti briefly occupied the Dominican Republic) or of ambivalence toward the country's racial identity. Among the merengue's most salient features is its African-derived *cinquillo* (syncopated five-note) rhythmic cell. *Salves* and *bailes de plato* are associated with Afro-Dominican Catholic worship.

Cuban (and, to a lesser extent, Puerto Rican and Dominican) dance music provides the basis of various commercial styles that have become popular not only in the Caribbean but also internationally. In late eighteenth and early nineteenth century Havana, black musicians dominated the profession. Residents preferred them for the capital's frequent social dances. At first, the repertory included many European-derived dances. The CONTRADANZA began that way, took on a home-grown, Africanized rhythmic flavor, and eventually became popular in the rest of the Hispanic Caribbean and beyond. In the late 1800's, *charanga* orchestras of flute, violins, piano, and TIMBALES (Afro-Caribbean percussion instrument) popularized the DANZÓN. In the early 1900's, the *son*, a rural song genre accompanied by guitars and percussion, reached Havana, where it was performed by small CONJUNTOS that added trumpet and bass. The *son* has a two-part form that includes a narrative first section followed by a *montuno* featuring responsorial vocal parts.

By the 1930's, the *son* had overtaken the *danzón* in popularity. Innovations introduced by blind *tres* player Arsenio Rodríguez (1911-1970) gave birth to modern Cuban dance music (later called SALSA, a term that engenders some controversy). Besides the *son*, Cuban dance music incorporated many other genres, including GUARACHA, rumba, BOLERO (slow romantic ballad), *cha-cha-chá*, MAMBO, and others.

During the 1950's, the still-vital *charanga* orchestras popularized *cha-cha-chá*, while the American-style big-band arrangements of band-leader Pérez PRADO (1916-1989) helped popularize the mambo in

Tito Puente was one of the bandleaders responsible for popularizing Caribbean music in the United States. (AP/Wide World Photos)

Cuba, Mexico, and the United States. Salsa dominated Puerto Rican popular music, both on the island and in U.S. urban areas—especially in New York City, where bandleaders Tito PUENTE (b. 1923), MACHITO (1912-1984), Arsenio RODRÍGUEZ, and others led the mambo fad. Puerto Rican musicians Cesar Concepción and Rafael Cortijo (d. 1983) incorporated the *plena* and *bomba* into the salsa repertoire during the 1940's and 1950's.

The Cuban diaspora following the 1959 revolution has ensured the continuing vitality of salsa in U.S. urban areas (especially New York and Miami). The 1970's saw increased commercial success for the genre. To the roster of established performers such as Johnny Pacheco (b. 1935), Celia CRUZ, and Eddie Palmieri (1927-1988) were added new talents such as Willie COLÓN (b. 1950) and Rubén BLADES (b. 1948). The Panamanian-born Blades's innovations to the genre include topical, socially conscious lyrics and the use of synthesizers and more complex arrangements.

During the 1980's, the Dominican merengue dominated salsa among Puerto Ricans and Central Americans. Although primarily a rural, guitar-based genre, the merengue enjoyed a brief vogue as urban dance music performed by Dominican *charanga* orchestras during the late 1800's; however, it was suppressed by Eurocentric elements of the Dominican elite. Another dance-band instrumentation that included saxophones gained popularity from 1870 into the Trujillo era. In contemporary salsa music, the merengue is characterized by duple meter (two-beat measure), fast tempos, and saxophone arrangements employing fast-note passagework. Among the stars of 1980's merengue were performers Johnny Ventura and Wilfredo Vargas.

—*José Manuel Lezcano*

SUGGESTED READINGS:

• Bloch, Peter. *La-Le-Lo-Lai: Puerto Rican Music and Its Performers.* New York: Plus Ultra Educational Publishers, 1973. Survey of Puerto Rican composers, performers, and genres (both classical and popular). Contains an index and photos.

• Diaz Ayala, Cristobal. *Música Cubana del Areyto a la Nueva Trova.* San Juan, Puerto Rico: Editorial Cubanacan, 1981. A survey of Cuban music from the Taino Indians to the 1980's. Contains an index and photos.

• Jorge, Bernarda. *La Música Dominicana.* Santo Domingo, Dominican Republic: Editora de la Universidad Autónoma de Santo Domingo, 1982. A survey of nineteenth and twentieth century music. Discusses classical, folk, and dance music genres, instruments, and composers. Includes photos, indexes, and lists of composers' works.

• Manuel, Peter. *Popular Musics of the Non-Western World.* New York: Oxford University Press, 1988. In chapter 2, "Latin America and the Caribbean," Manuel surveys the principal genres, their musical characteristics, and their social and political contexts. Excellent notes and bibliography.

• Roberts, John Storm. *The Latin Tinge.* New York: Oxford University Press, 1979. A survey of major Latin American genres, composers, and performers and their impact on U.S. music. Includes glossary, discography, and index.

Music and musicians, Central American: Central American music became increasingly visible within Latino communities after the late 1970's, as immigrants reproduced traditional music from the isthmus. Several Central American musicians also achieved national and continental stature as performers of pan-Latino musical styles.

Although Central American music and musicians can be documented in the United States before the twentieth century, two factors have impeded the flourishing of an identifiably Central American musical culture in North America. First, large-scale immigration into the United States and Canada from the seven Central American republics did not occur until the mid-1970's, when political repression, war, and economic destruction forced many people to abandon their homelands. In addition, because so many Central Americans had an undocumented status in the United States and feared a forced return to a possibly dangerous situation in their home countries, they maintained a low profile and attempted to blend in with other Latinos.

Traditional and Folk-Based Music. The most readily identifiable instrument from Central America is the MARIMBA, which is found in varying sizes between the southernmost area of Mexico and Costa Rica. The marimba, originally from Africa, is a wooden-keyed xylophone struck with mallets. It is considered the national instrument of Guatemala and is important in both the Mayan and ladino (mestizo) populations. Guatemalans in the United States have imported or constructed their own marimbas, and where there is a large community (in Los Angeles, for example), groups perform for private functions as well as in restaurants and other venues.

The first major exposure of Central American music in the United States dates from tours of large Guatema-

A marimba band composed of young Guatemalans performs in Miami, Florida. (AP/Wide World Photos)

lan marimba orchestras at the end of the nineteenth century. Presentations by these ensembles spurred the adaptation of the concert marimba, first in symphony orchestras and later in jazz and other music. Concert marimbas, however, lack the unique buzzing sound that distinguishes Latin American and African marimbas. This sound is produced by a small piece of stretched membrane attached with beeswax on the bottom of the resonator that hangs under each wooden key.

Guatemalan marimbas are usually large enough for several musicians. The most typical Guatemalan marimba ensemble is called a *marimba pura* (pure marimba). It combines a stand-up bass and trap drum set with a *marimba grande* (big marimba) that accommodates four players and a smaller *marimba tenor* (tenor marimba) with two or three players. The repertoire of the *marimba pura* is extensive, from song and dance forms such as the Guatemalan SON *chapín* and *son barreño* and adaptations of European waltzes and polkas, to interpretations of classical music by more sophisticated ensembles. Often marimba groups add trumpets, saxophones, and additional percussion to perform contemporary popular dance styles such as CUMBIAS and MERENGUES.

The smaller *marimba de arco* (marimba with an arc) is popular in Nicaragua. The *marimba de arco* has twenty-two keys and is played by a single musician seated at the instrument, always accompanied by a guitar and a small, four-stringed *guitarilla*. Music of the *marimba de arco* trio accompanies Nicaragua's best-known folk dances and is regularly featured in celebrations in Miami's large Nicaraguan community.

Two music styles from Mexico first became immensely popular throughout Central America and then in U.S. and Canadian communities: the mariachi and trio. Mariachis also accompany singers in the CANCIÓN *ranchera*, another popular form. Other folk-based musical styles that use one or more singers with guitar accompaniment include the Mexican-derived CORRIDO and HUAPANGO, the *sique* from Honduras, the *son nica* from Nicaragua, and the *pasillo* and *parrandera* from Costa Rica. Brass bands are used for religious and festive occasions, particularly the Nicaraguan *chichero* brass bands in Miami.

The two Afro-Central American communities from the eastern coast of Central America have made an impact. *Palo de mayo* (Maypole), a song and dance form of the English Creole-speaking population in Nicaragua, has been a favorite in the Nicaraguan American community. *Punta*, a similar style, originated with the GARIFUNA people, the mixed African and Carib population from the Atlantic coast of Honduras and Belize. Several *punta* groups from the New York and Los Angeles areas enjoyed popularity in the late 1980's. These groups integrated Spanish and Garifuna lyrics and mixed traditional Garifuna rhythms with popular Caribbean musical styles, particularly merengue. Most *punta* groups use large mahogany drums tuned with wooden pegs. These drums are similar to several types of West African drums. Groups that perform Atlantic Coast music have revitalized and brought recognition to Afro-Central American culture, in both Central and North America.

Popular and Classical Music and Musicians. Central American musical styles had not achieved a high profile in either the Latino or the non-Latino North American population by the 1990's. Many Central American musicians, however, have specialized in non-Central American musical styles that are popular throughout the North American Latino community and Latin America and the Caribbean as a whole.

The best-known Central American musician in the early 1990's was Rubén BLADES. Born in Panama, Blades lived for many years in New York City and obtained a law degree from Harvard University. He joined with trombonist and bandleader Willie COLÓN in the mid-1970's to launch his career as a SALSA singer and composer. Backed by his own group, Blades continued to be one of the most popular and creative salsa musicians. His compositions are notable for their musical originality and thoughtful lyrics containing social messages and commentary. His consistent call for pan-Latino and United States unity helped to propel salsa as a common musical bond among Latinos in the United States.

Two other important musicians of Central American descent were Luis Enrique, from Nicaragua, and "El General," from Panama. Luis Enrique, a singer-songwriter and percussionist in the *salsa romántica* (romantic salsa) popular style, had several hits beginning in the late 1980's. Afro-Panamanian El General (Edgardo A. Franco) was in the forefront of Spanish-language rap sometimes labeled dance-hall reggae-español, an offshoot of the Jamaican reggae dance-hall style. El General has recorded separate versions of songs in English and in Spanish and occasionally mixes both languages in the same song.

The *nueva canción* (new song) movement has been an important vehicle for exposing North American audiences to elements of Central American music and social reality. *Nueva canción* draws from Central

Rubén Blades. (AP/Wide World Photos)

American and other Latin American and Caribbean folk and popular music styles. Its lyrics emphasize revolutionary political change and social justice. Local bands have formed in several North American cities, usually including non-Central Americans.

There has been little development of European classical music in Central America compared to the rest of the Americas. The two most prominent classical composers of Central American origin residing in the United States were Salvadoran pianist Hugo Calderón, who writes in a neoromantic, nationalist style, and conductor Roque Cordero, probably the first Central American composer to use serial technique (a modern compositional approach that does not utilize tonality).

—*T. M. Scruggs*

SUGGESTED READINGS: • Chenoweth, Vida. *The Marimbas of Guatemala*. Lexington: University of Kentucky Press, 1964. • Holston, Mark. "The Rap on the Raperos." *Américas* 44, no. 5 (1992): 4. • Miller, Amy. "Teaching the World to Punta." *The Beat* 10, no. 4 (1991): 39-41, 54. • Parker, Robert A. "The Vision of Rubén Blades." *Américas* 37 (March/April, 1985): 15-19. • Randel, Don Michael. "Crossing Over with Rubén Blades." *Journal of the American Musicological Society* 44 (Summer, 1991): 301-323.

Music and musicians, Mexican American: Mexican American music combines elements from the two cultures of Mexico and the United States. Three major regional forms emerged historically among Mexican Americans: the CONJUNTO, the *orquesta*, and the CORRIDO. *Conjunto* (ensemble) and *orquesta* (orchestra) are ensemble styles; the *corrido* is a narrative ballad. All three are unique to the Mexican American experience, and each keys on different aspects of the Mexican and U.S. cultures to create a powerful artistic form.

Mexican Americans trace their history in the Southwest from 1598, when Spanish Mexicans founded the province of New Mexico. Even after the region was annexed by the United States, following the MEXICAN AMERICAN WAR of 1846-1848, immigration from Mexico continued; in the twentieth century it exploded, as Mexico's economy stagnated and a tide of immigrants swept northward in search of work.

From their earliest days in the Southwest, Mexicans practiced the musical traditions they brought with them, such as the *romance*, a narrative ballad brought originally from Spain, and the *jota*, which was popular throughout Mexico. In the nineteenth century, dancing became such a passion in the Hispanic Southwest that if a few people gathered during the day and a guitarist or violinist could be summoned, dancing usually began.

The nineteenth century witnessed the invasion of the "Anglos," as Mexicans called the North Americans. The annexation of the Southwest by the United States generated considerable conflict between the natives and the Anglo newcomers, triggering forms of cultural reaction, including music, among the defeated Mexicans. Continuing emigration from Mexico deepened the interethnic tension, which further contributed to the production of cultural expressions keyed on interethnic conflict, especially from the Mexicans, who were the subordinate group in the struggle between the two peoples.

The Corrido. Among the most important artistic forms to arise out of the interethnic conflict was the *corrido*. *Corridos* dealing with intercultural conflict proliferated in the latter part of the nineteenth century and the early twentieth century. Emerging out of the ancient *romance* tradition but possessing its own structure (a four-line stanza with octosyllabic, *abcd* rhyme patterns) and its own theme (intercultural conflict), the Mexican American *corrido* reigned supreme, at least until the 1960's. It provided a strong artistic outlet for Mexican Americans' continuing conflict with Anglos.

"El Corrido de Gregorio Cortez" epitomizes the *corrido* of intercultural conflict. The events it depicts took place in Texas in 1901. It was composed by an anonymous *corridista* (*corrido* singer) to celebrate the deeds of a man who killed a sheriff in self-defense and who eluded his captors for many days, until he was turned in by another Mexican. In the *corrido*, CORTEZ is portrayed as a larger than life hero, while his pursuers, the Texas Rangers, are seen as cowards. The following translated lyrics provide a feel for the tone and substance of the *corrido* of intercultural conflict: "They turned the hound dogs loose/ so they could follow the trail,/ but to reach Cortez/ was like trying to reach a star./ He took off toward Gonzalez/ without any fear whatsoever:/ 'Follow me, you cowardly Rangers,/ I am Gregorio Cortez.'"

The *corrido* underwent transformations as society changed. For example, in the 1960's and 1970's, when the United Farm Workers union was most active, the *corrido* was used to rally Mexican Americans around the farmworkers' plight. At that time, the larger than life hero was replaced by helpless victims brutalized by police officers or other agents of the dominant system. This portrayal aroused Mexican Americans and motivated them to fight for the rights of the lowly Mexican farmworkers. By the 1980's, however, *corri-*

dos had devolved into fictional narratives invented for films, and many glamorized drug smugglers and other criminals. A few *corridos* still depicted the lives of real people, especially farmworkers.

The Conjunto. The second major musical tradition in the Hispanic Southwest is the *conjunto*. Anchored by the diatonic button accordion and a twelve-string bass guitar known as a *bajo sexto*, the *conjunto* traces its roots to the 1860's, when the accordion was introduced into northern Mexico by German immigrants settling in Monterrey, Nuevo León. The accordion was adopted by the poorer rural folk for their dance celebrations, and association with rural life spawned the label *música ranchera*, or "country music." Strengthening its country flavor was its repertoire, much of it derived from European folk music such as the polka, schottische, and redowa. The *HUAPANGO*, a type of music originating in northern Mexico, rounded out the repertoire.

The *conjunto* quickly spread across the border into South Texas, where it evolved into a powerful ensemble, first shedding its German identity and then, as a uniquely Mexican American style, acquiring widespread popularity. Among the leading innovators in the Texas-Mexican tradition was Narciso Martínez, who was born in 1911 in Matamoros, Tamaulipas, Mexico, but was reared in Texas. As the "father" of the modern ensemble, Martínez was the first to break with the German accordion style by developing a new right-hand technique. Santiago Jiménez, Sr., born in 1913 in Piedras Negras but reared in San Antonio, Texas, is another pioneer. He was the first to use the contrabass in the evolving ensemble.

The next generation of *CONJUNTO* musicians carried the style to maturity, cementing its popularity among working-class Texas-Mexicans. Accordionist Valerio Longoria, born in 1924 in Kenedy, Texas, added the *CANCIÓN* (a tune with lyrics) to the *conjunto* ensemble. Tony de la Rosa, born in 1931 in Sarita, Texas, added drums, rounding out what became the standard ensemble—accordion, *bajo sexto*, drums, and bass. Paulino Bernal, born in 1939 in McAllen, Texas, took the *conjunto* style to its highest levels of technical performance. Finally, Leonardo "Flaco" JIMÉNEZ, born in San Antonio, Texas, in 1945, popularized the music beyond its Texas-Mexican base, especially through his association with the TEXAS TORNADOS, a hybrid group that combined the traditional elements of the *conjunto* with country-western music.

In the 1960's, northern Mexicans became important contributors to the evolving style. Two musical groups,

Los Relámpagos del Norte (the lightning from the North) and Los Bravos del Norte (the brave ones from the North), achieved phenomenal popularity on both sides of the border. From the 1960's to the 1990's, *conjuntos* from Mexico were principally responsible for the spreading popularity of the style. The solid support of a large immigrant population ensured the continuing dominance of the *conjunto* among Mexicans and Mexican Americans in the United States. At the end of the twentieth century, after more than a century of development, *conjunto* music showed few signs of decline. Like the *CORRIDO*, the conjunto early acquired an association with the poorer classes in Texas and northern Mexico. As Texas-Mexican society evolved in the twentieth century and a strong middle class emerged, the conjunto came to represent a working-class aesthetic that in many ways was pitted against the tastes of middle-class Mexican Americans. In the 1960's, when the *conjunto* began to spread beyond Texas, it took root among the lower classes in other regions. Wherever the *conjunto* spread, its association with working-class Mexicans accompanied it; as a result, it acquired a symbolic charge that contrasted sharply with the more sophisticated *orquesta*.

The Orquesta. The history of the *orquesta* can be divided into two periods, the first lasting from the nineteenth century until the 1930's, with the violin as the *orquesta*'s lead instrument, and the modern period, when the *orquesta* featured trumpets and saxophones. Early *orquestas* were mostly improvisational in nature, owing to the general economic instability of Mexican American society prior to the 1930's. In the 1930's, as a result of an emerging, more stable, middle class, a new and better-organized *orquesta* appeared, combining elements of modern U.S. dance bands and the Mexican dance *orquesta*.

The most important leaders in the modern *orquesta* tradition came from the active Texas tradition. One was Beto Villa, born in 1915 in Falfurrias, Texas. Besides adopting a dual repertoire that included tunes from American dance bands and Mexican bands, Villa's *orquesta* moved into the *conjunto*'s territory, appropriating some of its *ranchero* elements as well. Why Villa would adopt a style that was so opposed to the *orquesta* and the more middle-class tastes it represented has to do with the nature of Mexican American middle-class society itself.

Wishing to distance itself from the more agrarian and Mexicanized culture of the poorer people, the middle class had gravitated toward more sophisticated forms of artistic culture, such as the *orquesta*, while favoring a more urban, "Americanized" lifestyle. As a result of discrimination practiced against Mexicans by non-Hispanic whites throughout much of the twentieth century, middle-class Mexican Americans were frustrated in their attempts to be accepted as equal citizens of the United States and were thus continually forced to reaffirm their Mexicanness in an Anglo-dominated society.

The solution to this frustrated desire to be simply "American" was to be both "Mexican" and "American," or bicultural. This biculturalism, involving both acculturation and resistance, gave rise to the bimusical *orquesta*, an ensemble that, like its creators, swung between the stylistic poles represented by Mexican and American music. *Música* RANCHERA (country music) reconnected Mexican Americans to their "roots," and *música jaitona* (hightone music) helped them to feel more "middle class" and "American."

Orquesta's uniqueness lay in bimusicality, or the ability to combine Mexican and U.S. music. From the *conjunto* repertoire the *orquesta* borrowed the polka and the HUAPANGO; from middle-class orchestras in the United States it adopted the swing and fox-trot; and from Mexican *orquestas* it appropriated the BOLERO, the DANZÓN, and other genres.

After Villa certified the *ranchero-jaitón* combination as the norm for the Mexican American *orquesta*, others followed. Isidro López, born in 1933 in Bishop, Texas, synthesized Mexican and American musical elements much more than Villa did. He was an important transitional figure who bridged two musical generations—the Mexican American, active between about 1930 and 1960, and the Chicano, active from about 1965 to 1985. Beto Villa epitomized the former generation; the latter was represented by Little Joe Hernández, born in 1940 in Temple, Texas.

The era represented by Little Joe and his *orquesta*, known as La Familia, marked a new stage in the *orquesta* tradition in the Southwest. During this stage, known as *La Onda Chicana*, the *orquesta* completely synthesized elements from various musics—American, Mexican, RANCHERA, and *jaitón*—to create a hybrid style that enjoyed phenomenal success among the Chicano generation. *La Onda Chicana* reflected a changed cultural climate in the Hispanic Southwest. Dissatisfied with what they saw as the older generation's lack of ethnic pride, the Chicanos discarded their elders' desire to be accepted by non-Hispanic whites. They proudly accepted their ethnic, working-class roots while adopting those elements from U.S. culture that served their purposes.

La Onda Chicana reflected this pragmatic, pick-and-choose attitude, but in its stylistic combinations it went beyond mere selection. It synthesized all the musical elements mentioned earlier to achieve a highly innovative bimusical sound that combined *ranchera* and *jaitón* within the same piece. In this fusion, Little Joe y la Familia took the undisputed lead, dominating the field throughout the 1960's and 1970's as the musical voice of the Chicano generation.

Other important *orquestas* from *La Onda Chicana* include Sunny Ozuna (born in 1943 in San Antonio, Texas) and the Sunliners, Tony "Ham" Guerrero (born in 1944 in San Angelo, Texas) and the Tortilla Factory, and Jimmy Edward Treviño (born in 1951 in San Antonio). In their collective efforts, the *orquestas* that created *La Onda Chicana* represent one of the most innovative eras in American ethnic music.

—*Manuel Peña*

SUGGESTED READINGS:

• Loza, Steven. *Barrio Rhythm: Mexican American Music in Los Angeles*. Urbana: University of Illinois Press, 1993. A comprehensive history of Mexican American music in an urban setting.

• Paredes, Americo. *A Texas-Mexican Cancionero*. Urbana: University of Illinois Press, 1976. Excellent history of the *corrido* and other folk songs of the Southwest.

• Paredes, Americo. *"With His Pistol in His Hand"*: *A Border Ballad and Its Hero*. Austin: University of Texas Press, 1958. Traces the history of the *corrido*, using the ballad of Gregorio Cortez as the focus.

• Peña, Manuel. *The Texas-Mexican Conjunto*. Austin: University of Texas Press, 1985. An interpretive history of the *conjunto*.

Music and musicians, South American: South American music and musicians form a tradition extending to the pre-Conquest period. Early forms of music have been carried forward or modified, and music of the twentieth century shows influences of the past.

The Pre-Columbian Era. Archaeological evidence and early chroniclers indicate that several pre-Columbian civilizations had strong musical traditions. Although string instruments were unknown, wind and percussion instruments were plentiful. The ubiquitous panpipes of the Andean region were played by the Incas and their predecessors, the Mochica and Nazca peoples. Musical war trophies, such as *quenas* (notched end-blown flutes) made from enemies' bones, are described by chronicler Garciliaso de la Vega. The Aztecs used music to accompany human sacrifice.

A Bolivian group plays panpipes. (Claire Rydell)

Among pre-Columbian peoples, music was used in rituals and generally was believed to possess magical powers. Pre-Columbian practices and beliefs survived among indigenous communities of the late twentieth century. Some of these communities, for example, used music in cattle-marking ceremonies or for supernatural aid in courtship.

The Colonial Era. After the SPANISH CONQUEST, many musical practices of the Indians were forbidden and instruments were destroyed. During the colonial era, church authorities favored polyphonic choral music composed by Europeans or by immigrant and native-born composers in the European style. Important composers of sacred music include Hernando Franco (1532-1585) in Mexico and Gutierre Fernandez-Hidalgo (c. 1555-1627) in Colombia. Among secular genres, the *villancico* and *negrillo* are significant for incorporating black or Indian dialects and musical characteristics. Gaspar Fernandes (c. 1566-1629) is the best-known composer of *negrillos.*

Independence. In South America, the period between 1810 and 1825 saw many former Spanish colonies gain their independence. Sacred music declined in importance. Cathedral music libraries fell into ruin, and previously high performance standards dropped sharply. Concurrently, there was a surge in secular music, particularly opera. Italian opera was extremely popular, and lavish opera houses were built in South American cities.

The preferred operas were composed by Italians or by South Americans who composed in the Italian style. Brazilian Carlos Gomez (1836-1896) wrote many successful operas, including *Il Guarani,* based on Amazon legends.

Salon music for the piano, consisting of short sentimental pieces of moderate difficulty, enjoyed favor among the elite, who preferred European dances including the minuet, polka, waltz, and contredanse, on which the CONTRADANZA is based. Many South American dances were derived from European models. For example, both the Argentine RANCHERA and the Mexican *jarabe* evolved from the mazurka. Nineteenth century South American composers continued to follow European stylistic models. A few composers, such as Peru's Daniel Alomía Robles (1871-1942), ventured to quote folk music.

The Twentieth Century. During the 1900's, many South American composers were nationalists, using folkloric materials within the traditions of European concert music. In Brazil, Heitor Villa-Lobos (1887-1959) achieved international recognition. His series of *Bachianas Brasileiras* explored the similarities between the music of Johann Sebastian Bach and the folk music of northern Brazil. Mexican composer Carlos Chávez earned recognition for such nationalist works as his *Sinfonia India* for orchestra, which quotes Yaqui Indian melodies and includes Indian percussion. Alberto Ginastera of Argentina began as a nationalist composer with the ballets *Panambi* (1937) and *Estancia* (1941), then later adopted techniques of the European avant-garde.

Many South American composers who avoided nationalist elements in their compositions embraced what they believed to be universal musical values. They incorporated European and North American avant-garde trends such as atonality (the lack of a tonal center) and aleatoricism (composition by using chance methods).

Folk Music. South America's folk music traditions are nourished by a rich intermingling of cultures drawn from three major ethnic groups: the descendants of European settlers, Indians, and African slaves. Many specific musical traditions are syncretic, or show a blending of multiple influences.

The most prominent European musical influences in South America are from the Iberian Peninsula. Spain and Portugal contributed musical elements including "colonial rhythm" (meter of two beats against three), melodies in parallel thirds (intervals of three scale-tones), and European harmony and scales. Iberian folk-song genres such as the *villancico* (Christmas carol), CANCIÓN de cuna (cradle song), narrative *romance*, and *copla* survived in South America under various names.

South American dances evolved from European genres including the polka, contredanse, jota, and mazurka. Guitars, harps, and violins are among the most popular European-derived string instruments. Variants of the guitar include the Mexican bass *guitarron*, the diminutive Andean CHARANGO, and the Venezuelan CUATRO. In Argentine tango, the *bandoneon*, a button accordion, is a prominent solo instrument.

In the Andean region, which includes those countries once part of the Inca empire, music of the Highland Indian and mestizo people draws from both Inca and Spanish traditions. Drums, panpipes, and other wind instruments of pre-Columbian origin are played separately or in consort with guitars, *charangos*, and other string instruments of European derivation. Harmony is either European or in the pre-Columbian tradition of parallel fifths and fourths, although melodies in thirds are common in mestizo music. Andean melodies are based on scales of three, five, or seven tones. They feature syncopation (off-beat accents) and are repeated with minimal variation. Among the most popular genres are the quick huayno and the slow yaravi.

Musical styles showing varying degrees of African retention are common in South America, especially in coastal regions to which Europeans brought Africans as slaves in the largest numbers. Countries with folk musics showing strong retention of African traits include Brazil, Colombia, Venezuela, Surinam, Guyana, and French Guiana. African-derived traits are less marked in the musics of Uruguay, Argentina, Peru, and Ecuador.

Among the most prominent African-derived musical characteristics are the use of syncopation, additive rhythm (rhythms based on mixed groupings of two and three beats), ostinato (repeated) rhythmic and melodic phrases, extensive use of percussion, and call-and-response form (in which a leader sings a phrase and a chorus answers with a refrain). The least acculturated African-derived styles often feature percussion ensembles including drums, gourd rattlers, and bells, as in the cult music of Bahía, Brazil. More acculturated African-derived styles, such as SALSA and the Brazilian urban SAMBA, may use Western-derived instrumentation similar to that of jazz or rock bands, including brass instruments, saxophones, electric basses and guitars, and drum trap sets. Afro-Caribbean percussion instruments such as conga drums and TIMBALES are also common in salsa.   —*José Manuel Lezcano*

SUGGESTED READINGS: • Béhague, Gerard. "Afro-American Folk Music in North and Latin America." In *Folk and Traditional Music of the Western Continents*, edited by Bruno Nettl. 3d ed. Englewood Cliffs, N.J.: Prentice-Hall, 1990. • Béhague, Gerard. "Latin American Folk Music." In *Folk and Traditional Music of the Western Continents*, edited by Bruno Nettl. 3d ed. Englewood Cliffs, N.J.: Prentice-Hall, 1990. • Chase, Gilbert. *A Guide to the Music of Latin America.* 2d ed. Washington, D.C.: Pan American Union, 1962. • Manuel, Peter. "Latin America and the Caribbean." In *Popular Musics of the Non-Western World*, edited by Peter Manuel. New York: Oxford University Press, 1988. • Olsen, Dale. "Folk Music of South America—A Musical Mosaic." In *Musics of Many Cultures*, edited by Elizabeth May. Los Angeles: University of California Press, 1980. • Slonimsky, Nicolas. *Music of Latin America*. New York: Thomas Y. Crowell, 1945.

Music and musicians, Spanish American: Music, musicians, and musical instruments from Spain arrived in the Americas with the first Spanish explorers; their influences can be found in later folk, classical, and popular music in Hispanic communities in the United States and throughout Latin America. Twentieth century composers and performers from Spain have also contributed significantly to music in the United States.

Origins. The first Spanish music arrived in the Americas in the sixteenth century in the form of vocal music for the Catholic Mass brought by Franciscan and Jesuit missionaries and folk songs and dances brought by soldiers, sailors, and settlers. Some of the finest church music from the sixteenth century was composed by Tomás Luis de Victoria (1548-1611), who studied in Rome with Giovanni Palestrina and later returned to Madrid to serve the Empress Marie. Hernando Franco (1532-1585), a Spanish-born composer, organist, and choir conductor, immigrated to Guatemala before moving to Mexico City, where he composed and directed music at the first cathedral there. Two hymns to the Virgin using a Nahuatl text (the language of the Aztecs) have been found that may have been composed by Franco; such songs illustrate the early and still-continuing evolution and blending of Spanish and American musical materials.

Sacred works from Spain, including masses, motets, psalm settings, organ works, and Magnificats (Christmas cantatas), spread with the missionary padres and later with trained musicians to churches in California and the American Southwest, where converted Native Americans learned to play European musical instruments and sing in choirs. These converts also composed and adapted church choral music using their own native languages as well as Spanish and Latin.

Folk Music. Folk songs also traveled to Spanish settlements throughout the New World, although the composers and lyricists are impossible to identify as a result of both the passage of time and blending with indigenous songs. For example, Latin American songs called ALABADOS, originally used to commemorate saints, have been traced back to southern Spain.

FLAMENCO song and dance, also associated with southern Spain and Andalusia, have a long and complex history that can be traced back through Spanish and Gypsy performers, perhaps to Jewish and Arab music. Highly emotional, expressive, and rhythmic, this music, associated with the guitar, continues to thrive in Hispanic regions of North America.

The *zaranzuela*, a popular Spanish opera form of the seventeenth and eighteenth centuries combining opera, spectacle, and spoken dialogue, was transplanted from Spain, as was the *tonadilla*, a later form of short comic operetta. Musical comedies and short plays performed by contemporary Chicano theaters in California and the American Southwest have their roots in these genres and in medieval morality plays.

Folk music by its nature involves absorption of several cultural styles, as evidenced by the still-popular CORRIDO, or ballad. *Corridos* are derived from an older ballad form, the *romancero* or ROMANCE, in Spain. One such ballad recounting the exploits of the eleventh century Spanish war hero El Cid has been found in New Mexico, where it is still sung. In the 1960's, a *corrido* honoring the exploits of activist César CHÁVEZ appeared in California and the American Southwest, indicating that the Spanish ballad continues within the context of a developing Mexican and Mexican American *corrido* form.

Classical, Opera, and Pop Music. Classical music by Spanish composers has long been popular with symphony concertgoers in the United States. Among the most notable composers is Joaquin Rodrigo, best known for his *Concierto de Aranjuez* and *Concierto Madrigal*, works for guitar and orchestra. Other significant Spanish composers whose works have been played regularly in the United States are Manuel de Falla (1875-1946), widely hailed for his ballet *The Three-Cornered Hat*, and Isaac Albeniz (1861-1909), who toured the United States and Mexico performing his piano work *Iberia*, a set of musical impressions of Spain. The popularity of these artists and their works in the United States has resulted from both the colorful rhythms and melodies associated with Spain and the virtuoso artistry of guitar players such as Pepe Romero and Andrés Segovia.

In the world of opera, Spanish tenor José Carreras has moved to the forefront of the world opera scene, having performed in New York, San Francisco, and Chicago and on international television with Italian tenor Luciano Pavarotti and Mexican tenor Placido

Lively dance forms accompany some types of Spanish music. (New Mexico Magazine, Mark Nohl)

Domingo. In pop vocal music, Julio IGLESIAS has sold millions of albums in the United States, in Mexico, and throughout Central America, South America, and Europe. Born in Madrid and trained as a lawyer and soccer goalkeeper, Iglesias took up singing and songwriting in the late 1960's. Iglesias, who performs in seven languages, is one of the best-known Spanish musicians in the world. His record sales of more than one hundred million have earned for him a place in the *Guinness Book of World Records.* —*Keith Atwater*

SUGGESTED READINGS: • Béhague, Gerard. *Music in Latin America: An Introduction.* Englewood Cliffs, N.J.: Prentice-Hall, 1979. • Chase, Gilbert. *The Music of Spain.* New York: W. W. Norton, 1941. • Espinosa, Aurelio M. *The Folklore of Spain in the American Southwest.* Norman: University of Oklahoma Press, 1985. • Livermore, Ann. *A Short History of Spanish Music.* New York: Vienna House, 1972. • Marco, Tomás. *Spanish Music in the Twentieth Century.* Translated by Cola Franzen. Cambridge, Mass.: Harvard University Press, 1993. • Slonimsky, Nicolas. *Music of Latin America.* New York: Thomas Y. Crowell, 1945.

Música norteña: Musical tradition characteristic of northern Mexico and the United States-Mexico border region. The term goes back to the nineteenth century, when the northern region of Mexico had been substantially settled. Such dance forms as the polka, the *mazurca*, the VALSE, and the *paso doble* are considered to be different types of *música norteña*. Typical ensembles feature the button-key accordion and the *bajo sexto* (large twelve-string bass guitar), two instruments widely spread at the time in the same region. The music bears close resemblance to the CANCIÓN ranchera, *canciones revolucionarias*, and CORRIDOS.

Música tropical: Generic term designating popular music of urban Latin America. *Música tropical* encompasses a wide array of music and dance forms that originated in the Caribbean region. *Música tropical* is performed by CONJUNTO bands of musicians featuring native instruments such as the GÜIRO, BONGOS, and MARACAS. All Afro-Cuban dance music forms, such as the SALSA, the SAMBA, the GUARACHA, the CONGA, the MAMBO, the *CUMBIA* of Colombia, and the MERENGUE of the Dominican Republic, are covered by this collective label.

Mustangs: Horses from the western United States. Mustangs, the horses that roamed free in the western United States, were brought by the Spaniards to the Southwest. Although the horse originated on the American continent, it became extinct there thousands of years ago and was absent until its reintroduction by the Spanish.

The origin of the mustangs in the Southwest probably dates to an expedition by Juan de OÑATE in 1598. He took 325 horses with him, and they proliferated. In 1680, natives attacked Santa Fe and killed hundreds of Spaniards. They captured many horses, but some escaped and ran wild. These horses and their descendants became the mustangs. The horse became an essential animal for the Indians of North America, who used them in hunting, warfare, and recreation.

Mutualistas: Mutual aid or mutual benefit societies. Mutual aid societies developed in the United States among ethnic minorities in the 1880's and 1890's and continued through the twentieth century. These organizations held a central position in U.S. ethnic life. In the absence of meaningful government assistance, mutual benefit societies formalized the help immigrants gave to persons from their country in times of need. They served as a cultural liaison between countries of origin and the new, adopted society of the United States.

Most mutual aid societies attempted to meet the material needs of their members with emergency loans and other forms of financial assistance, job-seeking services, and health and death insurance. Many organizations expanded their services to include sponsorship of civic affairs, newspapers, private schools, and popular community events for entertainment and socializing. These functions helped to establish a sense of belonging and refuge from an often hostile, xenophobic environment. Although men dominated most of these organizations, women also formed auxiliary societies or independent groups. Throughout much of the East, the Far West, and the Midwest, Italians, Poles, Czechs, and other Southern and Eastern European immigrants established benefit societies; in the Midwest, Southwest, and Far West, Mexican immigrants formed *mutualistas*.

Scholars of Chicano history have argued that *mutualistas* served as a major point of organizational unity for local and regional political struggles. Because of strong discrimination against Mexican people, *mutualistas* had to assert the civil rights of Mexican Americans. Dual wage scales and mistreatment of Mexican workers in the workplace often invoked responses from groups that otherwise would have confined their attention to insurance matters. Many *mutualistas* through-

Members of the Alianza Hispano-Americana in Tucson, Arizona, prepare for a parade. (Arizona Historical Society)

out the Southwest combined the functions of mutual aid societies with labor activism. Texas *mutualistas* of the 1910's and 1920's, such as El Congreso Mexicanista, La Gran Liga Mexicanista, La Sociedad Mutualista Protectora, and the Woodmen of the World, exhibited a particularly high level of involvement in labor struggles, also speaking out against police abuse against Mexican Americans and Mexican nationals living in the United States.

Aside from their own particular battles, *mutualistas* routinely endorsed the struggles of political action groups that operated in defense of Mexican American civil rights. In the 1930's, the LEAGUE OF UNITED LATIN AMERICAN CITIZENS (LULAC) easily won the support of mutual aid societies across the Southwest in its effort to improve educational facilities for Mexican American schoolchildren. The ALIANZA HISPANO-AMERICANA, the Federación Obreras Latino-Americana, the Order Hijos de America (SONS OF AMERICA), and the Sociedad Benito Juárez were only a few of the organizations that backed the LULAC struggle. The

Alianza Hispano-Americana, a *mutualista* founded in Tucson, Arizona, in 1894, also supported more radical labor organizations such as the Asociación Nacional Mexico-Americana (ANMA), an organization strongly influenced by the Communist Party. The Alianza Hispano-Americana joined with various groups, including the Congress of Industrial Organizations (CIO), the American Civil Liberties Union (ACLU), and African American newspapers to celebrate the ANMA's 1949 founding convention.

Mythical biography: The AZTECS chose AZTLÁN as the name for their empire and homeland. Many Mexican Americans still recognize Aztlán as their spiritual home. Although Mexico surrendered huge tracts of land to the United States in 1848 by the signing of the TREATY OF GUADALUPE HIDALGO, Mexicans and Mexican Americans have not forgotten that Texas, New Mexico, and California were once part of the Aztec empire of their ancestors. Some Mexican Americans speak longingly of a future return to Mexico and of the Mexico that once was, yet they continue living within the dominant white culture and struggling to retain their customs and their language.

Other Latinos visualize Aztlán as the symbol of a mythical promised land where members of La RAZA (the race) will live in unity and harmony. The humanistic, group-centered nature of this Aztlán contrasts with the acquisitive, individualistic nature of the "Colossus of the North" (the United States).

For Latinos, the dormant vision of Aztlán was reawakened as part of the struggle for minority rights during the Civil Rights movement of the 1960's. A separate identity for Latinos in the Anglo culture already existed, as evidenced by racial and economic stratification. The *MOJADO* (WETBACK) was always assigned to the lowest ranks in the economic structure. The brown skin of Latinos set them apart both from the white majority and from African Americans and other black-skinned people, who were struggling to achieve a new place within U.S. society while reclaiming pride in their African heritage.

Latinos kept history and folklore alive through the oral traditions of song and story. *Corridos*, ballads that celebrate the lives of Mexican American folk heroes, have been sung on both sides of the border since the late nineteenth century. The heroes of these songs fought against an unjust system of laws and drama-tized the unrewarded expectations of those who crossed the border.

In 1972, Rudolfo Alfonso ANAYA's novel *Bless Me, Ultima* created national and international awareness of the plight of Latinos living within the United States. Set in rural New Mexico in the mid-1940's, the story reflected the cultural conflict caused by the demands that post-World War II society imposed upon those living in the geographical area that once was Aztlán. The fate of the members of this world, which was destroyed by the dawning of the Atomic Age, is found in the sequel *Heart of Aztlán* (1976).

By the 1980's, at least two perspectives existed for Mexican Americans. One is exemplified in the pessimism of Genaro GONZÁLEZ, whose protagonist in the novel *Rainbow's End* (1988) finds death instead of honor at the end of the rainbow. Optimism can be found in the upsurge of interest in the Chicano experience reflected by international conferences in Paris in 1987, by the founding of the journal *Aztlán*, and by the passage of the NORTH AMERICAN FREE TRADE AGREEMENT, which recognized Mexico as an equal of the United States and Canada on the North American continent.

As the twenty-first century neared, many Chicanos rejected the idea of the permanence of the Rio Grande border. They invoked one name for the lands where Mexicans and Mexican Americans reside—Aztlán.

N

Nachos: Snack of tortilla chips with chiles and cheese. Nacho's Restaurant in Piedras Negras, Coahuila, Mexico, claims to have originated this snack, which has become popular along the U.S.-Mexico border and has been discovered by Anglo-Americans. Nachos consist of tortilla quarters fried until crisp, garnished with cheese and chile slices, then broiled just long enough to melt the cheese. This dish is far more popular in the United States than in Mexico.

Nacimiento: Nativity scene. *Nacimiento* (literally, "birth" in Spanish) refers to nativity scenes commonly found at Christmas time in Latin American homes. These scenes depict the story of Jesus' birth with figures made out of clay, plastic, or wood. They are set in three-dimensional surroundings depicting the stable, animals, and surrounding countryside. The styles vary depending on culture and availability of materials, but all contain the basic elements of the virgin birth.

NAFTA. *See* **North American Free Trade Agreement**

Narváez, Pánfilo de (c. 1470, Valladolid, Spain—1528, Gulf of Mexico): Explorer and conquistador. Narváez's first enterprise in the New World was the conquest and occupation of the island of Jamaica. In 1511, he went to Cuba. Under the leadership of Diego VELÁZQUEZ DE CUÉLLAR, he participated in the occupation and settlement of that island.

In 1520, Velázquez sent Narváez to arrest Hernán CORTÉS in Mexico. Cortés had gone to conquer Mexico in Velázquez's name but kept the colony for himself. Narváez, however, was unable to capture Cortés; instead, Cortés imprisoned Narváez until 1522.

Narváez's most famous expedition, beginning in 1528, was an attempt to discover, conquer, and settle FLORIDA. The expedition arrived in the area of Tampa Bay and made way inland. The natives did not receive the explorers well. After several attacks, Narváez and his party retreated to the coast and sailed away in makeshift barges. They headed west, following the coast of the Gulf of Mexico. Narváez's barge disappeared in a strong current, and it is believed that he died at sea.

In another barge was Álvar Núñez CABEZA DE VACA, the most famous member of that expedition. He survived eight years among the Indians and returned to Spain to tell his story.

Nascimento, Milton (b. Oct. 26, 1942, Rio de Janeiro, Brazil): Singer, songwriter, and bandleader. Nascimento grew up in a small town and was reared by adoptive parents. In 1965, he moved to São Paolo, where he struggled as a musician. He later met Brazilian singer Elis Regina, who got him into the recording studio.

In 1967, Nascimento skyrocketed into the national music scene, during the First International Pop Song Festival in Rio de Janeiro. Singer Agostihno dos Santos had encouraged him to submit some songs. Nascimento at first refused, because he had been involved in similar festivals and had hated the competitive atmosphere and egoism involved. Dos Santos nevertheless asked Nascimento for three songs, which he taped at home and sent to the festival. When the festival was over, Nascimento found out that he had been the only artist allowed to present three songs.

Between 1970 and 1980, Nascimento recorded several albums, including *Travessia*, *Cravo E Canela*, *Native Dancer*, and *Geraes*, with the Chilean group Agua and singer Mercedes Sosa. He has also recorded with Flora PURIM, Airto MOREIRA, Paul Simon, and Herbie Hancock. He has written film scores and has appeared in several films. His music is a unique blend of ethnic Afro-Brazilian, jazz, and rock elements tinged with melancholy.

National Agricultural Workers Union (NAWU): Labor union. The NAWU was created by a renaming of the NATIONAL FARM LABOR UNION in 1952. This union continued the struggle to ensure that farmworkers would receive the minimum wage, unemployment insurance, and better working and living conditions. The presence of larger unions such as the Agricultural Workers Organizing Committee, along with the government-sponsored BRACERO PROGRAM, made it impossible for the union to flourish. In 1964, the Amalgamated Meat Cutters and Butchers Workmen of America took over the union through a merger.

National Alliance of Spanish-Speaking People for Equality (NASSPE): Nonprofit civil rights organization. Founded in 1970, the NASSPE is designed to assist professional journalists and others of Hispanic descent working in the mass media industries in the United States, though its activities work on behalf of a wider constituency.

NASSPE headquarters are in Washington, D.C. The alliance is affiliated with the CONGRESSIONAL HISPANIC CAUCUS, the Consortium of National Hispanic Organizations, and the NATIONAL COUNCIL OF LA RAZA. NASSPE gathers and disseminates information on topics of interest to the Hispanic community both to the media and to Hispanic organizations. Some of these topics include housing, health, education, immigration law, and U.S. foreign policy in Central America.

The alliance's major goal is equal rights for Hispanic people throughout the United States. It works to publicize the views of the Hispanic community and is dedicated to creating networks among Hispanic organizations and U.S. government officials. It conducts lectures and maintains listings of speakers who discuss issues related to the Hispanic community.

National Association of Cuban-American Women: Advocacy group. This group, founded in 1972, carries the full name of Asociación Nacional de Mujeres Cubanoamericanas, de los Estados Unidos de America. In 1986, it absorbed the National Association of Cuban Women and Men of the United States. Membership in 1994 exceeded five thousand.

This national association addresses issues concerning problems affecting Hispanic and minority women and works to achieve such goals as equal education, fair immigration policies, and meaningful work with adequate compensation. It provides direct services to its constituents and seeks to increase awareness among its members about numerous opportunities provided by local, state, and federal agencies. The organization is funded by local, state, and federal grants.

The association disseminates information on postsecondary educational opportunities and sources of financial aid in particular cities. It produces a biweekly bilingual radio program and maintains a library of more than two thousand volumes on subjects such as Cuban history, Cubans in the United States, and human rights violations in Cuba. It also conducts placement services and bestows awards to people who advance the general interests of the organization. It encourages participation in task forces dealing with legislative activities and professional endeavors and acts as a clearinghouse and referral center.

National Association of Hispanic Journalists (NAHJ): Professional association. The NAHJ, founded in 1984, organizes and provides support for Hispanic journalists in English, Spanish, and bilingual news media.

The NAHJ had a membership of nearly two thousand as of the early 1990's. Its state and regional affiliates are connected to a headquarters in Washington, D.C.

The association encourages the study and practice of JOURNALISM and communications by Hispanics. It gives recognition to Hispanic members of the media professions and promotes fair and accurate media treatment of Hispanics. It opposes job discrimination and demeaning stereotypes and is involved in increasing educational and career opportunities and development for Hispanics in the field, offering placement services to Hispanic students. It seeks to foster greater awareness and recognition of members' cultural identity, interests, and concerns. It provides a united voice for Hispanic journalists with the aim of achieving national visibility. Activities of the NAHJ include a census of Hispanic media professionals nationwide, a writing contest, and publication of a job exchange newsletter. The Premio Triunfo recognizes journalism excellence in print, radio, television, and photojournalism.

National Association of Hispanic Publications (NAHP): Professional association. The nonprofit group, founded in 1982 and renamed as the National Federation of Hispanic Owned Newspapers in 1992, promotes the use of Hispanic print media as a valuable means of communication.

The NAHP, headquartered in Orlando, Florida, had a 1991 membership of 103 publishers and editors representing Hispanic-oriented newspapers printed in the United States. The group recruits and trains print journalists and provides information on current as well as out-of-print Hispanic publications, maintaining a library of those publications.

The Hispanic press was generally thriving in the early 1990's, growing in number of publications and revenue twice as quickly as the English-language print media. Growth resulted from rapid and continuing increase in the Hispanic population and the fact that Hispanic newspapers and magazines addressed the needs and interests of their target audience, filling a gap left by the mainstream press.

Members of the organization believe that despite the dramatic growth of the Hispanic press, their newspapers are being largely overlooked by corporate advertisers. They see misperception of Hispanic consumers as one reason for the failure of the Spanish-language press to receive more advertising from large corporate clients.

National Association of Latino Elected and Appointed Officials (NALEO): National organization of

Hispanic officeholders. NALEO was established in 1976 as an avenue for Latinos who served in both elected and appointed office—including local, state, and national levels—to come together in a cohesive manner. NALEO is a national, nonpartisan, nonprofit Hispanic civic research and action organization, concerned with a broad range of issues affecting the Hispanic community. The organization attempts to address issues such as children in poverty, federal employment of Hispanics, citizenship, and amnesty.

NALEO is the foremost advocate of increased access to U.S. citizenship for legal permanent residents. Additionally, NALEO informs Hispanic voters on issues affecting the Hispanic community and registers Hispanic voters. The organization also maintains a clearinghouse of citizenship materials.

National Chicano Health Organization (NCHO): Professional organization. The NCHO encourages and prepares Chicano high school and college students for careers in health care. It was established in the early 1970's by Chicano medical students. Its founders noticed that Chicanos were underrepresented in schools teaching the health professions and attributed this fact to poor self-esteem, inadequate mentoring and guidance of students (especially culturally relevant techniques), and lack of information or misinformation given to prospective applicants. NCHO linked the poor health and high infant mortality in Chicano barrios to the lack of health care workers there. The group has devised programs for high schools to recruit and prepare Chicano students for careers in medicine and public health. On the college level, it has recruited students and helped secure financial aid for health care schooling.

National Chicano Moratorium on Vietnam: A peaceful antiwar demonstration protesting the involvement of Mexican Americans in the Vietnam War. On August 29, 1970, a Mexican American anti-Vietnam War rally took place in EAST LOS ANGELES, California, a district about eight miles east of downtown Los Angeles in which about one million Mexican Americans resided. The rally, called the National Chicano Moratorium on Vietnam, was organized by the National Chicano Moratorium Committee to protest what it considered to be a disproportionate number of Mexican Americans serving on the front lines in Vietnam. The organizers called for Mexican Americans to fight for social reform and equality at home and not to fight in Vietnam.

The demonstration was the largest event organized by Mexican Americans in East Los Angeles history. About seven thousand protesters carried signs calling for peace and criticizing what they regarded as President Richard Nixon's racist policies on Vietnam. The demonstrators marched peacefully into Laguna Park for an afternoon rally following a five-mile walk through East Los Angeles.

Rioting erupted at the rally as approximately three hundred police officers dressed in riot gear descended on demonstrators. The trouble began near the site of the rally, although accounts vary as to the initial spark that ignited the violence. Organizers of the rally denounced the violence and denied any involvement in starting it. According to police reports, the trouble started when several youths tried to loot a nearby liquor store and attacked officers who were summoned to the scene. The police claimed that some demonstrators from the park joined the melee in front of the liquor store. Two hundred police officers were then called in to secure the park and to assist the officers monitoring the rally. As the police moved in, the crowd of demonstrators spilled onto Whittier Boulevard, a main artery in the business district. Demonstrators and police clashed for four hours as officers used tear gas to disperse crowds and demonstrators burned buildings and smashed store windows. The riot resulted in more than two hundred arrests, at least one death, at least fifty injuries, and extensive property damage. Some estimates put the number of people involved as high as twenty thousand. Journalist Rubén SALAZAR was an indirect casualty, killed by being hit in the head with a tear gas canister while inside a business near the rioting.

National Chicano Survey: Survey of the Chicano population. Conducted in 1979, the National Chicano Survey interviewed 991 persons of Mexican origin. The survey covered all states except those with Mexican-origin populations composing less than 1 percent of the state's total population. The survey focused on the Southwest and Chicago, Illinois. Researchers led by principal investigator Carlos Arce gathered data concerning language, culture, literacy, immigration experiences and patterns, family roles, labor force activity, and political activity. The survey was the first of its kind to focus specifically on the situation of Chicanos. The resulting data were used in planning for the Chicano community.

National Coalition of Hispanic Health and Human Services Organizations: Organization of mental health professionals. Founded in 1973 as the Coalition of Spanish-Speaking Mental Health Organizations, this group still is known as COSSMHO. Membership by 1994 included more than 250 institutions and agencies and more than 800 professional individuals.

The group's primary mission is to help Hispanic community-based organizations to develop new model programs, strengthen local infrastructures, and conduct studies. This private nonprofit organization receives federal grants and contracts, foundation support, corporate support, and membership dues. Private funding has increased from 1 percent at the agency's founding to more than one-third of the agency's budget. The agency accepts no funding from tobacco or alcohol companies.

The agency has been involved in AIDS education projects among Hispanics and has been in the forefront of women's health issues. It advocates expanding the base of basic health research, which has concentrated on white males. Agency activities focus on increasing awareness of emerging issues among decision makers, increasing funding for community-based programs, providing direct funding and technical assistance to community-based organizations, and other community-based demonstrations and programs.

National Conference of Puerto Rican Women: Women's advocacy group. This group, founded in 1972, had a 1994 membership in excess of three thousand. It included seventeen state groups and a national headquarters in Washington, D.C., that encouraged the formation of more local chapters and fostered closer ties among them. The organization's main goals are first, to promote the full participation of Puerto Rican and other Hispanic women in the economic, social, and political life of the United States and Puerto Rico, and second, to collaborate with other organizations promoting equal rights. Its political and lobbying activities are performed in concert with those of other civil rights organizations.

Three times a year, the organization publishes *Ecos Nacionales*, a newsletter covering issues affecting Puerto Rican and other Hispanic women. The publication also includes association news, book reviews, local chapter news, and listings of employment opportunities. The organization also publishes various speeches, books, and articles.

National Congress for Puerto Rican Rights: Civil rights organization. The National Congress for Puerto Rican Rights was established in 1981 and had a 1994

The National Congress for Puerto Rican Rights promotes a variety of civil rights causes. (Richard B. Levine)

membership of more than three thousand, with five affiliates. The organization acts as an advocate for the civil and human rights of Puerto Ricans in regard to education, labor, voting, housing, women's issues, the media, health, and justice. It also opposes U.S. governmental intervention in Latin America and the Caribbean.

The group maintains a speakers bureau, compiles statistics, and publishes *Convention Document*, a summary of the findings of the group's biennial conference. It also publishes a quarterly newsletter entitled *Unidad Borinqueña*.

The organization sponsors task forces on labor and women's issues. These task forces work to alleviate discrimination against Puerto Ricans and to monitor legislation affecting Puerto Ricans. The group uses lobbying and supports demonstrations as part of its efforts to achieve its goals at both the national and local levels.

National Council of Hispanic Women: Advocacy group. This national organization, with approximately two thousand members in 1994, is dedicated to enhancing the role of Hispanic women in American society. There are institutional as well as individual members including Hispanic women and men, corporations, universities, and government representatives. The common bond and philosophical backbone of the organization is the conception that Hispanics in general and Hispanic women in particular are not participating as they should in various levels of society. One concern is the relatively low economic status of the Hispanic population of the United States.

This organization seeks to express the concerns and interests of Hispanic women by participating in the decision-making process, promoting ideals that will keep the United States safe and strong, and improving the economic and social conditions of Hispanics. The organization works to bring Hispanics in general and Hispanic women in particular into the mainstream of American society.

These aims are pursued through promoting the exchange of ideas and creating forums for these exchanges to take place. The group sponsors public forums, public policy debates, television interviews, and other means of mass communication.

National Council of La Raza (NCLR): The NCLR is a nonprofit organization founded in 1968 to provide technical assistance to Latino community groups and engage in research, policy analysis, and advocacy on issues important to Latinos. Established in Arizona as the Southwest Council of La Raza, the organization moved its headquarters to its Washington, D.C., office, which was opened in 1970. The group's name was changed to the National Council of La Raza in 1972.

The NCLR's early efforts resulted in greater Latino participation in federal programs such as the Manpower Development Training Act (MDTA), Comprehensive Employment and Training Act (CETA), and Job Training Partnership Act (JTPA). The NCLR worked with emerging Latino organizations in the late 1960's and the 1970's, assisting with funding as well as staff and board development. The NCLR continues to provide training and seed grants to affiliate organizations, which numbered about 150 in the early 1990's.

The NCLR has provided investment capital to numerous Latino entrepreneurs and community development corporations, including the Mexican American Unity Council in San Antonio, Texas; Chicanos por la Causa in Phoenix, Arizona; and The East Los Angeles Community Union. It also has supported housing development by participating in projects such as Project PARAR (Proyecto de Asistencia y Rehacimiento de Alojamiento Rural), Project IDEA (Proyecto Industria, Desarrollo, Entrenamiento y Asistencia), and the Rio Grande Valley Development Project.

Beginning in 1979, the NCLR attempted to influence federal policy on education by publishing analyses of dropout prevention programs, migrant education, and bilingual education. It helped create reauthorization language for the Bilingual Education Act in 1984, 1986, and 1988. In 1984, it began Project EXCEL, a community-based effort to reform and supplement public school systems. This project developed education models such as Project Success, an after-school and summer program to increase high school completion and college entrance rates, and Project Second Chance, a dropout recovery program. In 1987, the NCLR authored the English Literacy Grants Program, and between 1988 and 1990, it promoted President George Bush's Executive Order on Hispanic Educational Excellence. Other NCLR projects address Latino issues such as health care, poverty, the elderly, civil rights, and employment.

The NCLR is governed by a twenty-six-member board of directors that must reflect the diversity of the Latino population. In 1994, Raúl Yzaguirre had been president and chief executive officer since 1974, overseeing a budget of $7 million dollars and a staff of sixty-four people.

National Farm Labor Union (NFLU): Labor union. The NFLU was founded in 1947 from remnants of the Southern Tenant Farmers Union, founded in 1934. The NFLU was headed by Hank Hasiwar and Ernesto GALARZA in California. The union organized a strike against the Di Giorgio Corporation in 1947, demanding higher wages and improvements in working and living conditions (*see* DI GIORGIO FRUIT CORPORATION STRIKE). The corporation successfully discredited the union, stating that it had a handful of members, no grievances, and no contracts. The union also headed unsuccessful strikes against melon growers in the Imperial Valley in 1951-1952 and the Schenley Corporation (grape growers) in 1952. The union was renamed as the NATIONAL AGRICULTURAL WORKERS UNION in 1952 and had a peak membership of about four thousand. It dwindled to about two hundred members by the mid-1960's. In 1964, it merged with the Amalgamated Meat Cutters and Butchers Workmen of America.

National Farm Workers Association (NFWA): Labor union. The NFWA was originally named the Farm Workers Association (FWA). César CHÁVEZ founded the FWA in 1962 in Delano, California, to improve the wages and living situation of farmworkers and their families. In 1965, the organization changed its name to the National Farm Workers Association. The union established a cooperative grocery store, drug store, health clinic, gas station, and credit union. It successfully negotiated with Schenley Industries for a farmworkers' wage increase. In 1967, the Agricultural Workers Organizing Committee and the NFWA merged to form the United Farm Workers Organizing Committee (UFWOC). In 1972, the organization's

The National Farm Workers Association organized a march from Delano to Sacramento, California, in 1966 as part of its protest against grape growers. (AP/Wide World Photos)

name was changed to the UNITED FARM WORKERS OF AMERICA (UFW).

National Hispanic Media Coalition (founded 1986): Professional association. The coalition promotes employment of Hispanics in radio, television, and film as well as portrayal of positive images of Hispanic Americans in these media.

As of 1994, the coalition had fifty-five thousand members and an annual budget of $75,000. The coalition was formed as a community response to media-related issues. Founding members in Los Angeles, California, objected to local news coverage that focused on gang violence and issues of illegal immigration and ignored positive cultural events. The group also objected to the lack of Hispanic weeknight anchors.

In 1993, the coalition hosted the screening of two new films created under the auspices of the Hispanic Film Project and Universal Studios. The project became a stand-alone nonprofit foundation and intended to expand its work to include other film studios. The coalition, in partnership with African American and other groups within the Caucus for Media Diversity, protested against the sale of *The New York Post* to Rupert Murdoch. Members have testified before U.S. civil rights hearings in Los Angeles regarding minority representations in the media.

National Labor Relations Act (1935): Labor law. Also known as the Wagner Act in honor of its sponsor, Senator Robert Wagner of New York, the act established the right of workers to bargain collectively for better wages and working conditions. The act also established a federal agency known as the National Labor Relations Board (NLRB) to serve as a court of appeals to investigate and resolve charges of unfair labor practices and bargaining disputes. The NLRB did not recognize unions as legal organizations but only as bargaining agents for workers. The board's role in mediation made it more difficult for unions to use the threat of strikes as an effective weapon to achieve change.

National Puerto Rican Coalition (NPRC): Nonprofit public interest organization. The NPRC fosters the social, economic, and political well-being of all Puerto Ricans, evaluates the potential impact of legislative and government proposals and policies on the Puerto Rican community, and provides technical assistance and training to Puerto Rican organizations.

In 1977, a group of forty community representatives met in Washington, D.C., at the invitation of the U.S. Commission on Civil Rights to discuss the future of the stateside Puerto Rican community. The commission had released a report in 1976 titled *Puerto Ricans in the United States: An Uncertain Future*. It convened the meeting to discuss what community leaders could do to offer a more promising future.

A consensus emerged that there was a need for an organization in Washington, D.C., to represent the interests of Puerto Ricans before national policymakers. The NPRC was incorporated as a membership organization in 1977 and received tax-exempt status early in 1980. That year, a two-year contract from the U.S. Department of Housing and Urban Development enabled the NPRC to begin full-time operations.

By the early 1990's, the NPRC consisted of more than eighty organizations located throughout the United States and in Puerto Rico. To further its mission, the NPRC has developed programs in three broad areas. Programs in advocacy, research, and policy analysis are carried out primarily in Washington, D.C. Programs designed to enhance the image of Puerto Ricans in the United States, such as the Life Achievement Awards, are conducted nationally. Partnership projects in community economic development are carried out locally. All programs are designed with the goal of empowering the community to effectively influence public policies and their implementation.

Among the NPRC's major achievements has been the reduction of barriers to both economic and political participation. Throughout its history, the organization has taken concrete steps to strengthen its capacity to provide technical assistance and support to other Puerto Rican organizations and to ensure input into national policy decisions that affect the Puerto Rican community. The NPRC worked with the U.S. Bureau of the Census to ensure adequate Puerto Rican participation at the community level in the bureau's various outreach programs, particularly the local Complete Count committees that coordinated the 1990 census. Its continuous advocacy efforts have been successful in grassroots organization and coalition building focused on welfare reform, education program reauthorization, housing, gun control, and health reform.

The national office of the NPRC is in Washington, D.C. In 1994, NPRC membership exceeded five hundred, including both individual and corporate members. The organization published an annual report, individual status reports (policy analysis, community networking, technical assistance, and membership services advocacy), and a monthly newsletter titled *NPRC Reports*.

National Puerto Rican Forum: Service organization. Founded in 1957, this organization has gone through a downsizing process in order to refocus its activities and reshape its agenda. Its purposes include identifying the obstacles that block the advancement of Hispanics. It is concerned with the overall improvement of Puerto Rican communities throughout the United States. The agency designs and implements programs to provide job counseling, training, and placement as well as teaching English as a second language. Na-

tional career services and job placement efforts focus on bilingual secretaries, clerical workers, and data entry workers.

During the early 1990's, the center operated a translation service for the New York State Department of Social Services. Other services provided were English skills training, world-of-work orientation, high school equivalency preparation, and job counseling.

The agency also focused on advocacy and the creation of a national Puerto Rican agenda. Along with several other Puerto Rican agencies, it sponsored the National Puerto Rican Summit in Washington, D.C., in September of 1994.

Job placement is a major goal of the National Puerto Rican Forum. (Jim West)

Nava-Villarreal, Hector Rolando (b. May 23, 1943, Nuevo Laredo, Tamaulipas, Mexico): Oncologist and medical researcher. Nava-Villarreal's medical research concentrates on oncology, or the study of cancer. He received his training in Mexico, including his M.D. degree, which he received from the medical faculty of the Universidad de Nuevo León in 1967. He did his internship in Corpus Christi, Texas, and his residency at the Roswell Park Cancer Institute in Buffalo, New York, where he also served as a fellow in surgical oncology from 1974 to 1976. From 1968 to 1970, Nava-Villarreal served in Vietnam in the U.S. Army as a battalion surgeon. He began work as a cancer researcher at the Roswell Park Cancer Institute in 1976. He is noted for pioneering work in the use of lasers to treat cancer.

Navarro, Gabriel (b. Guadalajara, Mexico): Playwright, journalist, and actor. Navarro spent twelve years in the Mexican Army in Veracruz and Sonora during the Mexican Revolution. He went to Los Angeles in 1922 in the Compañía Nuevo México and soon started his own Compañía de Operetas, Dramas, Zarzuelas y Revistas Méxicanas. His numerous *revistas* included *Los Angeles al día* (1922, with frequent collaborator Eduardo Carrillo), *La ciudad de los extras* (1922), *Su excelencia, el amor* (1923), *México quiere paz* (1926), *La ciudad de irás y no volverás* (1927), and *Loco amor* (1932).

In the 1930's, Navarro came to deplore the nearly pornographic burlesque performances that abounded in the Los Angeles theater and called for more serious drama. His own plays included dramas and historical epics such as *Los emigrados* (1928), *El sacrificio* (1931), and *Alma yaqui* (1932). As a journalist, Navarro launched a magazine, *La Revista de Los Angeles*, in Los Angeles in 1923, wrote for *El Hispano Americano* in San Diego during the late 1920's, and was theater critic for *La Opinión* in Los Angeles in the 1930's. In that position, he called the public's attention to the plight of theatrical artists during the Depression.

Navarro, José Antonio (Feb. 27, 1795, San Antonio, Tex.—Jan. 13, 1871, San Antonio, Tex.): Politician. Born to a Spanish émigré who became a merchant on the Texas frontier, Navarro spent his early years in northern Mexico, central Texas, and Louisiana. He returned to San Antonio in 1816 and became widely known because of his commercial activities.

Navarro's election to the state legislature in 1821 launched his political career. He unsuccessfully attempted to ease tensions between Tejano and Anglo settlers in the early 1830's. A believer in federalism, Navarro was one of three Tejanos who signed Texas' declaration of conditional independence from Mexico in 1835. He later helped write the constitution for the new republic of Texas.

Navarro served as one of the four commissioners in the ill-fated SANTA FE EXPEDITION of 1841. He was captured and condemned to death as a traitor, but his sentence was later commuted to life imprisonment. Navarro escaped from prison and returned to Texas following the ouster of Antonio López de Santa Anna as Mexico's president in 1845.

Navarro took an active part in Texas politics during the next four years, but the increasing racial intolerance of many Americans led him to retire from public life in 1849. He died of cancer in 1871.

Negrete, Jorge (1911, Guanajuato, Mexico—Dec. 5, 1953, Los Angeles, Calif.): Singer and actor. As a young man, Negrete began a military career, but he soon gave up his training for singing. In the early 1930's, he began appearing on radio programs in Mexico City.

In 1938, Negrete made his first film, *La madrina del diablo*, about a hero rescuing a lady from the convent where her father had confined her. His acting career included more than two dozen films. In addition to possessing a charming baritone voice, Negrete was also handsome and soon became popular among female audiences.

In 1941, during the golden age of Mexican cinema, Negrete portrayed the character of the Mexican singing caballero in *¡Ay Jalisco no te rajes!* The role made him a matinee idol. He embodied the *charro Mexicano* and sang the RANCHERA MUSIC his fans demanded.

Among Negrete's films are *Juntos pero no revueltos* (1939), *Silk, Blood, and Sun* (1943), and *Tierra de pasiones* (1944). Negrete was one of the founders of the National Association of Actors and was instrumental in obtaining recognition and benefits for his fellow Mexican actors.

Neruda, Pablo (Neftalí Ricardo Reyes Basoalto; July 12, 1904, Parral, Chile—Sept. 23, 1973, Santiago, Chile): Poet. Neruda was the son of José Del Carmen Reyes, a farmer and railroad worker, and Rosa Basoalto. Following the death of Neruda's mother from tuberculosis within days of his birth, Neruda and his father moved to the nearby town of Temuco. His father remarried in 1906.

Pablo Neruda (right) accepts the Nobel Prize in Literature. (AP/Wide World Photos)

When he was nine years old, Neruda studied humanities at Temuco Boys' Academy. He was graduated in 1920, and in that year he moved to Santiago, where he entered the Pedagogical Institute to study French. He remained there only through the third year.

Although he began writing poetry in 1914, Neruda did not publish his first book of poems, *Crepusculario*, until 1923. He had already adopted the pseudonym of Pablo Neruda. He published a short novel, numerous essays, and numerous newspaper articles but is known primarily for his poetry. In his work Neruda expressed, as no one had before him, the metaphysical anguish of Latin Americans and their material decline as a result of exploitation, poverty, and disease.

Neruda's major volumes of poetry include *Veinte poemas de amor y una canción desesperada* (1924; *Twenty Love Poems and a Song of Despair*, 1969), *Residencia en la tierra* (1925-1931; *Residence on Earth, and Other Poems*, 1946), *Canto general* (1950; English translation, 1991), *Odas elementales* (1954, 1956, 1957; *Elemental Odes*, 1961), *Los versos del Capitán* (1953, 1963; *The Captain's Verses*, 1972), and *Cien sonetos de amor* (1959; *One Hundred Love Sonnets*, 1986). Neruda won the Nobel Prize in Literature in 1971.

Nevada: State in the American Southwest. Although Hispanics have resided in Nevada for centuries, the majority living there in the 1990's had arrived in recent times. Mexicans came in the thousands in the early 1900's to become farm, mine, and railroad workers. They eventually settled in and around Elko, Ely, Sparks, and Las Vegas, where their assimilated descendants enjoyed a comfortable middle-class lifestyle.

In 1990, Nevada's Hispanic population of approximately 124,000 represented the state's fastest-growing minority. About 85,000 of them were Mexican Americans, with Cuban Americans another 29,000. Many of the Cuban Americans arrived shortly after Fidel Castro came to power in Cuba.

New Deal: The presidential administration of Franklin D. Roosevelt acted on many fronts in its attempts to reverse the Great DEPRESSION. The administration acted in the areas of banking, agriculture, industry, and labor relations in its attempts to bring relief to the destitute, promote economic recovery in business and farming, initiate reforms that would prevent future depressions, and open opportunities for members of the lower socioeconomic classes.

When Roosevelt took the office of the presidency in March, 1933, the United States was at the depths of the Great Depression. As a product of the Progressive era, Roosevelt was a conservative who believed in the American free enterprise system and rejected proposals from intellectuals that the United States move toward SOCIALISM. Roosevelt believed that capitalism needed to be resurrected, but with government aid. His New Deal programs contained three goals: relief, recovery, and reform.

Relief legislation included the Civilian Conservation Corps (CCC) of 1933 and the WORKS PROGRESS ADMINISTRATION (WPA) of 1935. The CCC, as a means of providing temporary jobs, paid young men to plant trees, prevent erosion, and build parks. Thousands of Latinos joined these efforts. The WPA provided work relief on a large scale. Nearly four million persons, primarily unskilled laborers, were put to work on infrastructural projects including roads, parks, dams, and public buildings. Another branch of the WPA employed artists, actors, and scholars. Latino scholars were among those encouraged to write histories and other works. Many Latino artists of murals and other forms received support for their work. Murals by Latino artists began to appear on public buildings.

Recovery efforts aided various industries. The Farm Credit Administration was created in 1933 to save the land and homes of farmers by extending credit to them on favorable terms. The Reconstruction Finance Corporation made loans to railroads to install modern equipment. To encourage business, western railways lowered their passenger rates.

Reform measures attempted to prevent future depressions. The Social Security Act of 1935 provided programs to protect people in their old age and to compensate them should they become unemployed or disabled. The Federal Deposit Insurance Corporation was created in 1933 to guarantee the safety of bank deposits.

New Deal programs affected many areas of American economic life but left others untouched. Benefits were directed largely toward the middle and upper classes, the owners of businesses. The most needy and the least organized had difficulty obtaining their share of governmental largesse. Labor legislation attempted to make unions and workers more powerful, but the unions tended to exclude Latino workers, leaving them no better off. Widespread unemployment, in fact, encouraged discrimination against Latino workers, who were relatively defenseless.

New Jersey: The Latino population of New Jersey grew by 50.4 percent between 1980 and 1990. New

Jersey's nearly 740,000 Latino residents ranked it among the ten states with the largest Hispanic populations. Latinos in New Jersey, according to 1990 census data, represented close to 10 percent of the state's population. Like its neighbors in the Northeast, New Jersey hosted a mixed Hispanic population. Puerto Ricans were the majority, with more than 320,000 composing 43 percent of the state's Latino population. Cuban Americans numbered in excess of 85,000 (12 percent), making New Jersey home to one of America's largest Cuban enclaves after Florida. Mexican Americans (28,759) made up only 4 percent of New Jersey's Latinos. More than 300,000 Latinos identified themselves as "Other Hispanic," making this category the second-largest segment of the state's Latino population.

In its publication *New Jersey Population Profile* issued in November, 1991, the Midwest Northeast Voter Registration Education Project (MNVREP) reported that Latinos resided in each of the state's twenty-one counties. In eleven counties, the majority Hispanic group was Puerto Rican. The Cuban American population was concentrated in Hudson, Union, and Bergen counties. Sizable populations of Mexican Americans could found in Essex, Middlesex, and Monmouth counties. The MNVREP found that Hispanics were concentrated primarily in the urban centers of Newark, Union City, and Elizabeth.

LATINO POPULATION OF NEW JERSEY, 1990

Total number of Latinos = 739,861; 10% of population

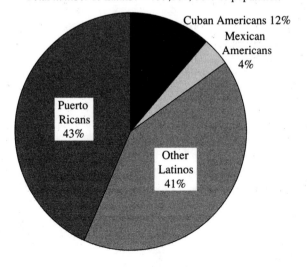

Source: Data are from Marlita A. Reddy, ed., *Statistical Record of Hispanic Americans* (Detroit: Gale Research, 1993), Table 106.

The Center for Hispanic Policy, Research, and Development, a division of the New Jersey Department of Community Affairs, published a *Status Report on Hispanic Initiatives* in August, 1993. Among the factors that affected the quality of life for New Jersey's Latino population were income levels and high poverty rates. Latinos in urban areas, where almost 90 percent of the state's Latinos lived, had the lowest per capita income and a higher unemployment rate than other groups. Research also pointed to an increase in their POVERTY rate, citing a 2 percent increase from 1990 to 1991. Research indicated that among Hispanic subgroups, New Jersey's Puerto Ricans suffered the worst housing conditions. With a relatively high percentage of renters, Latinos in urban areas of New Jersey generally have been vulnerable to involuntary displacements and GENTRIFICATION.

Relatively low levels of educational attainment among Latino children were linked to inadequate funding, fear of crime, and the relative lack of Hispanic teachers in New Jersey's urban schools. This situation was complicated by the limited English proficiency of many Latino parents. The state began a number of initiatives to address Latino educational concerns, including English as a second language (ESL) and bilingual education programs. The low income levels of New Jersey's Latinos have had a direct effect on the quality of health care available to them. Lack of adequate health insurance and the relatively few culturally sensitive health care providers have hindered access to health care for Latinos. The threat of AIDS had begun reaching into Latino communities within the state's urban areas.

Statistics compiled by the NATIONAL ASSOCIATION OF LATINO ELECTED AND APPOINTED OFFICIALS indicated that the number of Hispanic elected officials in New Jersey grew from twelve in 1984 to forty-four in 1993. New Jersey gained distinction when Robert Menendez joined the U.S. Congress as its first Cuban American Democrat.

New Mexico: The fifth-largest and thirty-seventh most populous U.S. state (1990 census). New Mexico is home to a distinctive Latino community that traces its history to the Spanish colonial era.

History. New Mexico was first explored by the Spanish in the middle of the sixteenth century. The first explorer was Fray Marcos de Niza, who came north from Mexico in search of the fabled cities of CÍBOLA. Francisco Vázquez de CORONADO established Spanish dominion over the native populations in the

Taos was one of the first Spanish settlements in New Mexico. (Justine Hill)

1540's. Silver strikes in Zacatecas in the 1550's sparked interest in possible mineral wealth in New Mexico.

First Settlements. In 1598, Juan de OÑATE brought the first colonists to establish a settlement at San Juan Pueblo, and the capital villa in SANTA FE was erected twelve years later. New Mexican colonial life during the 1600's was characterized by the exploitation of native labor, the appropriation of goods as tribute, and forced religious conversion on a wide scale. The Pueblo Revolt of 1680 rid the New Mexico territory of Spanish colonists, but the Spanish returned in 1692. That year, Diego de Vargas was appointed governor of New Mexico, and Spanish settlement was renewed, amid sporadic fighting with the native population through the beginning of the eighteenth century.

The Spanish government began an extensive program of land grants to new settlers—to individuals, extended families, and larger town groups—conditional upon three years' occupation. The new settlers were called *Españoles Mexicanos* (Mexican Spaniards). The land-grant program effectively spread the immigrant population across the territory rather than centralizing new settlement in a few large cities.

In 1821, the Mexican Republic was established. There were approximately sixty thousand people of Spanish or mixed Spanish, Mexican, and native descent in New Mexico at that time. Newly independent Mexico feared U.S. expansion and encouraged further settlement of its northern territory. Spain had kept New Mexico almost completely isolated; Mexico opened the territory's northern border, and the famed SANTA FE TRAIL was established as a conduit for people and goods from the east. The next two decades were a period of immense growth and change for New Mexico, with increases in population, commerce, and sophistication.

The U.S. Colonial Period. Mexican fears of U.S. designs were well founded. The MEXICAN AMERICAN WAR began in May, 1846, and in August, General Stephen Kearny of the U.S. Army marched into Santa Fe and easily occupied New Mexico. Two years later, the U.S. and Mexican governments signed the TREATY OF GUADALUPE HIDALGO, dictating the terms of the territorial cession and the rights of the people in the conquered territory. At the time of the U.S. conquest, Hispanic New Mexicans so outnumbered Anglos that

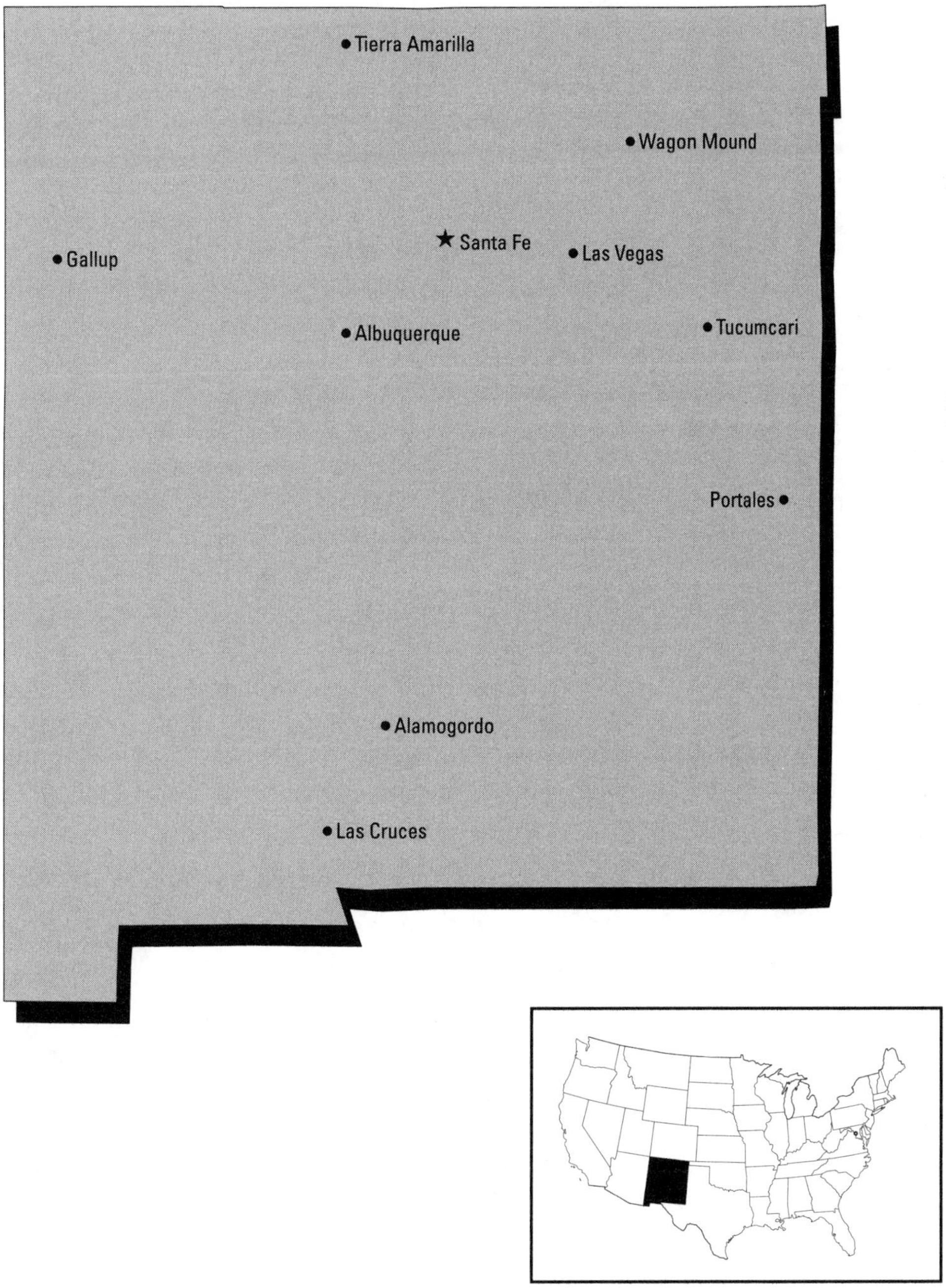

- Tierra Amarilla
- Wagon Mound
- ★ Santa Fe
- Las Vegas
- Gallup
- Tucumcari
- Albuquerque
- Portales
- Alamogordo
- Las Cruces

Governor Toney Anaya appeared on Meet the Press *in 1984 as chairman of Hispanic Force '84.* (AP/Wide World Photos)

there was no immediate subjugation of the non-Anglo population, as had occurred in Texas and California.

During the U.S. colonial period, there was great confusion over land grants and ownership. In 1895, the situation was complicated by the imposition of land taxes. In addition, the arrival of railroads and the discovery of gold in the 1890's accelerated the territory's growth. The consequent arrival of Anglo settlers created Anglo-Hispanic rivalries in many New Mexico communities.

Politics. During the late eighteenth century, the territory made many attempts to obtain statehood. In 1902, a congressional subcommittee on New Mexican statehood focused on the prevalent use of the Spanish language in New Mexican society. The overwhelming Spanish majority, in the eyes of Anglo lawmakers, made the territory a less than perfect candidate for entry into the Union. Nevertheless, on August 21, 1912, New Mexico became the forty-seventh state.

From the beginning of statehood, Hispanics have been extremely active in New Mexican politics. Latinos have served as judges, mayors, county commissioners, state legislators, and heads of local, state, and federal agencies. Manuel A. Otero, Jr., the son of a prominent New Mexican businessman, served as territorial governor. Dennis CHÁVEZ represented New Mexico in the U.S. House of Representatives from 1931 to 1935 and in the Senate from 1935 to 1962. Jerry APODACA was elected governor in 1975, followed by Toney ANAYA in 1983. Other prominent Hispanic politicians include Senator Joseph M. MONTOYA and Representative Antonio Fernandez. For many years, representatives from New Mexico were the only Spanish-speaking members of Congress, even though California, Texas, and Florida had larger Spanish-speaking constituencies.

During the U.S. colonial period and the early years of statehood, the Spanish language and Hispanic culture were at times suppressed by the powerful Anglo minority. The state constitution, however, was fortified with strong recognition of the presence and influence of Hispanics in New Mexico. Article 7 guarantees equal rights to English and Spanish speakers. Article 12 provides for BILINGUAL EDUCATION and encourages teacher BILINGUALISM, an especially important provision considering that most schools prior to statehood were church-sponsored. Article 20 requires that all laws be published in both English and Spanish.

Land. Since the first Spanish settlers came to New Mexico, the region's politics have revolved around land issues. (*See* LAND TENURE ISSUES.) The Treaty of Guadalupe Hidalgo guaranteed that the U.S. government would respect Spanish land grants, some of which dated back to the reign of Philip II in Spain, but that guarantee proved to be weak. Much land was appropriated for federal parks and forests; other parcels were taken over by business interests. Grants that had been large when conferred had with time been subdivided and dispersed among family and community members.

The peasant population of New Mexico has always had deep roots in the land, especially in the Chama and San Juan Valleys in the northern part of the state. Indignation over the loss of lands sparked vigilante activism through the early decades of the twentieth century. Two loose groups, the GORRAS BLANCAS (white caps) and Manos Negras (black hands), roamed the countryside under cover of night, cutting fences, burning barns, and destroying livestock on appropriated grant lands.

In the 1960's, continuing inaction on the issue led to the establishment of the grassroots Alianza Federal de Mercedes (Federal Alliance of Land Grants), under the leadership of a former preacher and boxer named Reies López TIJERINA. The organization, which soon became the Alianza Federal de Pueblos Libres (Federal Alliance of Free Villages), researched the history of land grants, uncovered legal title documents, and sought to invoke original property rights for the descendants of the grantees through official judicial channels.

When those methods failed, the Alianza turned to more extreme measures. On October 15, 1966, López Tijerina led the Alianza in the KIT CARSON NATIONAL FOREST TAKEOVER, a short-lived armed takeover of grant land in north-central New Mexico. The following June, an attempt to perform a citizen's arrest on the state's district attorney in the northern village of Tierra Amarilla led to armed conflict, and a deputy was seriously injured. The incident was sensationalized in the press as a raid: It gained publicity for the cause, but it cast those seeking the restoration of land grants in a bad light. Although some reparations have been made, the issue of land and land grants is still a volatile one for Latinos in New Mexico.

Culture. By 1990, only 38 percent of New Mexicans were Latino. From a Latino point of view, the state is divided into two regions. The southern part, reaching as far north as Albuquerque, is considered "Little Texas," reflecting the Anglo majority and the influence of Anglo-American and Texan culture. The political and social outlook tends to be more conservative, affluent, and Protestant. The northern part of the state is home to the traditional Latino culture, which tends to be more liberal, impoverished, and Catholic. Since the early part of the twentieth century, New Mexico's Latinos have generally preferred to think of themselves as Spanish Americans or HISPANOS rather than as Mexican Americans, reflecting a purer Iberian lineage and heritage. Although such a perception is true to a degree, from the beginning of colonization, New Mexicans of Spanish descent have intermarried with native populations and with other immigrant groups.

Northern New Mexico has tended to be culturally and economically isolated, but these conditions have changed with improvements in communications and transportation. Ethnic pride, poverty, and isolation have characterized the Latino communities of New Mexico. Religion has always been an important element of New Mexico village life. The *moradas* (meeting houses) built by the monklike Hermanos PENITENTES, a religious fellowship that developed and flourished during the 1800's, are still in use in several dozen communities. Traditional religious arts are still practiced. The

LATINO POPULATION OF NEW MEXICO, 1990

Total number of Latinos = 579,224; 38% of population

Puerto Ricans 0.4% Cuban Americans 0.2%

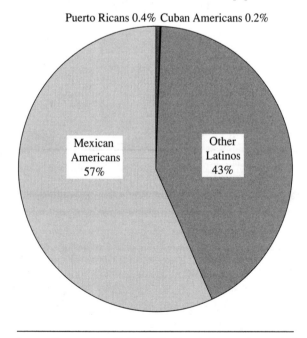

Mexican Americans 57%

Other Latinos 43%

Source: Data are from Marlita A. Reddy, ed., *Statistical Record of Hispanic Americans* (Detroit: Gale Research, 1993), Table 106.

Note: Percentages are rounded to the nearest whole number except for Cuban Americans and Puerto Ricans, for whom rounding is to the nearest 0.1%.

1980's witnessed a threefold growth in the number of Hispanic artists working in traditional crafts. That increase is linked to the emergence of the tourist industry in the state. In some areas, old-fashioned pastoral plays are presented in village halls, and many villages retain the traditional ADOBE style of architecture. The Spanish spoken in New Mexico is still peppered with archaic, centuries-old Iberian expressions not heard among Spanish speakers elsewhere in the Western Hemisphere.

The Future. With the expansion of modern ways and values, the traditional New Mexican HISPANO lifestyle and culture face possible extinction. The cycle of feast days has become obsolete or of purely anthropological and touristic interest. The annual Fiesta de Santa Fe exemplifies the more secular celebrations that honor the state's Spanish heritage. World War II brought defense plants, and employment opportunities and military service drew young Latinos away. The postwar period also saw a massive influx of settlers, primarily from Texas, Oklahoma, and Kansas. Since 1950, the northern counties of New Mexico have been the only regions in the nation with large Latino communities to experience substantial population losses. Seasonal farming, native artistry, and self-sufficiency have given way to urban service jobs, cultivation of the tourist industry, and integration into the state economy and mainstream way of life.   —*Barry Mann*

SUGGESTED READINGS:

• Roberts, Calvin A., and Susan A. Roberts. *New Mexico.* Albuquerque: University of New Mexico Press, 1988. An overview of the state and its history. Written for the general reader, with generous photographs.

• Sanchez, George I. *Forgotten People: A Study of New Mexicans.* Albuquerque: University of New Mexico Press, 1940. A classic in the literature on the people of New Mexico, this is an "interpretive study of the social and economic conditions" of Spanish New Mexicans, with a focus on Taos as a representative Hispano community. A somewhat sentimental and politically loaded essay that examines such issues as poverty, illiteracy, land, and inequities in provision of public services. Illustrations.

• Swadesh, Frances Leon. *Los Primeros Pobladores: Hispanic Americans of the Ute Frontier.* Notre Dame, Ind.: University of Notre Dame Press, 1974. A painstaking historical study of the settlement and cultural patterns of the Chama Valley. A carefully documented anthropological and sociological treatise. Good notes, glossary, bibliography, and index.

• Vigil, Maurilio E. *Los Patrones: Profiles of Hispanic Political Leaders in New Mexico*. Washington, D.C.: University Press of America, 1980. Vigil profiles twenty-eight Hispanic leaders in New Mexican history and includes short essays on the three periods to which they belong.

• Warren, Nancy Hunter. *Villages of Hispanic New Mexico*. Santa Fe, N.Mex.: School of American Research Press, 1987. Warren offers a personal and nostalgic journey into New Mexico village culture, examining history, people, customs, lifestyles, religion, art, and architecture. An enjoyable narrative essay with more than ninety photographs.

• Weyr, Thomas. *Hispanic U.S.A.: Breaking the Melting Pot*. New York: Harper & Row, 1988. Examines the people and politics of U.S. Hispanic communities in general, with numerous references and one descriptive section devoted to New Mexico's people and language. Interviews and travel anecdotes provide a personal perspective.

New Mexico Rebellion (1837): Also known as the Chimayó Rebellion. Native New Mexicans and Pueblo Indians rebelled against unfair taxation in a manifestation of increasing animosity toward local authorities and the Mexican government.

On August 3, 1837, in the Chimayó-Santa Cruz de la Cañada region of northern New Mexico, native New Mexicans, the descendants of the original Spanish settlers, initiated a successful political rebellion against the local government. The revolt occurred following an unpopular political appointment and the implementation of a new system of taxation.

The uprising was the bloody culmination of New Mexicans' increasing resentment toward the inefficiency of Mexican rule. After the signing of the Treaty of Córdova on August 24, 1821, Mexico secured its independence from Spain, and New Mexico became a part of the Mexican nation. Turmoil within Mexico itself—civil wars, unstable political administrations, and threats of foreign invasion—contributed to undermining its ability to govern New Mexico satisfactorily. New Mexico's boundaries were never firmly established, and its status changed three times between 1821 and 1824, when it became a separate territory (a region under the jurisdiction of a particular country that is not granted official statehood). Because New Mexico lay far away from the capital, Mexico City, the central government of Mexico managed affairs loosely and maintained virtually no control over local officials. Moreover, the central government allocated no

revenue to administer the territory. At the same time, Anglo traders, trappers, and entrepreneurs involved in the Santa Fe trade arrived in the region. The opening of the SANTA FE TRAIL, an important trade route from Independence, Missouri, to Santa Fe, affected the regional economy and linked New Mexico with the United States. As a result of these factors, the residents of New Mexico felt little loyalty to Mexico.

In 1835, the Mexican government appointed Colonel Albino Pérez as the new *jefe político*, or governor, of New Mexico. Pérez was unpopular because he was a military officer and an outsider. At the order of the Mexican government, he instituted a system of direct taxation that adversely affected the economic well-being of both New Mexico's native population and the Anglo traders. An underground anti-Pérez movement began to form.

The spark that ignited the rebellion was the jailing of Juan José Esquibel, a native New Mexican official, on corruption charges. When Esquibel was imprisoned in La Cañada, anti-Pérez forces mobilized, marched into La Cañada and freed Esquibel. Next they drew up a plan demanding statehood status under Mexico. The plan included a refusal to pay taxes or to obey the officials who collected them. Unable to quell the revolt, Pérez fled south with other members of his government. He was captured and beheaded by Pueblo Indians. On August 10, two days after the successful conclusion of their rebellion, the rebels met and chose José González as the new governor.

The rebellion of 1837 was the first in a series of events that undermined Mexico's control over New Mexico and led to New Mexico's acquisition by the United States. Political unrest and mismanagement continued after the rebellion. By September, 1837, González was ousted from power and executed, along with members of his cabinet. In 1841, the president of the new Republic of Texas sent forces to New Mexico to take possession of the capital. The invasion was a failure, and New Mexico continued to experience political and social instability while under threat of invasion from the United States. In 1846, New Mexican officials surrendered to U.S. forces and New Mexico officially became a territory of the United States.

New Orleans, Louisiana: According to the 1990 U.S. Census, New Orleans, at the mouth of the Mississippi River, had a population of about 497,000. The metropolitan area population was approximated at 1,239,000. About 4.3% of those people were Latinos. No single Latino group predominated.

LATINO POPULATION OF
NEW ORLEANS, LOUISIANA, 1990

Total number of Latinos = 53,226; 4.3% of population

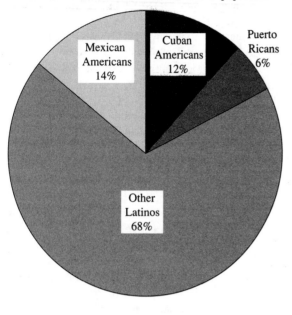

Source: Data are from Marlita A. Reddy, ed., *Statistical Record of Hispanic Americans* (Detroit: Gale Research, 1993), Table 111.

Note: Figures represent the population of the Metropolitan Statistical Area as delineated by the U.S. Bureau of the Census.

The Mississippi River was explored by Spaniards early in the sixteenth century. The first European attempt to establish a permanent settlement began in 1682, when René-Robert Cavalier, Sieur de La Salle, claimed what was later known as the Louisiana Territory for France, under the name of King Louis XIV.

Relationships with the native population were generally far from friendly, and little trace of the native culture remains. For almost a century, the area was controlled by France, and French was the working language of most of the population. The port of New Orleans was established in 1719. In 1762, the territory was ceded to Charles III, King of Spain, a cousin of the French king. The Spanish controlled the area until 1800, when Napoleon Bonaparte annexed the territory. Napoleon gave up the area when he decided he needed cash more than an American colony. He sold the land to the United States in the LOUISIANA PURCHASE of 1803.

During this time, most of what is now the central United States, stretching from the Mississippi River to the Rocky Mountains, as far west as Montana, was controlled by the French. The Spanish and French also controlled most of the Caribbean islands. As a result, New Orleans has a heritage that is unique in the United States, involving African, Caribbean, Central and South American, and European culture. By the time LOUISIANA became a state in 1812, French Creole was the established language of most of the population. There was also a second French culture. After the French and Indian War, when Great Britain gained control of Canada, several thousand French exiles from Nova Scotia moved to New Orleans and surrounding areas.

Modern New Orleans presents a blend of cultures. Apart from the French influence, Spanish architecture is evident. During the nineteenth century, there were large migrations from many parts of Europe and Latin America. There is a strong African influence as well. Many slaves came to the port of New Orleans from the Caribbean region rather than directly from Africa. In addition, there were many free black people, as emancipation was far easier to achieve under French and Spanish rule than under American rule.

The French Creole language is a mixture of archaic French, West Indian and Mexican Spanish, English, and various African tongues. VODUN, imported from Haiti, is regularly practiced in the area, despite the fact that the area is overwhelmingly Roman Catholic. By the latter half of the twentieth century, English had replaced French as the most common language, but it was still not difficult to find people who were more comfortable speaking Creole, and a few older people did not speak English at all.

Perhaps the most surprising fact about New Orleans is that the 1990 census reported only 4.3 percent of the population as Hispanic. There has been some recent immigration from Cuba and other Caribbean nations, but the most significant Hispanic influence in New Orleans is centuries old. Much of the modern population considers itself to be of French, or simply American, background.

New Spain: Colonial term for Mexico. New Spain was the name Hernán CORTÉS applied to the area he conquered in his defeat of the Aztec empire. The name was, at first, applied to all the Spanish territories in North America. New Spain's borders became unclear when new colonies were founded, such as New Galicia and New Vizcaya. Politically, however, the new colonies were part of the viceroyalty of New Spain. The most prominent of the Spanish colonies in the New World, it became the independent country of Mexico.

New York City: Largest city in North America. The population of New York City varied between seven and eight million between 1960 and 1990. The expanding metropolitan area, estimated in the 1990 census to have a population of eighteen million, spans parts of three states. The Hispanic population is estimated to be approximately one million within the city limits, with another half million in nearby suburbs and upstate New York. These estimates are that and no more, as the definition of where a metropolitan area begins and ends varies among sources of data. In addition, minority populations tend to be inaccurately reported.

Historical Background. New York City has always been a city of many cultures and many neighborhoods dominated by these cultures. The original American Indian population of the area was largely exterminated or forced to move west and north. The original European settlers were primarily English and Dutch, although even in the seventeenth century, dozens of languages were spoken in the city.

During the nineteenth century, New York became the major gateway for a huge tide of immigrants coming through Ellis Island, mostly from various parts of Europe. It was not until the latter half of the twentieth century, however, that New York gained a significant Latino population. Puerto Ricans, the dominant Latino group in New York, became citizens of the United States in 1917 through the JONES ACT, but few could afford to travel to the mainland. After World War II, however, travel became considerably more reliable and less expensive, and Puerto Ricans and other people of the Caribbean region began to arrive in New York City in large numbers.

Demographics. The 1990 Latino population of New York City was almost entirely from the Caribbean islands, with only a few people with Mexican, Central American, and South American origins present. Latino populations have lived in many parts of the city; neighborhoods in New York City changed ethnic backgrounds rapidly. Following the first major wave of Puerto Ricans, following World War II, certain neighborhoods remained distinctly Latino. The greatest concentrations of Latinos are in El Barrio (SPANISH HARLEM, on the upper East Side of Manhattan), the South Bronx, and the Bedford-Stuyvesant and Flatbush areas of Brooklyn.

Within these neighborhoods and others, there are distinct enclaves of particular national origin, sometimes only a few blocks long. The population of New York City is extremely concentrated geographically, so that what might appear to be a tiny neighborhood may actually have thousands of residents.

Although the city's Latino population is largely of Puerto Rican background, there is diversity. Reliable statistics are difficult to compile, it should be noted, because many residents are undocumented immigrants and do not respond to the census. Dominicans make up a significant part of the city's Latino culture. Starting in the 1960's and accelerating in the decades following, there was an influx of Cubans. The overwhelming majority of Latinos in New York City, however, are of Puerto Rican origin. When one speaks of Latinos in New York, this group is usually the major focus.

The Puerto Rican Ethnic Group. PUERTO RICANS are unique among the "immigrant" populations of the United States because in their home country they are American citizens and are not subject to the same immigration laws that apply to other groups. They are a distinct nationality with a complex historical background.

Puerto Rico originally had an indigenous American Indian population related to the natives of South America. When Spaniards conquered the island, however, much of the native population was killed. Most of

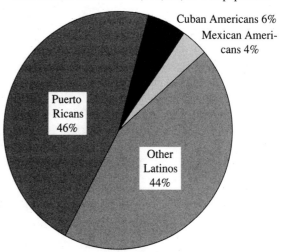

LATINO POPULATION OF NEW YORK, NEW YORK, 1990

Total number of Latinos = 2,777,951; 15% of population

Cuban Americans 6%
Mexican Americans 4%
Puerto Ricans 46%
Other Latinos 44%

Source: Data are from Marlita A. Reddy, ed., *Statistical Record of Hispanic Americans* (Detroit: Gale Research, 1993), Table 111.
Note: Figures represent the population of the New York-northern New Jersey-Long Island Consolidated Metropolitan Statistical Area as delineated by the U.S. Bureau of the Census.

President Lyndon B. Johnson signed the Immigration and Nationality Act of 1965 in New York City, at Liberty Island. (LBJ Library)

the survivors left the island for other Caribbean islands or the American mainlands. The native cultural influence never completely disappeared, however, and there were intermarriages, so that by the time the Spanish were in complete control, native words had entered the language and native customs had entered the social atmosphere.

The Spaniards brought in black slaves from Africa to replace the native work force they had destroyed. Intermixing resulted in many Puerto Ricans having some African heritage and black skin color.

The Puerto Rican people are a mixture of the populations of three continents and a wide variety of cultural heritages. Spanish has been the only language in general use for centuries, but it is a Spanish intermixed with African and American vocabulary and with a pronunciation at least as different from that of Spain as American English is from that of England. When Puerto Ricans move to New York City or elsewhere in North America, they have yet another culture to assimilate.

Religion and Culture. Most Puerto Ricans, like most people of the Caribbean, are Catholic. There is, however, a significant influence of the SANTERÍA religion, which is older than Christianity and was transported from Africa with the slave trade. Santería is common in New York City, where BOTÁNICAS, specialized stores in Hispanic neighborhoods, sell herbs and icons used in Santería rites.

Although many second- and third-generation Puerto Ricans speak English at least as well as they speak Spanish, or speak a mixture of the two languages often referred to as "SPANGLISH," Spanish is still the working language of the barrio, and business is often conducted in that language. Many Puerto Ricans have become part of English-speaking society, but in general, assimilation has been slow and difficult, and Spanish-speaking enclaves persist.

Some problems of assimilation stem from the ambiguous national identity of Puerto Ricans. They are officially Americans, though those who still live in Puerto Rico do not have the right to vote in U.S. federal elections. Many of those who live in New York City consider themselves to be Puerto Ricans rather than Americans. The political future of Puerto Rico has long been an issue, with some suggesting statehood, others hoping for independence, and still others promoting continuance of Puerto Rico's commonwealth status. This is complicated by the fact that, according to 1990 figures, there were more Puerto Ricans in New York City than in San Juan, Puerto Rico's capital. The North American population of Puerto Ricans rivaled that of the island itself.

Life within the barrio can be festive, despite the deprivations of the citizens. Particularly during the summer, there seems to be a constant street festival in progress, with singing, dancing, and people playing music on bongos, guitars, and even tin cans.

Economic Conditions. Government statistics, especially unemployment figures, are not good indications of the true situation among New York City's Latinos. Unemployment statistics, for example, count only those people actively seeking work. Those who have given up looking and live on public assistance or by other means do not figure into unemployment statistics. By all accounts, the Puerto Rican community in New York City is in the worst shape of all groups in the city.

Many businesses in Hispanic neighborhoods are owned by Puerto Ricans and other Latinos, but they are generally not very profitable. Many fail or yield only a marginal living for the owners. Many of these small operations conduct business in Spanish, and the customers are almost exclusively from the neighborhood.

Although it is possible for a Latino to move out of the barrio and into the mainstream of society, language barriers and prejudice make this difficult. Despite the cultural diversity of New York City and the publication of books, magazines, and newspapers in dozens of languages, the working language of the middle and upper classes is English. Someone whose command of English is uncertain has a difficult time. First-generation immigrants therefore face particular problems.

Many of the city's Latinos live in crowded, substandard housing, infested by cockroaches and rats. Families are often large, with one or both parents working at low wages. Health conditions are often poor because of housing conditions and because medical care may be an unaffordable luxury for the many Latino workers and unemployed people without medical insurance.

Education. Puerto Rican children of the 1990's and earlier had the highest dropout rate and the lowest educational achievement of any racial or ethnic group in New York City. Language barriers (shared with many ethnic groups) combined with low economic status to produce these results. Until the last decades of the twentieth century, virtually all elementary and high school education, in both public and parochial schools, was conducted in English. Someone without a good command of that language was likely to fail. At the end of the twentieth century, a movement toward BILIN-

Children parade in the annual festivities surrounding Three Kings Day. (Odette Lupis)

GUAL EDUCATION began, but the intent of the board of education was still to assimilate Puerto Ricans into English culture. Parents, many of whom did not speak English well or at all, were often of little help in assimilation.

Crime. Crime is rampant in New York City's Hispanic neighborhoods, especially the poorest, including SPANISH HARLEM and the South Bronx. Part of the reason is poverty, but the problem is intensified by a general disrespect for the legal system. Few police officers in Spanish neighborhoods are Latinos themselves, and communication is difficult. The police are considered by many Latinos to be invading enemies. Bias against Latinos by some police officers contributes to the antagonism and lack of respect for the law.

As in most urban ghetto areas, drug use and the crimes committed to pay for it are an increasing problem. GANGS and gang violence are common. Most of the crime remains within the confines of the barrio, where the police are not welcome. A certain amount of tolerance toward drug dealing, prostitution, and other crime is exhibited by the police force, which is over-whelmed by the level of crime in these areas and focuses only on the most severe problems.

Conclusion. Despite efforts to develop understanding and peaceful relations among Latinos and other groups in New York City, and despite development and education programs of various types, Latinos, especially Puerto Ricans, are in desperate straits. Much of the city's Puerto Rican population came from slums in San Juan, where conditions were even worse. Although they are better off, their status merits improvement.

The Latino influence on New York City's culture is considerable. Caribbean, Mexican, and other Hispanic restaurants exist in many parts of the city, and Latino entertainers abound. In large part, however, Latinos in New York City constitute a foreign culture trapped within a city that has assimilated many other cultures over the centuries. Latinos as a whole are far from assimilation. The influx since the 1950's of Cubans, whose economic condition is generally better than that of Puerto Ricans, has not helped the situation in any significant way, because the two groups have not inter-

By the 1950's, Puerto Ricans had established an enclave in New York City. (Library of Congress)

mingled. Puerto Ricans often resent the influx of other Latinos higher on the socioeconomic scale.

—*Marc Goldstein*

SUGGESTED READINGS:

• Lewis, Oscar. *A Study of Slum Culture: Backgrounds for La Vida*. New York: Random House, 1968. A sociological study of slum life in Puerto Rican neighborhoods of San Juan and New York City. This is a study of one hundred families in four San Juan slums and fifty families in New York City. Contains statistical reports as well as individual family stories.

• Lopez, Alfredo. *The Puerto Rican Papers: Notes on the Re-Emergence of a Nation*. New York: Bobbs-Merrill, 1973. A discussion of the history and culture of Puerto Ricans, from their ancestral beginnings to the present. Told in first-person narration by a New York Puerto Rican. Includes a number of firsthand accounts of conditions.

• Rivera, Edward. *Family Installments: Memories of Growing Up Hispanic*. New York: William Morrow, 1982. A series of autobiographical sketches about life in Spanish Harlem, including family stories and legends as well as firsthand accounts of life in the barrios of New York.

• Shorris, Earl. *Latinos: A Biography of the People*. New York: W. W. Norton & Co., 1992. Describes a variety of Latino cultures in the United States. Included are many individual reports by people from various Latino cultures living in a variety of places in the country.

• Thomas, Piri. *Down These Mean Streets*. New York: Knopf, 1967. An autobiographical account of life in Spanish Harlem. The author has established a reputable living as a writer, but as a teenager and young adult he was a drug addict and spent time in jail. Addresses many of the problems faced by Puerto Ricans and other Latinos in New York City.

• Wakefield, Dan. *Island in the City: The World of Spanish Harlem*. New York: Arno Press, 1975. A description of life in the area of highest concentration of Puerto Ricans in the United States. Includes a history of Puerto Ricans in New York City and elsewhere and expresses the points of view of a variety of people and groups, including both barrio dwellers and English-speaking people who have interacted with them.

• Weyr, Thomas. *Hispanic U.S.A.: Breaking the Melting Pot*. New York: Harper & Row, 1988. A general discussion of Hispanic populations in the United States, with an emphasis on the reasons why Latinos have had a harder time than most immigrant groups in assimilating into mainstream United States culture.

The influence of Hispanic culture on mainstream culture is examined.

Newspapers and magazines: Latinos have made many contributions in the areas of print media and journalism, collecting, writing, and presenting news and information of cultural interest to Latinos and the Spanish-speaking peoples of the United States. This article will focus on the contributions of Chicanos/Mexican Americans, Cuban Americans, Puerto Ricans, and Spanish immigrants as the most visible. Periodicals slanted toward and produced by other Latinos are likely to become increasingly prominent.

Introduction. The Latino press has been studied in many different ways. It has been viewed both as an exile press and as an immigrant press. Some research has focused on contributions in English, and other work has concentrated on publications in Spanish. The Latino press in all of its forms has been invaluable in the study of various aspects of Latino history and culture.

Although Latino publications and publishing efforts are often lumped together, many scholars believe that there is instead a separate press for each Latino subgroup. These presses have served various functions. They have been institutions of social control, institutions of activism, and media for reflection on the state of the Latino community.

This article provides a roughly chronological discussion of various facets of the Latino press. The first section is a discussion of the early Mexican press and early presses in the United States. A brief overview of the press during the Mexican American War follows. Next, the article discusses the primarily Mexican press of New Mexico, Arizona, Texas, and California, covering the period up to the Mexican Revolution. A separate section on the Mexican Revolution is included because that event had such large effects on the Latino press. Following this discussion are separate sections on the publications of Spanish immigrants, Cuban Americans, and Puerto Ricans. Next, the Chicano and Latino press in the Midwest is examined. The section on the period from the 1930's to the 1950's discusses the presses of several Latino subgroups, as does the final section on the post-1960 Latino press.

The Early Mexican Press. The publication of periodicals in Mexico began with *volantes* or *hojas volantes* (literally, flying pages). These broadsides were published as early as 1542. They contained news from Europe, the Caribbean, and South America. Prototypical Mexican newspapers and their founding dates include *La Gaceta de México* (1722), *Gaceta General* (1666), *Mercurio Volante* (1772), and *Diario de México* (1805).

The Early Press of Louisiana and Texas. The Spanish-language press in the United States has origins in the press of Texas and Louisiana in the early 1800's. The oldest Spanish-language newspaper in the United States is *El Misisipí*, published in New Orleans, Louisiana, beginning in 1808. The following year, Joaquín de Lisa and Joseph Antonio Boniquet began publishing *El Mensagero [Luisanés]*.

The city of El Paso, Texas, was important to the Mexican American press. Between 1890 and 1920, more than twenty Spanish-language daily and weekly newspapers targeted the Mexican community there. Much of the Mexican immigrant press of that period concentrated on the Mexican Revolution (1910-1921). As early as 1891, notices for contract labor appeared in such El Paso newspapers as *El Latinoamericano*; along with these notices were critiques of Mexican labor contractors. *El Clarín del Norte*, for example, frequently attacked labor contractors for their maltreatment of Mexican workers. In the early 1900's, protests against Porfirio Díaz began to be raised, particularly in the newspapers associated with Ricardo FLORES MAGÓN and the Mexican Liberal Party.

El Bejareño (1855) is one of the earliest papers that can be used to study the historical development of San Antonio. *El Regidor*, founded in 1888 by Pablo Cruz, was one of San Antonio's more important early papers. It focused attention on the community and, of all papers appearing in the state before 1913, was probably the most popular and most significant.

La Prensa, published in San Antonio, Texas, between 1913 and 1959, is an important source of information on the history of the Latino press. The editors of *La Prensa* reported in 1938 that between 1813 and 1937, 431 Spanish-language newspapers had been published in the United States. Most were in the Southwest, but New York, Florida, Illinois, Missouri, Pennsylvania, Louisiana, and other states were represented by Latino print outlets.

The Press of New Mexico. Ramón Abreu established the first press in the state in 1834. Among the state's first newspapers were *La Verdad* (1844) and *El Payo de Nuevo Méjico* (1845). *El Crepúsculo de la Libertad* was published prior to the election of deputies to the Mexican Congress in October, 1834.

Urbano Chacón, an early Spanish-language journalist, is tied closely to the history of the press in both northern New Mexico and southern Colorado. He was the editor of *El Explorador*, *El Espejo*, and *La Aurora*. His son, Felipe Maximiliano CHACÓN, was a noted New Mexico writer who also continued his father's newspaper work. Early in the twentieth century, he edited, managed, and wrote for *La Voz del Pueblo*, *El Faro del Río Grande*, *El Independiente*, *El Eco del Norte*, and *La Bandera Americana*.

The period from 1879 to 1900 saw a proliferation of Hispanic journalism and a resurgence of the New Mexico press. The city of Las Vegas was an important center for this resurgence, with forty-four newspapers appearing in that city. Among them were *La Voz del Pueblo* (1891-1895), *El Defensor del Pueblo* (1891-1892), and *El Independiente* (1891-1895). *La Voz del Pueblo* was founded in Santa Fe by Nestor Montoya and later moved to Las Vegas when Felix Montoya joined the staff. *El Defensor del Pueblo* was directed by Juan José Herrera. It was founded in Albuquerque in 1891 and was the official organ of the Knights of Labor. *El Independiente*, founded by Lorenzo López, was an offshoot of *La Voz del Pueblo*.

Several other noteworthy papers appeared early in the twentieth century. These include *La Aurora* (1902-1914), *La Bandera Americana* (1917-1936), and *La Voz del Río Grande* (1926-1937).

The Press of Arizona. The press of this state, as in others of the Southwest, is tied to the state's Mexican-origin community. About a dozen Arizona papers existed between 1877 and the end of the nineteenth century; about twenty more existed between 1900 and the 1950's.

The first Spanish-language paper in Arizona was Carlos Tully's *Las Dos Republicas* (1877-1878). Tully also founded *La Colonia Mexicana* (1885), *La Alianza* (1889), and *La Voz* (1895). None of his papers enjoyed the success of Tucson's *El Fronterizo* and *El Tucsonense* (established 1915). *El Fronterizo* (1878-1914) was published by Carlos Velasco, who was part of a community of middle-class Mexican American artists and intellectuals and was the founder of the ALIANZA HISPANO-AMERICANA. The paper campaigned against discrimination aimed at Latinos.

The Early California Press. There were no newspapers printed in California prior to the invasion and military occupation by the United States in 1848. Following the takeover of California, the Zamorano press produced *The Californian*, closely associated with the invaders of California.

The early history of the Spanish-language press in the state is usually divided into the Californio press and the Mexican immigrant or populist press. Among

El Tucsonense *was one of the more successful Spanish-language newspapers of the early twentieth century.* (Arizona Historical Society)

the Californio papers is *El Clamor Público*, which evolved out of the Spanish section of the *Los Angeles Star*. It was one of the most militant and important Spanish-language papers of the 1850's. It was founded in Los Angeles in 1855 and was first edited by José E. González and Francisco P. Ramírez, who was only seventeen years old when he became editor.

Ramírez was important in protesting what was perceived as the Anglo theft of California lands and in speaking out against the injustices committed against Mexicanos in California and throughout the Southwest. He favored emancipation of slaves and argued for better treatment for California Indians. He was interested in changes occurring in the community and in issues of language and bilingualism. *El Clamor Público* was not able to withstand competition from the *Los Angeles Star* and ceased publication in 1859.

Two others Californio papers, *La Crónica* (1861-1892) and *Las Dos Republicas* (1892-1898), also circulated widely, the former in Arizona and northern Mexico as well as in California. Both of these papers were associated with the elites of society but also addressed issues important to the mainstream of the Spanish-speaking communities of their time.

The "Mexican immigrant" or populist press tended to be more nationalistic. (It should be noted that the term "Mexican immigrant" press is in part a misnomer because many Mexicans became U.S. citizens not through immigration but through annexation of territory by the United States.) Examples of papers from this press are *La Voz de la Justicia*, *El Eco de la Patria*, and *El Eco de México*. Between the Californio and populist presses, about sixteen newspapers were published in California between 1860 and 1900.

The Mexican Revolution. The Mexican Revolution stimulated the Spanish-language press of the United States, with militant sociopolitical activity spilling into the United States from Mexico. Political exiles and economic refugees fled to such cities as El Paso and San Antonio, Texas, and Los Angeles, California. Political exiles published newspapers in the United States that represented various Mexican factions, such as those in favor of Porfirio Díaz or Francisco Madero. Particularly important among the political papers were those associated with the Mexican Liberal Party and the brothers Ricardo and Enrique FLORES MAGÓN.

The press of this era can be divided into two types, general and activist. The general press is represented by two Los Angeles papers, *La Prensa* (founded in 1912) and *El Heraldo de México* (1916-1920). *La Prensa* was founded by Adolfo Carrillo and had state-wide circulation. *El Heraldo de México* contained news from Mexico, particularly about the revolution; information on the status of Mexican immigrants in the United States; and news and information on local events of interest to Mexicans, Mexican Americans, and other Latinos living in the Los Angeles area.

Regeneración, published by the Flores Magón brothers, was important among the activist or militant papers. From 1900 to 1901, the paper was published in Mexico City and joined many other liberal publications in a campaign against Porfirio Díaz. The government in turn attacked the papers, many of which closed down as a result. Many of those responsible for their production were jailed or forced into exile. In 1904, Ricardo Flores Magón and his followers were forced into exile in the United States, where they resumed publishing. *Regeneración* appeared in several U.S. cities, among them San Antonio, Texas (1904); St. Louis, Missouri (1905-1906); and Los Angeles, California (1910-1918). Other important activist publications were *Huelga General* and *El Rebelde*, both linked to the INDUSTRIAL WORKERS OF THE WORLD, a major labor union. The monthlies *La Fuerza Consciente* and *La Pluma Roja* were associated with anarchist thought.

The Magonistas (people associated with the Flores Magón brothers) maintained contact with most radical and labor newspapers, in both Spanish and English. They also were linked to important networks of newspapers published by women in the Southwest. Andrea Villarreal González and her sister published *La Mujer Moderna* (founded 1910). One of the earliest papers published by women and associated with the Magonistas was *La Voz de la Mujer*, which appeared in El Paso, Texas, in 1907.

The arrival in the United States of political exiles from Mexico changed the content and audience of newspapers. For example, Mariano AZUELA, noted Mexican novelist of the Mexican Revolution, published in 1915 the newspaper serial adventures that became the novel *Los de abajo* (1916; *The Underdogs*, 1929). Many of the papers published in the United States also found their way into Mexico.

One of the most important Spanish-language papers of the late twentieth century has its origins in the Mexican Revolution. Ignacio Eugenio LOZANO, Sr., a refugee from the revolution, founded *La Prensa* in San Antonio, Texas. The publication began as an exile paper but later focused on U.S. news. In 1926, Lozano established *La Opinión* in Los Angeles. That paper remained under the direction of the Lozano family into the 1990's.

Spanish Immigrants and Their Press. Spanish exiles and immigrants began to make important contributions to the Spanish-language press of the United States late in the nineteenth century. They worked on newspapers alongside other Latinos and frequently were involved with labor and radical publications, particularly anarchist newspapers.

El Despertar was one of the first anarchist papers published in the United States. It circulated in New York and New Jersey from 1891 to 1902 and contained articles by many noted Spanish anarchists, including Anselmo Lorenzo and Federico Urales. *Brazo y Cerebro* (1912-1914) was edited by Juan Martinez and published in New York. *Cultura Obrera* (1911-1927) was the official organ of the Firemen and Ship Stockers Union and contained information about Spain as well as on the Mexican Liberal Party. *Cultura Proliteria* (1910-1959) was one of the longest-running anarchist papers published in the United States. Noted Spanish anarchist Pedro Esteve worked on this paper; he also edited *Doctrina Anarquista Socialista*, which was published in Paterson, New Jersey, in 1905.

The outbreak of the Spanish Civil War in 1936 sent many Spanish exiles to the United States, particularly those opposed to Francisco Franco. Among the important papers of the civil war period are *España Republicana*, *España Libre*, and *Pueblos Hispanos*.

The Cuban American Press. By the 1830's, Cuban Americans had established large communities in Florida, particularly near Key West and Tampa. Political insurrection and independence movements in Cuba from 1868 forward took many Cuban exiles and intellectuals to the United States. Cuban Americans contributed much to the Spanish-speaking press of the United States, particularly after the end of the nineteenth century. Cuban Americans often worked with Spanish immigrants and Puerto Ricans on various periodicals.

Some of the earliest Cuban American papers were associated with the independence movement. Many had close contact with activist organizations such as the tobacco and cigar workers' unions, as was the case of *El Internacional*, the most important labor paper published in YBOR CITY. La Sociedad de Torcedores de Tampa was an important cigar workers' union in Tampa. It was associated with many radical and labor Spanish-language newspapers, including *La Tribuna del Pueblo*, *Boletin Obrero*, *La Defensa*, and *El Despertar*, among others.

The largest waves of Cuban immigration to the United States occurred in the wake of the CUBAN REVOLUTION in 1959. Cubans formed large communities in Florida, particularly in DADE COUNTY. Among the important Cuban American newspapers of the post-revolution period are *El Diario de las Americas* (founded 1953) and *El Miami Herald*.

The Puerto Rican Press. Puerto Ricans have a well-developed press both on the island and on the mainland; the press contains both general and activist branches. The history of the Puerto Rican labor and radical press is tied intimately to migration of Puerto Rican workers from the island to the mainland. Examples of the labor and radical press on the island include *El Eco Proletario*, *La Miseria*, *La Huelga*, *Yo Acuso*, *El Pan del Pobre*, *Unión Obrera*, *Justicia*, and *Consciencia Popular*.

The annexation of Puerto Rico to the United States as a result of the SPANISH-AMERICAN WAR (1898) led to social and political changes on the island and to the first large migrations to the mainland. The beginning of the twentieth century marked the launch of the Puerto Rican labor and radical press. The most important paper of this period was *La Correspondencia de Puerto Rico*, published in San Juan from 1890 to 1943. It is one of the oldest and most important Puerto Rican papers and is crucial for studying the immigration of Puerto Ricans to Hawaii and elsewhere.

Many of the early emigrants from Puerto Rico settled in El Barrio, or SPANISH HARLEM, a section of New York City. Among the important newspaper writers of that area was Bernardo VEGA, a Puerto Rican political and labor activist who arrived in New York in 1916.

La Voz de Puerto Rico (1874) was one of the first papers specifically oriented to a Puerto Rican audience in the United States. *Novedades* was founded in 1887, followed by *La Prensa* in 1913. *La Prensa* merged with *El Diario* to form *La Prensa-El Diario*, one of the most important papers in New York. *Claridad* (founded 1959) is published in San Juan and New York; the New York edition is bilingual. The paper presents Marxist and *independentista* perspectives on news and current events.

The Midwestern Chicano and Latino Press. Many important Spanish-language periodicals appeared in the Midwest, particularly in the area of Chicago, Illinois, which has a large Puerto Rican community. Among the papers of the Midwest are *México* (1922), edited by Francisco Bulnes; *El Correo de México* (1922), edited by J. Espinoza; *La Defensa* (1933), edited by Jose de Mora; *El Centinela* (1959-1960); *Prensa Libre*; *La Gaseta* (1964); and the notable *El*

Puertorriqueño, published from 1965 well into the 1980's.

The Post-1960 Latino Press. In terms of the Latino experience, the period beginning in 1960 is perhaps most notable for the large immigration of Cubans to the United States. In response to Fidel Castro's 1959 takeover of the island, many well-educated professionals from the upper and middle classes immigrated to the United States as political exiles and refugees. The majority settled in Florida, New York, and New Jersey. Most of the early political exiles were anti-Castro and anti-Communist. A very different kind of Cuban came to the United States in the MARIEL BOAT LIFT (1980). The *marielitos*, some of whom were political undesirables and criminals sent by Castro, provided an injection of contemporary Cuban culture and caused Cuban culture and arts to flourish.

The contemporary Cuban press in the United States can be characterized as politically less differentiated than the Chicano or Puerto Rican press; it is primarily an exile press. Cuban immigrants quickly became part of the U.S. professional culture, including the realm of academia. Cubans also went on to establish presses

and publishing houses, book companies, newspapers, reviews, and newsletters.

A useful tool for the study of the Cuban exile press is the Cuban Exile Periodical Collection at the University of Miami. Some of the most important publications in this collection are *America Libre*, *El Avance Criollo*, *Bohemia Libre*, *Alacrán Azul*, *Exilio*, *La Revista Cubana*, *Economia*, *Noticias de Arte*, and *Revista Ideal*.

The late 1960's through the mid-1970's witnessed the rise of the CHICANO MOVEMENT. The Chicano movement is marked by a break with, indeed a rejection of, the earlier Mexican American period. In particular, the Chicano movement pointed out the failure of integrationist strategies. Most aspects of this movement were documented by the Chicano press. More than two hundred newspapers emerged during this period. Perhaps the most recognized was *El Malcriado*, published in an English edition from 1969 to 1976 and in Spanish from 1969 to 1975. *El Malcriado* was the official voice of the UNITED FARM WORKERS union and also provided a variety of cultural expression.

The CRUSADE FOR JUSTICE, led by Rodolfo "Corky" GONZÁLES, was a major urban organization in Denver,

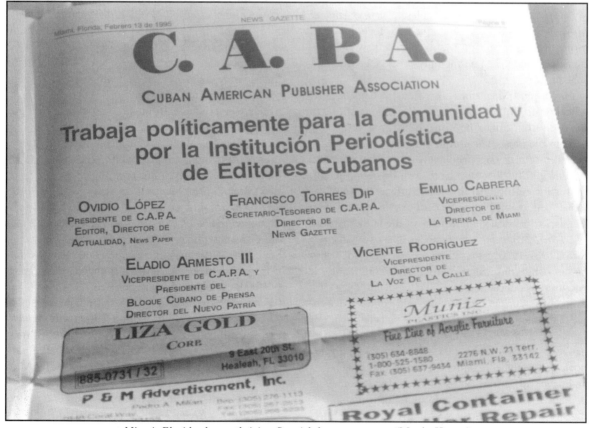

Miami, Florida, has a thriving Spanish-language press. (Martin Hutner)

Colorado. The organizational mouthpiece of the Crusade, published between 1968 and 1980, was *El Gallo*. In northern New Mexico, *El Grito del Norte* (1968-1973), established by Betita Martínez, was a progressive bilingual newspaper that provided coverage of a multitude of injustices suffered by Chicanos, including the land grant struggles. Newspapers such as *Catolicos de la Raza* (1970) in Los Angeles called for the creation of a commission on Mexican American affairs within the hierarchy of the Roman Catholic church; such a commission would plan and carry out socially relevant programs in the Chicano community. *Basta Ya* (1969-1971) chronicled Latino struggles within San Francisco's Mission District.

The Midwest is represented by *Renacimiento*, established in Lansing, Michigan, in 1969. It was dedicated in part to "education, to providing information and a creative outlet." Another longstanding Midwest newspaper was *El Informador* (1973-1980), published in Chicago.

Newspapers edited and published by Chicano student organizations also proliferated. Perhaps the oldest Chicano student newspapers are *El Popo* at California State University-Northridge and *La Gente* at the University of California, Los Angeles. *Chicano Student Movement* (1968-1969) attempted to document and promote this movement. Many of these new publications were published on monthly, weekly, or irregular schedules.

Magazines. Magazines also flourished as a periodical form. In 1968, *Con Safos: Reflections of Life in the Barrio* burst onto the scene in Los Angeles. It was perhaps the most radical in its attempt to create a Chicano aesthetic. It contained many forms of expression, including critical essays, short stories, poetry, humor, satire, art, graffiti, and cartoons. Perhaps the most famous "reflections" were the cartoons and "barriology exams," which tested knowledge of life in the barrio.

La Raza Magazine, an offshoot of the newspaper *La Raza* (1967-1970), focused on documenting socioeconomic conditions within the Chicano community. It was used by educators committed to developing a Chicano curriculum in high schools and colleges. It provided detailed coverage of activities and candidates of La RAZA UNIDA PARTY, an important third-party alternative in the Southwest. In 1968, it published a yearbook that included examples from Latino magazines and newspapers from across the country. It contained perhaps the best photographic journalism documenting the NATIONAL CHICANO MORATORIUM ON VIETNAM (1970).

Agenda and *La Luz* attempted to reach a general national audience. *Agenda* (1976-1980) began as a bulletin for the Southwest Council of La Raza, then expanded to a magazine published by the group, renamed the NATIONAL COUNCIL OF LA RAZA. Coverage included social, political, and economic matters. *La Luz* (1972-1980) was launched after considering the audience for a Latino magazine. The monthly from Denver, Colorado, sought to build a corporate structure and actively solicited advertisements from large corporations. It tried to incorporate items of interest to Latinos from various subgroups.

In 1967, QUINTO SOL published the first issue of *El Grito*, a journal best known for its critiques of stereotypes of Chicanos. The academic journal focused on connecting the Mexican American experience to a historical past. It was joined in 1970 by *Aztlán: Chicano Journal of Social Sciences and the Arts*, published by the Mexican American Cultural Center at the University of California, Los Angeles. *Aztlán* published some creative works, but its primary contributions were in history and the social sciences. Also at UCLA, the *Chicano Law Review*, established in 1972, documented legal rulings of interest to the Latino community.

De Colores: Journal of Emerging Raza Philosophy and *Caracol* provided outlets for cultural expression and for examination of the philosophy of La RAZA. *Caracol* also carried some of the debates involved in the Chicano movement. *Revista Chicano Riqueña*, perhaps the most successful Latino journal, began publication in 1973 in Gary, Indiana. It sought to promote a dialogue among Latinos. Although its focus is contemporary creative expression, it has considered more traditional cultural expressions and has published critical essays.

Chicana perspectives are represented in *Imagenes de la Chicana* from Stanford University and *La Razon Mestiza* in San Francisco. Sylvia Castillo began publishing *Intercambios Femeniles* as a newsletter at Stanford University; it later became a magazine focused on the success of Latinas in education and business. *Latina*, a glossy magazine aimed at a middle-class Latina constituency, took a similar approach.

PUERTO RICAN NATIONALISM and other issues also received attention in the Latino press. THE YOUNG LORDS, a militant organization in New York City, published *El Palante* from 1969 to 1974 and *El Young Lord* (1971, from Milwaukee, Wisconsin). The Midwest Council of Puerto Rican Studies published a scholarly journal titled *The Rican: Journal of Contemporary Puerto Rican Thought* (1971-1975). In 1986, the Center for Puerto Rican Studies at Hunter College of the City University of New York began publishing *Centro Boletin*, a journal mixing scholarly information with a popular format. It covers topics such as the media, history, women, and the economy.

Decline of the Latino Press. The Latino press suffered a marked decline in the mid-1970's. Many student and community periodicals folded. Some of their editors and writers entered journalism school and became journalists at more established mainstream publications.

Many publications changed their names to reflect a new emphasis to match the changing times. In 1975, *Aztlán* changed its subtitle from *Chicano Journal of Social Sciences and the Arts* to *International Journal of Chicano Studies Research*, reflecting commitment to the development of Chicano studies rather than a traditional orientation. After an internal battle, *El Grito* changed its name in 1976 to *Grito del Sol* and began primarily to publish literature. In 1981, *Revista Chicano Riqueña* moved from Gary, Indiana, to Houston, Texas; in 1986, it took the name *Americas Review: A Review of Hispanic Literature and Art in the USA*.

Publications continued to emerge, even though the Latino press in general was in decline. Reflecting the government's introduction and use of the term "Hispanic," some new professional magazines used the term in their titles. These include *Hispanic*, *Hispanic Business*, and *Hispanic Engineer*. *Nuestro: The Magazine for Latinos* emerged in 1977 but had folded by 1987. *Somos* began publishing in 1978 as a regional magazine covering the Chicano community in Southern California; it ceased publication in 1980.

The Department of Chicano Studies at California State University-Los Angeles in 1981 launched a short-lived journal titled *Campo Libre: Journal of Chicano Studies*. Other literary journals produced in this period include *Crítica: A Journal of Critical Essays*, launched in 1984 at the University of California, San Diego. That journal had a national and international focus on cultural production. The Center for Mexican American Affairs at the University of Texas at Austin began publishing *Ethnic Affairs* in 1987. That journal acted as a forum of objective scholarship that built on prior investigation as well as stimulating discussion of major social, political, and economic problems and trends. The *Latino Studies Journal*, under the leadership of Felix Padilla at De Paul University in Chicago, concentrated on critical essays and scholarly articles. *The Puerto Rican Journal* appeared briefly in Chicago in 1982; it covered other Latino groups as well as Puerto Ricans.

Dailies such as *La Opinión*, *La Prensa*, and the *Miami Herald* continued to provide Spanish-language coverage of news events both within the Latino communities and in the countries of origin. These newspapers reached the Latino communities of the United States to a larger extent than did magazines and journals.

Conclusion. This article has not discussed the presses of all Latino subgroups; instead, it has documented the publishing efforts of the largest numbers of Latinos. Certain journals, such as *Revista Chicano-Riqueña* and *Latino Studies*, have encouraged collaboration by various groups of Latinos. Latinos from various subgroups have long cooperated in newspaper publishing.

Various issues have played roles in the history of the Latino press. Women and women's issues have played significant roles in the Spanish-language and Latino press of the United States from the early Spanish immigrant radical and labor press (primarily from an anarchist perspective), to the Latino and Chicana press in the years surrounding the Mexican Revolution, to the feminist publications of the late twentieth century. Independence rhetoric was a large part of the Cuban American and Puerto Rican press early in the twentieth century. During the 1960's, the Chicano movement spurred publication of ideas related to cultural nationalism and the reclaiming of ethnic heritage. The Latino press will no doubt change its content and form, but there can be little doubt that it will continue to act as a mechanism to advance community interests and as a chronicler of the Latino experience.

—Rafael Chabrán and Richard Chabrán

SUGGESTED READINGS:

• Chabrán, Rafael. "Spaniards." In *The Immigrant Labor Press in North America, 1840's-1870's: An Annotated Bibliography*, edited by Dirk Horerder. 3 vols. New York: Greenwood Press, 1987. An annotated bibliography of Spanish-language newspapers that focus on labor-related issues.

• Chabrán, Rafael, and Richard Chabrán. "The Spanish-Language and Latino Press of the United States: Newspapers and Periodicals." In *Handbook of Hispanic Cultures in the United States: Literature and Art*, edited by Francisco Lomelí, Nicolás Kanellos, and Claudio Esteva-Fabregat. Houston: Arte Público Press, 1993. A general survey of the Spanish-language and Latino press of the United States.

• Chabrán, Richard. "Production of Chicano Writings." In *Biblio-Politica*, edited by Francisco Garcia-Ayvens and Richard Chabrán. Berkeley: University of

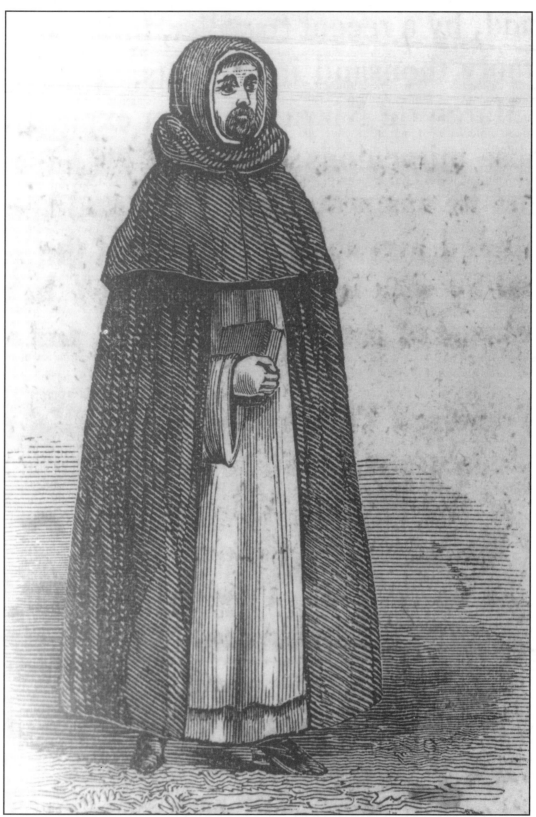

Fray Marcos de Niza is a noted sixteenth century explorer. (Institute of Texan Cultures)

California Press, 1984. An interpretive survey of Chicano publications.

• Cortes, Carlos E. "The Mexican-American Press." In *The Ethnic Press in the United States: A Historical Analysis and Handbook*, edited by Sally M. Miller. Westport, Conn.: Greenwood Press, 1987. A brief historical overview of the Mexican American press.

• Del Olmo, Frank. "Voices for the Chicano Movement." *The Quill* 59 (October, 1971): 9. A journalistic account of Chicano newspapers published during the 1960's.

• Gutierrez, Felix. "Spanish Language Media in America: Background, Resources, History." *Journalism History* 4 (Summer, 1977): 4. A major survey of the Spanish-language press in the United States.

• MacCurdy, Raymond R. *A History and Bibliography of Spanish-Language Newspapers and Magazines in Louisiana, 1808-1945*. Albuquerque: University of New Mexico, 1951. A historical study of the Spanish-language press in New Mexico.

• Rios-C., Herminio, and Lupe Castillo. "Toward a True Chicano Bibliography: Mexican-American Newspapers, 1848-1942." *El Grito* 3 (Summer, 1970): 17-24. A listing of Spanish-language newspapers.

• Rios-C., Herminio. "Toward a True Chicano Bibliography: Part II." *El Grito* 5 (Summer, 1972): 38-47. A continuation of the 1970 article cited above.

• Stratton, Porter A. *The Territorial Press of New Mexico, 1834-1912*. Albuquerque: University of New Mexico Press, 1969. A historical study of the New Mexico Press.

Niggli, Josephina (b. July 13, 1910, Monterrey, Nuevo León, Mexico): Playwright and novelist. The daughter of Frederick Ferdinand Niggli (a cement manufacturer) and Goldie Morgan Niggli, Josephina was educated at the Incarnate World College, where she received her B.A. in 1931. She received an M.A. from the University of North Carolina in 1937 and attended the Old Vic Theatre School in 1955.

Niggli was an instructor in radio at the University of North Carolina, Chapel Hill, and worked as a writer at Metro-Goldwyn-Mayer Studios in 1951 and 1952. She was an assistant professor of drama at the University of North Carolina Women's College from 1955 to 1956 and also taught at Western Carolina University.

Although Niggli has won critical acclaim for her one-act plays and has written for film, she is perhaps best known for her first novel, *Mexican Village* (1945), hailed as a classic portrait of small-town Mexico. She also published a second novel, *Step Down, Elder Brother* (1947), in which she evokes the sense of being of an entire community, and a children's book, *A Miracle for Mexico* (1964). Niggli's work affords readers a vivid, authentic depiction of Mexican life in all of its local color.

Niza, Fray Marcos de (c. 1495, Nice, Savoy—Mar. 25, 1558, Mexico): Priest. Fray Marcos de Niza was a Catholic priest from Nice, in the duchy of Savoy (modern France). He went to the New World in 1531 with Francisco PIZARRO, who conquered Peru. In 1538, Fray Marcos went to New Galicia, a colony north of New Spain governed by Francisco Vázquez de CORONADO.

In 1539, Fray Marcos led an expedition north to unknown territories. He was accompanied by Estevanico, the African slave who, with Álvar Núñez CABEZA DE VACA and two other Spaniards, had survived Pánfilo de NARVÁEZ's ill-fated expedition to settle Florida.

During the journey, Estevanico (identified in some sources as Esteban and Estevan) went ahead and reached an Indian pueblo that belonged to a larger complex believed to be CÍBOLA, a mythical complex of seven rich cities. The residents of the pueblo killed Estevanico. When Fray Marcos heard the news, he decided not to enter the city, but he managed to get a glimpse from a distance. It is probable that he saw Hawikuh, the southernmost Zuni pueblo.

After his return, Fray Marcos reported that he had seen a wealthy city. He emphasized that the structures had turquoise. This sparked the imagination of other explorers and conquistadores. Fray Marcos was named provincial of his order in 1540, and he moved to Mexico City.

Nopales: Edible pads of the prickly pear cactus. The fleshy, oval pads of the prickly pear cactus (genus *Opuntia*) are eaten in Mexico, especially in its western, central, and northern portions. The spines of a *nopal* are removed, and sometimes tough parts of the skin are removed. The *nopal* is then boiled, baked, or scored and grilled. Undercooked *nopales* contain a mucilaginous fluid (*baba*) that can make them unpalatable. Cooked *nopales* can be eaten as is or sliced and included in various dishes. Cut-up *nopales* are available canned and usually are called *nopalitos* in this form.

North American Free Trade Agreement (NAFTA): NAFTA, passed in 1993 and effective on January 1,

1994, eradicated or reduced all tariffs among Canada, the United States, and Mexico, permitting freer trade. Free trade with the United States and its neighbors to the north and south, Canada and Mexico, has been discussed for decades. As agitation grew in Europe for the establishment of the Common Market early in the 1990's, so, too, did many Americans speculate that a common market of sorts would benefit the three nations included in NAFTA.

The Democratic Party was divided on NAFTA; Republicans largely favored passage. Michigan's Senator, Donald Riegle, a Democrat, called NAFTA a poisoned cup the George Bush Administration had passed to President Bill Clinton. Senate Majority Leader George Mitchell, however, contended that NAFTA clearly solidified U.S. leadership in the Western Hemisphere and throughout the world.

Clinton, who had met earlier with Mexico's president Carlos Salinas de Gortari, met in Seattle with Canadian prime minister Jean Chrétien on November 18, 1993, to work out final sticking points before the U.S. Senate voted on the act, which had passed in the U.S. House of Representatives on November 17, 1993. Canada already had ratified NAFTA, on June 23. The U.S. Senate approved NAFTA on November 20, 1993, by a vote of sixty-one to thirty-eight. On December 8, Clinton signed the document that made NAFTA effective on January 1, 1994.

Although Mexico was the last of the three countries to vote for passage, ratification in Mexico seemed ensured because Salinas' Institutional Revolutionary Party held all but three seats in Mexico's Senate. Mexico's vote on November 22, 1993, was fifty-six in favor, two opposed.

Numerous groups lobbied and demonstrated in attempts to prevent U.S. acceptance of the North American Free Trade Agreement. (Impact Visuals, Fred Chase)

NAFTA eliminates, for a period of fifteen years, many tariffs among the three countries included in it. It calls for a gradual phasing out of textile, apparel, automobile, and automotive parts tariffs. Immediately cut were 57 percent of all agricultural tariffs; tariffs on U.S. corn and Mexican peanuts, orange juice, and sugar were reduced gradually.

Foreign investors from NAFTA countries are treated equally with domestic investors except in the U.S. airline and radio communication industries, Mexican energy and railway industries, and Canadian culture industries. By the year 2000, all limits on investment in Mexican banks were to cease for U.S. and Canadian banks, securities brokers, and insurers.

By 1999, truckers would be able to cross the U.S.-Mexico border freely. Intellectual property enjoys protection consistent with each country's standards. In purchasing, NAFTA member companies could compete in government bidding. The act established commissions to monitor environmental abuses and to impose fines.

NAFTA established a North American Development Bank to aid communities adversely affected by the act and to aid environmental projects on the U.S.-Mexico border. The United States pledged $90 million to retrain workers laid off before July, 1995, as a result of NAFTA.

NAFTA interlocked the world's largest, eighth-largest, and thirteenth-largest economies. The combined market created by NAFTA comprised 360 million people with combined annual purchasing power in excess of $6 trillion. As Latin America enters a growth phase, it is likely that NAFTA will be expanded to include other Latin American nations.

North American Indians: Since the arrival of Europeans in the Americas, the lives and cultures of the original native populations have mingled with those of the new arrivals. Food, language, and religious customs of the Indians and the Spanish and later European conquerors have affected one another, and there is a large intermixture of racial ancestry.

First Contacts. Apart from a failed Viking invasion that left little mark on North American culture, the first Europeans to land on American shores were Spaniards. The intent of these first explorers and conquerors was to find a new route to India, and the early explorers thought they had arrived near the Indian coast. This is why the American natives were called Indians and the islands first visited by Christopher Columbus and explorers of that time are called the West Indies. It did

not take long for the Europeans to realize that they had not landed among the advanced Indian civilization they had expected. Instead, they found a land inhabited by people of a variety of cultures and speaking a variety of languages unrelated to Spanish or any other language known in Europe.

The wealth of gold that the explorers sought did not exist in North America, though some gold was found. The Aztec and Inca civilizations were destroyed in the process of taking gold from their lands. In the West Indies and on the coasts of North America, there was little to be found in the way of material riches.

The Europeans of the time considered any non-Christian, nonwhite race as inherently inferior. As they had in Africa, they attempted to enslave the population. This effort met with little success. The Indians resisted, and mortality rates were high. In addition to the deliberate slaughter of Indians unwilling to give up their lands, the Europeans indirectly caused EPIDEMICS of a variety of diseases. The native populations had no natural resistance to these diseases and were decimated. Many of the survivors fled to South and Central America, and to Mexico and Florida. The response of the Europeans was to bring in slaves from Africa.

The earliest explorers came without women and took Indian wives. Their offspring were referred to as MESTIZO, a mixture of Indian and European ancestry. Many or most Latinos have both Indian and European roots.

Areas of Contact. After the Caribbean islands were explored and found to hold little of value to the Spaniards, other areas were colonized. With the most important exception of Brazil, which was colonized by Portugal, most of Central and South America is dominated by Spanish-speaking culture, although native languages and cultures persist in some of the less accessible areas of the interior. The Caribbean islands are also predominantly Spanish, with the exception of the country of Haiti, which was colonized by the French.

In mainland North America, Spain controlled what is now Mexico and the states of California, Nevada, Utah, New Mexico, and Arizona, as well as parts of Colorado, Wyoming, Kansas, and Oklahoma. When Mexico gained its independence from Spain in 1821, it held all this territory. Texas was part of Mexico until it gained independence in 1836, and it became part of the United States in 1845. The states mentioned above were ceded to the United States in 1848 after the MEXICAN AMERICAN WAR. Before that time, they made up fully half the territory of Mexico.

Indians at missions often engaged in crafts such as rope making and basket weaving. (Institute of Texan Cultures)

This Mexican Cession has important linguistic implications. The Spanish, and even the Mexicans, were largely unsuccessful in replacing native languages with Spanish. Many American Indians did learn at least some Spanish, long before encounters with English-speaking European settlers. Modern Indian languages persist, but with much borrowed Spanish vocabulary. The introduction of writing was welcomed by many Indian tribes and adapted for use in native languages.

Cultural Exchanges. The Spanish explorers and their English and French successors held extreme cultural biases. Any group of people that had not accepted Christianity and did not speak a European language was considered automatically inferior. There were even philosophical debates as to whether Indians were human beings. The general tendency was to try to impose European culture on the "savages."

By the middle of the twentieth century, most Indians in North America were practicing Christians, although tribal rituals persisted. Except in the most remote regions, Spanish and English became the predominant languages. The European culture was superior in material and especially military terms, and when peaceful relations were established, Indians realized they had much to gain from European knowledge. The conquerors, however, also gained.

A good example of Indian influence on Europeans is in the area of dietary habits. When the Europeans arrived, they had to live primarily on the native diet. Corn, potatoes, tomatoes, chocolate, and a variety of beans and peppers were unknown to Europeans before contact with the American natives. On the other hand, Christopher Columbus, in his second voyage to the West Indies in 1493, brought pigs, cows, goats, and sheep, animals unknown to the natives. Horses were also introduced by the Spanish.

Much of the food considered to be from Latino cultures has American Indian as well as Spanish roots. For example, a beef taco, a common Mexican food in the United States, is actually a European meat wrapped in the product of an American plant. The foods most identified with the West Indies are heavily based on beans native to the Americas. The hot peppers so important to a number of Latino cooking styles are American in origin.

The music called Latino and sometimes Spanish is also heavily influenced by American Indian culture. The driving, syncopated rhythm heard in many Latin American songs is heavily influenced by American Indian tribal songs and dances.

Religion. By far the most common religion among Latinos is Catholicism, the dominant religion of Spanish, Portuguese, and French explorers and colonists.

Some of the first Europeans in the Americas were missionaries who considered it their duty to bring Catholicism to the "heathen" natives. The Christianity practiced by American Indians, however, remained tinged by tribal beliefs.

Unlike Christians, who consider it a major point of faith that there is only one God, people of American Indian cultures had a multitude of gods and spirits. Thus it has never been necessary for an American Indian to give up tribal religious culture in order to accept Christianity. In American Indian ceremonies, there is often an admixture of native religion and Christianity. It is not unusual for a ceremony to begin with traditional evocations of the gods and spirits of animals, earth, water, and sky, followed by the Lord's Prayer. This was a source of frustration to many missionaries, who saw this mixture of cultures as blasphe-mous. The mixture of religions has affected Latinos who do not consider themselves to be Indians and have little or no direct knowledge of the Indian religions that some of their ancestors followed.

An example of this influence is SANTERÍA, a religion practiced by many Latinos, particularly those from the West Indies. Santería is older than Christianity. Its origins are obscure, but it appears to span the cultures of three continents. Santería, a form of religion and healing, has roots in Africa and was brought to the Caribbean by black slaves. It was then altered to suit American culture, as native American herbs were substituted in medicinal mixtures for African herbs that were difficult or impossible to obtain. Finally, as Christianity become dominant, often by force, the names of Christian saints were used to represent the ancient gods.

Dennis Banks (standing), a leader of the American Indian Movement, was the chancellor of Deganawidah-Quetzalcoatl University, which offered classes focusing on American Indians. (AP/Wide World Photos)

Santería is still practiced in the United States. Shops called BOTÁNICAS sell the herbs and icons necessary for Santería rites. *Botánicas* exist in many cities and neighborhoods with large Latino populations. Even many Catholic Latinos practice Santería.

Conclusion. The greatest proportion of Indians in the United States who still hold to their ancient customs is in the Southwest. There, the Spanish influence was greatest. Immigration from Mexico to the region is extensive. The American Indian languages still in regular use are heavily influenced by Spanish, much more than they are influenced by English.

There are few North American Indians who are of "pure blood." Spanish ancestry is common among them, and because the Spaniards and Mexicans who moved into the Southwest were already far from purely European in ancestry, there is also Caribbean and African influence.

Virtually every Hispanic American has some Indian ancestry, and Indian culture has shaped Latino culture. Puerto Ricans go to BODEGAS (grocery stores) to buy foods originally used by Indians. Mexican Americans have brought with them a diet that is Spanish and Indian. The Spanish spoken by Latinos contains American Indian words.

In general, it is impossible to separate the Latino and Indian cultures in any meaningful way. North American Indians of the late twentieth century were more likely to speak English than Spanish, but their customs were more heavily influenced by the early Spanish cultural exchange than by the much later encounters with English culture. In turn, Hispanic cultures are heavily influenced by the native cultures that the Spanish invaders of the Americas encountered.

Except in the Southwest, where they are concentrated, American Indians are often mistaken for people of Hispanic origin. There are linguistic differences, but the cultures are strongly connected in both directions, and the racial mixtures are almost identical. Latino foods are as much a part of native American culture as of Spanish culture. Religious rituals among Latinos are influenced by Indian customs.

The two-way cultural exchange is clear. Cultures intermixed long before the United States existed and long before English-speaking colonists encountered the indigenous population of the United States.

—*Marc Goldstein*

SUGGESTED READINGS:
• Hudson, Charles. *The Southeastern Indians.* Knoxville: University of Tennessee Press, 1976. A study of the Indians of the southeastern United States, from prehistorical evidence through modern times. Emphasizes the Indians' contact with European settlers and the differences these encounters have made in native cultures.

• Meltzer, Milton. *The Hispanic Americans.* New York: Thomas Y. Crowell, 1982. A description of the various Hispanic populations in the United States. Illustrated with photographs, this book contains a variety of stories from particular Hispanic families in the United States.

• Shorris, Earl. *Latinos: A Biography of the People.* New York: W. W. Norton & Co., 1992. Describes a variety of Latino cultures in the United States. Included are many individual reports from various Latino cultures in a variety of places.

• Spicer, Edward H. *Cycles of Conquest.* Tucson: University of Arizona Press, 1962. A long, detailed discussion of the relationships between European explorers and conquerors and the native American population. Illustrated with maps and charts.

• Viola, Herman J. *After Columbus: The Smithsonian Chronicles of the American Indians.* Washington, D.C.: Smithsonian Books, 1990. A history of North American Indian cultures, with a particular emphasis on changes in those cultures resulting from European influences.

Nosotros: Entertainers' organization. Nosotros was founded in 1969 by Mexican-born actor Ricardo MONTALBAN. It works to increase opportunities in films and television for Latino actors and to improve the image of Latinos in the industry. In 1970, Nosotros initiated the Golden Eagle Awards, which are presented to outstanding Latino entertainers annually. The group developed its own theater to produce Latino plays. By the 1990's, it accepted scripts from Latino playwrights, offered acting classes, held membership meetings open to the public on a limited basis, and had a cable-access show called *Nosotros Today.*

Novarro, Ramón (Ramón Samaniegos; Feb. 6, 1899, Durango, Mexico—Oct. 31, 1968, Hollywood, Calif.): Actor. A child of Mexican aristocrats and a cousin of actress Dolores DEL RIO, Novarro made his film debut in 1916. He strongly objected to the images of Mexicans prevalent in early films, and throughout his career he turned down many roles. In the 1920's, he emerged as a popular romantic lead in the "Latin lover" style. His credits include *A Small Town Idol* (1921), *The Four Horsemen of the Apocalypse* (1921), *The Prisoner of Zenda* (1922), *Scaramouche* (1923), *Ben Hur*

Ramón Novarro. (AP/Wide World Photos)

President George Bush congratulates Surgeon General Antonia Coello Novello after her swearing-in ceremony. (AP/Wide World Photos)

(1926), *The Student Prince* (1927), *The Pagan* (1929), *Mata Hari* (1931), *The Cat and the Fiddle* (1934), and *The Sheik Steps Out* (1937).

With the advent of sound in films, Novarro's imperfect English limited his career in Hollywood. Through the 1930's and 1940's, he worked largely in Spanish and French films, including *La Sevillana* (1930) and *Contra la corriente* (1937). He did two Westerns in 1950, *The Outriders* and *Crisis*, and made his last film, *Heller in Pink Tights*, in 1960. A lifelong homosexual, Novarro refused to conceal his sexual orientation despite studio pressure. In 1968, he was brutally murdered in his home in Hollywood.

Novello, Antonia Coello (b. Aug. 23, 1944, Fajardo, Puerto Rico): Government official. Novello was nominated as the U.S. surgeon general in 1989, following C. Everett Koop's announcement that he would retire from that position. Prior to becoming surgeon general, Novello had been deputy director of the National Institute of Child Health and Human Development at the National Institutes of Health. Novello was the first woman and the first Latino to hold the position of surgeon general. As surgeon general, Novello addressed such problems as teenage drinking, children infected with AIDS, and smoking, along with targeting women's health issues.

Novello suffered from a congenital colon condition that was not corrected until she was eighteen years old. She based her decision to become a doctor in part on the desire to help those who suffered as she had. She earned B.S. and M.D. degrees from the University of Puerto Rico. She did her internship and residency at the University of Michigan Medical Center in Ann Arbor, from 1970 to 1973. In 1971, she became the first woman to win the University of Michigan Pediatrics Department's Intern of the Year Award. In 1974, Novello joined the staff of Georgetown University Hospital in Washington, D.C. She later served with the National Institutes of Health as a staff physician, as a project officer at the National Institute of Arthritis, Metabolism, and Digestive Diseases, and as executive secretary in the Division of Research Grants. She earned a master's degree in public health from The Johns Hopkins University in 1982.

Nueva canción: Fusion of folk and popular music. *Nueva canción* was produced by a new generation of popular poets motivated by revolutionary activities in Latin America. They were active in national folkloric movements and raised questions about people's struggle for sociopolitical equality. *Nueva canción* is most notable in the work of the Chilean Violeta Parra (1917-1967). She wrote her own new folk songs, based on rural folk songs and dances, in the 1950's, influencing the coming generation of musicians, including Inti-Illimani, a group that drew on music and instruments from all of Latin America.

Nueva trova: New Cuban song. The *nueva trova* shares many aspects with the Latin American music of resistance, or *nueva canción*. In Cuba, however, the *nueva trova* is not considered protest music; it is recognized and supported by the government as an art form. Touching on themes of love and social struggle, the *nueva trova* is sung by *trovadores* acting as social commentators, not as political propagandists. Accompanied by guitar and voice, the *trovadores* compose using elements from the GUARACHA, CANCIÓN, GUAJIRA, and SON, as well as drawing from international musical trends. The *nueva trova* is seen as a cultural product of the Cuban Revolution.

Nuns and priests: From 1493 onward, the Spanish Crown wanted to extend Catholicism to the Americas. Beginning with the second voyage of Christopher Columbus, "fighting priests" were members of the colonizing expeditions. The priests' mission was to convert the conquered natives from their Indian religions to Catholicism. These early missionaries were required by their rulers, Isabella and Ferdinand and later Charles I, to ask the Indian groups they encountered to accept Catholicism freely, before the conquistadores made war on them; this was known as the *requerimiento* (the requirement). Unfortunately, the Indians often did not understand what was asked of them, and many abuses of the policy occurred.

One of the early champions of the Indians, Father Bartolomé DE LAS CASAS, pleaded with King Charles V (Carlos V) to impose stricter standards upon the conquistadores concerning the treatment of the Indians. Early religious reforms included attempts to translate bibles and prayer books into native languages; some reformers also sought a degree of tolerance for Indian religious practices that coexisted with Catholicism. By the mid-sixteenth century, many priests had been born in the Americas, and these clerics generally exhibited greater understanding of American customs.

Young women often saw membership in a religious community (a convent) as an alternative to arranged marriages and became sisters (nuns). Until early in the twentieth century, women in traditional communities

The archbishop of San Antonio, Texas, performs a baptism. (James Shaffer)

generally had only two career choices—marriage or the convent. Arranged marriages held little attraction for many young women, because the male partner could be elderly or ill; in other cases, the wife was obligated to move to her husband's *estancia* (ranch or dwelling), which typically was at a great distance from the wife's family or from the benefits of city living. Before the twentieth century, the average life span for women was quite short, and many deaths happened as the result of pregnancies or childbirth. These dangers were heightened for women living in the country with no access to medical attention; thus, life in the convent often held greater attraction than marriage.

There was much work to be done by religious communities. Education and health care in Latin America and in Latino communities traditionally has been in the hands of priests and nuns. It was considered an honor to have one son enter the priesthood and one daughter enter the convent.

Latino priests and nuns play an important role in the modern Roman CATHOLIC CHURCH. Masses, funerals, marriages, and prayer services in Spanish happen not only in large U.S. coastal cities and on the Texas border but also in the northern tier of agricultural states, especially during summer, when migrant farmworkers populate the region. Outreach programs for Spanish-speaking Catholics who live throughout the United States and Canada were central to the mission of the Catholic church in the late twentieth century.

Nutrition: Along with medical care, other indicators of health status are genetic inheritance, lifestyle, and environment. Lifestyle includes diet and nutrition, exercise, and hours of sleep. Good nutrition is important not only for physical well-being but also for learning.

The War on Poverty of the 1960's introduced the importance of nutrition in the learning process. One of its programs provided subsidized lunches at schools. Since then, numerous studies have measured the effects of nutrition on health.

Obesity, HYPERTENSION, and DIABETES are all associated with diet and nutrition. A nutritious diet contributes to the control of weight, hypertension, and diabetes. The HISPANIC HEALTH AND NUTRITION EX-

AMINATION SURVEY, conducted in the 1980's, provided the basis for examining nutrition and obesity among Latinos. A relationship was discovered between socioeconomic status and obesity. Latinos were found to be more likely to be overweight than were non-Hispanic whites, with Mexican Americans having the highest prevalence, among Latinos, of being overweight.

The Hispanic Health and Nutrition Examination Survey also found that people of lower socioeconomic status tended to have rounder body shapes, with subcutaneous fat concentrated around the midsection. Puerto Rican males were an exception to this finding. Latinos have reported lower cholesterol measurements than low-income non-Hispanic whites.

A few studies have focused on nutrition and Latino children. In a study conducted for the Centers for Disease Control, no association was found between the cholesterol levels of Latino children and obesity. Another study published in 1990 examined the effect of vitamin and mineral supplements on Latino children. There was no significant difference between those who were given vitamins and those who were not. The researchers indicated that the addition of an educational component to reduce the high intake of protein, sodium, and carbonated drinks could help improve the feeding practices of Latino mothers.

Several studies have examined the dietary calcium intake of Latinos, non-Hispanic whites, and non-Hispanic blacks, finding that the calcium intakes in the three largest Latino groups (Mexican Americans, Cuban Americans, and Puerto Ricans) were similar but that the sources of calcium were different. As an example, tortillas were an important source of calcium for Mexican Americans but less important for the other groups. The level of calcium consumed by women in general was less than the recommended daily allowance. Latinos also reported higher energy intakes from carbohydrates and a lower percentage of energy intake from fat than non-Hispanic blacks or whites. Later studies began to examine the relationship between nutrition and pregnancy outcomes among Latinas.

Although it can be assumed that Latinos need to examine their eating habits because of the high incidence of hypertension and diabetes in this population, research had provided little guidance by the early 1990's. Dietary research may also provide insight into educational outcomes.

Nuyorican Poets' Café (New York, N.Y.): Performance center. The café was established on Manhattan's East Side by owner/university professor Miguel ALGARÍN. The café served as a venue for the emerging Nuyorican poetry, theater, and writing of the 1960's, work that crosses many genres but expresses the sentiment of Puerto Rican artists from working-class New York. Poetry was the natural medium for many Nuyorican artists who were reared within the oral tradition, and the café provided a forum for performance. Poets associated with the café in the 1960's included Tato LAVIERA and Miguel PIÑERO. The café continues as a space for poetry readings, music, comedy, and plays.

Nuyoricans: "Nuyorican" is a term that has been used since the 1970's to describe a Puerto Rican born or living in New York City. Puerto Rican writers living in the United States were the first to call themselves Nuyoricans. More than 2.5 million people of Puerto Rican descent lived in the United States in 1990, and about half lived in NEW YORK CITY and surrounding areas. Attempts to popularize the term "Neo-Rican" for all Puerto Ricans living in the United States failed.

Historical Background. On April 21, 1898, the United States of America declared war against Spain and its colonies in the New World. On July 28, 1898, U.S. military troops under the command of General Nelson Miles invaded Puerto Rico. Puerto Rico was taken as war bounty and became a territory of the United States.

In 1917, the JONES ACT was approved by the U.S. Congress and signed by President Woodrow Wilson. This law gave the people of Puerto Rico United States citizenship and established Puerto Rico as a territory. Two months after its approval came the military draft for all male U.S. citizens aged eighteen years and older.

World War I claimed the lives of many U.S. citizens, including Puerto Ricans. The years that followed were years of economic hardship in Puerto Rico, caused in part by hurricanes that devastated the island but more substantially by the worldwide economic depression.

During the depression years, tumbling prices for sugarcane and tobacco dealt the Puerto Rican economy serious blows. In an attempt to rebuild the economy and regain Puerto Rican support, the American government appointed Jesús T. PIÑERO as the first native Puerto Rican governor in 1946. He was not very successful, and in 1947, under the administration of President Franklin D. Roosevelt, the United States gave Puerto Rico the right to elect its own government.

Operation Bootstrap. In November, 1948, Luis MUÑOZ MARÍN became the first Puerto Rican governor to be chosen in free elections. His tenure brought

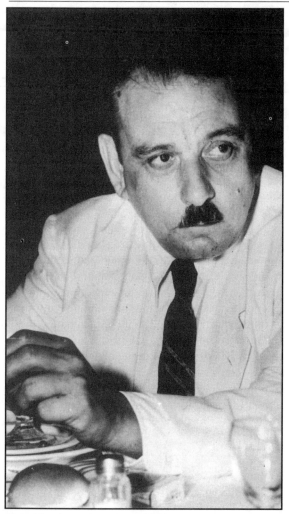

Luis Muñoz Marín, as governor of Puerto Rico, increased industrial activity on the island. (AP/Wide World Photos)

rapid changes to Puerto Rico's economy. Important among these was Law Number 936, granting U.S. investors tax breaks for ten to seventeen years if they established factories on the island. During the next two decades, hundreds of factories moved to the island, and Puerto Rico's economy changed rapidly from agricultural (sugarcane and tobacco) to primarily industrial.

The factories established on the island often required little technology but were labor intensive. Factories facing labor shortages promised to train workers at no cost to them. To support the industrialization process, the Puerto Rican government offered incentives such as housing and land at low cost in or near the cities. The Puerto Rican government's overall program of industrialization, begun in 1944, became known as OPERATION BOOTSTRAP. It included a goal of reducing

unemployment, partly through industrialization and partly through encouraging workers to leave the island to take jobs in the United States.

Many unemployed farmworkers moved from their rural lands into the cities seeking the opportunities promised by industry and the Puerto Rican government. A significant number of factories produced clothing. Women hoping to find jobs in the sewing industry urged their husbands to move into the cities. The 1940's and 1950's saw a massive internal migration from the countryside to the cities.

Puerto Ricans in New York. After World War II, rumors began to spread in Puerto Rico of higher wages in the United States for similar work. Falling air fares and an extensive recruitment program by U.S. firms helped to bring more migrant workers to the mainland. These workers were often brought to the United States on one-year contracts to pick fruits and vegetables.

The new immigrants established themselves primarily in large urban industrial centers. The largest group of Puerto Rican immigrants went to New York City and settled in the communities of Manhattan, Brooklyn, and the Bronx. At that time, many U.S. cities, especially in the Northeast, were experiencing a process of urban flight. Those who could afford to move relocated to the suburbs, which were made attractive by the mass production of cars and the construction of highways.

Buildings left vacant in the cities were often divided into small units and rented to immigrants, many of them Puerto Ricans. Many newcomers were soon confronted with a host of problems previously unknown to them. The buildings were often in bad condition and lacked heating or needed expensive repairs. The few skills that immigrants had acquired in their previous urban experiences on their tropical island were often not sufficient to cope with the new environment. Racial tension, which was low in Puerto Rico, added to the problems of the period, as did the need to learn a new language and cope with climatic changes.

Nuyoricans. Children and teenagers growing up in the Puerto Rican communities witnessed their parents' puzzled reaction to their new home. These children developed their own lifestyle, combining elements of Puerto Rican and American culture with relative ease.

Facing racial tensions, some of them formed youth gangs that declared territorial dominion over certain streets or parks. These gangs became widely known through the film *West Side Story* (1961) and later cinematic efforts that created a stereotype of young Puerto Ricans in New York City.

Casita Maria, in East Harlem, conducted classes in English after World War II. (AP/Wide World Photos)

The second and third generation of Puerto Ricans born in New York adopted different ways of living. Some left the old Puerto Rican communities behind, giving way to new Latin American groups of immigrants. Some stayed and climbed the social ladder, becoming professionals, politicians, and artists. Others, sadly, remained mired in impoverished conditions.

Around 1970, writers including Juan FLORES and Miguel ALGARÍN began to call themselves Nuyoricans. They took pride in the term, which differentiated them and their writings as coming from the Puerto Rican experience in the United States rather than from observers with a more distant perspective.

Writings of Puerto Rican authors such as Pedro Juan SOTO (*Spiks*, 1956) and René Marqués (*La carreta*, 1951-1952) were challenged by firsthand Nuyorican experiences such as *La carreta made a U-turn* (1979) by Tato LAVIERA and *Mendoza's Dreams* (1987) by Ed VEGA. After 1990, the term Nuyorican became accepted and respected. It was, however, well understood that inside—perhaps deep inside—every Nuyorican remains a Puerto Rican.   —*Juana Iris Goergen*

SUGGESTED READINGS: • Algarín, Miguel, and Miguel Piñero, eds. *Nuyorican Poetry*. New York: William Morrow, 1975. • Flores, Juan. *Divided Borders*. Houston, Tex.: Arte Público, 1993. • Mohr, Eugene. *The Nuyorican Experience*. Westport, Conn.: Greenwood Press, 1982. • Picó, Francisco. *Historia general de Puerto Rico*. Río Piedras, Puerto Rico: Huracán, 1986. • Turner, Faythe, ed. *Puerto Rican Writers at Home in the USA*. Seattle, Wash.: Open Hand, 1991.

O

Obledo, Mario Guerra (b. Apr. 9, 1932, San Antonio, Tex.): Public official. Obledo served in the Korean War. He earned a degree in pharmacology from the University of Texas in 1957, then a bachelor's degree and a doctor of law degree at St. Mary's University in San Antonio. He has dedicated his life to organizing Latinos and helping others to recognize the benefits of political organizing. Obledo held the presidency of the LEAGUE OF UNITED LATIN AMERICAN CITIZENS as well as other local, district, state, and national offices in that organization. He became an assistant attorney general in Texas in 1965 and has taught law at Harvard University.

Obledo was a cofounder of the HISPANIC NATIONAL BAR ASSOCIATION and the MEXICAN AMERICAN LEGAL DEFENSE AND EDUCATION FUND, two organizations that offer tremendous benefits to Latinos. He also participated in the SOUTHWEST VOTER REGISTRATION

Governor Edmund G. Brown, Jr., in 1975 appointed Harvard Law School professor Mario Obledo as secretary of the California Department of Health and Welfare. (AP/ Wide World Photos)

EDUCATION PROJECT. Obledo brought his pharmaceutical experience to his work as secretary of the California Department of Health and Welfare. He was appointed head of that agency in 1975.

Obra bufa cubana: Cuban genre of blackface farce. The *obra bufa* (from an Italian phrase meaning "to puff out one's cheeks in mockery") originated in Paris and traveled to Cuba from Spain in the 1870's. The *obra bufa cubana* follows a basic sketch format revolving around the *bufo*, a quick-witted and unscrupulous black person, a master of satire who is aided by his comic mulatto girlfriend in getting the better of a newly arrived and stupid Galician. The form traveled to the United States, where it became popular in the 1930's. Later, *obras bufas musicales* appeared, including song and dance forms such as the GUAJIRA and GUARACHA. Other *obras bufas cubanas* raised questions about labor.

Ocampo, Silvina (b. 1906, Buenos Aires, Argentina): Poet and short-story writer. Ocampo received a good overall education that focused on European and European-style high culture. Much of it was acquired informally through family and friends. Her family pursued a cosmopolitan ideal, providing the children with a thorough grounding in French and English. Ocampo pursued art lessons for a time, studying painting and drawing, but her interest soon shifted to literature.

In 1940, Ocampo married novelist and short-story writer Adolfo Bioy Casares. In the years leading up to their marriage, Ocampo and Bioy Casares spent much time with writer Jorge Luis Borges, and after the marriage the three continued their close association, from which a number of collaborative projects emerged. Ocampo and her husband collaborated on the 1946 detective novel *Los que aman, odian*. All three appeared as co-editors of two important anthologies: *Antología de la literatura fantástica* (1940; *The Book of Fantasy*, 1988) and *Antología poética argentina* (1941). Ocampo's collections of short stories include *Autobiografía de Irene* (1948); *Las invitadas* (1961), and *Leopoldina's Dream* (1988). Ocampo has written short fiction that is considered outstanding in its rigorous construction and manifestation of imagination, keeping its humanistic qualities covertly present beneath a display of ingenuity.

OCCUPATIONAL CLASSIFICATIONS OF LATINO WORKERS, 1990

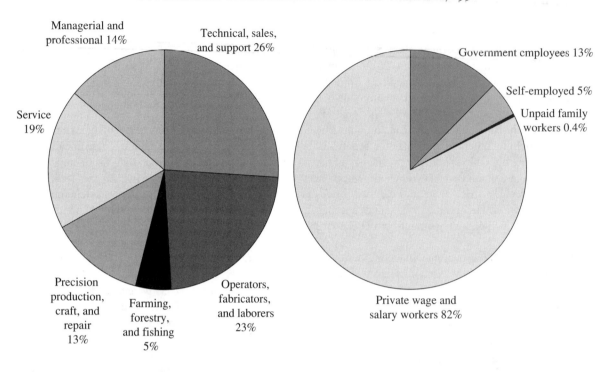

Source: Data are from Bureau of the Census, *1990 Census of Population: Persons of Hispanic Origin in the United States* (Washington, D.C.: Bureau of the Census, 1993), Table 4.

Occupations and occupational trends: The Latino population of the early 1990's was the fastest-growing subpopulation in the United States and the fastest growing segment of the labor force. The Latino population was also comparatively young, with a median age of about twenty-six years, compared to about thirty-four for the rest of the population. Latino men in particular had high labor force participation rates.

There were about ten million Latinos in the U.S. civilian labor force as of 1990. The Latino work force had increased 65 percent since 1980, a growth rate four times that of the non-Hispanic work force.

Trends. Even though Latino workers saw improvements after 1960, Latinos generally have occupied the lower-paid, less skilled, less stable, and most dangerous occupations. In part, the lower occupational standing of Latinos reflects lower levels of skills and of job training, which in turn reflect lower educational attainment and poor English-language proficiency, particularly among foreign-born Latinos. Latinos also have less experience in the job market, in part because on average they are younger than other workers.

The lower occupational standing of Latinos may reflect different labor market conditions in areas where Latinos live; it may also result from general discrimination, exclusion from job opportunities, segregation into low-income neighborhoods, and consequent poorer educational opportunities.

The 1990 census showed that high proportions of Latino adults were born outside the United States. Studies show that recent immigrants tend to occupy the least desirable occupations, at least until they have time to acquire the knowledge and skills necessary to function in the U.S. labor market.

Latino women tended to have occupations different from those of men, though both have been concentrated in lower-paid, less-skilled occupations. To understand occupational change among Latinos, it is important to consider men and women separately. It is also important to consider place of birth, inside or outside the United States. Finally, because the occupational classification system changed significantly for the 1980 census, caution should be exercised in making comparisons over time.

Mexican Americans. The 1990 census showed that persons of Mexican origin were by far the largest

Latino group in the U.S. labor force. There were nearly six million Mexican Americans in the work force (3.6 million males and 2.3 million females), of whom 54 percent (3.2 million) were born in the United States.

Mexican American Men. There is a clear pattern of upgrading in the occupational distribution of U.S.-born Mexican American men. The proportion of men in managerial, professional, and technical occupations (the highest categories) increased from 8.7 percent in 1960 to 15.4 percent in 1990. Similarly, the proportion in lower-status white-collar occupations (clerical and sales) increased from 8.6 to 16.9 percent during the same period. There was also a slight increase in the proportion of jobs in upper-blue-collar or craft (16.4 to 22.8 percent) and service occupations (8.0 to 14.0 percent). The largest and most dramatic declines were in lower-blue-collar occupations (operatives, laborers, and farmers), which declined from 46.3 to 28.5 percent. Farm labor jobs also declined, from 12.1 to 2.3 percent, during the period.

Foreign-born Mexican American men show smaller increases in white-collar positions between 1960 and 1980, then a slight decline in 1990. On the other hand,

Mexican American men increasingly hold technical jobs. (David Bacon)

craft (12.6 to 22.3 percent) and service (7.5 to 16.6 percent) jobs increased substantially between 1960 and 1990. Lower-blue-collar occupations also increased, from 38.7 percent in 1960 to 44.8 percent in 1980, but they then declined to 38.7 percent in 1990. The most dramatic decline was in farm labor, which declined from 31.4 percent in 1960 to 9.3 percent in 1990.

Many of these changes are a result of a large influx of Mexican workers during the 1980's. According to the 1990 census, nearly half of all foreign-born Mexican workers in 1990 had entered the United States between 1980 and 1990.

Mexican American Women. Mexican American women, particularly those born in the United States, also exhibited a trend of occupational upgrading. Upper-

white-collar occupations (managerial, professional, and technical) increased from 5.9 percent of jobs in 1960 to 15.0 percent in 1990. Lower-white-collar jobs increased from 29.2 to 35.2 percent during the same period. Craft occupations increased slightly, from about 1.0 percent in 1960 to 3.8 percent in 1990, while lower-blue-collar occupations declined from 29.8 to 19.0 percent. Jobs in the service sector fluctuated between 23 and 26 percent, and farm labor decreased from 7.7 to 2.7 percent.

The 1990 census showed that 62 percent of female Mexican American workers in 1990 were born in the United States. U.S.-born Mexican American women were more likely to have white-collar (and less likely to have blue-collar, service, and farm labor occupations) than their foreign-born counterparts.

A Puerto Rican woman trains for a career as an architect. (Hazel Hankin)

Puerto Ricans. Puerto Ricans are the second-largest Latino group in the U.S. labor force. Puerto Ricans are U.S. citizens at birth, whether born in Puerto Rico or on the mainland, but they share many characteristics with other Latinos who are not U.S. citizens by birth.

Puerto Rican Men. Nearly 57 percent of the male Puerto Rican work force in the United States was born outside the mainland, according to the 1990 census. Puerto Rican males born on the mainland experienced virtually no change in the proportion in the upper-white-collar occupations between 1970 and 1990, with about 17.6 percent employed in those occupations, but showed some unsteady growth in the lower-white-collar (19.4 percent in 1960 to 23.3 percent in 1990) and service (15.6 to 19.3 percent) occupations. Conversely, lower-blue-collar occupations declined from 37.6 percent in 1960 to 23.6 percent in 1990. The proportion of mainland-born Puerto Rican men engaged in farm labor was very small throughout the period.

Fewer Puerto Rican men born outside the United States had upper-white-collar occupations than their U.S.-born counterparts. The proportion engaged in these occupations rose from 5.5 percent in 1960 to 13.9 percent in 1990. The proportions in lower-white-collar (10.4 percent in 1960 to 15.4 percent in 1990) and in upper-blue-collar or craft positions (from 9.3 to 18.5 percent) also rose significantly. Conversely, more than half (52.6 percent) of island-born Puerto Rican men worked in lower-blue-collar jobs in 1960, but that proportion dropped to 31.8 percent in 1990. There was also a small decline in farm labor (3.8 percent in 1960 and 1.0 percent in 1990). Service jobs fluctuated between 18.6 and 19.8 percent during this period, ending at 19.3 percent in 1990.

Puerto Rican Women. Puerto Rican women, particularly those born on the mainland, experienced an occupational upgrade. Upper-white-collar occupations increased from 4.1 percent in 1960 to 20.8 percent in 1990. Lower-white-collar occupations increased from 17.0 to 42.5 percent. Upper-blue-collar or craft occupations changed very little (2.0 percent in 1960 and 3.2 percent in 1990). Lower-blue-collar occupations declined from 68.9 to 14.7 percent. Service jobs increased from 7.6 to 18.4 percent. According to the 1990 census, about 53 percent of Puerto Rican women workers were born outside the United States. Puerto Rican women born in the United States were somewhat more likely to have white-collar occupations and less likely to have blue-collar and service occupations than their island-born counterparts.

Cuban Americans. The first major wave of Cuban immigrants to the United States, unlike other Latino groups, was motivated to emigrate primarily by political, rather than economic, conditions. These ensued from the 1959 revolution in Cuba. High proportions of Cuban refugees were from the middle and upper classes. Cuban immigrants held a relatively advantaged position in comparison to other Latinos.

The 1990 census showed that 82.0 percent of Cuban workers were born outside the United States but that only 25 percent entered the country during the 1980's. This suggests that three-quarters of foreign-born Cuban workers have had some time to gain skills and knowledge of the U.S. labor market.

Cuban American Men. The proportion of U.S.-born Cuban American men holding upper-white-collar occupations fluctuated between 1960 and 1990 (24.2 percent in 1960 and 1980, 29.1 percent in 1970, and 27.2 percent in 1990). Lower-white-collar occupations increased from 9.9 percent in 1960 to 26.3 percent in 1990. Conversely, upper- and lower-blue-collar occupations dropped dramatically during the period (24.2 to 14.3 percent and 26.4 to 16.2 percent, respectively). The proportion of U.S.-born Cuban men employed in service occupations remained about 15.4 percent throughout the period, except when it dipped to 9.4 percent in 1970.

The upgrading in occupational status is more evident among foreign-born Cuban workers. The proportion in upper- and lower-white-collar occupations rose for the most part between 1960 and 1990. Upper-white-collar occupations increased from 12.5 percent in 1960 to 27.6 percent in 1980 but then declined to 23.6 percent in 1990. Lower-white-collar occupations rose from 10.2 percent in 1960 to 20.5 percent in 1990. Upper-blue-collar or craft occupations fluctuated between 17.4 and 20.7 percent. There were large declines in lower-blue-collar occupations (38.1 percent in 1960 to 22.3 percent in 1990) and service occupations (20.4 percent in 1960 to 11.8 percent in 1980 and 12.5 percent in 1990).

Cuban American Women. Like Mexican American and Puerto Rican women, Cuban American women experienced an occupational upgrade. Upper-white-collar occupations increased from 9.3 percent in 1960 to 24.2 percent in 1990. The proportion in lower-white-collar occupations increased from 25.1 to 43.7 percent during the period. Upper-blue-collar or craft occupations increased slightly, from 1.8 percent in 1960 to 3.7 percent in 1990. Lower-blue-collar occupations declined precipitously, from 50.9 to 14.3 percent. Service jobs fluctuated between 12 and 14 percent during this period.

According to the 1990 census, only 20 percent of female Cuban American workers were born in the United States. They were somewhat more likely to have white-collar occupations and less likely to have blue-collar and service occupations than their foreign-born counterparts.

Dominicans and Central and South Americans. Previous work on occupational trends has combined people of Central American, South American, and Dominican origin into one group. For historical comparability, this is done here. The 1990 census shows that 90 percent of workers in this group were born outside the United States and that 57 percent entered the country between 1980 and 1990.

Dominican, Central American, and South American Men. U.S.-born members of this group, like Cuban Americans, have had high proportions in white-collar occupations since 1960. The proportion of upper-white-collar jobs fluctuated, from 27.8 percent in 1960, to 23.2 percent in 1970, to 29.5 percent in 1980, and finally to 22.5 percent in 1990. Lower-white-collar occupations increased over the same period (22.2 percent in 1960 to 27.5 percent in 1990). On the other hand, the proportions in upper- and lower-blue-collar occupations declined over this period (crafts went from 20.6 percent in 1960 to 12.8 percent in 1990 and lower-blue-collar jobs from 23.1 percent to 18.9 percent). Service jobs also increased substantially, from 6.3 percent in 1960 to 17.9 percent in 1990. Farming occupations played a very small role throughout the period.

Contrary to the experience of other groups, there is a clear pattern of occupational downgrading among foreign-born workers with Central and South American or Dominican origins. This results in part from the changing composition of immigrants with these origins. Civil unrest in Central America caused a much broader socioeconomic spectrum of immigrants to arrive in the United States than previously was the case. The proportion of upper- and lower-white-collar occupations declined between 1960 and 1990 (from 27.8 to 15.1 percent and 22.2 to 15.0 percent, respectively). Upper-blue-collar or craft occupations fluctuated between 18 and 21 percent, while lower-blue-collar jobs increased from 23.1 to 29.4 percent. Service occupations increased dramatically, from 6.3 percent in 1960 to 19.3 percent in 1990. Farm labor jobs had only a small, but increasing, role over this period.

Dominican, Central American, and South American

Women. Central and South American women, unlike other Latino women, did not show a strong pattern of occupational upgrading. Upper-white-collar occupations increased slightly, from 12.1 percent in 1960 to 15.5 percent in 1990. The percentage of lower-white-collar occupations decreased from 39.0 to 29.9 percent. Upper-blue-collar jobs increased slightly, from 1.1 percent in 1960 to 4.0 percent in 1990. Lower-blue-collar occupations increased from 29.1 percent in 1960 to 32.3 percent in 1980, then declined to 19.7 percent in 1990. Service occupations increased from 18.8 percent to 30.9 percent, mostly after 1980. The 1990 census shows that only 10.5 percent of female U.S. workers of Dominican, Central American, and South American origin were born in the United States. They were somewhat more likely than their foreign-born counterparts to have white-collar occupations and less likely to have blue-collar and service jobs.

Central Americans. According to the 1990 census, there were more than 700,000 Central American workers in the U.S. civilian labor force, but very few (8 percent) were native to the United States. Two-thirds of those born outside the United States entered the country between 1980 and 1990. Among Central Americans, Salvadoran workers were the most numerous (318,000), followed by Guatemalans (153,000) and Nicaraguans (108,000). U.S.-born Central American men were much more likely than their foreign-born counterparts to have white-collar occupations. Similarly, U.S.-born Central American women were much more likely to have white-collar occupations than were their foreign-born counterparts.

South Americans. There were nearly 600,000 workers of South American origin in the civilian U.S. labor force according to the 1990 census. Very few South Americans (12 percent) were native to the United States. Nearly half of foreign-born South Americans (47 percent) entered the country between 1980 and 1990. Colombians were the largest group (213,000) among South American workers, followed by Ecuadorans (109,000) and Peruvians (102,000). Both native and foreign-born South American men had high proportions in white-collar occupations, but native men were more likely to have lower-white-collar jobs, while their foreign-born counterparts were much more likely to have blue-collar jobs. U.S.-born South American women were much more likely than were their foreign-born counterparts to have white-collar occupations.

Dominican Americans. The 1990 census showed more than 233,000 workers from the Dominican Republic in the U.S. civilian labor force. Only about 11 percent of Dominican Americans were born in the United States. Half of the foreign-born Dominicans entered the United States between 1980 and 1990. Native Dominican men were more likely than foreign-born counterparts to have white-collar occupations. Similarly, native Dominican women were more likely than their foreign-born counterparts to have white-collar occupations. —*Jorge del Pinal*

SUGGESTED READINGS:

• Bean, Frank D., and Marta Tienda. *The Hispanic Population of the United States.* New York: Russell Sage Foundation, 1987. One of the 1980 census monographs commissioned by the Russell Sage Foundation and one of the most comprehensive analyses of the Latino population in existence.

• Cattan, Peter. "The Diversity of Hispanics in the U.S. Work Force." *Monthly Labor Review* 116 (August, 1993): 3. A report from the Bureau of Labor Statistics detailing the changes and composition of the Latino work force in the United States. Based on averages of monthly surveys of the U.S. labor force as opposed to single cross-sectional views from decennial censuses.

• Del Pinal, Jorge, and Jesus M. Garcia. *Hispanic Americans Today.* Current Population Reports, Population Characteristics, P23-183. Washington, D.C.: Government Printing Office, 1993. This chart book presents some of the latest information available from the Census Bureau about the Latino population and also has a guide to census products with information about Latinos.

• Garcia, Jesus M. *The Hispanic Population in the United States: March 1992.* Current Population Reports, Population Characteristics, P20-465RV. Washington, D.C.: Government Printing Office, 1993. Part of an annual series presenting information on Latinos. Based on the Current Population Survey taken in March of each year.

• Newman, Morris J. "A Profile of Hispanics in the U.S. Work Force." *Monthly Labor Review* 101 (December, 1993): 3-14. A Bureau of Labor Statistics report detailing the changes and composition of the Latino work force in the United States.

• U.S. Department of Commerce. Bureau of the Census. *Detailed Occupation and Other Characteristics from the EEO File for the United States.* 1990 Census of Population, 1990 CP-S-1-1. Washington, D.C.: Government Printing Office, 1992. Presents the most detailed information about occupations of Latinos as a group. Based on the 1990 Census of

Population and Housing.

• U.S. Department of Commerce. Bureau of the Census. *Persons of Hispanic Origin in the United States.* Census of Population, 1990 CP-3-3. Washington, D.C.: Government Printing Office, 1993. Presents a wealth of statistical information about Latino groups. Based on the 1990 Census of Population and Housing.

Ochoa, Ellen (b. May 10, 1958, Los Angeles, Calif.): Astronaut. Ochoa, a Mexican American, attended San Diego State University as an undergraduate and changed majors five times before obtaining a bachelor's degree in physics. She then earned a master's degree and a doctorate in electrical engineering from Stanford University. At Stanford, she received a Stanford engineering fellowship as well as an IBM predoctoral fellowship.

Ochoa was a research engineer in the Imaging Technology Branch at Sandia National Laboratories in Livermore, California, from 1985 to 1988. She obtained three patents in optical processing. She began work with the National Aeronautics and Space Administration (NASA) in 1988, as a researcher, later becoming chief of the Intelligent Systems Technology Branch at the Ames Research Center. Her accomplishments were recognized by the 1989 Hispanic Engineer National Achievement Award for the most promising engineer in government.

Ochoa became interested in flying after her older brother got a private pilot's license. She got her own license, for small-engine planes, in 1988. She thought that learning more about aviation would aid in her quest to become an astronaut. Ochoa had first applied to work with NASA as an astronaut in 1985. She was named one of the one hundred finalists in 1987 and was graduated in the class of 1990, becoming the first Latina astronaut.

Ochoa, Esteban (Mar. 17, 1831, Chihuahua, Mexico—Oct. 27, 1888, Tucson, Ariz.): Businessman and politician. Born into an important ranching and mining family, Ochoa grew up on the New Mexico frontier, where he learned the freighting business. After being educated in Missouri, Ochoa returned to New Mexico and became a successful entrepreneur. His reputation was such that in 1859 he was elected chairman of a committee that sought to create an Arizona territory separate from New Mexico. At that time, he moved to Tucson, Arizona, which he made the headquarters of his business interests.

Ochoa left Tucson during the Civil War, as he re-

Esteban Ochoa. (Arizona Historical Society)

fused to take an oath of allegiance to the Confederacy. Upon returning to Tucson after the war, he organized the leading freight company in the Southwest. Ochoa's position made him a natural spokesman for the Spanish-speaking population of southern Arizona. He acted as a broker between it and Anglo society and was elected both to the Arizona territorial legislature and as mayor of Tucson. Ochoa was instrumental in the establishment of a public school system in the Arizona Territory. The expansion of the railroad in the 1880's severely affected his business interests. He died a relatively poor, but highly respected, man.

Ochoa, Victor (b. 1948, Los Angeles, Calif.): Muralist. During the mid-1960's, an interstate highway project displaced about five thousand Chicano families in the Balboa Park area of San Diego, California. Several Chicano artists, including Ochoa, protested this action and vowed to paint the columns of the highway bridge. The San Diego Parks and Recreation department ceded a building to the artists. By 1969, the artists had turned the building into a cultural center and were painting murals. Two murals eventually were completed on the highway bridge abutments. Ochoa's monumental mural *Gerónimo* is on display in Balboa Park.

In 1971, Ochoa, Salvador Robert Torres, David Ulivares, and Alberta Ybarra held an art exhibition, along with an exhibition by a dance group that shared the building, in the cultural center. They later broke away from the dance group and formed the Congreso de Arte Chicano en Aztlán in Logan Heights, California.

Ochoa's work combines Hispanic and Native American cultural elements. Much of his work is painted in public places, with the purpose of reaching the common people, educating them about their heritage, and inspiring their ethnic pride. Ochoa is known for his role in the Southern California Chicano empowerment mural movement.

O'Farrill, Alberto (b. 1899, Santa Clara, Cuba): Playwright and actor. O'Farrill began acting and writing in 1921 in Havana, where he performed with the Teatro Esmeralda. O'Farrill built his career on the broad, blackface comedy style of the OBRA BUFA CUBANA. He went to New York City in the mid-1920's and performed as the *negrito* in blackface comedies. As a member of the Compañía de Bufos Cubanos, he wrote plays and ZARZUELAS that explored Afro-Cuban culture, religion, beliefs, and music.

O'Farrill's *Un doctor accidental* played at the Apollo Theater in 1926. One of his most popular works was *Kid Chocolate*, based on a famous Cuban boxer. His other works include *Un negro en Andalucía*, *Los misterios de Changó*, and *Una viuda como no hay dos*.

While in Havana, O'Farrill edited a literary journal called *Proteo*, and beginning in 1927 he edited *El Gráfico*, a newspaper that became an important organ for literature and theater in New York. He worked with the companies of the Teatro Variedades and the Teatro Campoamor into the 1930's.

Ogilvie, Ben (Benjamin Ambrosio Ogilvie; b. Feb. 11, 1949, Colon, Panama): Baseball player. Ogilvie, a tall left-handed-hitting outfielder, made his major league

Ben Ogilvie hits a home run against St. Louis Cardinals pitcher Joaquín Andujar in the 1982 World Series. (AP/ Wide World Photos)

debut with the Boston Red Sox in 1971. After three seasons as a part-time player, he was traded to the Detroit Tigers and over the course of four seasons gradually won regular status. In 1978, he was traded to Milwaukee, where he finally emerged as a star. He batted .303 in his first season with the Brewers, hit 29 home runs the next year, and led the American League with 41 home runs in 1980. In 1982, he hit 34 home runs and drove in 102 runs for the Brewers' American League champions. A three-time All-Star, Ogilvie retired after the 1986 season with a lifetime .273 batting average and 235 career home runs.

O'Higgins, Pablo (1904, Salt Lake City, Utah—1983, Mexico City, Mexico): Muralist and art historian. O'Higgins formally studied art for a brief time, at the Art Academy in San Diego, California. He divided his professional time between the United States and Mexico. In 1922, he cofounded an independent atelier in California with two fellow students, Kenneth Slaughter and Miguel Foncerrado. When he returned from Mexico in 1925, he exhibited for the first time in San Francisco. He exhibited in New York City in 1927, 1931, and 1936 exhibitions.

In 1926, O'Higgins joined the staff of the bilingual magazine *Mexico Folkways*, which specialized in Mexican art in the United States. In 1930, he collaborated on a publication about Mexican artist José Guadalupe Posada. He spent 1945 as a welder in a San Francisco shipyard as an antifascist act.

Diego RIVERA invited O'Higgins to Mexico in 1924. O'Higgins painted wall murals there for four years, then returned in 1933. A 1965 retrospective, his last exhibition, was in the Palace of Fine Arts in Mexico City in 1971. He died preparing a mural for the University of Colima.

O'Higgins was a member of the Mexican Union of Painters, Sculptors and Graphic Artists. In 1927, he joined the Mexican Communist Party. He was a founding member of Liga de Escritores y Artistas Revolucionarios (LEAR) and spent two years on a wall painting with LEAR. In 1937 he founded the anti-Fascist Taller de la Gráfica Popular (TGP) with Leopoldo Mendea and Luis Arenal.

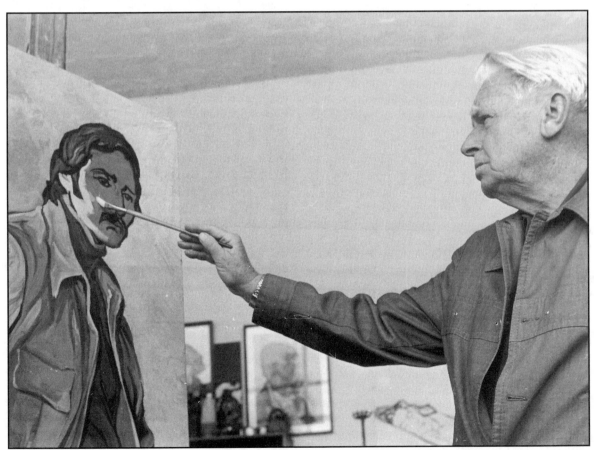

Pablo O'Higgins completes a painting in 1975. (AP/Wide World Photos)

In 1931-1932, O'Higgins received a grant to work in Moscow. He visited again in 1968, during a tour that included several European countries. O'Higgins served as a link between the United States and Mexican art scenes and exemplified the mix of artistic and political goals. Mexico recognized him with honorary Mexican nationality for services to art and education.

Old Spanish Trail: Route through the American Southwest between Santa Fe, New Mexico, and Los Angeles, California. New Mexicans seem to have been the first to acknowledge the possibilities for trade between the two states. Antonio Armijo, with at least thirty of his countrymen, began the journey from Abiquiu, New Mexico, to San Bernardino, California, in 1829. They survived the harsh Mojave Desert by eating horse and mule flesh, ultimately profiting from the trade of their woolen goods. Thereafter, a caravan of pack mules annually made the arduous two-month journey in each direction. The trail, in a larger sense, became an extension of the Santa Fe trade between Missouri and Santa Fe, thus facilitating the exchange of American and Mexican products. It was little used after the Mexican American War (1846-1848) except as a route for driving sheep and other livestock.

Older Latinos: Latinos have become the fastest-growing U.S. minority population. Older Latinos are the fastest-growing subgroup of that population.

Attitudes Toward Older Latinos. Older Latinos are held in high esteem in their roles as *la abuela* (grandmother) and *el abuelo* (grandfather). The Latino elderly and their families commonly help one another. Family structures serve as the primary source of self-worth and may provide economic and social support. As geographic mobility increases, however, and as Latino families acculturate, the family may provide less financial and emotional support to its older members.

The majority of older Latinos do not participate in the political processes of the United States. Less than half were registered to vote in the early 1990's. The strength of the senior lobby, therefore, lay with non-Hispanic voters, sometimes resulting in neglect of the needs of elderly Latinos and other minorities.

Health Issues. The health of older Latinos is generally worse than that of nonminority elders. Diet as well as harsh working conditions while employed have contributed to shorter life spans. In 1989, 96 percent of all elderly persons were covered by Medicare, but only 83 percent of older Latinos were covered; 8 percent of

Latino elderly had no health insurance, compared with only 1 percent of all elderly persons.

Older persons from minority groups are more likely to experience psychological and social stress than are older Americans as a whole. The lack of data on psychological problems among the Latino elderly has hindered efforts of mental health professionals to develop effective programs for them.

Economic Issues. As is true of Americans as a whole, among the Latino population women tend to live longer than men. During late adulthood, therefore, some Latinas face the deaths of male family members and spouses who provided financial support. Federal and state programs provide some support, and many Latinas sell craft items to supplement their income.

Retired Latinos lose the ability to earn money and in some cases also lose a sense of self-worth associated with paid employment. Latino men in particular have been taught to regard household chores, child care, nurturance, and interpersonal relationships as demeaning. The roles of Latinas change less as they age, as they associate more with work in the home throughout their lives.

Older Latinos are more likely to live in the community and are less likely to be institutionalized than are non-Hispanic older people. Latino elders in need of assistance avoid relying on outsiders except as a last resort. They rely on other Latinos, particularly family members.

Comparisons Among Subgroups. According to data from the early 1990's, older Mexican Americans were more likely to have been born in the United States and to speak English than were older Latinos of Cuban and Puerto Rican descent. Of older Mexican Americans, 75 percent had less than an eighth grade education. Most older Mexican Americans (98 percent) had qualified for Social Security benefits as members of the U.S. labor force.

Most older Cuban Americans (98 percent) were first-generation immigrants. They were less likely to speak English and less likely to receive Social Security benefits. More than 98 percent of Puerto Rican elderly living in the United States as of the early 1990's were born in Puerto Rico and entered the United States before reaching the age of forty-five.

Access to Services. A lack of formal education has constituted a barrier to access to services. Many elderly Latinos are literate in neither English nor Spanish and may lack knowledge about social services. A survey conducted in 1987 found that use of health care services increased when bilingual staff members were available.

Pride, reluctance to admit need, complicated procedures, and fear of being poorly received also have been cited as barriers to use of social services by older Latinos. Caring for elderly relatives can impose a heavy burden on a family's resources. Therefore, older Latinos will require increasing amounts of social services.

Trends Regarding Older Latinos. Some Latinos have departed from traditional roles of caring for elderly parents. Mobility and acculturation have begun to separate generations of Latino families, with the elderly often living isolated lives in urban barrios where housing is less expensive. As younger Latinos raise their economic status, they tend to move away from such neighborhoods.

Organizations for Older Latinos. Because fewer older Latinos are able to obtain a sense of self-worth and belonging from membership in the extended family, senior citizen centers have become increasingly

Many older Latinos do not participate in politics; this Mexican American man displays evidence that he does. (James Shaffer)

A volunteer for a "meals on wheels" program prepares food packages to be taken to elderly people. (Bob Daemmrich)

LATINOS AGED 65 AND OLDER, 1989-1990

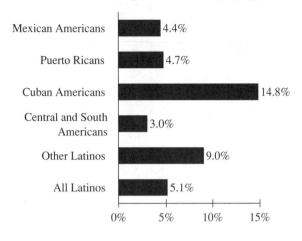

Mexican Americans 4.4%

Puerto Ricans 4.7%

Cuban Americans 14.8%

Central and South Americans 3.0%

Other Latinos 9.0%

All Latinos 5.1%

0%   5%   10%   15%

Source: Data are from Bureau of the Census, *Statistical Abstract of the United States 1992* (Washington, D.C.: U.S. Bureau of the Census, 1992), Table 44. That table was constructed with data from U.S. Bureau of the Census, *Current Population Reports*, P-60 (No. 174) and P-20 (No. 455).

important. Activities provide a means of coping with various obstacles and offer means for older Latinos to come to terms with their aging.

Latino senior centers provide food, transportation, and other services for the elderly. Murals may be painted on the walls to reflect Latino culture and the historical experiences of the community. Walls often feature posters in Spanish and English containing information about health issues such as high blood pressure, heart disease, diabetes, and the importance of a nutritional diet. Senior citizen centers hold special meaning for some Latinos. Centers provide the opportunity to remain active and engage in new experiences such as attending concerts, going to a circus, visiting museums, and taking trips.

Participation in various activities enables Latinas in particular to be respected and honored, establishing a sense of self-worth. Women often form groups based on gender-identified tasks and activities such as crochet, planning associated with religious and traditional holidays, and arts-and-crafts projects.

Senior citizen organizations are a relatively recent phenomenon among Latinos. THE ASOCIACIÓN NACIONAL PRO PERSONAS MAYORES (National Advocacy Association for Spanish-Speaking Elderly) was the first major group founded for older Latinos. Its establishment in 1975 resulted in a significant increase in the proportion of older Latinos who are members of an organization.

Older Latinos, like other senior citizens, are concerned with the image they project to others. They do not want to appear weak, dependent, or nonproductive. Senior citizen organizations allow them to demonstrate their competence and ability to learn new roles. For some, these groups fill a psychological and social void, providing outlets for needs and desires that might otherwise have no mode of realization.

—*María L. Alonzo*

SUGGESTED READINGS: • Bacerra, Rosina M. "The Mexican-American: Aging in a Changing Culture." In *Aging in Minority Groups*, edited by R. L. McNeely and J. N. Colen. Beverly Hills, Calif.: Sage Publications, 1983. • Facio, Elisa. "Gender and the Life Course: A Case Study of Chicana Elderly." In *Building with Our Hands: New Directions in Chicana Studies*, edited by Adela de la Torre and Beatriz M. Pesquera. Berkeley: University of California Press, 1993. • Galarza, E. "Forecasting Future Cohorts of Mexican Elderly." In *Chicano Aging and Mental Health*, edited by M. R. Miranda and R. A. Ruiz. Rockville, Md.: U.S. Department of Health and Human Services, Public Health Service, Alcohol, Drug Abuse, and Mental Health Administration, National Institute of Mental Health, 1981. • Mahara, R. "Elderly Puerto Rican Women in the Continental United States." In *The Psychosocial Development of Puerto Rican Women*, edited by C. Garcia Coll and L. Mattei. New York: Praeger, 1989. • Schmidt, Adeny, and Amado M. Padilla. "Grandparent-Grandchild Interaction in a Mexican American Group." *Hispanic Journal of Behavioral Sciences* 5 (1983): 181-198. • Torres-Gil, Fernando M. *Politics of Aging Among Elder Hispanics*. Washington, D.C.: University Press of America, 1982.

Oliva, Tomas (b. 1930, Guanabacoa, Cuba): Artist. Oliva was graduated from the San Alejandro Academy in Havana in 1952 with a degree in painting and sculpture. He had also taken a class in plastic animation for films in Havana. He continued his artistic training, attending the Royal School of Ceramics in Madrid, Spain, in 1953 and studying at an art school in Paris, France, beginning in 1954.

Oliva returned to Cuba in 1962. Before becoming an exile in 1968, he took classes in stage design and taught drawing and design at the School of Architecture of the National University in Havana as well as courses in materials and design at the School of Arts, Crafts, and Set Design of the National Academy (formerly San Alejandro Academy). He eventually settled in Miami, Florida, after leaving Cuba in 1968.

Oliva began participating in group exhibitions in the mid-1950's and had several one-man shows in Havana. By the 1960's, he was exhibiting around the world. He has created sculptures for monuments in Cuba, Czechoslovakia, and Spain. Oliva is known for using all sculptural materials, although he favors painted metals. His expansive figures appear to be floating despite their size or mass.

Oliva, Tony (Pedro Oliva y Lopez; b. July 20, 1940, Pinar del Rio, Cuba): Baseball player. Oliva, the son of a Cuban plantation worker, was offered a tryout by a scout for the Minnesota Twins in 1960. Oliva, then known as Pedro, borrowed a passport for the trip to the United States from his brother Tony, and the name stuck. He made rapid progress through the minor leagues, posting batting averages of .410, .350, and .304 before earning a major league job with the Twins in 1964.

A left-handed-hitting outfielder, Oliva had a sensational rookie season, hitting .323 to become the first rookie to win the American League batting title. He also led the league in hits, doubles, and runs scored and belted thirty-one home runs, easily winning the league's Rookie of the Year Award. An eight-time All-Star, Oliva repeated as batting champ in 1965 and 1971 and also led the league in hits in 1965, 1966, 1969, and 1970; he led the league in doubles in 1967, 1969, and 1970. In 1966, he won a Gold Glove Award for fielding excellence. He was a key member of Minnesota's 1965 American League champions and 1969 and 1970 Western division champions, but a series of knee injuries hampered him throughout his fifteen-year career. He retired after the 1976 season with a lifetime .304 batting average and 220 career home runs.

Olivares, Julian (b. Dec. 6, 1940, San Antonio, Tex.): Literary critic. Olivares, a Mexican American, is the son of a theater concession superintendent, his father, and a garment worker, his mother. He received a B.A. from California State College, Los Angeles, in 1968, and an M.A. and Ph.D. from the University of Texas at Austin in 1974 and 1977, respectively.

He was an assistant professor of Spanish at Bridgewater State College in Bridgewater, Massachusetts, from

During spring training for the 1975 season, Tony Oliva works on his swing. (AP/Wide World Photos)

1978 to 1981, then an assistant professor at the University of Texas at Houston from 1981 to 1986, when he was promoted to associate professor. He began serving as an associate editor of Arte Público Press in 1982 and has edited *Chicano-Riquena*, the oldest and most respected review dedicated to the expression of Hispanic creativity in the United States.

As a teacher and literary critic, Olivares has focused on the literature of Spain from the sixteenth and seventeenth centuries. Olivares' major works of literary criticism include *The Love Poetry of Francisco de Quevedo* (1983) and *The Sacred and Moral Verse of Francisco de Quevedo* (1988). He has also contributed to numerous periodicals and several collections of critical essays. Olivares' critical works on Quevedo are considered a major contribution to the understanding of seventeenth century Spanish poetry.

Olivares, Luis (1934, San Antonio, Tex.—Mar. 18, 1993): Roman Catholic priest. As the charismatic pastor at La Placita, Los Angeles' oldest church, Olivares created a haven for Latino street vendors, immigrants, day laborers, and the poor. Olivares died from complications of AIDS, contracted in El Salvador from a contaminated needle.

Olivares advanced quickly in the Claretian order and at one time was given the responsibility of being provincial treasurer. His encounter with the UNITED FARM WORKERS in the 1970's began his political and spiritual quest. During his time as pastor of La Placita, from 1981 to 1990, Olivares championed the dignity and rights of the poor and disenfranchised.

Olivares viewed La Placita as a vital community center. In opposition to his order and the police, he defended the street vendors who flocked to La Placita offering their goods to Sunday parishioners. During President Ronald Reagan's Central American intervention, Olivares proclaimed La Placita a sanctuary for the homeless and political refugees. He defied the 1986 IMMIGRATION REFORM AND CONTROL ACT by hiring undocumented workers.

Olivares, as president of the UNITED NEIGHBORHOODS ORGANIZATION, led the fight against insurance "redlining" in the inner city and worked for an increased minimum wage. He delivered sermons against human rights abuses abroad and in the United States and was often arrested in civil disobedience marches. He continued his activities despite opposition from his religious superiors, U.S. government agencies, and Salvadoran death squads. Olivares enriched the historical and spiritual legacy of La Placita's community by his ministry of struggle and justice, becoming perhaps the most controversial church figure in Los Angeles history.

Olivárez, Graciela (May 9, 1928, near Phoenix, Ariz.—1987): Public official. After dropping out of high school, Olivárez attended business school and became famous as the first female disc jockey in Phoenix. Her political activity led Olivárez, a Mexican American, to the position of state director of the Office of Economic Opportunity, the precursor to such programs as Head Start, VOLUNTEERS IN SERVICE TO AMERICA (VISTA), and the Job Corps.

During the Civil Rights movement, Olivárez's record impressed University of Notre Dame president Theodore Hesburgh, who invited her to apply to the law school there. In 1970, she was its first female graduate. She returned to New Mexico and became the state's director of planning in 1975. Her work against poverty caught the attention of President Jimmy Carter, who in 1977 appointed her director of the Community Services Administration. She left her government service in 1980 to become a senior consultant with the United Way of America. She continued her service to people through nonprofit organizations such as the American Cancer Society and the League of Women Voters. She also ran a television station.

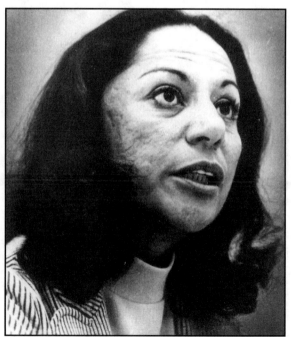

As an appointee in the Jimmy Carter Administration, Graciela Olivárez hoped to revitalize the anti-poverty effort begun in the 1960's. (AP/Wide World Photos)

Olivas, Michael (b. 1951): Educator and attorney. Olivas earned a bachelor's degree in 1972 and a master's degree in 1974 from Pontifical College in Columbus, Ohio. He then went to Ohio State University to earn a Ph.D. in 1977 and to Georgetown University School of Law, where he received his law degree in 1981.

As a member of the League of UNITED LATIN AMERican Citizens (LULAC), Olivas raised his visibility and recognized the necessity of political organizing to address issues of concern to the Latino community. He served as the director of resources for the LULAC Education Resource Center in Washington, D.C., from 1979 to 1982.

In 1982, Olivas began teaching law at the University of Houston Law School. He later served as the director of the Institute for Higher Education, Law and Governance at that university and was named associate dean in 1990.

Oller, Francisco (1833, San Juan, Puerto Rico—1917, San Juan, Puerto Rico): Painter and musician. Early in his career in Puerto Rico, Oller copied portraits by famous native artists and did caricatures. At the age of fourteen, he refused an offer to study in Rome because his mother disapproved. He loved music and sang with the Philharmonic Society of San Juan and local opera, later performing baritone roles in Paris and with an Italian troupe in the 1850's.

Oller first studied art in Madrid, with Federico Madrazo in 1851-1852. In 1858, he went to Paris to study with Thomas Couture. He spent 1861 at the Academie Suisse with Antoine Guillemet. He also served as a copyist at the Louvre. In 1868, he married Isabel Tinajero, with whom he had two daughters.

Oller divided his professional time among Puerto Rico, Spain, and France. After studying in Spain, Oller returned in 1853 to Puerto Rico, where he exhibited and won local prizes. After his return to Europe in 1858, he submitted to the Paris Salons of 1865, 1867, and 1875, though he returned to Puerto Rico in 1865. He received government funding to go to the Vienna Universal Exposition in 1873. Back in France in 1874, Oller began to do open-air painting and became a friend of Paul Cézanne, Camille Pissarro, Édouard Manet, Pierre-Auguste Renoir, and Claude Monet. He consciously emulated Gustave Courbet. He was inducted into the Order of King Charles III of Spain and served as court painter to King Amadeo.

Known for the Puerto Rican and creole content of his realist-impressionist works, Oller is considered to be the greatest Hispanic painter of the mid-nineteenth

century. Dividing his time between countries, he changed style according to the norms of each country. He is best known for his portraits. The vast majority of his works are lost or have been destroyed. In 1971, exhibitions of his works were undertaken in Ponce and Río Piedras, Puerto Rico; New York, New York; Springfield, Massachusetts, and Washington, D.C.

Olmecs: The first great Mesoamerican culture (sometimes called the first American civilization). The Olmecs helped lay the foundation for later civilizations that developed in Mexico and Central America.

The Olmec culture evolved along the southwestern coast of the Gulf of Mexico in the regions of Tabasco and southern Veracruz, on the northern Isthmus of Tehuantepec. Its origin dates back to at least 1250 B.C.E. San Lorenzo, La Venta, and Tres Zapotes were Olmec centers, and they have undergone the most intensive archaeological excavation. Olmecs may have spoken a language related to Mayan or Mixe-Zoque.

Olmec peoples produced an artistic style that provided the original archaeological definition of their civilization. Their art included colossal stone heads, figures of humans and animals, bas-reliefs, and large flat-topped platforms and pyramid-like structures on which altars were mounted. Figures of the fire serpent and werejaguar became common motifs in much of pre-Columbian Mesoamerican art. Some of the great carved basalt heads were more than six feet in height, weighed many tons, and were transported substantial distances to the locations where archaeologists discovered them.

No Olmec site has been completely excavated and studied; this accounts in part for speculation concerning the Olmecs' origins. One nineteenth century scholar noted that one of the colossal heads seemed "Ethiopian" in appearance and concluded that the Olmecs were African. Subsequent study discredited such migrationist theories, although they continued to find their way into print.

Archaeologists in the late twentieth century held that the Olmecs developed out of indigenous Mesoamerican roots and gave less weight to art in defining the characteristics of the culture. (*See* MESOAMERICAN NATIVE COMMUNITIES.) Judging from material remains, their society was nonegalitarian, with some individuals, such as chieftains and priests, possessing greater wealth and larger dwellings. In political terms, the Olmec region was neither an empire nor a theocracy but independent territories ruled by chieftains or more institutionalized states. This is shown, for example, in

This Olmec carving is in Villahermosa, Mexico. (Claire Rydell)

the quarrying, carving, and transportation of the colossal heads, tasks that required significant political
centralization. Furthermore, the urban area of La
Venta drew upon the resources of an extensive hinter-
land.

Famed for their long-distance trade, the Olmecs obtained precious jade and obsidian for blades from Central America. Iron ore, ceramics, and turtle, armadillo,
and marine shells were also important merchandise.
Such trade probably contributed to inequalities within
Olmec society, with luxury items reinforcing elite
status. The Olmecs practiced a more sophisticated agriculture than primitive slash-and-burn techniques.
MAIZE was a dietary staple, and the Olmecs may also
have cultivated MANIOC.

Other important features of Mesoamerican civilization had roots among the Olmecs. The Olmecs probably contributed iconography and many important beliefs to ancient Mesoamerican religions, including a
view of history emphasizing cycles of creation and
destruction and the cult of the feathered-serpent deity,
QUETZALCÓATL. The late Olmec period, around the
time La Venta and San Lorenzo were abandoned
(c. 400 B.C.E.), holds hints of the elaborate calendar
and writing systems that the Maya developed to their
highest expression during the Classic period (300 to
800 C.E.).

Much of the knowledge concerning Olmec culture
remained speculative at the end of the twentieth century, because it was based on incomplete archaeological data. Nevertheless, the Olmecs clearly constituted
a prime intellectual, material, and artistic source for
pre-Columbian Mesoamerica and thus for the indigenous component of Latino culture.

Olmedo, Alejandro "Alex" (b. Mar. 24, 1936, Arequipa, Peru): Tennis player. Olmedo learned to play
tennis as a small child while his father served as a

Alex Olmedo in competition at the 1959 U.S. National Championships. (AP/Wide World Photos)

Edward James Olmos holds his 1989 Nosotros Golden Eagle Award, given for being the outstanding actor in a television series. (AP/Wide World Photos)

caretaker for a local tennis club. In the late 1950's, he attended the University of Southern California (USC), where he was nicknamed "Chief" for his Incan features. While at USC, Olmedo won National Collegiate Athletic Association (NCAA) singles titles in 1956 and 1958.

These wins drew the attention of U.S. Davis Cup Team captain Perry Jones, who sought Olmedo for the team. Olmedo was not a U.S. citizen, however, and his selection was controversial. Jones contended that Olmedo should be allowed to play for the United States because Peru had no team. Olmedo was allowed to play, and he helped the U.S. team to capture the 1958 Davis Cup title.

Olmedo's 1959 singles and doubles wins at the U.S. Indoor Championship were the first by a South American. That same year, he won the Wimbledon and Australian Championship singles titles and reached the finals of the U.S. National Championship. In 1960, he began a successful professional career. A Peruvian national hero, he received his country's Order of Sports award. He was selected to the International Tennis Hall of Fame in 1987.

Olmos, Edward James (b. Feb. 24, 1947, Los Angeles, Calif.): Actor, director, and producer. Olmos, a Mexican American, studied sociology at California State University. He had his first major Broadway role in Luis Valdez's *Zoot Suit*. For that role, he received a 1978 Tony Award nomination, a Los Angeles Drama Critics Circle Award, and a Theatre World Award.

For his portrayal of Los Angeles schoolteacher Jaime ESCALANTE in *Stand and Deliver* (1988), Olmos was nominated for an Academy Award and appeared on the cover of *Time* magazine. He starred in and helped produce *The Ballad of Gregorio Cortez* (1982) and directed and coproduced *American Me* (1992). His other films include *Wolfen* (1981), *Blade Runner* (1982), *Saving Grace* (1986), *Triumph of the Spirit* (1989), *Maria's Story* (1990), and *A Talent for the Game* (1991).

From 1984 to 1988, Olmos played Lieutenant Castillo on television's *Miami Vice*, for which he received Golden Globe and Emmy Awards as best supporting actor. Deeply concerned with Los Angeles' Hispanic communities, Olmos received considerable publicity for his calls for peace and rebuilding in the wake of the 1992 Los Angeles riots.

Oñate, Juan de (1550, Guadalajara, Mexico—1630, Spain): Explorer and administrator. Oñate was the son of the Spanish governor of Nueva Galicia in Mexico. Wealthy from his father's silver mines and married to a granddaughter of the famous explorer Hernán CORTÉS, Oñate was given permission in a 1595 Spanish government contract to explore and settle the territory that became the modern state of New Mexico. He did this at his own expense, conquering and colonizing the territory by 1598. Oñate was then appointed governor of this territory, and he set up his capital at San Juan de los Caballeros.

Under Oñate, Franciscan priests converted many Pueblo Indians to Christianity, and several missions were established in the pueblos. The Spanish brought to the Pueblo tribes European and Mexican agricultural products such as grapes, melons, and other fruits, as well as horses and other draft animals, cattle, and chickens.

Ever curious and restless, Oñate explored widely, ranging as far afield as present-day Kansas. Eventually, Oñate's enemies persuaded the king of Spain to recall him. In 1607, an angry Oñate resigned as governor. He was tried and convicted of disobeying royal orders and of cruelty to the Pueblo Indians. This led to Oñate's exile from New Mexico. He settled in Spain.

O'Neill, Gonzalo (1867-1942): Poet. During the 1920's and 1930's, O'Neill was a large part of Puerto Rican cultural life. As a cultural entrepreneur, he invested his money in the theater and offered support to other writers.

O'Neill began his literary training in Puerto Rico, working with the magazine *El palenque de la juventud* (the young people's arena). His first published book, *La indiana borinqueña* (1922, the Indians of Puerto Rican), was a dramatic dialogue written in verse form. The work shows his commitment to Puerto Rican independence from the United States. In 1923, his three-act play *Moncho Reyes* was published in book form. Following that, in 1924 he published a book of nationalistic poetry titled *Sonoras bagatelas o sicilianas* (sonorous bagatelles or Sicilian verses). His most famous play is *Bajo una sola bandera* (1928; *Under Just One Flag*), which was produced in New York as well as in Puerto Rico. He continued to write, but most of his work has been lost. His only other known play is *Amoríos borincanos*, produced in 1938.

Onetti, Juan Carlos (b. July 1, 1909, Montevideo, Uruguay): Writer. Onetti was the son of Carlos Onetti, a customs employee, and Honoria Borges, a young woman from the south of Brazil. His early schooling was irregular and frequently interrupted by his family's moving from place to place. In high school he abandoned formal study and began to lead an unconventional, bohemian life, working at many different jobs. During those years, he became an avid reader.

In 1931, Onetti completed the manuscript of *El Pozo* (1939; *The Pit*, 1991), his first novel. It was recognized as an existential novel prefiguring the technical and narrative changes that would culminate in the "new novel" of the 1960's in Latin America. His major novels include *Tierra de nadie* (1941), *Para esta noche* (1943; *Tonight*, 1991), *La vida breve* (1950; *A Brief Life*, 1976), *Los adioses* (1951; *Farewells*, 1992), *Una tumba sin nombre* (1959), *El astillero* (1961; *The*

Shipyard, 1968), *Juntacadáveres* (1964; *Body Snatcher*, 1991), *La muerte y la niña* (1972), *Dejemos hablar al viento* (1979), and *Cuando entonces* (1987). His short stories are collected in *Un sueño realizado y otros cuentos* (1951) and *Tiempo de abrazar y los cuentos de 1933 a 1950* (1974). In his fiction, Onetti has developed an innovative point of view along with a semantic change in narrative that, combined with his particular philosophy, produced a new kind of existential novel in Latin America.

Operation Bootstrap: Economic development plan begun in the 1940's under Luis MUÑOZ MARÍN. In 1942, two years after the election of Muñoz's Popular

In 1960, Luis Muñoz Marín hosted a visit by President Dwight D. Eisenhower. (Library of Congress)

Democratic Party (Partido Popular Democrático, or PPD), Puerto Rico began a series of severe economic reforms to convert its weak agricultural economy to an industrial economy. The plan involved creation of government-owned industries that used indigenous resources. The government also bought the utility companies, set up a bank and planning commission, built housing projects, and purchased and redistributed land.

These attempts at self-sufficiency did not succeed, for several reasons. Profits were not large enough to expand the industries, and unemployment persisted. Control by the United States of Puerto Rico's shipping costs and its trade and tariff laws severely limited the country's independent economic development. In addition, U.S. business interests and the U.S. government disapproved of government ownership of industry, referring to it as a "socialist experiment."

These pressures caused Muñoz to initiate a new economic plan, which he called Operation Bootstrap. Muñoz saw industrialization as the only solution to Puerto Rico's economic woes. He sought to establish a new type of autonomy from the United States by developing industry through capital-intensive foreign investment while retaining a high level of self-government. Under the new plan, the Puerto Rican government-owned industries were sold to private holders, and the proceeds were applied toward improving infrastructure. A campaign was begun to bring U.S. industry to the island. Major incentives included Puerto Rico's freedom from U.S. federal taxes, local tax breaks, a stable political environment, and a plentiful and low-wage labor force. The creation of the Caribe Hilton hotel, a profit-sharing venture between the government and Hilton, paved the way for new tourism ventures.

During the late 1940's and the 1950's, Puerto Rico's fledgling industrial economy boomed as U.S. businesses took advantage of these conditions, importing raw materials and manufacturing such goods as electronics and textiles. In the 1960's, the program emphasized heavy industry, such as petroleum processing. During the recession of the 1970's, Operation Bootstrap emphasized education and productivity as Puerto Rico lost its labor-cost advantage and fought to keep business on the island. In the 1980's, Puerto Rico became home to pharmaceutical, scientific, and high-tech businesses as well as many banks.

Since the beginning of Operation Bootstrap, Puerto Rico has weathered many business cycles, but overall the country's economy has grown immensely. The program diversified the Puerto Rican economy, created jobs, and increased per capita personal income. Critics of the program, however, state that in spite of impressive statistics and political autonomy, Operation Bootstrap increased Puerto Rico's economic dependence on the United States because of its foreign-owned, export-oriented nature.

Although Puerto Rico's gross national product increased, so did unemployment. Beginning in the late 1960's, many industries moved out of Puerto Rico to countries with lower labor costs but similar tax breaks. To balance this loss, the United States increased the number of grants-in-aid and the amount of food stamps administered to Puerto Rico. Many unemployed Puerto Ricans flocked to the mainland for work. The island also depends on foreign oil for industry and consumer use. By the early 1990's, agriculture had been downplayed to the extent that Puerto Rico imported most of the basic food products consumed there.

Operation Wetback (1954-1958): U.S. government deportation of undocumented residents. The status of undocumented residents of the United States, particularly those from Mexico, has changed over time. In times of labor shortages in the United States, the Immigration and Naturalization Service (INS) has allowed them to enter and work without fear of arrest. At times of labor surplus, however, the government has exercised its official right to apprehend and expel illegal residents.

During and following World War II, undocumented Mexican workers came to the United States in large numbers, mostly to work in agriculture and in factories in the Southwest, where the demand for labor was high. When the need for labor diminished, the government felt pressure to reduce the number of undocumented workers. The Department of Justice proposed a policy that included a roundup of illegal workers, called Operation Wetback, as well as a continuation of the Bracero Program, which admitted some Mexican workers under contracts arranged by the government. A legislation package known as the Wetback Bills, which would have apprehended employers of undocumented workers and seized vehicles used to transport these workers, was proposed but never enacted. The term "wetback," a derogatory name for an undocumented Mexican worker, referred to the fact that some immigrants swam or waded across the Rio Grande to enter the United States.

Operation Wetback was publicized widely before it actually began, in an attempt to encourage or intimi-

Border Patrol agents fingerprint undocumented workers prior to deporting them. (AP/Wide World Photos)

date illegal Mexican immigrants into returning home. Once it began, it was precisely and efficiently carried out by the INS, an organization that recently had been reorganized by its new head, General Joseph M. Swing. Operation Wetback began in June, 1954, along the U.S.-Mexico border in Southern California and western Arizona. In July, 1954, it extended to South Texas.

Early roundups were considered successful in terms of the large numbers of illegal residents collected and sent back to Mexico. Hoping to continue along these lines, the INS attempted roundups in Chicago in September and October of 1954. These were relatively unsuccessful for the INS; the urban surroundings made it difficult to find undocumented persons. The Department of Justice hailed the operation as an overall success, however, citing the total number of illegal residents apprehended in 1954 as more than one million. Undocumented workers continued to be deported in a similar manner through 1958, bringing the total number of deported people to more than 3.5 million. With the support of the Mexican government, deported people were repatriated to their home areas or somewhere nearby in Mexico. Some re-entered the United States illegally, and others re-entered legally through the Bracero Program, which was created to meet a need for agricultural workers.

Operation Wetback benefited some Mexican residents of the United States, namely farmworkers who no longer had to compete with undocumented workers who were willing to work for low wages. The round-ups, however, violated civil and human rights. Illegal residents were sometimes treated in a physically brusque manner, and family members were separated. Many people were deported without deportation hearings. Any person could legally be taken aside and questioned if he or she appeared to be an "illegal Mexican," and many American citizens were thus detained on the basis of their looks.

Oregon: The history of Oregon has been influenced by the presence of Latino people, primarily in the area of agriculture. By 1990, the permanent Latino population in Oregon was only 4 percent of the state's total, indicating that much of this effect is from the migrant population.

A strong Hispanic population did not develop in the northwestern United States until the early 1900's. Prior to that time, during the early 1850's, a few Latino men,

primarily from Mexico and the southwestern United States, traveled the area working as cowboys. With the growth of farming, ranching occupations gradually declined. From the 1860's to the 1880's, the increase in mining drew a few Latino men to the area.

The first large increase in the Latino population of Oregon began during the Depression years of the 1930's. At this time, Latinos came mostly from the southwestern United States and worked as itinerant agricultural laborers. They settled primarily in the Willamette Valley in west-central Oregon because the area offered opportunities for field work.

World War II brought another increase in the Latino population. The military draft caused a shortage of field laborers in various agriculture-dependent states, including Oregon. Under the BRACERO PROGRAM, many people came to the state from Mexico. Workers from Mexico continued seasonal work through this program until 1964, by which time the Latino population in Oregon was the largest minority population in the state.

The government of the state of Oregon and various organizations within the state have worked actively to improve living conditions for the Latino population. One such group was the Research Committee on Migrant Labor. This committee was formed in 1955 by the Oregon Council of Churches. Its members were concerned about the appalling conditions under which migrant workers lived, and they worked to remedy these conditions. Encouraged by public support and led by Representative Don S. Willner, in 1959 the Oregon legislature passed laws prohibiting agriculturalists from exploiting workers.

By 1961, the state had developed summer programs for Spanish-speaking children of migrant workers. These programs later included all Latino children. In 1964, President Lyndon B. Johnson created the Office of Economic Opportunity (OEO) to aid in the campaign against poverty. The Oregon Council of Churches obtained a grant from the OEO in 1965. With this money, it formed the Valley Migrant League, which set up Hispanic social service centers in six Oregon communities.

Public opinion toward the Latino community varied between support and antagonism. The community of Woodburn, which had a white majority, strongly opposed a Chicano Cultural Center established by the Roman Catholic church in Willamette Valley. Activities at the center included arts and crafts classes, a newspaper, a television program, and a class in police-community relations.

LATINO POPULATION OF OREGON, 1990

Total number of Latinos = 112,707; 4% of population

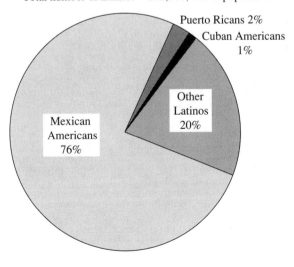

Source: Data are from Marlita A. Reddy, ed., *Statistical Record of Hispanic Americans* (Detroit: Gale Research, 1993), Table 106.
Note: Percentages are rounded to the nearest whole number.

Tony Orlando received a star on the Hollywood Walk of Fame in 1990. (AP/Wide World Photos)

By 1980, only 33 percent of the state's Latino population lived in the rural regions of Oregon. Continued educational and economic gains gave the Latino population of Oregon a greater voice in government and business. The Latino population grew to 112,707 people, as reported in the 1990 census.

Orendaín, Antonio (b. May 28, 1930, Etzatlán, Jalisco, Mexico): Labor leader. Throughout his career, Orendaín focused on the needs of farmworkers. In 1962, he helped establish and direct the NATIONAL FARM WORKERS ASSOCIATION. During the 1970's, he attempted to formally organize Texas farmworkers into a union. He had a good sense of how to use visible demonstrations to dramatize his points and gain public support. In 1977, he and hundreds of followers marched four hundred miles from the Rio Grande Valley to the state capital in Austin. Governor Dolph Briscoe formally received him and recognized the Texas Farm Workers Union, founded and directed by Orendaín. As the owner and manager of a construction company, Orendaín went on to organize packing house workers and electrical, radio, and machine workers. He served as a consultant to a juvenile probation program and for a time hosted a television program, *Contra Punto*.

Orlando, Tony (Michael Anthony Orlando Cassavitis; b. Apr. 3, 1944, New York, N.Y.): Singer and composer. Born to Greek and Spanish parents, Orlando began singing with Four Gents and the Milos. While studying mechanics, he was hired as a demo singer for the Brill Building Company.

In 1961, Orlando scored his first two U.S. Top 40 hit songs with "Halfway to Paradise" and "Bless You." After a short recording career that included the hit songs "Happy Times" (1961) and "Chills" (1962), Orlando began working in promotions in the record industry.

In 1970, Orlando returned to singing in a demo with Telma Hopkins and Joyce Vincent. After much persuasion, the trio recorded the song "Candida" under the name Dawn. The song became a national hit. Even though Orlando was immediately contacted for more recordings, he was hesitant because he had a secure job. He finally signed a contract, and in November Dawn recorded "Knock Three Times," which became an instant number one hit in the United States and the United Kingdom.

The group later changed its name to Tony Orlando and Dawn. More hit songs followed, among them "Tie a Yellow Ribbon 'Round the Ole Oak Tree" (1973), which *Billboard* magazine named as the top song of the year. The success of the song led to a prime time television series, *Tony Orlando and Dawn*, that ran from July, 1974, to December, 1976. Orlando retired from show business in 1977 but continued to give occasional solo performances.

Orozco, José Clemente (Nov. 23, 1883, Ciudad Guzmán, Mexico—Sept. 7, 1949, Mexico City, Mexico): Muralist. Orozco was graduated in 1890 from a Mexico City preparatory school, where a Vanegas Arroyo printing of illustrations had stimulated his interest in art. Still in Mexico City, he studied agronomy from 1897 to 1904 and architectural drawing from 1900 to 1904. He took courses at the Academy of Fine Arts and the National University from 1908 to 1914. Later, he worked as a draftsman in architectural firms. Beginning in 1911, he worked as a caricaturist for Mexico City newspapers. He was married to Margarita Valladares in 1923, and they had three children.

A critic of society, Orozco combined simple drawing with satire and the absurd. He counted among his early influences symbolist Julio Reulas and illustrator José Guadalupe Posada.

In 1922, Orozco painted his first murals at the National Preparatory School, Mexico City, returning to a more classic style with monumental and serene figures. The minister of education forced him to stop work in 1924 for two years. Orozco's style changed to a more emotional representation in later murals, such as those completed for Pomona College in California (1930), for Dartmouth College in New Hampshire (1932), and for the university, the government palace, and Cabanas Hospice in Guadalajara, Mexico (1936-1939).

The six panels Orozco did for the Museum of Modern Art in New York in 1940, at the same time as his exhibition of sketches and mural studies there, were his first move toward abstraction. His first outdoor mural was a six-story one at the National School for Teachers in Mexico City.

Orozco began a series of major exhibits in 1915. In 1946, he won the National Art Prize of Mexico. In 1947, he held an exhibition in the Palace of Fine Arts in Mexico City.

Orozco's artistic and political activities included membership in the Mexican Union of Painters, Sculptors, and Graphic Artists. He served as graphic artist for the movement's journal, *The Machete*. In 1943, he was a founder of the National College, which brought art and science personalities together.

José Clemente Orozco works on an oil painting in a New York studio in 1945. (AP/Wide World Photos)

Orozco is best known for his innovations in style, form, and material within the Mexican mural movement, which denounced and satirized the ills of his society. He is widely recognized as one of the finest artists of his generation, and his influence on U.S. muralists is undeniable. Along with those of Diego RIVERA, Orozco's ashes are in the Rotunda of Famous Men in the Civil Pantheon in Dolores.

Orphans: Legally, an orphan is a child under the age of sixteen who is without parents for one of three reasons: Both parents have died or abandoned the child, the child has been lost or separated from its parents, or a single parent is incapable of taking care of the child and has legally relinquished custody.

Throughout history orphans have been cared for in all societies by churches, government agencies, or individual families. The first Poor Law was passed in England in 1597. It became common for poor families to surrender their children to a poorhouse, to be taken care of by the state. The conditions of these establishments were often dismal and often the stigma and legacy of having been reared in one was passed on to the orphan's offspring.

Indigenous ethnic groups around the world have long practiced kinship fostering. An orphan would be taken in by relatives or the community in a form of de facto (nonlegal) adoption. This reflected and added to the strength of the extended family and community. American farm families from colonial times to the period of westward expansion enthusiastically accepted orphans into their homes. They had generous democratic natures and recognized the advantages of having as many household members as possible.

When industrialization took hold in Europe and the United States, the extended family lost its strength as members moved in small units to urban areas. Orphans lost their familial status and became more like temporary boarders, with little hope of finding adoptive parents.

Informal adoption of orphans has not been commonly practiced in modern time because legal procedures and regulations have been implemented. Orphanages concentrate their efforts on foster care provision. The orphanage provides a temporary home until a foster or adoptive parent can be found. Most orphanages concentrate their efforts on keeping families together. They take in some children for short periods of time, hoping that one parent or extended family member will be able to take each child home when family problems are solved.

Numbers of children in foster homes, living with nonrelatives, and being adopted are difficult to compile because the federal government has not kept cohesive and widespread records since the mid-1970's. Data on Latino orphans as a subgroup were not kept in printed records prior to 1970. Most numbers are gathered voluntarily by state social service agencies. Because private agencies and independent lawyers also arrange adoptions, it is difficult to count the numbers of foster children, orphans, and adoptions. Different tracking agencies generally agree, however, on their estimates. In 1990, there were estimated to be 101,000 adopted Hispanic children, 177,000 living with relatives other than the mother or father, and 54,000 living with nonrelatives only. Latino families, with their strong emphasis on the extended family, appear less likely than others to allow children to fall into the custody of nonrelatives.

Ortega, José Benito (1858-1941): Artist. Ortega was a true itinerant artist, traveling from town to town in New Mexico seeking patrons. He was one of several such artists serving Hispanos in the area. His santo figures were very simple and were painted in bright colors.

Much of Ortega's work was modeled on that of earlier periods in northern Mexico. One distinctive feature is that characters in the carvings are sized according to their importance rather than reflecting actual sizes. The saint in a figure therefore would be larger than any people, and people would be disproportionately large compared to animals.

Ortega, Katherine Davalos (b. July 16, 1934, Tularosa, N.Mex.): U.S. treasurer. As a ten-year-old girl, Ortega excelled at math and accounting, a foreshadowing of her later endeavors. Upon pursuing a teaching career, she found the way blocked by racial discrimination against Mexican Americans, so she decided to blaze her own path. Ortega began her own accounting firm and later served as a bank president. She was the first woman to be president of a California commercial bank.

Ortega eventually came back to the family accounting business and became increasingly involved in Republican politics. In 1982, she was selected by President Ronald Reagan to serve on a presidential advisory committee concerned with minority businesses. One year later, Ortega was appointed as treasurer of the United States, the second Hispanic woman to serve in that position. Although the post is largely ceremonial,

Katherine Ortega displays a 1986 $50 Gold American Eagle coin, the first investment-grade gold bullion coin ever issued by the U.S. Mint. (AP/Wide World Photos)

the treasurer supervises the Bureau of Engraving and Printing, the U.S. Mint, and the U.S. Savings Bond Division. In 1985, Ortega spearheaded a fund-raising project to restore the U.S. Statue of Liberty.

Ortega y Alberro, Maria Luisa "Malú" (b. Chicago, Ill.): A Mexican American reared in Chicago, Ortega y Alberro is associated with the Chicano art/empowerment movement there. She participated in the monumental mural *To Hope* on Benito Juárez High School in the Pilsen neighborhood (Chicago's Little Mexico) with Jaime Longoria, Marcos Raya, José Oscar Moya, and Salvador Vega.

Ortega y Alberro is best known as an interpreter of the Chicano experience. She says that a mural has the qualities of a poem, so she used the mural to abstract characteristic episodes of Chicano experience. She is best known as an interpreter of the Chicano experience within the Pilsen school.

Ortego y Gasca, Philip D. (b. Aug. 23, 1926, Blue Island, Ill.): Educator, poet, and publisher. In addition to several books, primarily concerning education or literature, Ortego is the author or coauthor of more than 150 poems, essays, short stories, and reviews. His play *Madre del Sol*, a dramatization of the Mexican American experience, was widely acclaimed both in the United States and in Mexico. In 1972, he was named senior editor and literary director of the magazine *La Luz*, and he has served as editor in chief of the *National Hispanic Reporter*. He is also the editor of *We Are Chicanos: An Anthology of Mexican-American Literature* (1973).

Ortego dropped out of junior high school to join the labor force, then served in the U.S. Marine Corps from 1944 to 1947. He attended the University of Pittsburgh from 1948 to 1952 under the G.I. Bill but joined the U.S. Air Force in 1953 before completing a degree. He continued his studies, receiving his bachelor's degree (in English and Spanish) in 1959 from Texas Western College. After resigning from the Air Force, he earned his M.A. in English in 1966 at the University of Texas at El Paso. In 1971, he earned his doctorate in English language and literature at the University of New Mexico. While pursuing his education, Ortego taught at New Mexico State University (1964-1970) and the University of Texas at El Paso (1970-1972), founding the Chicano studies program there. Later, he joined the faculty of the Mexican American graduate studies program at San Jose State University in California. In addition to his teaching, Ortego was chair of the Hispanic Foundation from 1982 to 1986.

Ortiz, Carlos (b. Sept. 9, 1936, Ponce, Puerto Rico): Boxer. When Ortiz moved to New York City at the age of nine, he did not know how to speak English. He did, however, already know how to box, and as a teenager he began a successful amateur career at the Madison Square Boxing Club. Named the outstanding boxer in the Police Athletic League for 1953, Ortiz won the Metropolitan Amateur Athletic Union lightweight title a year later.

After graduating from a vocational high school, the young fighter began a professional boxing career. Although undefeated in his first twenty-seven competitions and ranked among the leading lightweights, Ortiz could not get a fight for the lightweight title. In response, he moved to the junior welterweight class and took that title. He defended his title twice in 1960, losing it to Duilio Loi in September of that year.

Ortiz finally got his chance at the lightweight title in April, 1962, fighting against Joe Brown. Ortiz won the belt and defended it four times. He lost the title in a fifteen-round decision to Ismael Laguna in April, 1965, but won the rematch seven months later in a bout

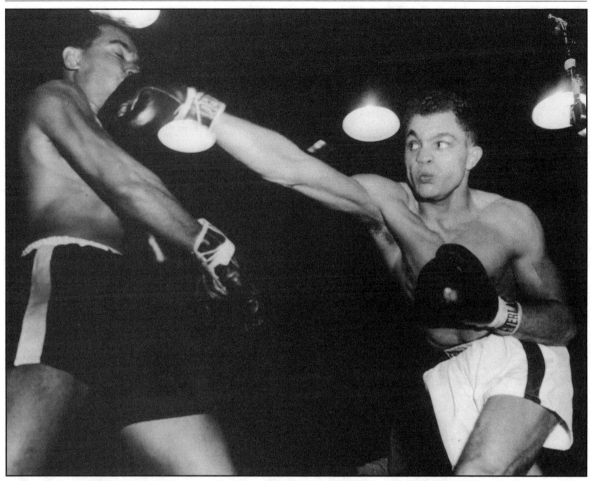

Carlos Ortiz lands a punch on Ray Portilla in a 1956 fight. (AP/Wide World Photos)

that drew the largest crowd in Puerto Rican boxing history. Ortiz held the title until June, 1968. While champion, Ortiz also made an unsuccessful bid for the New York State Senate in 1966. He retired in 1971 with a career record of 65-9-1, including thirty-seven knockouts. In 1991, he was inducted into the International Boxing Hall of Fame.

Ortiz, Francis V., Jr. (b. Mar. 14, 1926, Santa Fe, N.Mex.): Diplomat. Ortiz, a Mexican American, began his journey on the path to diplomacy by earning a degree from the School of Foreign Service at Georgetown University in Washington, D.C., in 1950. Ortiz began to pursue his diplomatic career after his graduation.

Prior to his schooling as a diplomat, Ortiz served in the United States Air Force (1944-1946), receiving the Air Medal for his distinguished service. He supplemented his education with a master's degree from George Washington University in 1967. Ortiz also

studied at the preeminent U.S. military educational institution, the National War College.

This assortment of knowledge and experience served him well in his foreign service posts in Ethiopia, Mexico, Peru, Uruguay, Argentina, Barbados, and Grenada. In 1979, Ortiz served as ambassador to Guatemala; from 1981 to 1983, as ambassador to Peru; and from 1983 to 1986, as ambassador to Argentina.

Ortiz, Manuel (July 2, 1916, Corona, Calif.—May 31, 1970, San Diego, Calif.): Boxer. Ortiz began his boxing career as a spectator—he was attending a boxing event when one of the contenders did not show up. Ortiz was recruited from the audience and knocked down his opponent, Bobby Hager, seventeen times.

By 1937, the Mexican American boxer had become the top Southern California amateur flyweight, winning Golden Gloves and national titles. A year later, he turned professional and in his second title bout took the bantamweight belt from Benny Goldberg.

Manuel Ortiz lost his bantamweight title to Vic Toweel in 1950. (AP/Wide World Photos)

Problems plagued the young boxer, however, and he lost several matches. Acquiring a new manager in 1941, Ortiz regained his form and took the bantamweight title from Tony Olivera in 1943. Over the next two years, he defended his title twelve times. After serving briefly in the military, Ortiz defended his title three more times in 1946, making fifteen consecutive successful title defenses.

Underdog Harold Dade unexpectedly took the title from Ortiz in January, 1947, in one of the sport's biggest upsets. Ortiz regained his title two months later and held it until 1950. He retired with a record of 97-28-3, including 49 knockouts.

Ortiz, Vilma (b. Apr. 15, 1954, New York, N.Y.): Scholar. Ortiz's early experiences in New York City's Puerto Rican community influenced her to pursue a career in the social sciences, studying the lives of Latinos. She received a B.A. from City College of New York in 1976 and a Ph.D. from New York University in 1981. She has held postdoctoral fellowships at Fordham University, the University of Michigan, the University of Wisconsin, and the Educational Testing Service. She joined the faculty of the University of California, Los Angeles (UCLA), in 1988.

Ortiz's research on the social conditions of Latinos in the United States focuses particularly on migration, employment, and family issues among Puerto Rican women as well as economic conditions among Latino immigrants in California. While at UCLA, she became involved in a thirty-year follow-up study of the landmark *The Mexican-American People: The Nation's Second Largest Minority* (1970), written by Leo Grebler, Joan W. Moore, and Ralph C. GUZMÁN. The follow-up attempted to locate and interview the original respondents as well as their adult children and grandchildren. This project was to produce the first major longitudinal and intergenerational study of Mexican Americans and examine questions regarding intra- and intergenerational mobility and ethnic change.

Ortiz Cofer, Judith (b. Feb. 24, 1952, Hormigueros, Puerto Rico): Poet and novelist. Ortiz Cofer is a widely anthologized poet and also an educator. As a child of a Navy sailor, she traveled back and forth from Puerto Rico to the United States. She immigrated to the United States in 1956 and earned college degrees in English literature. She has taught both literature and creative writing at universities throughout the South, and she received scholarships to the Bread Loaf Writers' Conference, a writing program at which she later

worked. Her childhood experiences of living in two different cultures are evident in her literary work. Her poems often deal with issues of cultural identity and relationships between women and men; her family and island homeland are also frequent subjects of her poetry.

Although primarily a poet, Cofer received critical attention for her first book, *The Line of the Sun* (1989). The book, which depicts a young bicultural girl's struggle to balance her Puerto Rican and American identities, garnered praise for its poetic lyricism.

Her works include the poetry volumes *Latin Women Pray* (1980), *The Native Dancer* (1981), *Among the Ancestors* (1981), *Peregrina* (1986), and *Terms of Survival* (1987). She also has a collection of personal essays titled *Silent Dancing* (1990) and a collection titled *The Latin Deli: Prose and Poetry* (1993).

Ortiz Montañez, Rafael (b. Jan. 30, 1934, New York, N.Y.): Sculptor and video artist. Ortiz Montañez, a Mexican American artist, is known professionally as Ralph Ortiz. He has redefined the roles of artist and artistic work, seeing the artist as a destroyer, reflecting the current state of society, rather than as a constructor of objects.

Ortiz Montañez performed his "Piano Destruction Concert" for a British Broadcasting Corporation television broadcast in 1966 and later performed the same piece for national broadcast in the United States. He is known for sculpture, exhibitions, concerts, theater performances, and lectures at universities, on the radio, and on television. His best-known work is *Montezuma*. He earned an M.F.A. from the Pratt Institute and a doctorate in education from Columbia University. In 1969 and 1970, he was director and curator of El Museo del Barrio in New York.

Ortiz Montañez became the leading destructive artist in the United States, keeping alive the 1960's concept. Through extensive use of the media, he has reached a wide international audience while addressing the ills of modern society through art. Later work focused on computers and their users.

Osorio, Carlos (b. 1927, Caguas, Puerto Rico): Cartoonist and illustrator. Osorio received much of his training in 1953 and 1954 at the School of Cartoonists and Illustrators, which later became part of the Visual Arts Department at New York College. He illustrated books and designed posters for the Division of community Education in San Juan, Puerto Rico, from 1956 to 1964. He lived on the U.S. mainland from 1964 to

1980. In 1969, he joined the Taller Boricua in New York, New York, and was a founding member of El Museo del Barrio in New York. He became known for his support of Puerto Rican artists in New York and for his own cartoons and illustrations, some of them stylistically similar to Japanese art. Osorio had visited Japan in 1951. He returned to Puerto Rico in 1980.

Oxnard sugar beet workers' strike (Feb. 28-Mar. 23, 1903): Labor stoppage. On February 28, 1903, thousands of Mexican and Japanese field workers in Oxnard, California, went on strike to protest low wages and ten-hour days in sugar beet fields owned by the Western Agricultural Contracting Company. The beet harvesters were paid in scrip and forced to buy food and clothing at a company store. The company also deducted wages to pay for services such as transportation to the fields and use of tools. The workers organized the Japanese-Mexican Workers Association to protest those practices.

On March 23, a demonstration ended in violence as police shot into a crowd of strikers, killing a union leader and wounding several dozen workers. After the shootings, negotiations began. The workers achieved a small victory. Beet growers in the area agreed to hire only members of the Sugar Beet and Farm Laborers Union. Wages improved slightly, but hours were not reduced. In a display of open prejudice, the leaders of the American Federation of Labor refused to accept the new union into its ranks.

P

Pachanga: Mexican party. *Pachangas* are parties, usually given for no other reason than having a good time. They usually are sponsored by a family, which provides food, beer, and music for dancing. The neighborhood or community is invited. Usually held on Friday or Saturday night by lower-income people, they are more prominent in Mexico than in the American Southwest. All ages participate, and sexes often are largely segregated. A special type of *pachanga*, the *tardiana*, is held in a public park or a closed-off street and serves as a place for young persons to meet and dance with members of the opposite sex under family supervision.

Pacheco, Romualdo (Oct. 31, 1831, Santa Barbara, Calif.—Jan. 23, 1899, Oakland, Calif.): Politician. The son of an army officer stationed in Santa Barbara, Pacheco worked on his stepfather's ships as a super-cargo when he reached the age of fifteen. He managed his mother's ranch in San Luis Obispo after the Mexican American War and became a state senator as a Democrat in 1858. During the Civil War, Pacheco served as brigadier general in a battalion of "Native Cavalry" formed by President Abraham Lincoln as a show of force in the Southwest.

In 1871, the Republican Party nominated Pacheco for lieutenant governor. He was elected, then took the governorship in 1875 when the incumbent, Newton Booth, took an interim seat in the U.S. Senate. Pacheco was little more than a figurehead in a caretaker government, but the Spanish-speaking population was proud of his accomplishment.

Republican leaders did not renominate Pacheco in the next election, and he turned to selling stocks in San Francisco. He served two terms in Washington, D.C., as Santa Clara's congressman between 1879 and 1883. Pacheco then returned to his business interests. The withdrawal of Pacheco and other CALIFORNIO leaders from local politics was unfortunate for the Spanish-speaking community, which was left without leaders actively pursuing that community's interests.

Pachuco: Mexican American urban youth type of the 1940's. Pachucos originated in the barrios of Los Angeles, California. Most were children of immigrants from Mexico, and most of their families had moved from rural to urban settings. As the first generation born in the United States, amid poverty and continued discrimination, these youths felt isolated from both American and Mexican culture. Consequently, they banded together in neighborhood gangs that provided camaraderie and friendship. The pachucos were known for their flashy style of dress, baggy zoot suits, and pompadour haircuts. They spoke CALÓ, a mixture of English and Spanish. Pachucos gained a negative reputation in Anglo culture and were stereotyped as being prone to violence and use of illegal drugs. This stereotype was reinforced during the zoot-suit riots that took place in 1943 (*see* SLEEPY LAGOON CASE). The 1940's-style pachuco, some believe, was a model for the "Vatos Locos" of the 1950's and the LOW RIDERS of the 1960's and 1970's.

The zoot suit was popular among pachucos of the 1940's. (AP/Wide World Photos)

Pacific Electric strike (April, 1903): Strike by Mexican railroad workers. Early in the spring of 1903, nine hundred track workers for the Los Angeles Pacific Electrical Railway Company organized La Union Federal Mexicana (Mexican Federal Union) and demanded a raise. The workers wanted three cents an hour more than the seventeen cents they were getting. The Los Angeles Merchants and Manufacturers Association and Citizens Alliance, dependent on streetcar lines for getting customers to and from stores, joined with the electric railway company to fight the union.

To break the strike, business leaders sent agents to El Paso, Texas, to recruit streetcar employees with a promise of twenty-two cents an hour. In Sonoratown, as the Mexican barrio in Los Angeles was called, the union pressed for a boycott of streetcars, but the business alliance proved too powerful. After a month, the strike ended. The Anglo community refused to support the strike and boycott, and the union effort collapsed. The strikers got their jobs back, and the replacement workers were sent home. The next year, Pacific Electric cut wages for all employees from $1.75 to $1.00 a day.

Padilla, Amado Manuel (b. Oct. 18, 1942, Albuquerque, N.Mex.): Educator. Padilla is the author of several books on issues of BILINGUAL EDUCATION and on Latino MENTAL HEALTH and identity, among other topics. Among his publications are *Crossing Cultures in Therapy: Pluralistic Counseling for the Hispanic* (1980, coauthored with Elaine Levine) and *Chicano Ethnicity* (1987).

Padilla earned his B.A. at New Mexico Highlands University (1964), his M.S. at Oklahoma State University (1966), and his Ph.D. at the University of New Mexico (1969). All of his degrees are in psychology. He began his teaching career at the State University of New York in 1969, moving to the University of California, Santa Barbara, in 1971. He was named a professor at the University of California, Los Angeles, in 1974 and moved to the faculty of Stanford University in 1988. Padilla was chosen as a senior lecturer in the Fulbright-Hays program at Pontifica Universidad Catolica de Peru for the 1977-1978 academic year. He was given the Distinguished Scholar Award by the American Educational Research Association in 1987 and the Distinguished Research Award by the same group in 1988.

Padilla, Benjamín (b. Guadalajara, Mexico): Writer. Padilla was a Mexican who lived in the United States. Writing in newspapers under the name "Kaskabel"

(rattlesnake), Padilla published numerous CRÓNICAS, or sketches of life in the Southwest, between 1910 and 1929.

Padilla, Heberto (b. Jan. 20, 1932, Pinar del Río, Cuba): Poet and novelist. Padilla grew up in Puerta de Golpe, Cuba. He completed his secondary education at the Institute of Secondary Teaching of Pinar del Río and Artemisa. Padilla studied law for three years at the University of Havana but never completed his degree.

During the reign of Fulgencio Batista, Padilla left Cuba. He returned when Fidel Castro assumed power in 1959. In 1968, Padilla's second book of poetry, *Fuera de juego* (1968), was awarded the first prize of the Cuban Union of Writers and Artists. On April 27, 1971, Padilla made a speech in which he denounced, as enemies of the Cuban Revolution, prominent Cuban and non-Cuban writers, journalists, economists, friends, and even his wife. After virtual ostracism, Padilla left the country in 1980 and took up residence with his family in the United States.

Padilla has published several volumes of poetry, including *El justo tiempo humano* (1962), *Fuera del juego*, and *El hombre junto al mar* (1981; *Legacies*, 1982). He also published the novel *En mi jardin pastan los heroes* (1982; *Heroes Are Grazing in My Garden*, 1984). Bridging the work of two generations of Cuban poets, Padilla's work moves away from the neo-baroque style of his contemporaries and embodies a new sensibility of clarity and austerity.

Padilla, Juan de (c. 1500, Andalusia, Spain—1542, Kansas): Priest and explorer. Fray Juan de Padilla prepared well for the hardships of the New World. He had been a fighting man in his youth before coming to Mexico. In Mexico, he was first guardian of Tulanzingo and Tzapotla in Jalisco. He also accompanied Pedro de Tovar on an expedition north to unknown territories, where they saw Moqui Indian villages. Padilla's fame comes from his journey with Francisco Vázquez de CORONADO to CÍBOLA and a later expedition to Quivira.

When Fray Marcos de NIZA returned from his trip to the Zuni pueblos in 1539, Coronado organized a new expedition that included Padilla. The expedition occupied Hawikuh, which Fray Marcos had seen and reported on, and Tiguex. Because the expedition found no gold or silver, a trip was organized to another region, Quivira.

When the expedition reached Quivira, located in modern Kansas, Padilla built a large cross. Again no

Heberto Padilla (center), surrounded by his family and Senator Edward Kennedy, addresses reporters after being allowed to leave Cuba in 1980. (AP/Wide World Photos)

gold or silver was found, so the expedition returned to Tiguex. When Coronado decided to return to Mexico, Padilla asked to stay behind to convert the Indians to Catholicism. He then returned to Quivira and found his cross intact. He began missionary work, but Indians killed him in 1542.

Padres Asociados por Derechos Religiosos, Educativos, y Sociales (Los PADRES): Religious activist group. Los PADRES was established in 1968 in San Antonio, Texas. Its membership consists primarily of Catholic priests, brothers, and deacons. Honorary membership is open to anyone who supports the goals of the group. In 1972, Los PADRES established a sister organization called the MEXICAN AMERICAN CULTURAL CENTER, which is nondenominational in nature and has no restrictions on membership.

The group's names translates as Fathers Associated for Religious, Educational, and Social Rights. Its objectives include developing a critical conscience whereby poor people—farmworkers in particular—see themselves as masters of their own destiny, capable of bringing about structural change. It advocates a supportive ministry and promotes Hispanic issues and rights within the CATHOLIC CHURCH. The organization seeks to incorporate the Mexican American cultural heritage within the Catholic church. An early and continuing goal was to achieve greater Hispanic representation in church leadership.

Padrino: Literally, "godfather." *Padrino* can designate a mentor or intermediary in business or political dealings. *Tener padrino* (to have a godfather) implies that a person has the means, through friendship or

Mentoring or padrino *relationships can begin early and involve sharing various types of knowledge and experience.* (James Shaffer)

influence, to achieve his or her personal or political goals. The relationship between mentor and protégé is called COMPADRAZGO. In colonial times in Latin America, a *padrino* was a white plantation owner or government official who, acting as a third party, tried to arrange a master's pardon for a runaway slave.

Padua Hills Theatre: Playhouse. The Padua Hills Theatre operated in the foothills of Claremont, California, from 1930 to 1974. The Anglo proprietors, Herman and Bess Garner, intended to run plays produced and directed by a local troupe.

By 1931, the Depression had nearly forced closure of the playhouse. The Garners experimented with productions of Mexican folk dance and song, performed by the Mexican employees hired to cook, clean, and serve at the dinner theater. The plays became such a success that the Garners gradually replaced their Anglo troupe with the Mexican Players of Padua Hills and expanded the repertoire to include romantic comedies and historical dramas. In addition to their new duties as performers, the Paduanos (the term used by the players to describe themselves) continued to serve in the dining room and at postproduction parties.

Facilitating communication between Anglo and Mexican American people was one of the main themes of the Padua Hills Theatre, and plays soon became recognized as much for their ability to create intercultural understanding as for their entertainment quality. Padua Hills Theatre eventually became the longest running Mexican American theater in the United States, and it produced many artists who performed on stage, film, and radio.

Paella: Spanish rice and seafood dish. *Paella* was created in Catalonian Spain and was brought to the Americas by the Spanish, but in the New World it has retained great popularity only in Puerto Rico. Basic Puerto Rican *paella* consists of some sort of seafood simmered in water with seasonings. Rice is added to absorb the water. The heart of *paella*, however, is the juxtaposition of tastes, and good *paellas* will have many ingredients. Usually included are several kinds of shellfish, chicken, sausage or ham, olives, red bell peppers, and pigeon peas. Puerto Ricans usually use ACHIOTE in place of saffron to color the rice. In New York City, Puerto Ricans sometimes refer to a sparse *paella* as *paellita*. *Paellas* often are served as party dishes.

Painting and painters: The history of North America contains a rich tradition of painting that is uniquely Latino, with techniques and styles as diverse as the collective cultures that created them. Indigenous, Spanish, European, African, and Mexican influences in painting helped shape the unique cultural expressions of Latinos of the late twentieth century.

Pre-Columbian Influences. Painting began for the indigenous peoples of North America as a form of communication and explanation for their experience in the world. They began by decorating pottery with meaningful designs, then developed expertise in murals and codices (illuminated manuscripts). The Classical Mayan period (300-900 C.E.) saw monumental frescoes (murals painted on fresh plaster), such as those in Bonampak, which adorned the interiors of many temple structures in the Lowland Maya area of the Yucatán and in TEOTIHUACÁN in Mexico. These interiors are decorated with nearly life-sized figures of warriors and priests and depict battle scenes, victory dances, sacrifices, processions, and ceremonies. The Mayan artists achieved skillful use of color; their figural style and draftsmanship are distinctive.

The Mayan, Aztec, and Mixtec codices that appear after 1000 C.E. seem to be miniature versions of murals and depict both historical and mythological themes. Long strips of bark paper treated with chalk and deerskin parchment are the supports used for native paints. The strips are folded like an accordion to maintain the continuity of a tribal history or ceremonial calendar. Only three Mayan codices have survived (in Paris, France; Dresden, Germany; and Madrid, Spain), because overzealous priests, during the SPANISH CONQUEST, thought that these exquisite histories were the work of the devil and destroyed all that they found.

Spanish and European Influences. When Hernán CORTÉS conquered the Aztecs in 1521, he destroyed an entire civilization and, in effect, the Amerindian civilizations. From the sixteenth century to the early nineteenth century, Spain possessed a colonial empire that spanned a large portion of the Western Hemisphere. The empire consisted of the viceroyalties of NEW SPAIN (Mexico) and Lima (Highland Bolivia and Peru), with an *audiencia* (colonial high court) in Buenos Aires.

In the sixteenth century, Spaniards made their earliest contact with the southwestern United States. Within twenty years, New Mexico was explored and claimed by Spain. Spanish colonists moved into the areas that are now Texas, Arizona, and California during the late seventeenth century and early eighteenth century. The existing political, social, and cultural structures of the native population were forced to change. As the Span-

Artwork at a San Luis, Colorado, church illustrates styles of early religious paintings. (James Shaffer)

ish and indigenous cultures mixed, a MESTIZO (mixed race) class emerged; mestizos became the laboring class. Spanish colonists attempted to copy the living conditions and cities of Spain; they rebuilt cities in the Spanish medieval and Renaissance style. Pre-Columbian styles of art and culture were pushed aside.

In its three centuries of existence, New Spain incorporated the styles of several great periods of European painting into native culture: the medieval, Renaissance, Baroque, mannerist, and neoclassical periods. Other elements also were introduced, such as Moorish and Asian forms. The Franciscan, Dominican, and Augustinian friars, there to Christianize the natives, set up artisan workshops and taught the natives how to paint in their methods. The friars needed religious images to teach stories of Christianity to the natives, so they used European engravings of paintings by Diego Velázquez and other Spanish and European painters as models. The natives reproduced many paintings, giv-

ing them a naïve quality. This became the start of a fusion of native and Spanish traditions.

During the medieval period, paintings were created in three formats: murals, panel paintings, and codices. Murals were painted on church and monastery walls instead of temple walls, although the fresco technique was still employed. Now the subject matter was Christian, but the highly decorative design and color scheme were native features. RETABLOS (panel paintings), made with wood and oil paints, became popular. These were of Italian and Flemish origin. Codices continued to chronicle the indigenous experience, as native peoples still used this method to write. Many recorded the main events of sixteenth century Mexico, everyday scenes, and native flora and fauna.

The remaining periods of New Spanish painting mirrored the styles coming from Europe, which appeared to be a series of reactions and counterreactions. The Renaissance period saw guilds and academies being established. Painting was characterized by brilliant and luminous color and strict rules followed by artists. The Baroque period of the seventeenth century was a reaction by the Catholic church meant to heighten its own appeal. Forms became realistic, dynamic, and emotional, and there was a new awareness of space. Neoclassicism reacted to the elaborateness of the Baroque period, using classical forms re-created with precision and controlled emotion.

The Mexican Influence. In 1821, New Spain gained its independence from Spain and called itself Mexico, after the name that the Aztecs called themselves—Mexicas. The nineteenth century saw a Mexican culture rich in artistic talent, producing the artists Juan Cordero (1824-1884), José María Velasco (1840-1912), and José Guadalupe Posada (1851-1913). The twentieth century saw Diego RIVERA (1886-1957), José Clemente OROZCO (1883-1949), David Alfaro SIQUEIROS (1896-1974), and Frida KAHLO (1907-1954). Whether self-taught or trained in Europe or the Mexican academy, each contributed a unique perspective on the Mexican experience.

Cordero and Velasco were masters in Mexican portraiture and landscape painting. Posada's contribution

Diego Rivera and Frida Kahlo were among the important Mexican and Mexican American painters of the early twentieth century. (AP/Wide World Photos)

was more in the graphic art arena. Posada deserves mention because he influenced Latino art with his social commentary and his development of motifs unique to Mexican life. Alive during the Mexican Revolution of 1910-1921, he wanted to educate people about war. He illustrated violent scenes, such as lynchings and execution squads, and drew hundreds of *calaveras* (skeletons) in various poses reminiscent of the death motifs of the Aztec and Maya.

The 1920's marked the beginning of the Mexican School of painting. Rivera, Siqueiros, Orozco, and others were commissioned by the Mexican government to create a national art that was based on Mexican reality, using native subjects. Soon, a manifesto was published that called for a revolutionary art that would reflect the geography, social conditions, and Amerindian heritage of Mexico while continuing the country's international participation in modern art.

Latino Painting. Hispanic America includes the Spanish borderlands area of the United States, Puerto Rico, Cuba, the Caribbean, and those areas in the United States populated by peoples of Hispanic descent. The peoples of these areas are a mixture of cultures: Native American, Spanish, European, African, and North American. Painting styles, subject matter, and purpose are as diverse as the artists who create works; however, some common characteristics can be observed. Many Latino painters want to create a national or cultural identity for their country or for their people. Moreover, they often employ "social realism" in narratives depicting the working class or social injustices. They illustrate the country's landscape or cityscape, everyday scenes, and folklore or mythology. Vibrant colors dominate. Differences occurred in how artists followed particular art movements (such as abstraction or surrealism) or were self-taught; personal experiences and messages also shaped their art.

Generally, the impetus to create a national art came from revolution and turmoil in a country. Puerto Rico, in 1898, became a United States possession; in 1902, Cuba gained independence from Spain; and the Mexican Revolution began in 1910. These countries attempted to retain their identity despite the turmoil.

With the influence of Francisco OLLER (1833-1917), Puerto Rican artists began to break away from the formal academic painting of Europe (*see* ART, PUERTO RICAN). Heavily influenced by French realist Gustave Courbet (1819-1877), Oller painted social realism scenes in a Puerto Rican context. In 1905, Ramón Frade (1875-1954), influenced by Oller, painted *Our Daily Bread*, an oil painting with monu-

mental forms, placed centrally against a Puerto Rican countryside. This became one of many national icons for Puerto Rico. Subsequently, Jorge SOTO (b. 1947) from New York City and Arnaldo ROCHE (b. 1955) from Chicago, Illinois, drew from their Puerto Rican heritage as they painted. A self-taught artist, Soto defines his forms with elaborate linear patterns. He is interested in conveying the Taino Indian and African aesthetic. Roche has a unique style involving "rubbings." He lays canvas or paper on an object that has been smeared with paint, rubs it, and elaborates on the distorted images.

Cuba's break from formal academic painting occurred in the 1930's (*see* ART, CUBAN AMERICAN). Víctor Manuel (1897-1969), Fidelio Ponce de León (1895-1949), Amelia Peláez (1897-1968), and Wilfredo Lam (1902-1982) painted in the new Cuban style, which focused on a national affirmation and an expression of self. Manuel expressed free use of color and form in his works. Ponce de León painted abstract, free-falling human forms with mystical, featureless faces. Peláez integrated flat planes of color and colonial motifs, drawing from Cuba's history. Lam combined the abstract cubism of Pablo Picasso with imagery from Africa and Oceania.

Cultural identity rather than national identity has been the main focus for Mexican American and Chicano painters (*see* ART, MEXICAN AMERICAN). Not being entirely Mexican or entirely American, Mexican Americans sought their own identity. Mexican American painters active between the 1930's and 1960's include Antonio García (b. 1901), Chelo González Amézcua (b. 1903), and Eugenio QUESADA (b. 1927). García, born in Mexico but living in the United States since he was eleven years old, painted Spanish Conquest and pre-Columbian themes. In his *Aztec Advance* (1929), García painted three Aztec warriors at a diagonal, with feathers shooting in opposite directions. This created drama and movement in the work. González Amézcua, born in Texas, also found inspiration in Mexican themes. A self-taught artist, she depicts Aztec rulers and mythological figures in a unique style that she called "filigree art." Her *El Magnífico Poeta Netzalhualcóyotl* (1969), done in this intricate style, took one month to finish. Quesada, born in Arizona, spent several years in Mexico to study the Mexican muralists. His oil paintings of Mexican subjects are painted in abstract forms with bold line and color.

The renaissance of the Chicano Art movement occurred in 1968, at the height of the Civil Rights movement in the United States. Driven to express the Chi-

The 1960's brought a revival of mural art. (Hazel Hankin)

cano experience, artists used various materials such as ink pens, watercolors, and spray paint to convey their message. They revived the mural but also painted in oils, gouache, watercolor, and multiple media. Subject matter often included skulls, farmworkers, religious symbols, serpents, the family unit, and their indigenous past. Melesio CASAS II (b. 1929), Frank ROMERO (b. 1941), Carmen LOMAS GARZA (b. 1948), and Yreina CERVÁNTEZ (b. 1952) are a few of the many artists from this period.

Casas was one of the pioneers of the Chicano Art movement. He began by painting the United Farm Worker logo (an eagle) and pre-Columbian motifs. He is best known for his popular "humanscape" paintings that give the feeling of being in a film theater. Romero, a member of the Los Angeles-based art group Los FOUR, focused on street scenes, many times painting low rider cars as the main subject. *The Closing of Whittier Boulevard* (1984) is a night scene giving a bird's-eye view of a police barricade in East Los Angeles. Lomas Garza paints about images from her childhood in southern Texas, using art to help heal the pain from the racism and discrimination she experienced. Her paintings of everyday events appear to be narratives, with a distinctive, naïve quality. The gouache painting *Curandera* (1977) displays flat, illustration-like forms and patterning. A watercolor by Yreina Cervántez, *Homenaje a Frida Kahlo* (1978), conveys the inspiration that Cervántez and other Chicana artists found in Kahlo. There is a surrealist quality to this work, with its fluid forms and vivid colors, depicting Kahlo and several native animals and plants.

—*Barbara Mendoza*

SUGGESTED READINGS:
• Beardsley, John, and Jane Livingston. *Hispanic Art in the United States: Thirty Contemporary Painters and Sculptors*. New York: Abbeville Press, 1987. Highlights thirty artists from Mexico, Cuba, Puerto Rico, Central America, and South America residing in the United States.
• Cancel, Luis R., et al. *The Latin American Spirit: Art and Artists in the United States, 1920-1970: Essays*. New York: Bronx Museum of the Arts, 1988. Focuses on the Latin American presence in the twentieth century art of the United States.
• Fuentes-Perez, Ileana, et al., eds. *Outside Cuba: Contemporary Cuban Visual Arts*. New Brunswick, N.J.: Rutgers, 1989. This exhibition catalog highlights second- to sixth-generation Cuban artists. Essays discuss the exile of artists and the exile of Cubans, among other topics.
• Griswold del Castillo, Richard, et al., eds. *Chicano Art: Resistance and Affirmation, 1965-1985*. Los Angeles: Wight Art Gallery, University of California, Los Angeles, 1991. This interpretive exhibition of the Chicano Art movement enlightens the reader on aspects of the Chicano experience as well as giving an overview of Chicano art.
• Quirarte, Jacinto. *Mexican American Artists*. Austin: University of Texas Press, 1973. Surveys twenty-seven Mexican American artists from the twentieth century. Antecedents to the art are discussed, primarily from the Spanish borderlands.

Palacios, Monica (b. June 14, 1959, San Jose, Calif.): Writer and performer. Palacios, who began writing short stories as an adolescent, earned a degree in film studies from San Francisco State University in 1984. Aware of the humor in her stories, she tried stand-up comedy in 1982 and soon found a gay cabaret where she could include material about her lesbianism. She began performing regularly at both mainstream and alternative clubs and events. In 1991, she developed a solo performance entitled *Latin Lezbo Comic*, with which she has toured throughout the United States. Her performances interweave autobiography, humor, and social awareness through theatricality and strong visual elements.

Palacios' other projects include *Greetings from a Queer Señorita*, a touring lecture/performance; *Deep in the Crotch of My Latino Psyche*, a collaboration with Luis Alfaro and Beto Araiza; *La llorona loca* and *Seagullita*, one-act plays; *Fierce Tongues/Women of Fire*, a festival of Latina artists; *Confessions*, a spoken-word and slide show; and ongoing work as a producer, writer, and performer with VIVA, an association of lesbian and gay Latino artists.

Palés Matos, Luis (Mar. 20, 1898, Guayama, Puerto Rico—Feb. 23, 1959, Santurce, Puerto Rico): Poet. Palés Matos' parents, Consuelo Matos and Vincente Palés Anés, were both romantic poets writing at the end of the nineteenth century. They surrounded their children with books of all sorts.

Because of debt incurred by the publication of his first book of poems, Palés Matos barely finished high school. In order to pay the debt, he was forced to work and became a self-educated man. His first two works, *Azaleas* and *Sonetos del Campo*, were published in 1915. A clear picture of his native city and early influences is found later in his unfinished novel, *El Litoral*, as well as in much of his poetry. His study of the black and mulatto dock and sugarcane workers in the coastal villages of Puerto Rico is evident in *Tuntún de pasa y grifería* (1937). His most complete collection of poetry is *Poesia 1915-1956* (1957). Palés Matos was the first Puerto Rican literary figure to achieve a broad and lasting influence on the evolution of Latin American literature, primarily through development of a poetic style inspired by the rhythms and sounds of African language and music of the Caribbean.

Paleta: Ice cream or fruit-flavored ice on a stick. A *paleta* is street food, usually purchased from a mobile vendor with an ice box on a bicycle or a hand cart. The *paleta* is any cold sweet on a stick, including ice cream and frozen fruit-flavored ices. The equivalent term in Puerto Rico is *limbel*.

Palmieri, Carlos Manuel "Charlie" (Nov. 21, 1927, Manhattan, N.Y.—Sept. 12, 1988, Bronx, N.Y.): Pianist, bandleader, and composer. Born to Puerto Rican parents, Palmieri and his brother Eddie grew up in the Bronx. Palmieri was musically gifted, with a perfect ear, and at an early age he could play any tune at the piano. He later went to the Juilliard School of Music in

A street vendor sells paletas *in downtown Los Angeles.* (Impact Visuals, Tom McKitterick)

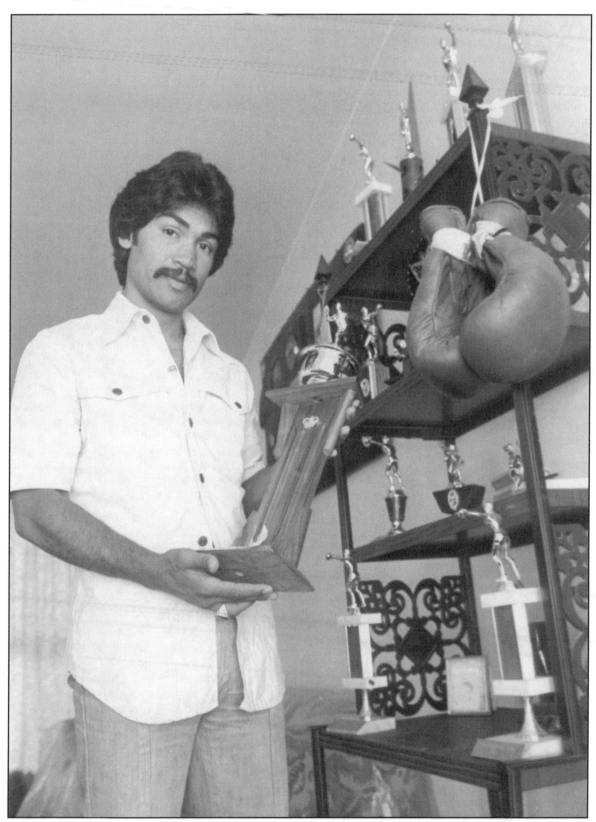

Carlos Palomino with some of his awards for boxing. (AP/Wide World Photos)

Manhattan. Between 1940 and the early 1950's, he played the piano and recorded with Rafael Muñoz, Pupi Campo, Xavier CUGAT, Tito PUENTE, and Vicentico Valdés, as well as with the Orquesta Ritmo Tropical, La Playa Sextet, and Conjunto Pin Pin.

Palmieri was influential among Latino musicians and contributed to the birth of SALSA. His first recording was "Let's Dance La Charanga!," which was followed by "Pachanga at the Caravana Club," "Viva Alegre," "Salsa Na' Ma for Alegre," and the legendary Cuban Jam Session albums, which included *El Gigante del Teclado*, *Vuelve el Gigante*, and *Adelante, Gigante*. Palmieri died of a heart attack at the age of sixty.

Palomino, Carlos (b. Aug. 10, 1949, San Luis, Mexico): Boxer. Palomino, one of the top welterweights of the 1970's, won the World Boxing Council (WBC) welterweight title in 1976 with a twelve-round defeat of John Stracey. He made seven subsequent successful title defenses before losing a 1979 decision to Wilfredo Benitez. After a loss on points to Roberto DURAN, he retired with a professional record of 27 wins, 3 losses, and 3 draws.

Palomino, Ernesto Ramírez (b. Dec. 21, 1933, Fresno, Calif.): Artist. Palomino has worked as a painter, sculptor, muralist, and filmmaker. His early charcoal drawings and a few oils were done between 1947 and 1955. He attended the San Francisco Art Institute on scholarship in 1954, then attended Fresno City College in 1956, Fresno State University in 1957, and San Francisco State University from 1960 to 1965. Palomino's early sculpture incorporated "found objects," and his master's thesis project at San Francisco State University was a 450-minute film titled *My Trip in a '52 Ford* that used objects as characters.

Between 1960 and 1965, Palomino concentrated on what he called GABACHO art, which used found objects and contained few references to the Chicano experience. He then worked with Luis VALDEZ of the TEATRO CAMPESINO as part of his interest in expressing Chicano points of view. Beginning in 1970, he taught in the La Raza Studies department at Fresno State University. Beginning in 1978, Palomino directed murals painted in summer programs by young people in California. He is known for his interpretations of the Chicano experience in various media and for his participation in the Chicano artistic movement in California.

Pan Americanism: The organizing spirit of Pan Americanism was born when the First International Conference of American States opened in Washington, D.C., in 1889. Its limited goal was to increase commerce among all countries of the Americas. Soon, the Commercial Bureau of the American Republics, later named the Pan American Union, became a permanent secretariat coordinating relations among members.

It was only in 1948 that something more ambitious emerged, the Organization of American States (OAS). OAS founders believed that a much wider range of inter-American issues should be overseen by a joint agency modeled after the United Nations (UN). Their concerns ranged from economic and cultural cooperation (matters of importance to the pre-1948 Pan American Union) to conflict resolution and collective security needs in the post-World War II era.

The OAS concept of collective security was aimed at preventing the obviously more powerful United States from dominating the rest of the Americas, both politically and militarily. The OAS charter thus emphasized the two-way nature of national security arrangements. In return for OAS members' general commitment to support U.S. leadership in the wider sphere of international relations, Washington would temper its role in Pan American conflicts.

By 1960, Pan Americanism appeared to be working. A number of disputes had been resolved through the auspices of the OAS, and its original goals were expanded to include shared economic and social development projects through a new Inter-American Development Bank. Despite obvious barriers to full agreement on U.S. sponsorship for wider Pan Americanism (which included Fidel Castro's Cuba), President John F. Kennedy won acceptance in 1961 of a new Charter of Punta del Este. This became the keystone for what he called the ALLIANCE FOR PROGRESS, based on economic aid.

In 1965, U.S. intervention in the Dominican Republic cooled Alliance for Progress presumptions of separation between politics and economic aid. Meanwhile, the 1969 American Convention on Human Rights called for an Inter-American Court on Human Rights. By the time this court was finally created in 1979, Pan Americanism was facing a turning point.

The decline in Pan American cooperation after the 1970's may have been sparked by Latin American perceptions of renewed U.S. determination to impose its political preferences in the Americas. Even before the 1983 U.S. invasion of Grenada and the 1989 ouster of General Manuel Noriega from Panama, Latin American-initiated alternatives to the historical Pan American model were being explored. The original

U.S. soldiers guard a food distribution center during the 1965 intervention in the Dominican Republic. (National Archives)

Rio Group (formed in 1983 at Contadora, Panama) could not successfully mediate Central American disputes without calling on the United States. Reorganized in 1986 as a forum for political consultation among nearly all South and Central American foreign ministries, the Rio Group entered the 1990's with plans for annual summit meetings. It also continued to serve as an independent caucus in larger international bodies in which the United States holds important, if not dominant, positions, such as the UN and the OAS.

Pan dulce: Mexican sweet roll. Mexican people as a rule love sweet rolls, and *panaderías* sell a large variety of them. Sweet rolls take on fanciful shapes and even more fanciful names, such as *besos* (kisses), *bigotes* (mustaches), and *monjas* (nuns). Many are topped with sugar, sesame seeds, or candied fruit, and some are made with yams, pumpkins, or other sweet vegetables. By non-Latino standards, many *panes dulces* are extremely sweet. One category of *pan dulce*, *pan de muertos*, is reserved for use on DÍA DE LOS MUERTOS (Day of the Dead). These sweet breads are decorated with representations of bones and skulls, reminding the living of their link to the dead. In parts of Oaxaca, the entire loaf is human shaped. In parts of West Mexico, *panes de muertos* depict *monos*, spirit beings that also are represented in the famous pictographs of Baja California. These *panes de muertos* are placed on home ALTARS during the Day of the Dead and may be taken to a cemetery for the nightlong celebration there.

Pantoja, Antonia (b. 1922, San Juan, Puerto Rico): Educator and administrator. Pantoja is known as a cofounder of ASPIRA and as the first president of the Universidad Boricua, which in 1973 became the first bilingual institution of higher learning to be established and controlled by Puerto Rican scholars.

Pantoja began work as a teacher in Puerto Rico after completing a two-year program at the University of Puerto Rico. Seeking to provide her family with a better economic life, she moved to New York, New York, in 1943 and took a factory job. She soon became involved in organizing workers to obtain better conditions. After earning a bachelor's degree in pre-social work from Hunter College of the City University of New York, she received a fellowship to attend Columbia University's School of Social Work.

Pantoja earned her master's degree in 1954 and worked for several years as supervisor of the adult division of a summer camp and as director of the Community Relations Division of the City of New York's Commission of Intergroup Relations. In 1958, Pantoja and several others organized the Puerto Rican Forum, Inc., an agency for business and career development for Puerto Ricans in New York City. That work led to the 1961 founding of ASPIRA, which promotes higher education for Puerto Ricans. While working with these groups, Pantoja also taught at Columbia University.

Pantoja returned to Puerto Rico in 1968 because of her asthma. She taught at the University of Puerto Rico and established ASPIRA clubs in that country. She returned to the United States in 1970 and soon secured funds to establish the Universidad Boricua and Puerto Rican Research and Resource Center in Washington, D.C. Her worsening asthma resulted in a move to San Diego, California, where she taught social policy and community development at San Diego State University. She founded, with Wilhelmina Perry, the Graduate School for Community Development, serving as its president. Pantoja returned to Puerto Rico in the mid-1980's and helped to develop Producir, Inc., a group that promotes self-sufficiency by creating jobs.

Paoli family: Antonio Paoli, a Puerto Rican vocal artist, acquired an international reputation during his operatic career. He and his elder sister Amalia captured the attention of Puerto Rican audiences and established a tradition of vocal excellence that extended for three generations.

Amalia Paoli was born on January 31, 1861, in Ponce, Puerto Rico, where she began to study the piano with Catalonian teacher José Forns and voice with Puerto Rican lyric soprano Isabel "Lizzie" Spence Graham. Her brother Antonio was also born in Ponce, on April 14, 1871.

Under the auspices of the Spanish government, Amalia and Antonio moved to Madrid in 1885 to pursue their studies. Amalia studied voice while Antonio pursued his regular school diploma. Puerto Rican statesman Julio Vizcarrondo, then resident in Madrid, arranged for Amalia to audition for the princess Doña Isabel. Amalia obtained a scholarship to study voice under well-known baritone Napoleón Vergez. Amalia started her voice lessons while Antonio attended sec-

ondary school as an intern in the monastery at the Escorial.

Amalia made her operatic debut at the Teatro Real de Madrid in 1891, in the opera *Aida*. She received favorable reviews from local music critics. Two years later, she had a successful operatic performance at the Teatro Manzoni in Milan, in Gaetano Donizetti's opera *La Favorita*.

In 1892, Antonio, back in Spain, started his studies for a military career. In 1895, Amalia's former voice teacher discovered her brother's impressive tenor voice and summoned her back to Spain. Vergez asked Amalia to assist and guide her younger brother's musical future.

Antonio soon also obtained a government scholarship, and in 1897 he moved with his sister to Italy for further voice studies. Within about two years he had finished his professional training. His impressive operatic debut came at the Paris Opera in 1899, in the role of Arnold in Gioacchino Rossini's opera *Guillaume Tell*. During his early career, he adopted the name Ermogene Imleghi Bascarán.

Antonio went to London for the 1900-1901 season at the Opera at Covent Garden. In 1901, he toured Puerto Rico, Cuba, and the United States. He has to his credit the first complete recorded version of the leading role of Canio in the opera *I Pagliacci* by Ruggero Leoncavallo (1907).

Antonio sang regularly in Central and South America, Europe, and Russia. His career reached a peak between 1908 and 1914 and slowed after World War I. In 1916, he moved with his family to London. In order to maintain his excellent physical condition, he tried a boxing career, but after a few fights he lost his voice and gave up the sport. After a year of intense studies and vocal exercises, he recovered his vocal powers and returned to the stage. He continued singing until 1928, when he retired to a teaching position at the University of Puerto Rico, after a last performance of his greatest role as Othello, with a visiting touring opera company from New York.

During his illustrious career, Paoli sang Othello in 570 performances and sang Manrico in *Il Trovatore* more than four hundred times.

Papaya: Tropical fruit native to the Caribbean and widely used in Latin America. It is not known when the papaya was first used in pre-Columbian America, but it had arrived in Peru by around 800 C.E., and it doubtless was eaten well before that in the Caribbean. Papayas can be boiled or baked as a vegetable when underripe, tasting much like a sweet squash, and the ripe fruit can be eaten raw or cooked as a dessert. The leaves also are edible as a cooked green, resembling dandelion greens. Papaya leaves and fruit contain papain, an enzyme that tenderizes meat, and they were used for this purpose in pre-Columbian Mexico.

Paque: Traditional Mexican confection. Also known as *pacle*, *paque* is a traditional confection prepared in the Mexican states of Tabasco, Veracruz, and Chiapas from the fruit of the *guapaque* tree and unrefined brown sugar. The fruit's tangy flavor is similar to that of tamarind. The name of the tree comes from the Aztec word *uapactle*. The *guapaque* is appreciated not only for its fruit but also for its fine, compact, hard, and weather-resistant wood, which is excellent for use in railroad track crossties and electrical poles. Its bark yields tanning and dyeing material.

Pardo, Jorge (b. 1951, Havana, Cuba): Sculptor. Pardo immigrated to the United States as a child, with his parents. His 1991 show in St. Petersburg, Florida, featured utilitarian objects altered in craftsmanlike ways, including a sofa and a chair made with copper tubing. Pardo often uses "found objects" in his works, such as *A Skateboard Ramp* and *Six Bank of America Counters, Altadena Calif.* He says that his work is influenced by French artist Marcel Duchamp. Much of his work consists of transformations of everyday and "found" objects into artworks that are aesthetically pleasing but no longer useful.

Paredes, Américo (b. Sept. 3, 1915, Brownsville, Tex.): Folklorist, educator, and writer. As a folklorist, Paredes served as editor of the *Journal of American Folklore* and the book *Folktales of Mexico* (1970), among others. Much of his work studies the folklorization of historic events. He has also written on folk music, with this work including his best-known publication, *"With His Pistol in His Hand": A Border Ballad and Its Hero* (1958), which concerns the ballad of Gregorio CORTEZ. His other publications include *George Washington Gómez: A Mexicotexan Novel* (1990) and *Between Two Worlds* (1991). His work brought scholarly attention to border culture, and he helped inspire the Chicano movement. Along with George I. SÁNCHEZ, he founded the University of Texas Mexican American studies program.

Paredes completed his A.A. at Brownsville Junior College in 1936. He began contributing poems to the weekly literary supplement to San Antonio's *La Prensa*

at about that time, publishing his first collection of poetry, *Cantos de adolescencia*, in 1937. Paredes entered the U.S. Army in 1944 and wrote for the military newspaper *Stars and Stripes*. He returned to Texas in 1950 to pursue his goal of becoming a professor of English. He earned his B.A. in 1951 from the University of Texas at Austin, then received his M.A. in 1953 and Ph.D. in 1956. After teaching at the University of Texas at El Paso, he joined the faculty of the University of Texas at Austin in 1951, teaching folklore and creative writing. He was director of the Folklore Center from 1957 to 1970, when he was named director of the Mexican American studies program.

Parentesco: Support relationship. *Parentesco* refers to a relationship between Latinos that offers kinship sentiment to kin or nonkin. In some Latin countries, the term is used only to signify relationships with family members and godparents, but in the United States and Canada, the term has been extended to include nonfamily individuals. People who have emigrated from the same city or region sometimes extend *parentesco* to one another in the form of friendship, monetary aid, and other support services. The social, cultural, and economic support system is particularly important if no relatives live nearby.

Parochial schools: Although the vast majority of Latinos are Roman Catholics, a relatively small proportion attend Catholic schools. They are, however, becoming an increasingly large and influential group within those organizations.

Catholic schools have existed in the United States since colonial times. The major reason for this was that until the 1963 federal ban on prayer in schools, religion played a large role in the public school system. In a country that was overwhelmingly Protestant, the prayers recited and the lessons taught were almost always of that religion.

It has been estimated that as of the early 1990's, approximately 70 to 80 percent of Latinos were Roman Catholics. About 20 percent of Latinos attended Catholic schools. The figure may seem low. One reason that Latinos do not send their children to parochial schools is economic. Latinos, statistically, are among the poorest people in the United States, and Catholic schools are relatively expensive. Some federal aid is provided to parochial schools, but never for religious materials, which form a significant part of the schools' costs. In addition, at least until the 1970's, most parochial schools taught in English. This was also true of

The parentesco *relationship in its broadest form can include support offered through networking, business, and social organizations.* (Martin Hutner)

Parochial schools may offer options of integration, curriculum, and discipline unavailable in public schools. (James Shaffer)

public schools, but the education provided there was free.

Latinos make up an increasingly large proportion of American Catholics, and the Catholic church, if it is to continue its school system, will have to adapt to this population. There are more Spanish-speaking teachers, and government funds are available to institute bilingual programs. Parents are becoming more likely to send their children to Catholic schools if they are affordable.

A number of positive influences, apart from religion, may exist in Catholic schools. Despite government attempts at integration, most children still go to neighborhood schools, and for Latino children, these neighborhoods are rarely integrated. Catholic schools are not run by the government, however, and they accept students of many nationalities, allowing parents to choose integrated schools. Catholic schools historically have had harsher disciplinary standards than have public schools. Urban families who face violence, drug addiction, and other criminal activities in daily life may see a stronger disciplinary environment

as beneficial. Evaluation of the relative benefits of bilingual Catholic schools and bilingual public schools will have to wait until the first generation of students educated in these schools reaches adulthood.

Parra, Catalina (b. Chile): Collage artist. Parra is the daughter of Chilean poet Nicanor Parra. She has lived in Germany and the United States.

Parra is known for her multimedia visual/word plays on advertising signs, such as *Plea-Sure* (1987), which examines the wording of cigarette ads. Parra directs her work toward a personal message rather than a mass media one. She speaks of her work as being as explicit as auditory language, but with different codes. Some of her works address the emotions brought on by the AIDS epidemic and by different kinds of victimization, as in her collage *Who's Next*. She and her father collaborated on a video to be shown on the Times Square light board in New York City. As in the video *USA Where Liberty Is a Statue*, Parra's works frequently deal with the concepts of freedom and democracy.

Parrandas: All-night parties. *Parrandas* are parties to celebrate a personal success such as a promotion, the purchase of a house, or a graduation. They are held in the house of the sponsor, who provides food, drink, and music for dancing. The food includes heavy snacks, since the party is to last until dawn. *Parrandas* of this sort are sponsored mostly by middle-class people from towns and cities. In some parts of the United States and Mexico, the term refers to a night of bar-hopping by young men, known as *parranderos*.

Parsons, Lucía. *See* **González Parsons, Lucía**

Parteras: Midwives. *Parteras* are a traditional part of Latino childbirth in the American Southwest. Midwives are trained to assist mothers in giving natural childbirth, which usually takes place at the mother's home. *Parteras* learn by apprenticing with an experienced midwife; knowledge is thus passed from generation to generation. The *partera* gets to know the mother during her pregnancy and eventually guides her through childbirth. She also encourages the woman's husband to participate in the birth. Many women choose to experience childbirth with the assistance of a *partera* so that the birth will take place in familiar surroundings. Many women find comforting the presence of another Spanish-speaking woman whom they know personally.

Partido: Livestock rental contract between the landless peasantry and the owners of animals on the Mexican frontier. In a *partido*, the owner of animals (mostly sheep) would loan them out for a set number of years, expecting in return that the herd would be increased by a certain amount yearly. Whatever surplus remained after the owner's conditions had been satisfied became the *partidario*, the caretaker's income. Profits and risks were always inequitably distributed, with the practice rarely producing more than a subsistence income for the borrower. In essence, this amounted to a sharecropping system for SHEEPHERDING on the Mexican frontier.

Partido Autonomista: Puerto Rican political party. While Puerto Rico was still governed by Spain, the issue of autonomy from European rule provoked intense feelings. Out of the heated debates came the establishment of the Partido Autonomista at an assembly that took place in Ponce, Puerto Rico, on March 10, 1887.

Román BALDORIOTY DE CASTRO was the founder and first president of this political party. The existing Liberal Party was divided and disorganized as a result of events in Spain and in Puerto Rico. Baldorioty de Castro was able to unite people behind the concept of self-rule under the banner of the Partido Autonomista.

The party platform and the type of government proposed by Baldorioty de Castro was known as the Plan of Ponce. Harassment by his political opponents and internal divisions within the party over strategy and ideology left many supporters disillusioned. Baldorioty de Castro's death in 1889 deprived the party of leadership, and it soon dissolved.

Partido Estadista Republicano (PER): Political party. The PER was a conservative, pro-statehood political party in Puerto Rico. It underwent several changes but remained a staunchly conservative force for U.S. statehood, contrary to many parties that advocated independence from the United States. José Celso BARBOSA is credited with founding the Partido Republicano in 1900, and Miguel Angel García was also an early leader. In 1932, the organization underwent its first modification to become the Unión Republicano. In 1948, it evolved into the Partido Estadista Republicano. The party is now obsolete because most of its leadership was absorbed by the New Progressive Party, which emerged in 1968.

Partido Independentista Puertorriqueño (PIP): Political party. The PIP was founded in 1946 by staunch, uncompromising *independentistas* (advocates of independence from the United States for Puerto Rico) within Luis MUÑOZ MARÍN's Popular Democratic Party (*see* PARTIDO POPULAR DEMOCRÁTICO). Many of the original members of the Popular Democratic Party, formed in 1938, were *independentistas*.

Because Muñoz Marín played down the issue of Puerto Rico's political status, the party attracted followers from other camps. By 1946, the more stringent *independentistas* split with the Populares. The PIP's greatest electoral success occurred in 1952, when it won 19 percent of the vote. The party declined and by the early 1990's usually received less than 10 percent of the vote. Much of the decline resulted from internal dissent over the electoral process and the strategy the party pursued. A prominent leader late in the twentieth century was Rubén Berrios, a passionate intellectual who led the party's turn toward SOCIALISM.

Partido Liberal Mexicano: Political party. In 1907, Ricardo FLORES MAGÓN and his brother Enrique established El Partido Liberal Mexicano, which found support in Southern California and in the Baja Peninsula of Mexico. One of the primary activities of this political party was to organize Mexican workers in the United States.

Ricardo Flores Magón is also known as a newspaper publisher. His first publication, *Liberación*, was a newspaper circulated in Mexico that was highly critical of the government of Porfirio Díaz. The Flores Magón brothers fled persecution by Mexican secret police and found refuge in San Antonio, Texas. In 1904, they published *Regeneración*. After moving their publication further north to St. Louis, Missouri, circulation reached six thousand by 1906.

Maintaining his criticisms and observations on Mexican government excesses, Ricardo Flores Magón was forced to leave St. Louis for Los Angeles. He was later imprisoned at San Quentin for violating U.S. neutrality laws.

Partido Nacionalista de Puerto Rico: Political party. The Partido Nacionalista de Puerto Rico was founded in 1922 to promote the cause of independence for Puerto Rico from the United States. It had little effect

Pedro Albizu Campos led the Partido Nacionalista de Puerto Rico through a period of militancy. (AP/Wide World Photos)

until the 1930's, when its leadership turned to acts of violence and militancy in an effort to achieve its goal of independence.

Pedro ALBIZU CAMPOS, a popular and charismatic figure, led the party during the period of militancy. In November of 1950, nationalists Oscar COLLAZO and Griselio Torresola attempted to assassinate U.S. President Harry S Truman. Puerto Rican governor Luis MUÑOZ MARÍN was also the target of a nationalist attack. The party attempted to initiate an armed revolt throughout the island around the same time. In 1954, four members of the party—Irving Flores, Lolita LEBRÓN SOTO, Rafael CANCEL MIRANDA, and Andrés FIGUEROA CORDERO—opened fire on members of Congress as they stood on the floor of the House of Representatives.

Partido Popular Democrático (PPD): Political party. The PPD was the dominant political party in Puerto Rico from 1940 through 1968. It was founded by Luis MUÑOZ MARÍN, who became governor in 1948. The PPD effectively became the first modern political party in Puerto Rico, mobilizing masses of people and pledging to modernize the government of the island.

The PPD practically converted the political system into a one-party system, winning nearly every elective office during its three-decade reign. The party was built around its reform program of the 1940's and Muñoz Marín, an extremely popular leader. This strength, however, turned into a liability when, in 1964, Muñoz Marín attempted to transfer power. A weakened and divided party lost the 1968 election. Recovery came after the 1972 election of Rafael Hernández Colón, who pledged to reorganize both the party and the government.

Partido Revolucionario Cubano: Cuban independence organization. In 1892, José MARTÍ, known as the father of Cuban independence, founded the Partido Revolucionario Cubano in Tampa, Florida. Exiled from his homeland because of his increasingly vocal anticolonial writings, Martí found many sympathizers among the Cuban cigar manufacturers and workers who lived in Key West and Tampa.

The movement to rid Cuba of Spanish rule gained momentum in 1868 with the uprising in the small town of Lares. El GRITO DE LARES came to symbolize the independence movement. Martí was only fifteen years old then but was deeply affected by this event.

Martí also found sympathizers for Cuban independence within the growing Puerto Rican community

Protesters gathered outside a meeting in Austin, Texas, at which Bill Clinton and Carlos Salinas discussed the North American Free Trade Agreement. (Impact Visuals, Fred Chase)

in New York. He arrived there in 1885. In 1892, the Cuba-Puerto Rican Mutual Aid Society was established there, as well as the Puerto Rican section of the Partido Revolucionario Cubano.

Partido Revolucionario Institucional (PRI): Mexican political party. The PRI took power in Mexico in 1929 and maintained it by silencing dissidents and incorporating those who challenged its power. Mexico was unique among Latin American countries in officially including labor in the ruling coalition.

The inclusion of labor and peasant movements within the PRI and the formal exclusion of organized business interests were symbolic commitments to mass representation. Voter apathy and abstention made effective representation of the people suspect.

The Mexican government and the PRI faced challenges from uprisings in the southern state of Chiapas in early 1994. These uprisings and electoral reforms enacted in 1993 and 1994 shaped the elections of August, 1994, as did the NORTH AMERICAN FREE TRADE AGREEMENT, signed by Mexican president Carlos Salinas Gortari and U.S. president Bill Clinton in

1992. PRI candidate Ernesto Zedillo won election to the presidency in the first elections in which national observers were mobilized and international visitors were invited. Prior to 1994, the PRI had been accused of electoral fraud.

Pascual, Camilo Alberto (b. Jan. 20, 1934, Havana, Cuba): Baseball player. One of the top American League pitchers of the late 1950's and early 1960's, Pascual debuted with the Washington Senators in 1954. The young right-hander, nicknamed "Little Patato" (his older brother Carlos, also a major league pitcher, was "Big Patato"), struggled in his first five seasons to a 28-66 record.

Pascual turned his career around in 1959, when he developed a forceful sidearm curve and improved his control over his fastball and other pitches. That year, he posted a 17-10 record for the last-place Senators and also led the league in shutouts.

In 1961, the Senators became the Minnesota Twins. That season, Pascual led the American League in strikeouts for the first of three consecutive seasons. He also led the league in shutouts in 1961 and 1962 and

Jaco Pastorius in a 1982 performance. (AP/Wide World Photos)

broke the twenty-win mark in both 1962 and 1963. Pascual stayed with the team until a late-season trade sent him to Cincinnati in 1969.

A five-time All-Star, Pascual retired in 1971 after spending seasons with Los Angeles and Cleveland. In his eighteen-year career, he compiled a 174-170 record with a 3.63 earned run average and 2,167 strikeouts.

Pasteles: Pies and similar dishes. Although the word *pastel* usually is rendered as "pie" in English, it covers a variety of preparations. In Puerto Rico, *pasteles* are *tamal*-like dough made of mashed root vegetables and filled with savory mixtures; they are wrapped in banana leaves and steamed or boiled. Throughout the rest of Spanish-speaking Latin America, *pasteles* are usually casseroles, often with layers of soft, precooked starches (rice, MASA, or corn kernels) and savory mixtures; occasionally they are sweetened and used as desserts. In Mexico, the word also refers to true sweet cakes or other pastries. The casserole-type *pastel* is known as *pastelón* in Puerto Rico, and fried *pasteles* everywhere are known as *pastellitos*.

Pastorius, Jaco (John Francis Anthony III; Dec. 1, 1951, Norristown, Pa.—Sept. 21, 1987, Fort Lauderdale, Fla.): Bass guitarist and bandleader. When Pastorius was seven years old, his family moved to Fort Lauderdale, Florida, where his father Jack pursued a career as a drummer and singer. Pastorius first learned to play drums but then switched to bass. He also played the piano occasionally. He was an excellent and hard-working student in school.

In 1976, Pastorius attracted attention with his first recording with the group Weather Report, an album titled *Heavy Weather*. With the group, he toured the world several times.

Pastorius was a talented and flamboyant performer. He was a virtuoso, a lyrical and original instrumentalist unanimously respected by music critics. He has been associated with bands including Las Olas Brass, Jubilee Roll Band, Uptown Funk All-Stars, Soul Incorporated, and Woodchuck, and he has recorded with artists Herbie Hancock, Joni Mitchell, Pat Metheny, Albert Mangelsdorf, Ian Hunter, and Ira Sullivan.

Pastorius' first solo album, *Jaco Pastorius*, was produced by Epic records, and his second, *Word of Mouth*, was released by Warner Brothers. These albums established him as an international artist. His style, a blend of rock and roll, jazz, blues, and Caribbean flavor, made him unique among Latino musicians. He became famous for his rapid fingering technique.

Paternosto, César Pedro (b. Nov. 29, 1931, La Plata, Buenos Aires, Argentina): Multimedia artist. Paternosto won first prize at the Third Biennial American Art (1966) and was chosen to be an exhibitor in the First Havana Biennial (1984), at the Museum of Modern Art in New York, New York. His best-known work is *Recuay* (1983), a sixty-inch-square acrylic and sand on canvas. His work is in the Museum of Modern Art in New York and the National Fine Arts Museum in Argentina.

Patlán, Raymond M. (b. 1946, Chicago, Ill.): Muralist. Patlán is a Mexican American who began his art career sharing a studio with Mario Castillo, one of the earliest U.S. muralists, in Chicago's Pilsen (Little Mexico) neighborhood. In 1965, Patlán began to work at Casa Aztlán, a Pilsen community center. He started to paint and direct murals there on a volunteer basis in 1970. The mural cycle *From My Fathers and Yours* was painted from ladders, without scaffolding, over the period of a year.

Patlán has directed numerous indoor and outdoor murals, all treating the Chicano experience. He directed *Reform and Liberty* as well as *Culture in Our Community* (1971-1972), painted by forty Neighborhood Youth Corps workers. He painted *History of Mexican American Worker* (1975) with Vicente Mendoza and José Nario (who conceived the idea). Legal problems with city advertising codes resulted from their use of the emblem of the United Farm Workers. Despite being vandalized, the huge (90 feet by 18 feet) public work incorporating street language, topical icons, and pre-Columbian motifs was easily deciphered by passersby.

Patlán spent 1976 in Berkeley, California, codirecting the Chicano Mural Workshop. He started the Chicago chapter of MARCH (the Chicano Artistic Movement) and spoke at the 1976 National Murals Conference in New York. He was one of the founders of the Pilsen school of Chicano education/empowerment, a mural movement in the 1960's. (*See* MURAL ART.) He was among its most experienced muralists.

Patriarchal ideology: System of ideas, beliefs, and behaviors that gives a man power and authority over his family. The idea of a man having automatic authority over his household is rooted in the Spanish ideology that called for racial and religious purity. The substantial power of the father/husband was seen as necessary to protect the family, especially the honor of women. The subordinate role ascribed to women has been seen as compromising their equality with men.

In Spanish and other Mediterranean societies, female honor was directly related to the social-class system. Female virtue was a high priority for the aristocracy; lower classes had less stringent sexual codes for women. Patriarchal values were based on the strict division of labor between men and women as well as in parental authority (particularly the father's) over children. Fathers had great authority in selecting appropriate marriage partners for their children. To preserve the structured order of society, the Spanish church and state supported patriarchy. This ideology was taken to the New World during colonial times. In Latin America, these ideas were shaped by indigenous beliefs and standards regarding GENDER ROLES, especially among the lower socioeconomic classes made up primarily of mestizos and Indians.

The concepts of machismo and *marianismo* are social reflections of patriarchal ideology. MACHISMO ideals relate to the power, rights, and behaviors of a man in the completion of duties as sole provider of his family's support, protection, discipline, and direction. *MARIANISMO* pertains to the expectation that Latinas use the VIRGIN MARY as a standard and role model. Women are honored and respected within the family because

Latino children are learning standards for behavior different from those of their parents. (James Shaffer)

of their influence in educating, forming, and guiding their children. They were traditionally free of responsibilities outside the home and had freedom within it.

In Latino communities in the United States, traditional patriarchal ideals and rigid gender roles have been undergoing important changes. Economic necessity has forced many women to leave their homes and join the work force to help support their families. As a result, traditional expectations regarding men's and women's roles were modified, although a double standard remained regarding sexual mores for men and women. Men are expected to be sexually experienced before marriage. Maleness is achieved in part by engaging in sexual activity, and there is a perception that men are unable to control themselves sexually. As a result, it is up to the woman to maintain proper sexual standards. Female premarital virginity and sexual innocence are highly valued. Among lower-income Latinos, sexual standards are not as rigid, and common-law unions and out-of-wedlock births are not uncommon.

The influence of patriarchal ideology is also evident in the political, professional, and business fields. Despite advances in education and experience, Latinas are often seen as helpmates to their male peers. During the CHICANO MOVEMENT, for example, it was argued that because of traditional ideas regarding gender roles, Latinos would not respond to women as leaders. Chicanas, it was thought, would better serve the cause by filling supportive roles. Increasing numbers of Latinas in the professions, academia, politics, and business are providing a unique voice that is slowly changing traditional patriarchal ideology.

Patrón-peón system: In nineteenth century Mexico, a landholding and social organizational system known as the hacienda (large rural estate) emerged. Estates encompassed huge amounts of land. One such enterprise in Chihuahua was as large as Costa Rica. One hacienda in Hidalgo had ninety miles of Central Railroad tracks pass through it; three haciendas stretched 180 miles between Saltillo and Zacatecas.

Nearly all haciendas were created through expropriations of land, on the theory that previous Spanish royal territories were held by people who had no title to them. Lands were taken from Indians on the grounds that Indians were unfit to control the land. Plantations owned by the Jesuit order after it was expelled from Mexico in 1767 were expropriated, as were lands of the Inquisition in 1813. Secular lay brothers' properties and other church lands were expropriated by the Benito Juárez regime in 1856.

The Porfirio Díaz regime used the HACIENDA SYSTEM to accelerate the country's move toward "progress." Thus, hacienda titles, including ownership of the inhabitants therein, were mostly granted or sold to favored supporters who became the new class of landholders called HACENDADOS (later known as *patróns*). The *hacendados* had complete control of the sparsely settled lands but had no obligations to the inhabitants or to later settlers. Thus, the domination that a private individual (the *patrón*) had over the land, with no legal responsibility to those who lived on it or sought to make a living from it, became the political, economic, and social system of the nineteenth century Mexican hacienda. The *patrón* had a labor source he could use however he saw fit. The resident laborers (*peónes*) were generally unable to go elsewhere, so they found every aspect of their lives subordinated to the *patrón*'s will. The *peónes* lacked the power to determine how they worked, where they lived, or how they prayed. The *patrón* decided all, even down to the services of a priest. The *patrón* paid with tokens cashable at the hacienda store (*tienda de raya*), where prices were typically too high for the *peónes* to pay. Credit was granted, and the *peón* and his children were thus forced to exist in perpetual debt bondage. The hacienda system came to an end in the cataclysm of the 1910 MEXICAN REVOLUTION.

Paz, Octavio (b. Mar. 31, 1914, Mexico City, Mexico): Writer. Both of Paz's grandfathers were well-known writers. His father, Octavio Paz, was a lawyer, diplomat, and journalist who represented Emiliano Zapata in the United States in 1916 and was one of the initiators of agrarian reform. His mother, Josefina Lozano, of Andalusian parents, was born in Mexico.

Paz was first educated in a French school run by Marist Brothers. He later transferred to an English school, then later to public schools. His father had a good library, and Paz read extensively. In 1933, he published his first book of poems, *Luna silvestre*. He began editing several literary magazines and in 1937 was invited by poet Pablo Neruda to come to Spain to the Second Antifascist Writers Congress. In Paris and then in Spain, Paz met many famous writers who influenced his own work.

Paz's major books of poetry and essays in English include *The Labyrinth of Solitude: Life and Thought in Mexico* (1961), *Collected Poems, 1957-1987* (1987), and *The Other Voice: Essays on Modern Poetry* (1991). Much of his work was first published in Spanish. His many awards and honors include the Nobel

Octavio Paz at the Metropolitan Museum of Art in New York City, prior to an evening honoring him. (AP/Wide World Photos)

Prize in Literature in 1990. Paz's influential work is concerned with the meaning of history, the predicament of modern man, and the significance of language.

Peanuts: Leguminous seeds used as nuts. Peanuts are native to South America, probably originating in Brazil. They were cultivated in Peru at least by 1100 C.E., and the Aztecs knew and used them by the sixteenth century arrival of Hernán Cortés. Peanuts have been incorporated into Mexican and Central American cuisines, roasted and salted as street snacks and ground as thickeners, but they are most prominent in Brazil. There, they flavor and thicken main dishes, as in *ximxim de galinha*; they also serve as snacks and even as flavoring for drinks, such as *batida de amendoim*. Peanuts are known as *cacahuete* in most of Latin America, as *cacahuate* in Mexico, as *maní* in Cuba, and as *amendoim* in Brazil.

Pearl Meadows Mushroom Farm, Inc. v. Alan Nelson (Aug. 24, 1989): Workplace litigation. The United States District Court for the Northern District of California heard this case (number C 82-1896 RPA). Pearl Meadows Mushroom Farm and four other employers sued to protest against workplace raids carried out under the authorization of Alan Nelson, commissioner of the IMMIGRATION AND NATURALIZATION SERVICE (INS). District Judge Aguilar found merit in employer and employee claims that the INS abused Hispanic workers and violated the Fourth Amendment.

This case resulted from a continuing pattern of problems with the INS experienced by California employers and their Hispanic workers. The plaintiffs obtained a preliminary injunction against workplace raids in 1985.

After hearing the plaintiffs' complaint against workplace searches and arrests directed against Hispanic workers, Aguilar refused a request by the INS to dismiss the complaint. He believed that the plaintiff companies and named Hispanic workers had the necessary legal standing to sue the INS.

Aguilar also concluded that the plaintiffs had demonstrated the following points. Actions had been directed against Hispanic workers without any cause to believe that they were undocumented aliens and based solely on their racial origin. The INS had used unreasonable force in detaining and arresting workers. The INS had shown a pattern of using constitutionally defective search warrants. The INS entered workplaces owned and operated by the five plaintiff companies without consent or with defective consent. The INS had detained entire work forces, without probable cause or reasonable suspicion to justify the action, by blocking both the entrances and exits to plants owned by the plaintiff companies. Unjustified warrantless arrests had taken place. Workers had been targeted by the INS because of their Hispanic appearance rather than because of any reasonable suspicion that they were illegal aliens. The INS had engaged in a pattern of repeated verbal and physical abuse directed against Hispanic workers. Finally, INS treatment of non-Hispanic workers was significantly different from treatment of Hispanic workers.

This decision discussed many crucial Fourth Amendment issues with implications far beyond the Hispanic community. The key Fourth Amendment issues in this case related to reasonable commercial expectations of privacy.

Skylark Nursery received court support for its view that the INS had violated its rights by entering areas of the business where public access was restricted. The court would have permitted a visual or aerial search, but it condemned the INS's entry into the protected portion of this workplace without a warrant and without consent.

Petaluma Mushroom Farm successfully contended that its reasonable expectations of privacy were violated. At this company, immigration officers crossed a concrete slab that surrounded company buildings and was used as a storage area.

Overall, the case highlighted the need to enforce the constitutional rights of Hispanic workers and their employers against dubious workplace search tactics of the INS.

Pecan Shellers' Strike (1938): Labor disruption. The Texas pecan industry, from its inception in the late nineteenth century, relied heavily on Mexican and Mexican American workers to gather, crack, and shell nuts. Much of the work was done from home, but many workers toiled in poorly lit and poorly ventilated factories. By the mid-1930's, the average wage for a pecan sheller in San Antonio was two dollars a week. Changes in labor law failed to help pecan workers because the pecan industry rejected codes set by the National Recovery Administration.

These conditions led to the formation of several labor unions by 1937. The unions represented ten to twelve thousand workers. In January, 1938, industry leaders announced a 15 percent wage cut, setting off a wave of strikes. Emma TENAYUCA was one of the powerful leaders of the strike movement.

Authorities treated the strike as a riot, arresting sixteen hundred workers. Conservative groups, including the League of United Latin American Citizens, failed to support the strike, which was perceived by some to be inspired by communism. The strike was settled in March, when arbitration gave the workers union recognition and a wage cut of 7.5 percent. The agreement was made obsolete in October by passage of the FAIR LABOR STANDARDS ACT, which set a minimum wage of twenty-five cents per hour. This increase in wages encouraged mechanization within the industry. Jobs disappeared quickly, and the union collapsed following World War II.

Pedreira, Antonio S. (June 13, 1898, San Juan, Puerto Rico—Oct. 23, 1939, San Juan, Puerto Rico): Literary critic, biographer, and essayist. Pedreira took his normal school degree in 1920 in teaching and his B.A. in 1923, both at the University of Puerto Rico. He earned an M.A. from Columbia University in New York in 1926. Six years later, he earned a Ph.D. in philosophy and letters at Madrid University.

After having taught Spanish language and literature at the University of Puerto Rico from 1921 to 1925, he lectured at Columbia University and at the Brookings Institution. He returned to the University of Puerto Rico in 1927 to establish and chair a department of Hispanic studies; he held the chair until his death. He also headed the university's Social Research Center and was co-founder of the influential cultural journal *Indice*.

Pedreira's biographies include *Un hombre del pueblo: José Celso Barbosa* (1937) and *Hostos, cuidadano de América* (1932). Among his numerous volumes of essays are *Insularismo: Ensayo de interpretación puertorriqueña* (1934), which analyzes the root causes of events in Puerto Rican history, and *La actualidad del jíbaro* (1935). Pedreira's bibliographies, biographies, and essays have contributed significantly to a greater understanding of the literature and national history of Puerto Rico.

Pelé (Edson Arantes do Nascimento; b. Oct. 23, 1940, Três Coraçoes, Brazil): Soccer player. Born into a poor Brazilian family, Pelé rose to achieve universal recognition as one of the world's premier soccer players. Making his professional debut with the Santos club in 1956, fifteen-year-old Pelé gained a reputation as a goal scorer. At the age of seventeen, he was selected to play for the Brazilian national team; a year later, he scored six goals in the World Cup tournament to help the country to its first international championship. Brazil also captured the World Cup in 1962 and 1970, although injuries kept Pelé from most of the 1962 competition.

International acclaim brought numerous offers from foreign clubs. To keep Pelé in Brazil, the nation's congress declared him a national treasure, an act that forbade his sale or trade. With Pelé, the Santos club shone throughout the 1960's, winning several major competitions.

By 1969, Pelé had scored more than one thousand career goals, adding his name to the record books as the third player to do so. A year later, he left the national team, and he announced his retirement in 1974. In 1975, however, he was lured out of retirement by a multimillion-dollar contract offer from the New York Cosmos of the fledgling North American Soccer League (NASL). As the NASL's biggest star, Pelé did much to popularize the sport in the United States before retiring permanently from competitive play in 1977.

A small man, standing 5 feet 8 inches and weighing 150 pounds, Pelé used his tremendous natural talent to make soccer an art. Fans flocked to see the star's

Pelé, the grand marshal of the 1981 Hispanic Day Parade in New York City, shakes hands with a young soccer player.
(Odette Lupis)

remarkable head shots and bicycle kick, and his skills and popularity earned him the 1973 Latin American Player of the Year Award. When he retired, he held world records for hat tricks (92) and international goals (92), and his career goal count (1,280) is the second highest of all time.

Pelli, Cesar (b. Oct. 12, 1926, Tucuman, Argentina): Architect. Pelli designed the Museum of Modern Art building (MOMA) in New York City. The MOMA building is considered to be one of the most innovative museums in the world. Pelli was also one of the first architects to use glass for nonstructural outer walls. Along with being a practicing architect, he was dean of the School of Architecture at Yale University from 1977 to 1984.

Peña, Amado Maurilio, Jr. (b. Oct. 1, 1943, Laredo, Tex.): Painter. Peña was born and reared in "the Valley," a southern Texas area heavily populated and influenced by Mexican Americans. He earned a B.A. in art and sociology (1965) and an M.A. (1971) from Texas Arts and Industries University. He began teaching high school in 1965, and in 1973 he moved to Austin, Texas, to work as a high-school teacher and print instructor.

Peña's early paintings are based on figures and objects, and they are painted in intense colors. During the 1960's, Peña participated in the CHICANO MOVEMENT, choosing militant topics. He spent some time in CRYSTAL CITY, TEXAS, working as an art consultant and teacher and becoming active in Chicano activism. He also began working on naïve drawings and prints.

Peña is particularly known for the use of metallic paints and gold inks and for acrylic paints on masonite and canvas. His later works deal with Native American life from Santa Fe, New Mexico, where he spent his summers. One of his best-known works is *La Raza* (1974).

Peña, Elizabeth (b. Sept. 23, 1959, Elizabeth, N.J.): Actress. Peña's family moved to Cuba when she was four months old but returned to the United States in 1968. Her father Mario was an actor, writer, director, and founder of the Latin American Theater Ensemble. Influenced by her father's involvement in the theater, Peña attended New York City's High School for the Performing Arts. On stage, she has appeared in *Blood Wedding* at New York's Public Theater, *Italian-American Reconciliation* in Los Angeles, and *Antigone* in San Francisco.

Peña made her major film debut in 1979 in *The Super*. She gained notoriety as the live-in maid Carmen in the hit 1985 comedy *Down and Out in Beverly Hills* and as Ritchie VALENS' abused sister-in-law in the 1987 film *La Bamba*. Peña's other films include *Times Square* (1980), *They All Laughed* (1981), *Crossover Dreams* (1984), *Batteries Not Included* (1987), *Vibes* (1988), *Blue Steel* (1989), *Jacob's Ladder* (1990), and *The Waterdance* (1992). On television, Peña has appeared in such diverse series as *One Life To Live*, *Tough Cookies*, *Shannon's Deal*, *Saturday Night Live*, *Hill Street Blues*, *Cagney and Lacey*, and *Crime and Punishment*. She starred in the television film *Drug Wars: The Camarena Story*.

Elizabeth Peña starred in the television series I Married Dora, *in which her character marries her employer to avoid deportation.* (AP/Wide World Photos)

Federico Peña chats with a family while touring the New York City subway system. (AP/Wide World Photos)

Peña, Federico (b. Mar. 15, 1947, Laredo, Tex.): Public official. Peña was reared and educated in Brownsville, Texas. He attended the University of Texas at Austin, where he was awarded undergraduate and law degrees.

At the age of thirty-six, Peña was elected mayor of Denver, Colorado. His efforts to strengthen and augment the local economy brought him into the national spotlight. Peña's economic programs caught the attention of Bill Clinton in 1992 as the president-elect scoured the nation for talent, particularly in the area of local economic development.

Clinton named Peña as the U.S. secretary of transportation. Peña actively pursued congressional votes on the president's economic package and the NORTH AMERICAN FREE TRADE AGREEMENT. Peña's efforts to redirect assets to improve the nation's transportation system received acclaim.

Peña, Tony (Antonio Francesco Peña y Padilla; b. June 4, 1957, Monte Cristi, Dominican Republic): Baseball player. Peña, a six-foot-tall catcher with a powerful throwing arm, made his major league debut with the Pittsburgh Pirates in 1980. In six full seasons with the Pirates, Peña received four All-Star nominations and won three consecutive Gold Glove Awards. A line-drive hitter with medium-range power, he hit .301 with fifteen home runs in 1983.

In 1987, Peña was traded to the St. Louis Cardinals; that year, he played for the Cardinals' National League pennant winners and batted .409 in St. Louis' World Series loss to the Minnesota Twins. In 1989, he was again named to the National League All-Star team; after the season, he signed as a free agent with the Boston Red Sox. In 1991, he won another Gold Glove Award while playing for Boston. In 1994, he signed as a free agent with the Cleveland Indians.

Penitentes: From early Christian times, penance has formed a central part of the Roman Catholic religion; it is one of the seven sacraments that church members may receive. During the reign of Isabella and Ferdinand, the Catholic monarchs of Spain, public demonstrations of penance were frequent and were used to deflect the suspicions of the Inquisition, which spread to the Americas in the fifteenth and sixteenth centuries. Penitents often selected their own punishment, but

Catcher Tony Peña tries to beat Baltimore Orioles batter Mike Devereaux to first base with his throw. (AP/Wide World Photos)

A Penitente group in New Mexico, around 1910. (Museum of New Mexico)

powerful judges and confessors of the church frequently decided upon penances.

Individual acts of penance, such as wearing coarse clothing (hair shirts or burlap), fasting, conducting vigils in damp, unheated churches, praying without sleep for long periods of time, and denying oneself luxuries, were considered ways to gain forgiveness of sins or signs of humility and sorrow well into the nineteenth century. The works of the greatest mystic writers of medieval Spain, Santa Teresa de Jesús and San Juan de la Cruz, contain examples of penances that believers practiced to become nearer to the medieval God.

In Mexico, the seventeenth century nun Sor Juana Inés de la CRUZ was the most brilliant writer of the colonial period. In writing about herself as a penitent, she told of denials of favorite foods and of cutting her hair as self-punishment for wrongs she believed she had committed. For the "sin" of correcting wrong ideas from a bishop's sermon, Sor Juana was ordered to sell her library, the best collection in the Americas, and spend the money on cholera victims of a Mexico City epidemic. Sor Juana completed this penance and nursed the sick until she fell victim to cholera and died.

Penitent religious individuals in Spain and the Americas say extra prayers or attend extra church services. Acts of public penance continue in the twentieth century during Holy Week and during other festivals of religious or historic importance. Statues of virgins and saints are carried through the streets in processions in the cities of the entire Spanish-speaking world. Such processions are important rituals for penitents. The women of the church dress the statues and adorn the platforms with flowers, and the men of the *confradía* (brotherhood) carry the decorated platforms through the streets as a public penance. The women and children follow the procession singing hymns and carrying palm, flowers, or lighted candles. In some smaller towns, one person is assigned to carry a cross in the Good Friday procession as a representative of the Christ figure.

The name "Penitentes" is also commonly applied to the religious order of the Brothers of Our Father Jesus Nazarite. The Penitentes, an organization of a few thousand members located primarily in New Mexico and Colorado, originated in the late eighteenth or early nineteenth century. The group earned its name from public processions in which members would perform various acts of ritual penitence. Following the expansion of Anglo culture into the region in the nineteenth and twentieth centuries, the order helped to preserve Hispanic cultural traditions in the area.

Perales, Alonso S. (1899, Alice, Tex.—May 9, 1960): Civil rights activist and lawyer. Perales faced poverty during his youth. After high school, he served in the

U.S. armed forces during World War I. At the same time, he started discussions with other Tejanos about founding an organization committed to championing the civil rights and welfare of Mexican Americans. These discussions culminated in the creation of the Order of SONS OF AMERICA (1921) and the League of Latin American Citizens (1927). Eventually these groups combined in 1929 as the LEAGUE OF UNITED LATIN AMERICAN CITIZENS (LULAC).

Perales was a leading figure in the growth of LULAC. While active in its early work, he realized his goal of earning a law degree and practicing law. The United States called on Perales to serve as a diplomat in the late 1920's and throughout the 1930's. In total, he served on thirteen missions to the West Indies, Mexico, South America, and Central America.

His first book, *El Mexicano Americano y la politica del sur de Texas* (1931), outlined thirty-five years of Tejano-Anglo relations. As a result of this work, Perales became an adviser on Mexican American concerns to President Franklin D. Roosevelt. His two-volume work describing the civil rights struggles of Mexican Americans, *En defensa de mi raza*, was published in 1936 and 1937. His other significant work, *Are We Good Neighbors?*, exposing inequities and civil rights injustices, was published in 1948. He also published a newspaper column in *La Verdad*, a San Antonio newspaper.

In March of 1952, the Spanish government awarded Perales the rank of commander in the Spanish Order of Civil Merit. He received the honor in response to his unfailing quest for civil rights and social equality for all Spanish-speaking peoples.

Perales, César A. (b. Nov. 12, 1940, New York, N.Y.): Public official. Perales built a public service career that combined his legal expertise with community activism. He completed his undergraduate studies at the City College of New York in 1962. Three years later, he earned his law degree at Fordham University School of Law.

Perales was a neighborhood legal services lawyer early in his career. He also worked as general counsel for the New York Model Cities Administration and helped found the PUERTO RICAN LEGAL DEFENSE AND EDUCATION FUND, serving as its president and general counsel during a landmark case regarding the 1981 redistricting of the New York City Council districts.

In 1980, President Jimmy Carter appointed Perales as assistant secretary for human development services. From 1983 to 1991, he served as a New York City

César Perales in 1976 as executive director of New York City's Criminal Justice Co-ordinating Council. (AP/Wide World Photos)

commissioner. Perales was appointed deputy mayor for health and human services by Mayor David Dinkins of New York in 1992.

Perera Soto, Hilda (b. Nov. 11, 1926, Cuba): Writer. Perera Soto is the daughter of Hilda Soto and José Francisco Perera, magistrate of Cuba's supreme court. While she was attending Baldor, an outstanding Havana secondary school, her literary vocation was encouraged by one of her teachers.

In 1948, Perera Soto obtained a scholarship at Western College for Women in Oxford, Ohio, from which she received a B.A. degree. In 1950, she received her Ph.D. from the University of Havana, and in 1970 she obtained an M.A. at the University of Miami. From 1948 to 1960 she directed the Spanish department at a secondary school in Havana. She also held a position with the United Nations Educational, Social, and Cultural Organization.

Deeply disappointed with Fidel Castro's regime, Perera Soto left Cuba in 1964 and smuggled out of the country pages of her most popular novel, *El sitio de nadie* (1972). Among her novels are *Mañana es 26* (1960), *Felices Pascuas* (1977), and *Plantado* (1981). One of her best-known books of short stories is *Cuentos de Apolo* (1974). She has also written novels and stories for children. The impact of Perera Soto's work lies not only in her innovative use of narrative structure and language but also in her vocal testimony against the human rights abuses in Castro's regime.

Pérez, Lisandro (b. c. 1949, Havana, Cuba): Sociologist. Pérez is known for his work on demographics and social change in Cuba and on the dynamics of the Cuban community in the United States. He immigrated to the United States in 1960 at the age of eleven.

Pérez holds a B.A. from the University of Miami and an M.A. and Ph.D. in sociology from the University of Florida. He served on the faculty of Louisiana State University for eleven years, until 1985, before joining the faculty of Florida International University, where he became director of the Cuban Research Institute. Pérez has contributed to numerous academic journals and has served as contributing editor for *The Handbook of Latin American Studies*, produced by the Library of Congress. He has written and published on demographics and infant mortality in the state of Louisiana, among other topics.

Perez, Pedro (b. 1951, Caibarien, Cuba): Artist. Perez's parents immigrated to the United States in 1966. They were granted exit visas in that year after having attempted to get them several times previously. Perez's father had publicly opposed the new pro-Soviet stance of the Cuban government under Fidel Castro and had been imprisoned for his views.

The family settled in Hackettstown, New Jersey. Perez left New Jersey in 1970 to attend the University of Tampa. He began his college education enrolled in a pre-engineering program but changed his major to art within a year. He earned his B.F.A. in 1974, spent two years in Tampa, Florida, and then enrolled on full scholarship in the Hoffberger School of Painting at the Maryland Institute of Art in Baltimore. He received his M.F.A. in 1978 and has taught at the Tyler School of Art in Philadelphia, Pennsylvania.

Perez sees his work as more in the American tradition than following Cuban forms, though he recognizes some specifically Cuban subjects, such as CARNAVAL celebrations, in his work. He has produced works in various forms, including paintings, sculptures, and drawings. His constructions of gold leaf, often reminiscent of Cuban festivals, show the influ-

ence of his childhood, when he watched his father work as a jewelry designer.

Pérez, Ruby Nelda (b. Feb. 17, 1954, Chicago, Ill.): Actress. Born in Chicago to a family of third-generation Chicanos, Pérez returned with her family to Texas at the age of five. She attended Texas Arts and Industrial University in Kingsville, studying to become a teacher, but also joined Teatro Bilingue, a bilingual theatrical company that toured southern Texas and Mexico.

In 1977, Pérez went to Houston as a founding member of the First Bilingual Theater of Houston. In 1979, she moved to Los Angeles, where she taught drama at the Plaza de la Raza, a Chicano cultural center. The following year, she joined TEATRO DE LA ESPERANZA, then based in Santa Barbara. She returned to Houston in 1982 as the Bilingual Theater's artistic project director. In 1981, she married Jorge Piña, and in 1984 the couple moved to San Antonio to work at the Guadalupe Cultural Arts Center.

Asked to perform at the Women's International Day Conference in 1985, Pérez created a one-woman show, *A Woman's Work*, exploring Chicana life and issues through poetry, monologue, and music. She has toured the show throughout the United States and in Mexico and Peru. In 1993, she premiered a second solo show, *Doña Rosita's Traveling Jalapeño Kitchen*, developed in collaboration with Teatro de la Ezperanza.

Perez, Tony (Atanasio Perez y Rigal; b. May 14, 1942, Camagüey, Cuba): Baseball player and manager. Perez made his major league debut in 1964 with the Cincinnati Reds. After three seasons as a part-time first baseman, he was moved to third base in 1967, and his career took off. From 1967 to 1975, Perez drove in more than 100 runs six times; he also hit as many as 40 home runs in a year and twice hit better than .300.

Perez was returned to first base in 1972. His potent hitting continued to make him one of the key components of the Cincinnati "Big Red Machine" that won four National League pennants and two World Series titles between 1970 and 1976. In the 1975 World Series against the Boston Red Sox, Perez hit three home runs.

After the 1976 season, Perez was traded to the Montreal Expos. A seven-time All-Star, Perez retired in 1986 after having played with the Expos, the Boston Red Sox, the Philadelphia Phillies, and the Reds again. Perez belted his final home run in 1986, tying Orlando CEPEDA for the most career home runs by a Latin player with 379.

Tony Perez. (AP/Wide World Photos)

Perez was named the Reds' manager in 1993. After the team got off to a 20-24 start, however, he was fired midway through the season.

Pérez-Méndez, Victor (b. Aug. 8, 1923, Guatemala City, Guatemala): Physicist. Pérez-Méndez is a noted expert in the area of experimental heavy ion physics. He received his B.S. in physics from Hebrew University in 1947 and his Ph.D. from Columbia University in 1951. After earning his Ph.D., he began work as a research scientist at the Lawrence Berkeley Laboratory. In 1969 he began serving as a professor of physics and radiology at the University of California, San Francisco. His areas of research are nuclear and high-energy physics, radiation detectors, and medical imaging.

Pershing Expedition (Mar. 15, 1916-Feb. 5, 1917): Expedition sent after Pancho VILLA. General John J. Pershing led a force of three thousand men into northern Mexico on March 15, 1916, in pursuit of Francisco "Pancho" Villa, in response to the massacre of seventeen people in Columbus, New Mexico. Villa was not caught, and the force left Mexico on February 5, 1917.

Villa was a leader of opposition to the Mexican government of Venustiano Carranza at the end of the MEXICAN REVOLUTION. He led a band of rebels that operated in northern Mexico, near the United States border. Villa's band was responsible for the deaths of U.S. citizens on both sides of the border.

President Carranza had invited eighteen engineers from the U.S. to operate mines in Mexico. They were killed by Villa's followers in the town of Santa Ysabel on January 10, 1916. U.S. citizens were also killed in several raids in Texas and New Mexico in the spring of 1916. These included a raid by Villa and 360 guerrillas on Columbus, New Mexico, on March 9, 1916, in which seventeen people were killed.

President Woodrow Wilson had been supportive of the Carranza government but had followed a policy of "watchful waiting," not wanting to become involved in Mexico's civil war. Because of the deaths of U.S. citizens, Congress put pressure on President Wilson to act. He decided to send an expedition of fifteen thousand men to pursue Villa into Mexico. Wilson also stationed a militia of 150,000 soldiers along the border with Mexico.

Pershing was selected to lead a force, known as the Pershing Expedition or the Punitive Expedition, into Mexico. On March 15, Pershing led three thousand men across the border at Paloma and into northern Mexico in pursuit of Villa.

General John J. Pershing led U.S. Cavalry forces into Mexico in pursuit of Pancho Villa. (Institute of Texan Cultures)

The presence of U.S. troops in Mexico aroused anti-American feelings and Carranza's opposition. Representatives of the two countries signed a proposal on November 24, 1916, to remove U.S. troops from Mexico and to position independent forces from each country to jointly guard the border. Carranza refused to ratify this proposal, and U.S. troops remained in Mexico.

President Wilson finally removed Pershing and his troops from Mexico on February 5, 1917, because they were needed in Europe to fight in World War I. A new Mexican constitution was proclaimed on the same day. Carranza was elected president of Mexico on March 11, 1917.

Different interpretations of the Pershing Expedition have emerged. Sources differ as to whether Carranza gave his approval to the expedition. Some consider the expedition justified because of the deaths of U.S. citizens; others believe that the United States used the massacre in Columbus, New Mexico, as an excuse to become involved in the Mexican Revolution on the government's side. Some believe that Villa deliberately provoked the United States so that its army would invade, building nationalist sentiment in support of Villa. The Pershing Expedition is considered by some as an invasion of Mexico by the United States.

Pescado: Fish. *Pescado*, or fish, is a staple of coastal peoples around the world, and a large percentage of Latin Americans live near a coast. Fish are prepared in many ways: fried and sold from market booths, cut up and simmered to make soups, wrapped in corn husks and steamed like tamales, and combined with other ingredients for stuffings. Most fish are eaten fresh, though Puerto Ricans make dried cod into many dishes, including BACALAITOS.